THE
Car Book
Value Guide

1 9 9 1 E D I T I O N

A guide to the prices of out-of-print Automotive, Motorcycle,
Model, Tractor, Truck and related subject books.
Incorporating a title, author and subject index.
Includes indexes to *Automobile Quarterly* and *Style Auto*.

Thomas E. Warth

Tew Press

Marine on St. Croix,
Minnesota 55047 USA.

FIRST PUBLISHED MARCH, 1991

ISBN 0-9625541-1-1

Printed in the United States of America
Published by Tew Press, Marine on St. Croix, Minnesota 55047 USA.
Copyright 1991 by Thomas E. Warth. All rights reserved. No part of this book may be
reproduced, stored in an information retrieval sysytem or transmitted by any means without prior written
permission from the publisher.

The use of trademarked names in descriptions of the books listed herein is for informational purposes only.
Cover photo and book production by M Design, Stillwater, MN.
Data files created by Rick Seymour.

COVER CONTEST
The person to most accurately describe the Automobilia included in the cover photo will have $100 donated to
his or her favorite charity and his or her name and address published in a future edition. Lamp, table, note pad and
books not included. Contest closes December 31, 1991. Send only written entries to the Publisher.

ADVERTISING
Please inquire for details concerning advertising space in future editions of this book.

DEDICATION

To the original customers of Classic Motorbooks.

CONTENTS

FOREWORD

I have been selling car books for over twenty five years. It has been my life. Running Classic Motorbooks, Inc. and now owning an out-of-print auto book business has enabled me to satisfy the one urge that seems to overide all others - the desire to hear the customer say - "Wow, I didn't know such a book existed", or, "I knew if you didn't have it, nobody would."

This book puts together much of the knowledge acquired over these twenty five years. I hope it elicits a few more "Wows".

Any profits from the publication of this book will be donated to Books For Africa, Inc., a non-profit corporation dedicated to sending used school text books to the English speaking countries of Africa.

Thomas E. Warth
Marine on St. Croix, Minnesota, USA
February 1991

INTRODUCTION

This book is not comprehensive. The information it contains is most accurate for automotive titles from the last thirty years. Titles not included are either in-print or titles with which we have no experience. The information is less complete for the peripheral subjects and for the pre-WW2 years.

The values are generally derived from actual sales and are the prices you would expect to pay when buying from a top quality, full service specialist automotive book dealer. Prices in general non-specialist, out-of-print book shops will be somewhat less.

Sellers can expect to receive anywhere from 5% to 60% of the value when selling to dealers. Prices offered will depend upon the dealer's inventory levels.

We feel that the principal demand comes from enthusiasts buying information and a secondary demand from book collectors.

With the exception of certain periodicals and annuals (where prices shown are for second- hand copies) all titles were believed to be out-of-print when this publication went to press. However, when shopping for these books, it is well to check for remaining new copies still for sale in book stores. Also be alert to the possibility that a new edition has been published.

We would appreciate corrections for incorporation in future editions.

GLOSSARY

Title   A book may have been issued in a variety of editions.   In most cases all are combined under one listing and the price is an average. The language of the book is the language of the title unless stated otherwise. E = Edition V = Volume

Author   Omitted if not known.

Pub Date   Date of publication of first edition. If + follows the year, then one or more later editions exist. 'S' following year indicates we assume book was published in that decade.

Subjects   For key to subject numbers shown in the Title and Author Index, see Index to Subject Numbers. Logic for subject category under which a book is listed is as follows: Priority in listing is given to marques, i.e., a biography of Bugatti will appear under MARQUES - Bugatti. Biographies otherwise appear under GENERAL - Biographies, MOTOR CYCLES - personalities (Henry Ford books have their own section under GENERAL.) Manufacturers that only made race cars, i.e., McLaren, are listed under RACING and the Nationality of the make. Books covering several makes are listed under GENERAL- Mixed Makes & the Nationality.

Publisher   Omitted if not known. When more than one entry, the first is the original publisher or creator of the title.

Series   Not indicated if series name is same as first word/words of title.

Bind   H = Hard binding S = Soft binding L = Leather binding X = Titles published in both hard and soft bound; Price is an average.

Price   Quoted price is for a copy in good (read, but well cared-for) condition. Value will vary up or down from this depending on condition. Recently out-of-print titles may increase in value quickly making our information less accurate.

Title	Author	Pub date	Subjects			Publisher	Series	Bind	Price
AA Book of Car	Jacobson M A I	70	405			Drive Pub		H	$10
Abarth Fiat/Simca/Porsche..........	Braden P/Schimidt G	83	151	152	136	Newport/Osprey		H	$70
Abtomo....(Russian)	Octpobc.../H	68	401			in Moscow		H	$30
AC (Foulis Mini Marque)	Watkins M	76	105	109		Haynes	Mini-Marque	H	$30
AC and Cobra	Mclellan J	82	105	109		Dalton Watson	Dalton Watson	H	$60
AC Cobra 1962-1969	Clarke R M	80	109			Brooklands	Brooklands	S	$30
AC Cobra 260-289-427(French)	Hazan P	84	109			EPA	Grand Tourisme	H	$50
AC(Shelby) Cobra Autohistory	McComb F W	84	109			Osprey	Autohistory	H	$40
Achievement of Excell...Rolls-Royce	Keith K/Hooker S	77	139			Newcomen Society		S	$30
Addio Bandini (Italian)	Lini F/Costantini L	67	205			LEA		S	$40
Adelaide Grand Prix Impact of Event	Burns J P A/Hatch J H	86	206			Centre for SA Econ Stud's		S	$30
Adventure on Wheels	Fitch J/Nolan W F	59	205			Putnam		H	$100
Adventurers Road	Nicholson T R	57	212			Rinehart		H	$30
Adventures In Rest Antique Cars	Mills B	78	401			Dodd/Mead		H	$30
Adventures of Vintage Car Collector	Radcliff A L	72	401			Seemann/Bonanza		H	$30
Advertising and Motor-car	Frostick M	70	503			Lund Humphries		H	$90
AEC - World Trucks No 10	Kennett P	80	303			PSL	World Trucks	H	$30
Afgan Trucks	Blanc J C	76	306			Stonehill		S	$30
Age of Automobile	Bishop G	77	401			Hamlyn		H	$20
Ahnen Unserer Autos	Granz P/Kirchberg P	75	408			Transpress VEB		H	$40
Ahrens-Fox Album	Sytsma J F	73	302			Sytsma, John F.		H	$200
Ahrens-Fox Rolls-Royce of F/E	Hass E	82	302			Hass		X	$80
Air-cooled Motor/Auto Engines	Mackerle J	61+	405			Cleaver-Hume/Halsted		H	$50
Airstream (trailers)	Landau R/Phillippi J	84	306			Gibbs M Smith		S	$30
AJ Foyt Racing Champion	Libby B	74	205			Hawthorn		H	$40
AJ Life My Life as Americas.......H	Foyt A J/Neeley W	83	205			Times Books		H	$40
AJ Life of Americas Greatest......S	Foyt A J/Neely W	83	205			Warner		S	$20
AJS and Matchless Postwar Models	Bacon R	83+	606			Osprey	Osprey Coll Lib	H	$50
AJS Hist of Great Motorcycle	Grant G	69	606			PSL		H	$40
Alain Prost (French)	Henry A	87	205			EPA	Toute L'Hist	S	$20
Alex Kow 40 Ans de Creation Pub....		78	504			L'Automobiliste		H	$100
Alf Francis Racing Mechanic	Lewis P	57+	205			Foulis/Motoraces BC		H	$60
Alfa Romeo (Ballantine)	Hull P	71	101			Ballantine Books	Ballantine #2	S	$20
Alfa Romeo (Green)	Green E	76	101			Evan Green Australia		H	$60
Alfa Romeo 164	Alfieri B	87	101			Automobilia		H	$90
Alfa Romeo 1980 (Japanese)		80	101			Neko		S	$40
Alfa Romeo 6C 2500 2nd Series Cat		40S	101			Clymer		S	$30
Alfa Romeo All Cars Fr 1910/Tutte..	Fusi L	78+	101			Emmetigraficia		H	$200
Alfa Romeo Car Grap Lib(Japanese)	Kobayashi S	70S	101			Car Graphic/Nigensha	Car Grap Lib 26	S	$40
Alfa Romeo Giulietta	Wilson E	82	101			Osprey		H	$125
Alfa Romeo History	Hull P/Slater R	64+	101			Cassell/Transport/Pksd		H	$90
Alfa Romeo Milano	Frostick M	74	101			Dalton Watson	Dalton Watson	H	$100
Alfa Romeo Spiders Autohistory	Owen D	82	101			Osprey	Autohistory	H	$50
Alfa Romeo Story	Wherry J H	67	101			Chilton	Sebring	H	$50
Alfa Romeo Tipo A Monoposto (Eng)	Fusi L	82	101			Emmetigrafica		H	$40
Alfa Romeo Zagato SZ TZ (Italian)	Minerbi M	85	101			La Mille Miglia Editrice		H	$90
Alfar Romeo 75 Anniversario	Grimaldi U A	80S	101			Edizioni Alfa Romeo		H	$100
Alfasud Collector's Guide	Owen D	85	101			MRP	Coll Gd	H	$40
Alfissimo!	Owen D	79	101			Osprey		H	$70
All About Electric & Hybrid Cars	Traisler R	82	417			Tab		H	$30
All About Motorcycles	Houlgate D	74	601			Scholastic		S	$10
All Arms and Elbows	Ireland I	67	205			Pelham Books		H	$80
All But My Life Stirling Moss H	Purdy K W	63+	205			Dutton/Kimber		H	$40
All But My Life Stirling Moss S	Purdy K W	63	205			Bantam		S	$20
All Color Book of Racing Cars	King B	73	297			Octopus Books		H	$10
All Color World of Cars	Drackett P	79	401			Mandarin/Octopus		H	$10
Allan Moffats Racing RX-7 Mazda		82	126			Garry Sparke Australia		H	$30
Allard	Kinsella D	77	105			Haynes		H	$40
Allard Inside Story	Lush T	77	105			MRP		H	$70
Allard to Zodiac Brit Prod Cars 60s	Jewell B	85	406			Alderman Press		H	$60
Alle Audi Automobile 1910-1980	Oswald W	80	124			Motorbuch Verlag		H	$60
Alle Fiat Automobile 1899-1986	Schmarbeck W	86	152			Motorbuch Verlag		H	$60
Alle Horch Automobile 1900-1945	Oswald W	82	124			Motorbuch Verlag		H	$70
Alle Peugeot Automobile 1889-1980	Schmarbeck W	81	120			Motobuch Verlag		H	$50
Alloys and Automobiles E Haynes	Gray R D	79	404			Indiana Historical Soc		S	$30
Alpine Classic Sunbeam	McGovern C	80	105			Gentry/Haynes		H	$90
Aluminum In Automobiles	Gorman R/Bond J R	59	405			Singer/Reynolds Metals Co		H	$40
Alvis in Thirties	Clarke R M	61	105			Brooklands	Brooklands	S	$30
Always in the Picture Velocette	Burgess R W/Clew J R	71	606			Goose		H	$50
Amateur Racing Driver	Cholmondeley Tapper T P	53	205			Foulis		H	$40
Amazing Bugattis	Garner P/Harvey M/Conway	79	107			Design Council/Barrons		S	$70
Amazing Mr Mohs	Mohs B	84	158			Mohs		S	$20
Amazing Porsche and VW Story	Nitske R	58	150	136		Comet Press Books		H	$50
America Adopts the Auto 1895-1910	Flink J J	70	419			MIT		H	$40
America Classic Cars (Japanese)	Kobayashi S	61	403			Nigensha Co. Ltd.		H	$150
American Auto Sales Lit 1928-1942	Tuthill R N	79	505			Bookman Dan		S	$40
American Automobile (Stein)	Stein R	75	403			Ridge/Random/Galahad		H	$40

Title	Author	Pub date	Subjects	Publisher	Series	Bind	Price
American Automobile Album	McGaughey W H	54	403	Dutton		H	$40
American Automobile Brief History	Rae J B	65	403	U of Chicago		H	$20
American Automobile Manufacturers	Rae J B	59	401	Chilton		H	$40
American Automobile Racing	Bochroch A	74+	297	Penguin/Viking/PSL		X	$50
American Automobiles 1925-1935	Bentley J	53	403	Fawcett		H	$30
American Automobiles of 50s and 60s	Martinez A/Nory J L	86	403	EPA/Vilol/MBI		H	$40
American Business Abroad Ford......	Wilkins M/Hill F E	64	169	Wayne		H	$40
American Car of 1921 (Motor Age)	Brigham R B	78	403	Brigham Press		S	$20
American Car Since 1775	Kimes B R	71	403	Automobile Quarterly		H	$50
American Car Spotter's Gd 1920-1939	Burness T	75+	403	MBI	Spotter	S	$60
American Car Spotter's Gd 1940-1965	Burness T	78	403	MBI	Spotter	S	$40
American Car Spotter's Gd 1966-1980	Burness T	81	403	MBI	Spotter	S	$30
American Cars (From Harrah's Coll)	Mandel L	82	403	Stewart, Tabori		H	$60
American Cars of 1930s	Vanderveen B H	71	403	Warne	Olyslager	H	$30
American Cars of 1940s	Vanderveen B H	72	403	Warne	Olyslager	H	$30
American Cars of 1950s	Vanderveen B H	73	403	Warne/Haynes	Olyslager	H	$30
American Cars of 1960s	Vanderveen B H	77	403	Haynes/Warne	Olyslager	H	$30
American Cars of 1970s	Bochroch A R	82	403	Warne/Haynes		H	$30
American Classic Cars:Survivors #2	Rasmussen H	77	403	Picturama	Survivors	H	$60
American Ford	Sorensen L	75	122	Silverado	Fordiana	H	$80
American Funeral Cars & Ambulances	McPherson T	73	304	Crestline	Crestline	H	$50
American Grilles	Salmieri S	79	403	Harcourt		H	$50
American Jeep in War & Peace	Willinger K/Gurney G	83	117	Crown		S	$30
American Motors Family Album	Conde J	69+	102	American Motors Corp.		S	$30
American Road Racing	Rueter J C	63	299	Barnes		H	$100
American Rolls-Royce	Soutter A W	76	139	Mowbray		H	$125
American Sports Car (Consumer Gd)	Consumer Gd	79	403	Publications Intl/Crown		H	$20
American Steam-Car Pioneers	Bacon J H	84	403 414	Newcomen		S	$40
American Supercar Dev of...........	Huntington R	83	403	H P Books		H	$30
American Truck Spotters Gd 1920-70	Burness T	78	301	MBI	Spotter	S	$30
American Trucking 75 Year Odyssey	Roll R M	79	301	MBI		H	$100
American Trucks 2	Jacobs D	82	301	Osprey	Col Lib	S	$30
American Trucks of Early Thirties	Vanderveen B H	74	301	Warne	Olyslager	H	$30
American Trucks of Late Thirties	Vanderveen B H	75	301	Warne	Olyslager	H	$30
American Trucks Photographic Essay	Jacobs D	80	301	Osprey	Osprey Col Lib	S	$30
American Vintage Cars	Betts Jr C	63	403	Sports Car Press/Crown	Mod Sports Car	S	$20
Americans at Le Mans	Bochroch A R	76	299 206	Aztex		H	$90
Americans on Road Autocamp to Motel	Belasco W J	79	419	MIT		S	$20
Amherst Villiers Superchargers	Amherst Villiers	30S	202	Eoin Young (reprint)		S	$30
Anatomy of Grand Prix Driver	Garrett R	70	297	Arthur Barker Ltd.		H	$20
And Then Came Ford	Merz C	29	415	Doubleday		H	$30
Andre Citroen Les Chevrons de la G	Sabates F/Schweitzer	80	153	EPA		H	$70
Andretti	Libby B	70	205	Grosset & Dunlap		X	$30
Annals of Mercedes-Benz Motor Veh	Nallinger F	61	130	Daimler-Benz		H	$50
Antique Auto Body Leather Work	Butler H J	82	405	Post	Vintage Craft	S	$20
Antique Auto Body Wood Work	Terry C W	69	405	Post	Vintage Craft	S	$20
Antique Automobile (Nixon)	Nixon S J C	56	401	Cassell		H	$50
Antique Automobile Body Const/Rest	Neubecker W	12+	405	Post		S	$30
Antique Automobiles (Bird)	Bird A	67+	401	Allen & Unwin/Treasure		H	$20
Antique Automobiles (Fawcett 168)	Bentley J	52	401	Fawcett	Fawcett	S	$10
Antique Automobiles 1896-1915	Bentley J	51	401	Fawcett		H	$30
Antique Automotive Collectibles	Martells J	80	507	Contemporary		H	$60
Antique and Classic Cars(Trend 193)	Wherry J H	60	401	Trend	Trend Book	S	$10
Antique Car Models Stories HT Make	Ross F	78	704	Lothrop		H	$20
Antique Cars	Sedgwick M	81	401	Exeter		H	$20
Antique Cars (Montagu)	Montagu	80S	401	Camden House	Golden Hglts	H	$10
Antique Cars (Morris)	Morris L	70	401	Casa Editore/Grosset		H	$10
Any Color so Long as it's Black	Roberts P	76	503	Morrow		H	$90
ARRC 1970 American Rd Rac Champions	Crow J T	71	204	Boojum Books		S	$20
ARRC 1971 & SCAA Road Racing Annual	Wolfson V	72	204	Haessner & Associates		S	$20
Ariel Postwar Models	Bacon R	83+	606	Osprey	Osprey Coll Lib	H	$50
Ariel Story	Hartley P	80	606	Argus Books Ltd		S	$30
Armstrong Siddeley Cars 1945-1960	Clarke R M	72	105	Brooklands	Brooklands	S	$30
Around Houses Hist MR West Aust	Walker T	80	298	Racing Car News		S	$30
Arrow 100th Anniv Meet 1978 issue	Weis B J	78	170	Pierce-Arrow Society		S	$30
Art Afons Fastest Man On Wheels	Katz F	65	211 205	Rutledge		H	$40
Art and Automobile	Tubbs D	78	504	Quarto/Arlington/Grosset		H	$50
Art and Science of GP Driving	Lauda N	77	203	Verlag Orac/MBI		H	$50
Art of Gordon Crosby	Garnier P	78	504	Hamlyn		H	$150
Art of Moto-cross	Smith J/Currie B	66	603	Cassell		H	$50
Art of Motorcycle Racing	Hailwood M/Walker M	63+	604	Cassell		H	$90
Art of Tin Toy	Pressland D	76	703	New Cavendish/Crown		H	$150
Assassination of Corvair	White A J	69	113	Readers Press		H	$40
Aston Martin (Autocar)	Garnier P	82	103	IPC/Hamlyn		H	$50
Aston Martin 1 1/2 International	Coram D	73	103	Horseless Carriage	Sports Car Peop	S	$50
Aston Martin 1914-1940 Pict. Review	Hunter I	76	103	Transport Bookman		H	$40
Aston Martin 1963-1972	Gershon D	75	103	Oxford Illustrated		H	$40

Title	Author	Pub date	Subjects	Publisher	Series	Bind	Price
Aston Martin and Lagonda	Frostick M	77	103 105	Dalton Watson	Dalton Watson	H	$60
Aston Martin Britain's Mst Colorful	Garnier P Editor	76	103	IPC Transport Press	Autocar	S	$40
Aston Martin Coll Rd Tests 1921-42	Feather A M	74	103	Feather		H	$30
Aston Martin Coll Rd Tests 1948-59	Feather A M	79	103	Feather		S	$30
Aston Martin Guide from 1948	Stowers R	79	103	Transport Bookman		S	$20
Aston Martin Postwar Road Cars	Rasmussen H	88	103	MBI/Haynes		H	$90
Aston Martin Register 1963	AMOC	63	103	AMOC		S	$70
Aston Martin Story of a Sports Car	Coram D	57	103	MRP		H	$300
Aston Martin V-8	Bowler M	85	103	Gentry/Arco		H	$40
Aston Martin V8s Autohistory	McComb F W	81	103	Osprey	Autohistory	H	$50
At Speed	Alexander J	72	297	R&T/Bond Parkhurst		H	$600
At Speed Special Limited edition	Alexander J	72	297	R&T/Bond Parkhurst		H	$1000
Atalanta	Davis S C H	55	205	Foulis		H	$60
Audi Quattro	Henry A	84	124	Cadogan/Arco	High Perfor....	H	$30
Audi Quattro Dev & Comp History	Walton J	84	124	Haynes		H	$70
Audi Une Tradition Sportive	Merlin D	81	124	Editia, S.A.		H	$30
Aurelia	Moon H	71	157	American Lancia Club		S	$50
Austerity Motoring 39-50 Shire 183	Lane A	87	406	Shire Pub	Shire Album	S	$10
Austin 1905-1952	Wyatt R J	81	105	David & Charles		H	$60
Austin A30 & A35 1951-1962	Clarke R M	83	105	Brooklands	Brooklands	S	$30
Austin Healey (Healey/Wisdom)	Healey D/Wisdom T/Boyd M	59	104	Cassell		H	$100
Austin Healey 100 1952-1959	Clarke R M	80	104	Brooklands	Brooklands	S	$30
Austin Healey Guide	Healey D/Wisdom T	59	104	Sports Car Press	Mod Sports Car	S	$30
Austin Healey Story Big Healeys	Healey G	77	104	Gentry/Haynes		H	$60
Austin Healey Year Book 1979-80	Skilleter P	80	104	Magpie		H	$30
Austin Seven 1922-1939	Wyatt R J	68+	105	David & Charles		H	$50
Austin Seven Cars 1930-1935	Clarke R M	71	105	Brooklands	Brooklands	S	$30
Austin Seven Companion		80	105	750 Motor Club		S	$40
Austin Seven in Thirties	Clarke R M	70	105	Brooklands	Brooklands	S	$30
Austin Ten 1932-1939	Clarke R M	74	105	Brooklands	Brooklands	S	$30
Australian Cars and Motoring	Goode J	72	402	Lansdowne		H	$20
Australian Competition Yearbook 74	Van Loon A J	74	204	Motoring News Intl		S	$70
Australian Competition Yearbook 75		75	204	Wheels Magazine		S	$70
Australian Motor Racing YB 79-80 #9		80	204	Motor Sport Press		H	$60
Australian Motor YB 80-81 #10		81	204	Motor Sport Press		H	$150
Australian Motoring Yearbook 73	Van Loon A J	73	204	Motoring News Intl		S	$80
Auto 1953	Di Ruffia C B	52	410	Alfieri Editore		H	$80
Auto 1954	Di Ruffia C B	53	410	Alfieri Editore/Tudor		H	$80
Auto 1956	Di Ruffia C B	56	410	Alfieri Editore/Tudor		H	$80
Auto Ads	Stern J/Stern M	78	503	David Obst/Random		H	$40
Auto Album	Burness T	83	401	Houghton Mifflin		S	$10
Auto as Art Form		75	506	Newport Harbor Art Mus		S	$20
Auto Da Corsa I Documentari	Bernabo F	68	298	Instituto Geografico.....		H	$90
Auto Engines of Tomorrow	Dark H E	75	405	Indiana		H	$30
Auto im Zeitblick Mercedes 1949-53	Zweigardt M	80	130	Gourmandise Verlag		S	$20
Auto in 1912	Auto Trade Journal	66	403	Iron Horse		S	$10
Auto Pioneering Story of R E Olds	Yarnell D	49	404	R E Olds		H	$50
Auto Racing Old and New(Fawcett 184	Lozier H	53	297	Fawcett		S	$10
Auto Racing/USA 1983	Taylor L A	84	204	Anlon		H	$80
Auto Racing/USA 1985	Taylor L A	86	204	Anlon/HP		H	$80
Auto Racing/USA 1987	Taylor L A	88	204	Stevenson F		H	$80
Auto Test Ferrari 1 1962-71(French)		83	121	EPA	Auto Test	S	$30
Auto Test Porsche 911 #1 (French)		83	136	EPA	Auto Test	S	$30
Auto-Biography My 40 Yrs of Motrng	Knowles A	70	205	Allen & Unwin		H	$30
Auto-Parade 1957(1st)(Int Auto Cat)	Logoz A	57	410	Int Auto Parade		S	$100
Auto-Parade 1958 (Vol II)	Logoz A	58	410	Int Auto Parade		H	$70
Auto-Parade 1960 #3	Logoz A	60	410	Int Auto Parade/Chilton		H	$60
Auto-Parade 1961 #4	Logoz A	61	410	Int Auto Parade/Chilton		H	$60
Auto-Parade 1962 #5	Logoz A	61	410	Int Auto Parade/Chilton		H	$60
Auto-Parade 1963 #6	Logoz A	62	410	Int Auto Parade/Macmillan		H	$60
Auto-Universum 1964	Logoz A	63	410	Int Auto Parade		H	$60
Auto-Universum 1965	Logoz A	65	410	Int Auto Parade/A Barker		H	$60
Auto-Universum 1966	Logoz A	65	410	Int Auto Parade		H	$60
Auto-Universum 1967	Logoz A	66	410	Int Auto Parade		H	$60
Auto-Universum 1968	Logoz A	67	410	Int Auto Parade			$60
Auto-Universum 1969	Logoz A	68	410	Int Auto Parade		H	$60
Auto-Universum 1970	Logas A	69	410	Int Auto Parade			$50
Auto-Universum 71	Logoz A	70	410	Int Auto Parade		H	$50
Autocourse 1959	Sporting Motorist Staff	60	204	Trafalgar Press		S	$300
Autocourse 1960-61 Part One	Eves E	60	204	Trafalgar/Victoria House		S	$180
Autocourse 1960-61 Part Two	Sporting Motorist Staff	61	204	Trafalgar/Victoria House		S	$180
Autocourse 1961-62	Sporting Motorist Staff	62	204	Trafalgar Press		H	$200
Autocourse 1962-63		63	204	Trafalgar Press		H	$200
Autocourse 1963-64	Gavin B	64	204	Autocourse Publications		H	$200
Autocourse 1964-65 (1965)	Phipps D	65	204	Haymarket		H	$300
Autocourse 1965-66 (1966)	Phipps D	66	204	Haymarket		H	$250
Autocourse 1966-67	Phipps D	67	204	Haymarket		H	$250

Title	Author	Pub date	Subjects	Publisher	Series	Bind	Price
Autocourse 1967-68	Phipps D	68	204	Haymarket		H	$200
Autocourse 1968-69	Phipps D	69	204	Haymarket		H	$250
Autocourse 1969-70	Phipps D	70	204	Haymarket		H	$250
Autocourse 1970-71	Phipps D	71	204	Haymarket		H	$200
Autocourse 1971-72	Phipps D	72	204	Haymarket		H	$250
Autocourse 1972-73	Kettlewell M	73	204	Haymarket		H	$300
Autocourse 1973-74	Kettlewell M	74	204	Haymarket		H	$400
Autocourse 1974-75	Kettlewell M	75	204	Haymarket		H	$400
Autocourse 1975-76	Kettlewell M	75	204	Hazleton		H	$180
Autocourse 1976-77	Kettlewell M	76	204	Hazleton		H	$150
Autocourse 1977-78	Kettlewell M	78	204	Hazleton		H	$180
Autocourse 1978-79	Kettlewell M	78	204	Hazleton		H	$300
Autocourse 1979-80	Hamilton M	80	204	Hazleton		H	$125
Autocourse 1980-81	Hamilton M	80	204	Hazleton		H	$125
Autocourse 1981-82	Hamilton M	82	204	Hazleton		H	$125
Autocourse 1981-82(French)	Hamilton M	81	204	Hazleton/Editions ACLA		H	$80
Autocourse 1982-83	Hamilton M	83	204	Hazleton		H	$180
Autocourse 1983-84	Hamilton M	83	204	Hazleton		H	$80
Autocourse 1984-85	Hamilton M	84	204	Hazleton		H	$80
Autocourse 1985-86	Hamilton M	85	204	Hazleton		H	$50
Autocourse 1986-87	Hamilton M	86	204	Hazleton		H	$90
Autocourse 1987-88	Hamilton M	87	204	Hazleton		H	$90
Autocourse 1988-1989	Henry A	88	204	Hazleton		H	$50
Autocourse 1989-90	Henry A	89	204	Hazleton		H	$80
Autocourse Hist of the GP Car 66-85	Nye D	86	297	Hazleton		H	$100
Autokind vs Mankind	Schneider K R	71	419	Norton		H	$30
Automania	Pettifer J/Turner N	84	419	Collins		H	$40
Automania Man & the Motor Car	Pettifer J	84	419	Little Brown		H	$40
Automobil Revue '51		51	410	Hallwag		S	$80
Automobil Revue '56		56	410	Hallwag		S	$70
Automobil Revue '59		59	410	Hallwag		S	$70
Automobil Revue '61		61	410	Hallwag		S	$60
Automobil Revue '62		62	410	Hallwag		S	$60
Automobil Revue '63		63	410	Hallwag		S	$60
Automobil Revue '64		64	410	Hallwag		S	$60
Automobil Revue '65		65	410	Hallwag		S	$60
Automobil Revue '66		66	410	Hallwag		S	$60
Automobil Revue '67		67	410	Hallwag		S	$60
Automobil Revue '68		68	410	Hallwag		S	$60
Automobil Revue '69		69	410	Hallwag		S	$60
Automobil Revue '70		70	410	Hallwag		S	$50
Automobil Revue '71		'71	410	Hallwag		S	$50
Automobil Revue '72		72	410	Hallwag		S	$50
Automobil Revue '73		73	410	Hallwag		S	$50
Automobil Revue '74		74	410	Hallwag		S	$50
Automobil Revue '75		75	410	Hallwag		S	$50
Automobil Revue '76		76	410	Hallwag		S	$50
Automobil Revue '78		78	410	Hallwag		S	$50
Automobil Revue '79		79	410	Hallwag		S	$50
Automobil Revue '80		80	410	Hallwag		S	$40
Automobil Revue '81		81	410	Hallwag		S	$40
Automobil Revue '82		82	410	Hallwag		S	$40
Automobil Revue '84		84	410	Hallwag		S	$40
Automobil Revue '85		85	410	Hallwag		S	$60
Automobil Revue '86		86	410	Hallwag		S	$60
Automobil Revue '87		87	410	Hallwag		S	$60
Automobil Revue '88		88	410	Hallwag		S	$60
Automobil Revue '89		89	410	Hallwag		S	$60
Automobil Revue '90		90	410	Hallwag		S	$60
Automobile & American Culture	Lewis D L	81	419	U of Mich Press		S	$50
Automobile Ads List - Life 60-69	Cottrill P K	80	503	Rigel		S	$20
Automobile Almanac 1967	Ash D	67	410	Essandess/Simon Schuster		S	$30
Automobile Almanac 1971	Ash D	70	410	Morrow		H	$20
Automobile Almanac 1972	Ash D	71	410	Automobile Almanac		S	$20
Automobile Almanac 1973	Ash D	73	410	Automobile Almanac/Crowel		H	$20
Automobile Almanac 1975	Ash D	75	410	Automobile Almanac		H	$20
Automobile Almanac 1977	Ash D	77	410	Automobile Almanac		S	$10
Automobile Archaeology	Burgess-Wise D	81	507	PSL		H	$40
Automobile and Regulation of Impact	Grad F P etc	75	419	Oklahoma		H	$30
Automobile Book	Sat Evening Post Editors	77	401	Curtis		H	$40
Automobile Brakes & Braking Systems	Newcomb T P/Spurr R T	69	405	Robert Bentley Inc.	Motor Manuals	H	$20
Automobile Connoisseur 01	Watkins M	69	410	Speed & Sports		H	$40
Automobile Connoisseur 03		70	410	Speed & Sports		H	$30
Automobile Connoisseur 04	Vyse H	70	410	Speed & Sports		H	$30
Automobile Connoisseur 05	Vyse H	71	410	Speed & Sport Pub. Ltd		H	$30
Automobile Design Great Designers..	Barker R/Harding A	70	502	David & Charles		S	$40
Automobile Driving Self-Taught (RP)	Russell T H	09+	203	Chilton		H	$10

Title	Author	Pub date	Subjects	Publisher	Series	Title Index Bind	Price
Automobile Engineers Reference Bk	Molloy E/Lanchester G H		405	Newnes		L	$70
Automobile Engines Today & Tomorrow	Stambler I	72	405	Grosset & Dunlap		H	$30
Automobile First Century	Burgess-Wise D/Boddy W	83	401	Orbis/Greenwich		H	$30
Automobile Illustration (Japanese)	Inomoto Y	71	504	Nigensha		H	$200
Automobile in America	Sears S W	77	401	American Heritage/S & S		H	$70
Automobile Museum Directory	Tavoletti G	76	401	ASI		S	$20
Automobile Quarterly Index 01-04		67	411	AQ	AQ	H	$30
Automobile Quarterly Index 01-20		85	411	AQ	AQ	H	$30
Automobile Quarterly Index 05-08		71	411	AQ	AQ	H	$20
Automobile Quarterly Index 09-12		75	411	AQ	AQ	H	$20
Automobile Quarterly Index 13-17		79	411	AQ	AQ	H	$20
Automobile Quarterly Index 21-25		89	411	AQ	AQ	H	$30
Automobile Quarterly Set thru V#25			411	AQ	AQ	H	$2000
Automobile Quarterly Vol 01-1		62	411	AQ	AQ	H	$40
Automobile Quarterly Vol 01-2		62	411	AQ	AQ	H	$80
Automobile Quarterly Vol 01-3		62	411	AQ	AQ	H	$30
Automobile Quarterly Vol 01-4		63	411	AQ	AQ	H	$80
Automobile Quarterly Vol 02-1		63	411	AQ	AQ	H	$50
Automobile Quarterly Vol 02-2		63	411	AQ	AQ	H	$40
Automobile Quarterly Vol 02-3		63	411	AQ	AQ	H	$30
Automobile Quarterly Vol 02-4		64	411	AQ	AQ	H	$50
Automobile Quarterly Vol 03-1		64	411	AQ	AQ	H	$100
Automobile Quarterly Vol 03-2		64	411	AQ	AQ	H	$40
Automobile Quarterly Vol 03-3		64	411	AQ	AQ	H	$20
Automobile Quarterly Vol 03-4		65	411	AQ	AQ	H	$50
Automobile Quarterly Vol 04-1		65	411	AQ	AQ	H	$50
Automobile Quarterly Vol 04-2		65	411	AQ	AQ	H	$20
Automobile Quarterly Vol 04-3		65	411	AQ	AQ	H	$90
Automobile Quarterly Vol 04-4		66	411	AQ	AQ	H	$150
Automobile Quarterly Vol 05-1		66	411	AQ	AQ	H	$40
Automobile Quarterly Vol 05-2		66	411	AQ	AQ	H	$80
Automobile Quarterly Vol 05-3		67	411	AQ	AQ	H	$70
Automobile Quarterly Vol 05-4		67	411	AQ	AQ	H	$40
Automobile Quarterly Vol 06-1		67	411	AQ	AQ	H	$40
Automobile Quarterly Vol 06-2		67	411	AQ	AQ	H	$40
Automobile Quarterly Vol 06-3		68	411	AQ	AQ	H	$40
Automobile Quarterly Vol 06-4		68	411	AQ	AQ	H	$80
Automobile Quarterly Vol 07-1		68	411	AQ	AQ	H	$40
Automobile Quarterly Vol 07-2		68	411	AQ	AQ	H	$70
Automobile Quarterly Vol 07-3		69	411	AQ	AQ	H	$20
Automobile Quarterly Vol 07-4		67	411	AQ	AQ	H	$70
Automobile Quarterly Vol 08-1		69	411	AQ	AQ	H	$40
Automobile Quarterly Vol 08-2		69	411	AQ	AQ	H	$20
Automobile Quarterly Vol 08-3		69	411	AQ	AQ	H	$80
Automobile Quarterly Vol 08-4		70	411	AQ	AQ	H	$90
Automobile Quarterly Vol 09-1		70	411	AQ	AQ	H	$90
Automobile Quarterly Vol 09-2		70	411	AQ	AQ	H	$20
Automobile Quarterly Vol 09-3		70	411	AQ	AQ	H	$70
Automobile Quarterly Vol 09-4		71	411	AQ	AQ	H	$70
Automobile Quarterly Vol 10-1		72	411	AQ	AQ	H	$50
Automobile Quarterly Vol 10-2		72	411	AQ	AQ	H	$20
Automobile Quarterly Vol 10-3		72	411	AQ	AQ	H	$20
Automobile Quarterly Vol 10-4		72	411	AQ	AQ	H	$30
Automobile Quarterly Vol 11-1		73	411	AQ	AQ	H	$20
Automobile Quarterly Vol 11-2		73	411	AQ	AQ	H	$20
Automobile Quarterly Vol 11-3		73	411	AQ	AQ	H	$30
Automobile Quarterly Vol 11-4		73	411	AQ	AQ	H	$20
Automobile Quarterly Vol 12-1		74	411	AQ	AQ	H	$20
Automobile Quarterly Vol 12-2		74	411	AQ	AQ	H	$20
Automobile Quarterly Vol 12-3		74	411	AQ	AQ	H	$30
Automobile Quarterly Vol 12-4		74	411	AQ	AQ	H	$20
Automobile Quarterly Vol 13-1		75	411	AQ	AQ	H	$30
Automobile Quarterly Vol 13-2		75	411	AQ	AQ	H	$40
Automobile Quarterly Vol 13-3		75	411	AQ	AQ	H	$30
Automobile Quarterly Vol 13-4		75	411	AQ	AQ	H	$20
Automobile Quarterly Vol 14-1		76	411	AQ	AQ	H	$20
Automobile Quarterly Vol 14-2		76	411	AQ	AQ	H	$20
Automobile Quarterly Vol 14-3		76	411	AQ	AQ	H	$30
Automobile Quarterly Vol 14-4		76	411	AQ	AQ	H	$20
Automobile Quarterly Vol 15-1		77	411	AQ	AQ	H	$20
Automobile Quarterly Vol 15-2		77	411	AQ	AQ	H	$30
Automobile Quarterly Vol 15-3		77	411	AQ	AQ	H	$20
Automobile Quarterly Vol 15-4		77	411	AQ	AQ	H	$20
Automobile Quarterly Vol 16-1		78	411	AQ	AQ	H	$40
Automobile Quarterly Vol 16-2		78	411	AQ	AQ	H	$30
Automobile Quarterly Vol 16-3		78	411	AQ	AQ	H	$40
Automobile Quarterly Vol 16-4		78	411	AQ	AQ	H	$30

Title	Author	Pub date	Subjects	Publisher	Series	Bind	Price
Automobile Quarterly Vol 17-1		79	411	AQ	AQ	H	$20
Automobile Quarterly Vol 17-2		79	411	AQ	AQ	H	$20
Automobile Quarterly Vol 17-3		79	411	AQ	AQ	H	$20
Automobile Quarterly Vol 17-4		79	411	AQ	AQ	H	$20
Automobile Quarterly Vol 18-1		80	411	AQ	AQ	H	$30
Automobile Quarterly Vol 18-2		80	411	AQ	AQ	H	$20
Automobile Quarterly Vol 18-3		80	411	AQ	AQ	H	$20
Automobile Quarterly Vol 18-4		80	411	AQ	AQ	H	$20
Automobile Quarterly Vol 19-1		81	411	AQ	AQ	H	$30
Automobile Quarterly Vol 19-2		81	411	AQ	AQ	H	$30
Automobile Quarterly Vol 19-3		81	411	AQ	AQ	H	$20
Automobile Quarterly Vol 19-4		81	411	AQ	AQ	H	$20
Automobile Quarterly Vol 20-1		82	411	AQ	AQ	H	$30
Automobile Quarterly Vol 20-2		82	411	AQ	AQ	H	$30
Automobile Quarterly Vol 20-3		82	411	AQ	AQ	H	$30
Automobile Quarterly Vol 20-4		82	411	AQ	AQ	H	$60
Automobile Quarterly Vol 21-1		83	411	AQ	AQ	H	$30
Automobile Quarterly Vol 21-2		83	411	AQ	AQ	H	$30
Automobile Quarterlys Vol 21-3		83	411	AQ	AQ	H	$50
Automobile Quarterlys Vol 21-4		83	411	AQ	AQ	H	$50
Automobile Quarterly Vol 22-1		84	411	AQ	AQ	H	$30
Automobile Quarterly Vol 22-2		84	411	AQ	AQ	H	$30
Automobile Quarterly Vol 22-3		84	411	AQ	AQ	H	$30
Automobile Quarterly Vol 22-4		84	411	AQ	AQ	H	$30
Automobile Quarterly Vol 23-1		85	411	AQ	AQ	H	$100
Automobile Quarterly Vol 23-2		85	411	AQ	AQ	H	$80
Automobile Quarterly Vol 23-3		85	411	AQ	AQ	H	$60
Automobile Quarterly Vol 23-4		85	411	AQ	AQ	H	$30
Automobile Quarterly Vol 24-1		86	411	AQ	AQ	H	$30
Automobile Quarterly Vol 24-2		86	411	AQ	AQ	H	$50
Automobile Quarterly Vol 24-3		86	411	AQ	AQ	H	$30
Automobile Quarterly Vol 24-4		86	411	AQ	AQ	H	$30
Automobile Quarterly Vol 25-1		87	411	AQ	AQ	H	$30
Automobile Quarterly Vol 25-2		87	411	AQ	AQ	H	$30
Automobile Quarterly Vol 25-3		87	411	AQ	AQ	H	$30
Automobile Quarterly Vol 25-4		87	411	AQ	AQ	H	$30
Automobile Quarterly Vol 26-1		87	411	AQ	AQ	H	$30
Automobile Quarterly Vol 26-2		88	411	AQ	AQ	H	$30
Automobile Quarterly Vol 26-3		88	411	AQ	AQ	H	$30
Automobile Quarterly Vol 26-4		88	411	AQ	AQ	H	$30
Automobile Quarterly Vol 27-1		89	411	AQ	AQ	H	$20
Automobile Quarterly Vol 27-2		89	411	AQ	AQ	H	$20
Automobile Quarterly Vol 27-3		89	411	AQ	AQ	H	$20
Automobile Quarterly Vol 27-4		89	411	AQ	AQ	H	$20
Automobile Quarterly Vol 28-1		90	411	AQ	AQ	H	$20
Automobile Quarterly Vol 28-2		90	411	AQ	AQ	H	$20
Automobile Quarterly Vol 28-3		90	411	AQ	AQ	H	$20
Automobile Quarterly Vol 28-4		90	411	AQ	AQ	H	$20
Automobile Quarterlys Gt Cars Gd Mq	Kimes B R	76	401	Aq/Bonanza		H	$40
Automobile Quarterlys World of Cars	Langworth R M	71	401	AQ		H	$20
Automobile Racing (Walkerley)	Walkerley R	62	298	Temple		H	$30
Automobile Racing 5E (Kuns)	Kuns R F	39	202	Kuns		S	$60
Automobile Racing 6E (Kuns)	Kuns R F	47	202	Kuns		S	$60
Automobile Refinishing Manual	Phillips V	78	405	Phillips		S	$20
Automobile Restoration Guide	Nowak S	81+	405	Tab	Mod Auto	S	$20
Automobile Sport 81-82	Bamsey I	81	204	Iconplan		H	$50
Automobile Sport 82-83	Bamsey I	82	204	Haynes		H	$40
Automobile Steering & Suspensn Q&A	Hartley J	77	405	Newnes		S	$20
Automobile Treasury of Ireland	Corry F	79	401	Dalton Watson		H	$30
Automobile Wheels and Tyres	I Mech E Papers	83	405	I Mech E		S	$60
Automobile Wooden Spoke Wheels	Hayes E		405	Oakcrest Machine Shop		S	$20
Automobile World 1969 see AUTO-UNIV			410				$60
Automobile Year 1953-54 #1(Auto Rev	Guichard A	53	204	Edita S.A.		S	$500
Automobile Year 1954-55 #2(Auto Rev	Guichard A	54	204	Edita S.A.		X	$800
Automobile Year 1955-56 #3(Auto Rev	Guichard A	56	204	Edita S.A.		H	$250
Automobile Year 1956-57 #4	Guichard A	57	204	Edita S.A./Doubleday		H	$150
Automobile Year 1957-58 #5 (1958)	Guichard A	58	204	Edita S.A./Doubleday		H	$150
Automobile Year 1958-59 #6	Guichard A	59	204	Edita S.A./Doubleday		H	$150
Automobile Year 1959-60 #7	Guichard A	59	204	Edita S.A.		H	$150
Automobile Year 1960-61 #8	Guichard A	61	204	Edita S.A.		H	$150
Automobile Year 1961-62 #9	Wilkins G	62	204	Edita S.A.		H	$250
Automobile Year 1962-63 #10	Molter G	63	204	Edita S.A.		H	$200
Automobile Year 1963-64 #11	Molter G	64	204	Edita S.A.		H	$125
Automobile Year 1964-65 #12	Molter G	65	204	Edita S.A.		H	$100
Automobile Year 1965-66 #13	Molter G	66	204	Edita S.A.		H	$150
Automobile Year 1966-67 #14	Wagner C L	67	204	Edita S.A.		H	$150
Automobile Year 1967-68 #15	Armstrong D	68	204	Edita S.A.		H	$150

Title	Author	Pub date	Subjects	Publisher	Series	Bind	Price
Book of the Triumph (motorcycles)	Brown E T/Davies A C	39+	606	Pitman	Mtr Cycl Lib	S	$40
Borgward Isabella Auto-Classic #6	Knittel S	80S	124	Podzun-Pallas	Auto Classic	S	$20
Borgward und seine Autos	Schmidt G	86	124	Motorbuch Verlag		H	$50
Bosch Electronics 1(Introduction)	Bosch	72	405	Bosch		S	$30
Bosch L-Jetronic Technical Inst(81)	Bosch	81	405	Bosch		S	$40
Bosch L-Jetronic Technical Inst(85)	Bosch	85	405	Bosch		S	$30
Boss 302 Registry	Ream R/Eby T	84	122	Ream/Eby		S	$30
Boss Ket Life of Charles Kettering	Young R	61	404	McKay		H	$40
Boss Kettering Wizard of GM	Leslie S W	83	160 404	Columbia		X	$40
Boss Wheels End of Supercar Era	Bowden R C	79	401	Tab		S	$20
Bourke Engine Documentary	Bourke L	68	405	DD Enterprises		S	$40
Bowser V1	Miklues R L	78	507	Miklues		S	$40
Boxer Ferrari Flat-12 Rac & GT Cars	Thompson J	81	121	Newport Press/Osprey		H	$60
Boy in the Model-T	Longstreet S	56	122	Simon & Schuester/Paperb		S	$20
Boyhood Photos of J-H Lartigue	Lartigue J H	66	510	Ami Guichard		H	$500
Boys Book of Motor Sport	Grant G	50S	213	Foulis		H	$50
Boys Book of Racing Cars		48	298	MRP		H	$30
BP Book of Motor Racing	Boyd M	60	297	Stanley Pauls		H	$30
BP Book of Racing Campbells	Hough R	60	205 211	S Paul		H	$50
BP Book of World Land Speed Records		63	211	Herbert Jenkins		H	$40
BRM H	Mays R/Roberts P	62+	298	Cassell		H	$60
BRM S	Mays R/Roberts P	64	298	Pan		S	$30
BRM Collection Christie Catalog		81	298	Christies		S	$50
BRM Story	Stanley L T	66	298	Parrish		H	$80
Brabham Grand Prix Cars	Henry A	85	298	Hazleton		H	$50
Brabham Story of Racing Team	Drackett P	85	298	Weidenfeld/Barker		H	$50
Brave Men	Tippette G	72	297	Macmillan		H	$30
Bricklin	Fredricks H A/Chambers A	77	173	Brunswick Press		H	$30
Bride and Bugatti(fiction)	De Buron N	58	107	Harvill/Norton		H	$40
Bright Wheels Rolling	Melton J/Purdy K	54	401	Macrae Smith		H	$30
Bristol Cars and Engines	Setright L J K	74	105	MRP		H	$180
British 250 Racer	Pickard D	84	603	Pickard		S	$10
British Car Owner's Handbook	Autocar	51	406	Clymer		S	$20
British Cars of Early Fifties	Voller D J	75	406	Olyslager/Warne/Haynes	Auto Library	H	$30
British Cars of Early Forties	Vanderveen B H	74	406	Olyslager/Warne/Haynes	Auto Library	H	$30
British Cars of Early Sixties	Voller D J	81	406	Warne/Haynes	Olyslager	H	$30
British Cars of Late Forties	Vanderveen B H	74	406	Warne/Haynes/Foulis	Olyslager	H	$30
British Cars of Late Sixties	Voller D J	82	406	Warne	Olyslager	H	$30
British Cars of Late Thirties	Vanderveen B H	73	406	Warne	Olyslager	H	$30
British Cars of Sixties	Nye D	70	406	Nelson		H	$40
British Cars(Neko)		82	406	Neko	Neko	S	$40
British Competition Car	Posthumus C	59	406	Batsford		H	$40
British Empire Trophy 1957(7" rec)	Bolster J	50S	206	Schofield Productions	Sound Stories		$20
British Grand Prix 1958(7" record)	Bolster J	50S	206	Schofield Productions	Sound Stories		$20
British Leyland Truth About Cars	Daniels J	80	105	Osprey		H	$60
British Light Wt Spts 78 (Japanese)	Inouye K	78	105	Neko	Neko	S	$700
British Lorries 1900-1945	Klapper C F	73	303	Ian Allen		H	$20
British Lorries 1945-1975	Stevens-Stratten S W	78	303	Ian Allen		H	$30
British Motor Bus, The	Booth	77		Ian Allan,Ltd.		H	$20
British Motor Cars	Speed J F	52	406	Foulis		H	$30
British Motor Cycles Since 1950 V1	Wilson S	82	606	PSL		H	$50
British Motor Cycles Since 1950 V2	Wilson S	83	606	PSL		H	$50
British Motor Cycles Since 1950 V4	Wilson S	87	606	PSL		H	$70
British Motorcycle Engines	Motor Cycle	50S	609	Iliffe/Clymer		S	$30
British Racing Cars	Posthumus C	48	298	Vitesse/Floyd Clymer		S	$20
British Racing Green 1946-1956	Klemantaski L	57	298	Bodley		H	$60
British RDC Silver Jubilee Book		52	298	BRDC		H	$100
British Road Racing (Dudley)	Dudley J	50	298	Ian Allen/Clymer		S	$30
British Scrambles Motorcycles	Venables R	86	603	Bruce Main-Smith		S	$50
British Sports Cars Since the War	Watkins M	73	406	Arco		H	$40
British Sports Cars(Grant)	Grant G	47+	406	Foulis/Clymer		X	$30
British Tractors for World Farming	Williams M	80	904	Blandford Press		S	$20
British Trials Motorcycles(Ven'bls)	Venables R	85	606	BMS		S	$30
Brooklands (Ballantine)	Wallace P J	71	206	Ballantine Books	Ballantine	S	$20
Brooklands and Beyond	Mortimer C	74	206	Goose & Son		H	$30
Brooklands Bikes in Twenties	Hartley P	80	604	Goose/Argus		S	$40
Brooklands Pictorial History	Georgano G N	78	206	Dalton Watson/Beaulieu		H	$30
Brough Superior Rolls-Royce of MCs	Clark R H	64+	606	Goose/Haynes		H	$50
Brown's Alchohol Motor Fuel Cookb'k	Brown M H	79+	417	Desert Publ		S	$30
Bruce McLaren Man & His Rac T'm	Young E S	71	298	Eyre & Spottiswoode		H	$60
Brush Runabout Sales Catalog			158	Clymer		S	$10
BSA Motorcycles 1935 to 1940		59	606	Temple/Hamlyn/BMS		S	$20
Bugatti (Ballantine)	Barker R	71	107	Ballantine Books	Ballantine #1	S	$20
Bugatti (Borgeson)	Borgeson G	81	107	Osprey		H	$90
Bugatti (Conway & Greilsamer)	Conway H G/Greilsamer J	78+	107	Editions Modelisme		H	$125
Bugatti Book	Eaglesfield B	54	107	MRP		H	$150
Bugatti Carlo-Rembrandt-Ettore ...	Dejean P	82	107	Rizzoli Int. Pub.		H	$200

Title	Author	Pub date	Subjects	Publisher	Series	Bind	Price
Bugatti Evolution of Style	Kestler P	77	107	Edita		H	$100
Bugatti Quality of Work/Art	Hallums E	79	107	Mithra Press		S	$100
Bugatti Story(Boddy)	Boddy W	60	107	Sports Car Press		S	$30
Bugatti Story(Bugatti)	Bugatti L	67	107	Chilton		H	$50
Bugatti Thoroughbreds From Molsheim	Dumont P	75	107	EPA/MBI/Albion Scott	Prestige.......	H	$125
Buggy-Go-Round (dune buggy racing)	Radlauer E/Radlauer R S	71	299 213	Collins		H	$20
Buick Cars 1929-39	Clarke R M	75	108	Brooklands	Brooklands	S	$40
Buick Golden Era 1903-1915	Therou F	71	108	Decir		H	$90
Buick Gran Sports GS Enthusiast....	Dove S L	89	108	Muscle Car Pubs		S	$40
Buick Gran Sports Source Book	Zavitz R P	84	108	Bookman	Source Book	S	$30
Buick Postwar Years	Norbye J P/Dunne J	78	108	MBI	Marques America	H	$50
Buick Riviera 1963-1978	Clarke R M	85	108	Brooklands	Brooklands	S	$30
Buick Riviera 1963-73 all series...	Wolfe C	86	108	MBI		S	$40
Buick V-8 & V-6 Performance Years	Schorr M L	83	108	Quicksilver		S	$20
Buick When Better Automobiles (Ads)	Mayborn M	72+	108	Highland		S	$20
Building and Operating Model Cars	Musciano W A	56	701	Funk & Wagnells		H	$30
Building and Racing Hot Rod	Hot Rod	66	202	Petersen/Signet/NAL		S	$10
Building Chevy Sprint Car Eng	Thawley J	80	111	Steve Smith		S	$20
Building Fire Truck (juvenile)	Bushey J	81	302	Carolrhoda		H	$20
Building Model Trucks	Jensen P	73	703	Auto-World/Haessner		H	$40
Built for Speed 24 Motorcycles	Griffith J	62	603	Temple		H	$40
Buses & Coaches 1945-1965	Gillham J	76		Almark		H	$20
Buses and Coaches from 1940	Vanderveen B H	74		Warne	Olyslager	H	$30
Buses and Trolleybuses 1919 to 1945	Kaye D	70		Blandford		H	$20
Buses and Trolleybuses Before 1919	Kaye D	72		Blandford		H	$20
Buses of World	Moses D	82		Ian Allan Ltd		H	$30
Buses on Continent 1898-1976	Kuipers J F J	77		Oakwood	Locomotion Pprs	S	$10
Buses Trolleys & Trams	Dunbar C S	67		Hamlyn		H	$10
Buyers Guide to European Autos	Shwetzer E L	54	412	Heinrich Klammes Press		S	$30
CART 1988-89 Men and Machines......	Hughes J	88	204	Autosport Intl		H	$70
CART 1989 Media Guide	CART	89	204	CART Pub Relations		S	$20
CART 1989-90 Men and Machines......	Hughes J	89	204	Autosport Intl		H	$60
Cabriolets	Thevenet J-P/Vann P	86	401	EPA/MBI		H	$40
Cadillac 1940-1984 ID Guide	Lehwald E A	84	110	Bookman Dan	ID Guide	S	$30
Cadillac 1950-59 (Automobile Hrtg)	Schneider R A	78	110	Automobile Heritage		H	$80
Cadillac Automobiles - 1904			110	Clymer (catalog reprint)		S	$10
Cadillac Data Bk & Price Gd 1960-69	Zavitz R P	85	110	Bookman		S	$30
Cadillac in Sixties No 1	Clarke R M	82	110	Brooklands	Brooklands	S	$20
Cadillac Participtn World War (I)	Cadillac	19	110 308	Cadillac		H	$125
Cadillac Standard of Excellence	Langworth R M	80	110	Publications Intl	Consumer Guide	S	$20
Cadillac Toute L'Histoire(French)	Robinson W F	85	110	EPA	Auto Histoire	S	$20
Cale Hazardous Life and Times of...	Yarborough C/Neeley W	86	205	Times		H	$30
California Classics Vol I	Meyer J C	77	401	Classic Car Club of SC		H	$30
California Classics Vol II	Meyer J C	78	401	Classic Car Club of SC		H	$30
California Classics Vol III	Meyer J C	80	401	Classic Car Club of SC		H	$30
Camaro (Gallery)	Wright N	85	111	Gallery/Smith		H	$20
Camaro 67-69 Fact Book	Dobbins M F	84	111	Dobbins		X	$40
Camaro Book From A Through Z28	Lamm M	84	111	Lamm-Morada		H	$70
Camaro From Challenger to Champion	Witzenburg G	81	111	Automobile Quarterly		H	$60
Camaro Full Story of Chevrolets....	Consumer Gd	83	111	Publications Intl	Consumer GGuide	S	$10
Camaro Three Gen Premier Perf Cars	Schorr M L	82	111	Quicksilver	Quicksilver	S	$20
Canada on Wheels Portfolio of......	Bondt J D	70	413	Oberon		H	$40
Canadian Cars 1946-1984	Zavitz R P	85	413	Bookman		S	$30
Canadian Motorsport Annual 1981-82	Chapman P	82	204	Wheelspin News		S	$30
Canadian Motorsport Annual 1983-84	Chapman P	84	204	Wheelspin News		S	$30
Capri Muscle Cars 1969-1983	Clarke R M	84	156	Brooklands	Brooklands	S	$30
Car and Driver Racing Annual 66-67	Davis D E	67	204	Ziff-Davis		S	$30
Car Badges of World	Nicholson T R	70	507	American Heritage/Cassell		H	$60
Car Book Consumer's Gd to Car Buyng		80	401	U S Dept of Transportatn		S	$10
Car Culture (Flink)	Flink J J	75	419	MIT		X	$20
Car Culture (Rambali)	Rambali B	84	419	Plexus		S	$20
Car Driving as Art	Davis S C H	52	203	Iliffe		H	$20
Car Facts & Feats - Guinness	Harding A	71+	412	Sterling/Guinness		H	$20
Car Maintenance & Repair	Judge A W	28+	405	Chapman & Hall/Bentley	Motor Manual	H	$20
Car Mascots Enthusiasts Guide	Di Sirignano G	77	507	Crescent		H	$80
Car of Kings	Lozier H	67	130	Chilton Book Co.		H	$350
Car Racing 1953 (52 season)	Gardner A T G	53	204	Country & Sporting		S	$50
Car Spotters Encyclopedia 1940-80	Consumer Gd	82	401	Publications Int		S	$40
Car Styling No 01	Fujimoto A	73	508	San'ei Shobo		H	$100
Car Styling No 02	Fujimoto A	73	508	San'ei Shobo		H	$100
Car Styling No 03	Fujimoto A	73	508	San'ei Shobo		H	$90
Car Styling No 04	Fujimoto A	73	508	San'ei Shobo		H	$90
Car Styling No 05	Fujimoto A	73	508	San'ei Shobo		H	$90
Car Styling No 06	Fujimoto A	73	508	San'ei Shobo		H	$80
Car Styling No 07	Fujimoto A	74	508	San'ei Shobo		H	$80
Car Styling No 08	Fujimoto A	74	508	San'ei Shobo		H	$80
Car Styling No 09	Fujimoto A	75	508	San'ei Shobo		H	$80

Title	Author	Pub date	Subjects		Publisher	Series	Bind	Price
Car Styling No 10	Fujimoto A	75	508		San'ei Shobo		H	$80
Car Styling No 11	Fujimoto A	75	508		San'ei Shobo		H	$70
Car Styling No 12	Fujimoto A	75	508		San'ei Shobo		H	$70
Car Styling No 13	Fujimoto A	76	508		San'ei Shobo		H	$70
Car Styling No 14	Fujimoto A	76	508		San'ei Shobo		H	$70
Car Styling No 15	Fujimoto A	76	508		San'ei Shobo		H	$70
Car Styling No 16	Fujimoto A	76	508		San'ei Shobo		H	$60
Car Styling No 17	Fujimoto A	77	508		San'ei Shobo		H	$60
Car Styling No 18	Fujimoto A	77	508		San'ei Shobo		H	$60
Car Styling No 19	Fujimoto A	77	508		San'ei Shobo		H	$50
Car Styling No 19 - Bertone	Fujimoto A	77	508		San'ei Shobo		H	$60
Car Styling No 20	Fujimoto A	77	508		San'ei Shobo		H	$60
Car Styling No 21	Fujimoto A	78	508		San'ei Shobo		H	$60
Car Styling No 22	Fujimoto A	78	508		San'ei Shobo		H	$60
Car Styling No 23	Fujimoto A	78	508		San'ei Shobo		X	$60
Car Styling No 24	Fujimoto A	78	508		San'ei Shobo		H	$60
Car Styling No 25	Fujimoto A	79	508		San'ei Shobo		H	$60
Car Styling No 26	Fujimoto A	79	508		San'ei Shobo		X	$60
Car Styling No 27	Fujimoto A	79	508		San'ei Shobo		X	$60
Car Styling No 28	Fujimoto A	79	508		San'ei Shobo		X	$60
Car Styling No 29	Fujimoto A	80	508		San'ei Shobo		H	$60
Car Styling No 30	Fujimoto A	80	508		San'ei Shobo		H	$60
Car Styling No 31	Fujimoto A	80	508		San'ei Shobo		H	$60
Car Styling No 31 1/2 Porsche/Desg	Fujimoto A	80	508	136	San'ei Shobo		S	$70
Car Styling No 32	Fujimoto A	80	508		San'ei Shobo		H	$60
Car Styling No 33	Fujimoto A	81	508		San'ei Shobo		H	$60
Car Styling No 34	Fujimoto A	81	508		San'ei Shobo		H	$50
Car Styling No 35	Fujimoto A	81	508		San'ei Shobo		H	$50
Car Styling No 35 1/2 - Giugiaro	Fujimoto A	81	508		San'ei Shobo		S	$70
Car Styling No 36	Fujimoto A	81	508		San'ei Shobo		H	$50
Car Styling No 37	Fujimoto A	82	508		San'ei Shobo		H	$50
Car Styling No 38	Fujimoto A	82	508		San'ei Shobo		H	$50
Car Styling No 39	Fujimoto A	82	508		San'ei Shobo		H	$50
Car Styling No 40	Fujimoto A	82	508		San'ei Shobo		H	$50
Car Styling No 41	Fujimoto A	83	508		San'ei Shobo		H	$50
Car Styling No 42	Fujimoto A	83	508		San'ei Shobo		H	$50
Car Styling No 43	Fujimoto A	83	508		San'ei Shobo		X	$50
Car Styling No 44	Fujimoto A	83	508		San'ei Shobo		H	$50
Car Styling No 45	Fujimoto A	84	508		San'ei Shobo		X	$50
Car Styling No 46	Fujimoto A	84	508		San'ei Shobo		S	$50
Car Styling No 47	Fujimoto A	84	508		San'ei Shobo		S	$50
Car Styling No 48	Fujimoto A	84	508		San'ei Shobo		S	$50
Car Styling No 49	Fujimoto A	85	508		San'ei Shobo		S	$50
Car Styling No 50	Fujimoto A	85	508		San'ei Shobo		S	$50
Car Styling No 51	Fujimoto A	85	508		San'ei Shobo		S	$50
Car Styling No 52	Fujimoto A	85	508		San'ei Shobo		S	$50
Car Styling No 53	Fujimoto A	86	508		San'ei Shobo		S	$50
Car Styling No 54	Fujimoto A	86	508		San'ei Shobo		S	$50
Car Styling No 55	Fujimoto A	86	508		San'ei Shobo		S	$50
Car Styling No 56	Fujimoto A	86	508		San'ei Shobo		S	$50
Car Styling No 57	Fujimoto A	87	508		San'ei Shobo		S	$50
Car Styling No 58	Fujimoto A	87	508		San'ei Shobo		S	$50
Car Styling No 59	Fujimoto A	87	508		San'ei Shobo		S	$50
Car Styling No 60	Fujimoto A	87	508		San'ei Shobo		S	$50
Car Styling No 61	Fujimoto A	87	508		San'ei Shobo		S	$50
Car Styling No 62	Fujimoto A	88	508		San'ei Shobo		S	$50
Car Styling No 63	Fujimoto A	88	508		San'ei Shobo		S	$50
Car Styling No 64	Fujimoto A	88	508		San'ei Shobo		S	$50
Car Styling No 65	Fujimoto A	88	508		San'ei Shobo		S	$50
Car Styling No 66	Fujimoto A	88	508		San'ei Shobo		S	$50
Car Styling No 67	Fujimoto A	88	508		San'ei Shobo		S	$50
Car Styling No 68	Fujimoto A	89	508		San'ei Shobo		S	$50
Cara Automobile	Pininfarina E	68	504				H	$250
Caracciola Mercedes Grand Prix Ace	Caracciola R	55	130	205	Foulis		H	$70
Carburation Lube & Eng Metallurgy	Giles J G	68	405		Iliffe Books	AutoTech	H	$10
Carburetors & Carburetion	Larew W B	67	405		Chilton		H	$30
Carburettors and Fuel Systems	Judge A W	25+	405		Chapman & Hall/Bentley	Motor Manuals	H	$20
Carl Benz and Motor Car	Nye D	73	130		Priory Press	Pioneers S & D	H	$40
Carlotti Takes the Wheel (juv fict)	Hawthorn M	59	213	207	Childrens Book Club		H	$50
Carriages Cars and Cycles	Remise J & F	84	703		Edita	Wld of Ant Toys	H	$100
Carroll Shelby Story	Shelby C/Bentley J	67	109		Pocket Books		S	$30
Carroll Shelbys Racing Cobra S	Friedman D/Christy J	86	109		Newport/Petersen		S	$20
Carrozzeria Italiana Culturae......	Anselmi A T	78	501		Alfieri/Automobilia		H	$60
Carrozzeria italiana Advancing Art	Anselmi A T	80	501		Automobilia		H	$100
Cars 1886-1930	Georgano G N	85	401		Nordbok/Beekman/Crown		H	$40
Cars and Coachbuilding 100 Years...	Oliver G A	81	501		Sotheby		H	$70
Cars at Speed	Daley R	61	297		Foulis/Collier/Lippincott		X	$30

Title	Author	Pub date	Subjects	Publisher	Series	Bind	Price
Cars Cars Cars Cars	Davis S C H	67	401	Hamlyn		H	$20
Cars For Kids (Bebe Auto)	Massucci E	82	703	Automobilia		H	$100
Cars in Color	Pick C	79	401	Octopus		H	$10
Cars in My Life	Bentley W O	63	139	Macmillan		H	$60
Cars in Profile 01 246 P4 Ferraris	Frere P	72	121	Profile Publications		S	$10
Cars in Profile 02 4.5 Lago-Talbot	Posthumus C	72	120	Profile Publications		S	$20
Cars in Profile 03 F1 Repco-Brabham	Nye D	72	298	Profile Publications		S	$10
Cars in Profile 04 Chaparral 2.....	Lyons P	72	299	Profile Publications		S	$20
Cars in Profile 05 Porsche 917	Frere P	73	136	Profile Publications		S	$20
Cars in Profile 06 Alfa Monoposto..	Hull P	73	101	Profile Publications		S	$10
Cars in Profile 07 Facel Vega	Sedgwick M	73	120	Profile Publications		S	$20
Cars in Profile 08 McLaren M8	Hodges D	73	298	Profile Publications		S	$20
Cars in Profile 09 4 1/2 Bentley	Berthon D/Stamer A	73	139	Profile Publications		S	$10
Cars in Profile 10 Matra MS80	Crombac G	73	120 298	Profile Publications		S	$10
Cars in Profile 11 Jaguar D-Type	Appleton J	73	127	Profile Publications		S	$10
Cars in Profile 12 Rolls-Royce P2	Oliver G A	73	139	Profile Publications		S	$10
Cars in Profile Coll. 1	Harding A	73	401	Profile Pulications		H	$30
Cars in Profile Coll. 2	Harding A	74	401	Profile Publications	Cars in Profile	H	$30
Cars New Classics	Harvey C	81	401	Hennerwood/Octopus/Treasu		H	$20
Cars Old Classics From Early Days..	Whyte A	83	401	Mandarin/Octopus		H	$20
Cars of 1923	Marvin K/Homan A L	57	403	Automobilists of UHV		S	$30
Cars of 1930's	Sedgwick M	70	401	Robert Bentley, Inc.		H	$40
Cars of 30s	Consumer Gd	80	403	Publications Intl		H	$30
Cars of 30s and 40s	Sedgwick M	80	401	Nordbok/Crown/Hamlyn		H	$40
Cars of 40s	Consumer Gd	79	403	Pub Intl/Crown/Beekman	Consumer Gd	X	$30
Cars of 50s	Consumer Gd	78	403	Pub Int/Crown	Consumer Guide	X	$30
Cars of 50s and 60s	Sedgwick M	83	401	Nordbok/Beekman/Crown		H	$40
Cars of 60s	Consumer Gd	79	403	Pub Int/Crown/Beekman	Consumer Gd	X	$20
Cars of Canada - Craven Foundation	Durnford H/Baechler G	73	413	McClelland & Stewart		H	$150
Cars of Connoisseur	Buckley J R	60	401	Batsford/Macmillan		H	$40
Cars of Early Thirties	Burness T	70	403	Chilton/Galahad		H	$40
Cars of Early Twenties	Burness T	68	403	Chilton		H	$40
Cars of Stars	Barris G/Scagnetti J	74	509	Jonathan David		H	$40
Cars of Stars & Movie Memories	Clymer F	54	509	Clymer		S	$30
Cars of World in Color	Scheel J D	64	401	Methuen/Dutton		H	$10
Cars That Got Away Ideas Exper.....	Frostick M	68	401	Cassell		H	$60
Cars That Henry Ford Built	Kimes B R	78	122	AQ		H	$40
Cars That Hudson Built	Conde J	80	163	Arnold-Porter		H	$60
Cars That Never Were Prototypes	Langworth R M	81	401	Pub Int/Beekman/Crown	Consumer Gd	H	$30
Cars Tin Toy Dreams	Kitihara T	84	703	Chronicle		S	$30
Cars to Remember 37 Great Autos....	Neeley W/Lamm J	75	401	Regnery		H	$40
Case Album	Brown E	82	901	Condie		S	$20
Case History	Smith N	58	298	Autosport		H	$40
Case History Story of Jaguar.......		64	127	Jaguar Cars		S	$40
Cast Iron Wonder Chevrolets Fab Six	Bell D	61	111	Clymer		S	$30
Castrol Rally Manual (1)	Browning P	71	209	PSL		H	$20
Castrol Rally Manual 2	Browning P	72	209	PSL		H	$20
Catalog of British Cars 1949-1950	Chambers P	49	406	Clymer		S	$20
Catalogue of Model Cars of World	Greilsamer J/Azema B	67	702	Edita/Haessner/PSL		H	$125
Cavallino No. 01 (Vol 01-1)		78	121	John W. Barnes		S	$500
Cavallino No. 01 (Vol 01-1) reprint		87	121	Barnes		S	$20
Cavallino No. 02 (Vol 01-2)		78	121	Barnes		S	$300
Cavallino No. 03 (Vol 01-3)		79	121	Barnes		S	$80
Cavallino No. 04 (Vol 01-4)		79	121	Barnes		S	$80
Cavallino No. 05 (Vol 01-5)		79	121	Barnes		S	$80
Cavallino No. 06 (Vol 01-6)		79	121	Barnes		S	$80
Cavallino No. 07 (Vol 02-1)		79	121	Barnes		S	$100
Cavallino No. 08 (Vol 02-8)		79	121	Barnes		S	$80
Cavallino No. 09		79	121	Barnes		S	$100
Cavallino No. 10		80	121	Barnes		S	$80
Cavallino No. 11		80	121	Barnes		S	$70
Cavallino No. 12		81	121	Barnes		S	$80
Cavallino No. 13		81	121	Barnes		S	$50
Cavallino No. 14		82	121	Barnes		S	$80
Cavallino No. 15		82	121	Barnes		S	$80
Cavallino No. 16		83	121	Cavallino		S	$80
Cavallino No. 17		83	121	Cavallino		S	$80
Cavallino No. 18		83	121	Cavallino		S	$80
Cavallino No. 19		83	121	Cavallino		S	$30
Cavallino No. 20		84	121	Cavallino		S	$30
Cavallino No. 21		84	121	Cavallino		S	$80
Cavallino No. 22		84	121	Cavallino		S	$80
Cavallino No. 23		84	121	Cavallino		S	$20
Cavallino No. 24		85	121	Cavallino		S	$20
Cavallino No. 25		85	121	Cavallino		S	$20
Cavallino No. 26		85	121	Cavallino		S	$80
Cavallino No. 27		85	121	Cavallino		S	$20

Title	Author	Pub date	Subjects	Publisher	Series	Bind	Price
Cavallino No. 28		85	121	Cavallino		S	$20
Cavallino No. 29		86	121	Cavallino		S	$20
Cavallino No. 30		86	121	Cavallino		S	$20
Cavallino No. 31		86	121	Cavallino		S	$20
Cavallino No. 32		86	121	Cavallino		S	$60
Cavallino No. 33		86	121	Cavallino		S	$80
Cavallino No. 34		86	121	Cavallino		S	$80
Cavallino No. 35		86	121	Cavallino		S	$80
Cavallino No. 36		86	121	Cavallino		S	$30
Cavallino No. 37		87	121	Cavallino		S	$20
Cavallino No. 38		87	121	Cavallino		S	$80
Cavallino No. 39		87	121	Cavallino		S	$80
Cavallino No. 40		87	121	Cavallino		S	$30
Cavallino No. 41		87	121	Cavallino		S	$60
Cavallino No. 42		87	121	Cavallino		S	$60
Cavallino No. 43		88	121	Cavallino		S	$60
Cavallino No. 44		88	121	Cavallino		S	$30
Cavallino No. 45		88	121	Cavallino		S	$30
Cavallino No. 46		88	121	Cavallino		S	$30
Cavallino No. 47		88	121	Cavallino		S	$30
Cavallino No. 48		88	121	Cavallino		S	$30
Cavallino No. 49		89	121	Cavallino		S	$60
Cavallino No. 50		89	121	Cavallino		S	$20
Cavallino No. 51		89	121	Cavallino		S	$30
Cavallino No. 52		89	121	Cavallino		S	$20
Cavallino No. 53		89	121	Cavallino		S	$60
Centenary of Car 1885-1985	Whyte A	84	401	Octopus/Longmeadow/Walden		H	$30
Century of Change - Caterpillar		84	906	Caterpillar World		S	$20
Century on Wheels Story of Am Auto	Miller E K	87	418	Pioneer		H	$40
Century on Wheels Story Studebaker	Longstreet S	52	145	Holt/Greenwood		H	$40
Certain Sound 30 Years of Motor Rac	Wyer J	81	298	Edita/Haynes		H	$125
Chain-Drive Frazer Nash	Thirlby T	65	105	Macdonald/MBC		H	$90
Chainless Wolverine			158	Clymer (reprint brochure)		S	$10
Challenge Me Race	Hawthorn M	58+	205	William Kimber		H	$40
Challenger Mickey Thompsons Story	Thompson M/Borgeson G	64	205 211	Prentice Hall		X	$40
Champion of World	Seidler E	70	205	Automobile Year		H	$80
Champion Year My Battle Wld Title	Hawthorn M	59	205	Kimber		H	$40
Champions at Speed	Corson R	79	205 213	Dodd Mead		H	$20
Champions of Indianapolis 500	Libby B	76	208	Dodd Mead		H	$20
Charger V2 Source Book	North P	85	115	Bookman	Source Boo	S	$20
Checkered Flag (Gault - juvenile)	Gault W C	64	213	Dutton		H	$20
Checkered Flag (Helck)	Helck P	61	504 297	Scribner/Castle		H	$200
Chequered Flag (Rutherford)	Rutherford D	56	298	Collins		H	$30
Chequered Year Story of GP Season	Simon T	71	297	Cassell		H	$40
Chevelle 64-73 Databook & Price Gd	Zavitz R P	86	111	Bookman Dan		S	$30
Chevelle SS Vol II A Source Book	Lehwald E A	85	111	Bookman	Source Boo	S	$30
Chevrolet 1911-1985	Langworth R M/Norbye J P	84	111	Publications Intl	Consumer Guide	H	$40
Chevrolet 1955-1957	Consumer Gd	87	111	Publications Intl/Crown		H	$20
Chevrolet Camaro Coll No 1 1967-73	Clarke R M	85	111	Brooklands	Brooklands	S	$20
Chevrolet Celebrating 75 Yrs Perf..	McGonegal R	86	111	Petersen	Magazine Spec'l	S	$10
Chevrolet Coming of Age 1911-42	Miller R	76	111	Evergreen		H	$80
Chevrolet Corvette 68-82 Autohist..	Falconer T	83	114	Osprey		H	$40
Chevrolet Performance Handbook	Ritch O C/Hot Rod Editors	63	111	Petersen	Hot Rod	S	$30
Chevrolet Power		78	111	Chevrolet Motors		S	$10
Chevrolet Racing Engine	Jenkins B	76	111	SA		S	$30
Chevrolet Small/Big Block Parts Gd		76	111	Phase III		S	$20
Chevrolet Speed Manual	Fisher B	54	111	Clymer		S	$30
Chevrolet=Racing 14 Years of.......	Van Valkenburgh P	72	111	Haessner		H	$180
Chevy El Camino 1959-82 Photofacts	Wood D F	82	111	MBI	CMB Photofacts	S	$40
Chevy Spotter's Guide 1920-1980	Burness T	81	111	MBI		S	$20
Chicago Fire Department Engines	Little K/Rosenhan K	72	302	Little/Rosenhan		S	$50
Chilton Automotive Multi-Guide		70+	405	Chilton		S	$20
Chiltons Comp Bk of Auto Facts	Norback C T	81	412	Chilton		X	$30
Chitty Chitty Bang Bang Magical Car	Fleming I	64	424	Random		H	$30
Chris Amon (Italian)	Tommasi T	69	205	L'Editrice Dell'Automobil		H	$20
Christophorus 1970 Yearbook	Von Frankenberg R	70	136	Porsche		S	$30
Chrome Colossus GM & Its Times	Cray E	80	160	McGraw		H	$40
Chrome Dreams Auto Styling Since 93	Wilson P C	76	502	Chilton		H	$30
Chrome Glamour Cars of Fifties	Laban B	82	401	Gallery/Orbis/Smith		H	$40
Chronicle of Auto Ind in Amer 93-46	Eaton Mfg	46	418	Eaton Mfg		S	$40
Chrysler & Imperial Postwar Years	Langworth R M	76	112	MBI		H	$60
Chrysler 300 1955-1961 Photofacts	Gunnell J	82	112	MBI	CMB Photofacts	S	$40
Chrysler 300 Source Book	Bonsall T E/Shields S A	81	112	Bookman	Source Book	S	$30
Chrysler Cars 1930-1939	Clarke R M	80	112	Brooklands	Brooklands	S	$30
Chrysler Corp Cars Perf Handbook	Martin W H/Hot Rod Eds	62	112	Petersen	Hot Rod	S	$30
Chrysler Corp Story of American Co	Chrysler	55	112	Chrysler		S	$30
Circuit Dust	Lyndon B	34	298	John Miles		H	$125

Title	Author	Pub date	Subjects		Publisher	Series	Bind	Price
Cisitalia	Balestra N/De Agostini C	80	118		Automobilia		H	$150
Citroen (Great Cars Series)	Broad R	75	153		Luscombe	Great Cars	H	$40
Citroen 2CV Collectors Guide	Taylor J	83	153		MRP	Coll Gd	H	$50
Citroen Great Marque of France	Dumont P	76	153		Interauto/MBI/EPA		H	$100
Citroen SM 1970-1975		85	153		EPA	Les Archives...	S	$40
Citroen SM Autohistory	Daniels J	81	153		Osprey	Autohistory	H	$50
Citroen Traction Avant 1934-1957	Sabates F	83	153		Vu Par La Presse	Coll Auto Achvs	S	$20
Citroen Traction Avant 34-39 (#3)	Sabates F/Didier L	83	153		Vu Par La Presse		S	$40
City of Flint Grows Up	Crow C	45	108		Harper		H	$30
Classic American Automobiles	Burgess Wise D	80	403		Albany/Galahad		H	$30
Classic American Cars	Nichols R	86	403		Bison/Bookthrift/Exeter		H	$20
Classic and Sportscar Lotus File	Hughes M	87	129		Bay View/Temple/Hamlyn		H	$50
Classic and Sportscar MG File	Buckley M	87	131		Bay View/Temple/Hamlyn		H	$50
Classic British Scramblers	Morley D	86	606		Osprey	Coll Lib	H	$50
Classic Car Profiles V1 1-24/3V set	Harding A	66	401		Profile Publications		H	$70
Classic Car Profiles V2 25-60/3V st	Harding A	67	401		Profile Publications		H	$125
Classic Car Profiles V3 61-96/3V st	Harding A	67	401		Profile Publications		H	$125
Classic Cars (Bishop)	Bishop G	79	401		Hamlyn/Crown/Crescent		H	$30
Classic Cars (in Col/Batsford Bk)	Buckley J R	64	401		Batsford/Viking	Batsford/Col Bk	H	$10
Classic Cars (Nichols)	Nichols R	84	401		Bison/Bookthrift/Exeter		H	$20
Classic Cars (Rand McNally)	Casucci P	78	412		Mondadori/Rand McNally	R-M Col Ill Gds	S	$20
Classic Cars 1930-40	Scott-Moncrieff D	63	401		Batsford/Bentley		H	$30
Classic Cars 50 Yrs Wlds Finest....	Brazendale K/Aceti E	79	401		Exeter/Bookthrift/Orbis		H	$30
Classic Cars and Antiques(Trend 111	Bowman H W/Gottlieb R J	53	401		Trend	Trend	S	$10
Classic Cars and Specials(Trend 135	Gottlieb R J	56	401		Trend	Trend	S	$10
Classic Cars Cadillac	Smith L/Hossain T	83	110		Col Lib Books		H	$30
Classic Cars in Profile V1 1-24	Harding A	67+	401		Profile/Doubleday		H	$70
Classic Cars in Profile V2 25-48	Harding A	67+	401		Profile/Doubleday		H	$70
Classic Cars in Profile V3 49-72	Harding A	67	401		Profile/Doubleday		H	$70
Classic Cars in Profile V4 73-96	Harding A	68	401		Profile/Doubleday		H	$125
Classic Cord	Post D R	52	116		Post		X	$70
Classic Corvette	Nichols R	83	114		Bookthrift/Exeter/Bison		H	$20
Classic Ferrari (Eaton)	Eaton G	83	121		Exeter/Bison/Bookthrift		H	$20
Classic Mercedes-Benz(Drackett)	Drackett P	83	130		Exeter/Bookthrift/Bison		H	$20
Classic MG	Aspden R	83	131		Bison/Bookthrift/Exeter		H	$20
Classic MG Yearbook 1973	Knudson R L	74	131		Motorcars Unlimited		H	$40
Classic Motorbooks 1970 Catalog		69	001				S	$50
Classic Motorbooks 1971 Catalog		70	001				S	$40
Classic Motorbooks 1972 Catalog		71	001				S	$40
Classic Motorbooks 1973 Catalog		72	001				S	$40
Classic Motorbooks 1974 Catalog		73	001				S	$40
Classic Motorbooks 1975 Catalog		74	001				S	$30
Classic Motorbooks 1976 Catalog		75	001				S	$30
Classic Motorbooks 1977 Catalog		76	001				S	$30
Classic Motorbooks 1978 Catalog		77	001				S	$30
Classic Motorbooks 1978 Mtcycl Cat		77	001				S	$20
Classic Motorbooks 1979 Catalog		78	001				S	$20
Classic Motorbooks 1980 Catalog		79	001				S	$20
Classic Motorbooks 1981 Catalog		80	001				S	$20
Classic Motorbooks 1982 Catalog		81	001				S	$20
Classic Motorbooks 1983 Catalog		82	001				S	$20
Classic Motorbooks 1984 Catalog		83	001				S	$10
Classic Motorbooks 1985 Catalog		84	001				S	$10
Classic Motorbooks 1986 Catalog		85	001				S	$10
Classic Motorcycle Racer Tests	Cathcart A	84	604		Osprey	Osprey Coll Lib	H	$50
Classic Motorcycles	Willoughby V	75	601		Hamlyn/Dial		H	$50
Classic Motorcycles in Australia	Dumble D B	77	601		Dumble		S	$20
Classic Porsche	McCarthy M	83	136		Bison/Fell/Exeter		H	$20
Classic Racing Cars	Posthumus C	77	297		Rand McNally/Hamlyn		H	$40
Classic Rolls-Royce	Georgano G N	83	139		Exeter/Bison		H	$20
Classic Single-Seaters Donington	Nye D	74	298		Macmillan		H	$50
Classic Sports Cars	Badre P/Martinez A	87	401		EPA/Bookthrift/Exeter		H	$20
Classic Supercharged Sports Cars	Perkins T J	84	401		Paradise		H	$60
Classic Tradition of Lincoln MC	Kimes B R	68	161		Automobile Quarterly		H	$50
Classic Twin-Cam Engine	Borgeson G	81	405		Dalton Watson	Dalton Watson	H	$100
Classics and Antiques - Trend	Bowman H W/Gottlieb R J	53	401		Trend	Trend Book	X	$20
Classics of the Road	Wise D B	78	401		Orbis		H	$20
Climax in Coventry My Life of Fine	Hassan W/Robson G	75	404		MRP		H	$40
Close Calls	Garlits D/Hicks D E	84	205	201	Huntington House		S	$20
Clubman Racer P2 Daytona (Japanese)	Ukon T	86	602		Neko		S	$30
Clutch & Flywheel Handbook	Monroe T	77	202		H P Books		S	$30
Coach Trimmers Art	Sherrington L F	81	405		Tab		X	$30
Coachbuilt Packard	Pfau H	73	159		Dalton Watson	Dalton Watson	H	$150
Coachwork of Erdmann & Rossi	Stuhlemmer R	79	501		Dalton Watson	Dalton Watson	H	$70
Coachwork on Rolls-Royce 1906-1939	Dalton L	75	139		Dalton Watson	Dalton Watson	H	$100
Coast to Coast in Brush Rnabout	Trinkle F M	52	158	212	Clymer		S	$30
Cobra (Legate)	Legate T	84	109		Chambers Green/Haynes/MBI		H	$90

Title	Author	Pub date	Subjects	Publisher	Series	Bind	Price
Cobra Story	Shelby C/Bentley J	65+	109	Trident/MBI		H	$50
Collecting & Rest Antique Fire Engs	Lichty R	81	302	Tab		S	$30
Collecting & Restoring Antique Cars	Wilk P	78	401	Book Creations/Cornerston		S	$20
Collecting Rstng Rdg Classic Mtcyls	Holmes T/Smith R	86+	609	PSL		S	$30
Collector's History of Automobile	Roberts P	78	401	Ottenheimer/Crown/Bon		H	$20
Collectors All Color Gd to Toy Cars	Gardiner G/O'Neill R	85	704	Salamander		H	$40
Collectors Cars	Brown J	85	401	Cavendish/Booksales/Chtwl		H	$20
Collectors Cars (Culpepper)	Culpepper L	79	401	Octopus		H	$20
Colonels Ferraris Maranello Con...	Nye D	80	121	Ampersand/Maranello		H	$40
Color Treasury of Autos & Model Crs	Massucci E	72	702	Orbis/Crescent		H	$20
Color Treasury of Formula 1 Cars		70S	297	Crescent Books		H	$10
Color Treasury of Racing Cars		71	297	Geografico/Orbis/Crescent		H	$10
Colorful World of Motorsport	Daniels J	80	297	Octopus		H	$20
Combat Motor Racing History	Lyndon B	33	298	Heinemann		H	$150
Combustion on Wheels	Cohn D L	44	419	Houghton Mifflin		H	$20
Comicar (automobile in comic strip)	Bertieri C	75	504	Editori Milano		H	$250
Comp Bk Automobile Body Des	Beattie I	77	502	Haynes		H	$30
Comp Bk Bldg/Coll Mod Autos	Hertz L H	70	702	Crown		H	$40
Comp Bk Collectible Cars 30-80	Langworth R M/Robson G	82+	401	Pub Int/Beekman/Crown	Consumer Guide	H	$40
Comp Bk Collectible Cars 40-80	Langworth R M	85	401	Publications Intl		H	$30
Comp Bk Electric Vehicles	Shacket S R	81+	417	Domus/Quality		X	$30
Comp Bk Fire Engines	Ditzel P C	82	302	Publications Intl	Consumer Gd	S	$10
Comp Bk Fuel & Gas Dragsters	Engel L K	68	201	Four Winds		H	$30
Comp Bk Horse Racing/Auto Racing	Brown G	80	297	NY Times/Arno/Bobbs	NY Times SB His	H	$30
Comp Bk Karting	Day D	61	214	Prentice-Hall		H	$30
Comp Bk Lamborghini	Lyons P	88	128	Pub Intl/Haynes/Guild	Consumer Guide	H	$40
Comp Bk Model Raceways & Rdways	Hertz L H	64	701	Crown		H	$40
Comp Bk NASCAR Stk Cr Rac	Engel L K	68	299	Four Winds/Scholastic		X	$30
Comp Bk Stock-Bod Drag Rac H	Engel L K	70	201	Four Winds		H	$30
Comp Bk Stock-Bod Drag Rac S	Engel L K	70	201	Scholastic		S	$10
Comp Car Modeller	Wingrove G	78	702	Crown/New Cav/Eyre Meth..		H	$90
Comp Catalog Japanese Motor Veh	Clymer F	61	420	Clymer		S	$50
Comp Catalogue of British Cars	Culshaw D/Hoffobin P	74	406	Walter Parrish/Morrow		H	$150
Comp Ency Comm Vehicles	Georgano G N	79	306	Krause		H	$80
Comp Ency of American Automobile	Ludvigsen K E/Wise D B	77+	403	Orbis		H	$30
Comp Ency of M/C(see NEW ENC)	Georgano G N	68+	401	Dutton		H	$50
Comp Gd Bolt-On Performance	Schreib L	78	202	SA		S	$30
Comp Gd Triumph TR7 & TR8	Kimberley W	81	146	Dalton Watson		H	$40
Comp Gd to American Cars 66-76	Lintern M	77	403	AutoMedia		S	$30
Comp Gd to Kit Cars	Kutner R M	77+	423	Auto Logic		S	$10
Comp Gd to Volvo 1800 Series	Creighton J	82	165	Dalton Watson		H	$40
Comp HB Front Wheel Drive Cars	Norbye J P	79	405	Tab		S	$20
Comp HB Model Car Racing	Aurora Plastics Corp	67	701	Prentice		H	$40
Comp HB Sand Blasting	Ammen C	79	405	Tab		S	$20
Comp Hist Chrysler Corp 1924-1985	Langworth R M/ Norbye J	85	112	Pub Intl/Beekman/Crown	Consumer Guide	X	$40
Comp Hist Ford Motor Company	Langworth R M	87	122	Pub Int/Beekman/Crown	Consumer Guide	H	$40
Comp Hist General Motors	Langworth R M/Norbye J P	86	160	Publications Intl	Consumer Guide	H	$50
Comp Hist German Car 1886..........	Norbye J P	87	408	Ervin/Crown/Portland		H	$30
Comp Hist Grand Prix Motor Racing	Cimarosti A	86+	298	Hallwag/Bateman/Crescent		H	$50
Comp Hist Japanese Car 1907-Pr	Ruiz M	86	126	Portland House/Crown		H	$20
Comp Ill Ency of World Motorcycles	Tragatsch E	77	601	Holt Rinehart Winston		H	$60
Comp Mercedes Story	Nitske R	55	130	Macmillan		H	$30
Comp Motorcycle Book	Engel L K	74	601	Four Winds		H	$20
Comp Pirelli Cal-see HEAVENLY B			510				$
Comp Rally Book	Hebb D	79	209	Stein & Day		S	$20
Comp Ray Kunz Auto Racing Book	Kuns R F	?	299	Ray Kuns		S	$50
Comp Van Book	Truscott L K	76	307	Harmony/Crown		S	$20
Competition Cars of Europe	Pritchard A	70	298	Bobbs-Merrill		H	$30
Competition Corvette	Consumer Gd	80	114	Publications Intl		S	$10
Competition Driv SEE Sports Car &..			203				$
Competition Driving	Marshall G	79	203	Foulsham		H	$20
Competitive Driving	Roberts P	64	203	Stanley Paul		H	$30
Compleat Hist Corvair for Nut V1	Wimpff J	78+	113	Clark's Corvair Parts		S	$40
Compleat Hist Corvair for Nut V2	Wimpff J	80	113	Vair Press		S	$30
Concise Cat. 1-75 Series Matchbox	Leake G	81	702	Leake		S	$20
Concise Dictionary of Motorsport	Bishop G	79	297	Bison/Mayflower		H	$20
Concise Ill Bk Modern Sports Cars	Ward L	89	401	Brian Trodd/W H Smith		H	$10
Concours d'Elegance	Wherry J H	69	401	Howell North		H	$30
Confessions of Automotive Stylist	Thomas B	84	502	Thomas		H	$60
Connoisseurs Choice-Racing/Spt/TrgC	Burgess J	79	401	Walker & Company		S	$20
Constant Search Coll Motoring Books	Mortimer C	82	507	Haynes		H	$60
Construction of Ford Specials	Mills J	60	156	Batsford		H	$40
Contemporary Classics Three........	Taylor R	74	401	Western	Golden Wheels	H	$10
Continental Circus	Mellors T/Davison G S	49	603	T T Special		H	$60
Continental Mark III		68	161	Ford Motor Co.		S	$30
Continental Sports Cars	Boddy W	51	401	Foulis		H	$40
Controlling Racing Car Team	Davis S C H	51	298	Foulis		H	$30

Title	Author	Pub date	Subjects	Publisher	Series	Bind	Price
Convert your Compact Car to Elec...	Jones C R	81	417	Domus		S	$20
Convertibles Complete Story	Gunnell J	84	401	Tab		S	$40
Cooper Cars	Nye D	83+	298	Osprey		H	$100
Cord Front Drive - O/M Mod.810-812		51	116	Floyd Clymer		S	$10
Cord Front-Drive	Huntington R	57+	116	Clymer/MBI		X	$40
Cord Sales Catalog			116	Floyd Clymer		S	$10
Corgi Toys Ones with Windows	Wieland J/Force E	81	702	MBI		S	$40
Corvair 1959-1968	Clarke R M	84	113	Brooklands	Brooklands	S	$30
Corvair Affair	Knepper M	82	113	MBI		H	$40
Corvair Decade	Fiore T	80	113	Corvair Society		H	$50
Corvair Hist & Restoration Guide	Artzberger B	84	113	Aztex		S	$50
Corvair Performance Handbook	Ritch O C	63	113	Petersen		S	$20
Corvair SAE Papers		79	113	SAE		S	$20
Corvette (Coleman)	Coleman B	83+	114	Wncmr/Smith/Gallery/CP		H	$20
Corvette Americas Only	Antonick M	78	114	Michael Bruce Associates		H	$50
Corvette Americas Only True Spts Cr	Consumer Gd	78	114	Publications Intl/Mayflwr	Consumer Gd	H	$10
Corvette Americas Only(leather)	Antonick M	78	114	Michael Bruce Associates		L	$150
Corvette Americas Sports Car (84)	Koblenz J	84	114	Pub Intl/Cons Gd/Beekman	Consumer Gd	H	$30
Corvette Body Repair Guide V2 68-82	Schiro R J	81	114	Glas-Ra		S	$70
Corvette Cars 1955-1964	Clarke R M	79	114	Brooklands	Brooklands	S	$30
Corvette Guide	Thompson D	58	114	Sports Car Press/Arco		H	$30
Corvette Past Present Future	Consumer Gd	84	114	Publications Intl	Consumer Guide	H	$10
Corvette Performance	Popular HR	77	114	Argus		H	$20
Corvette Restoration Srce Bk 53-67	Johnson R	78	114	Johnson		S	$60
Corvette Sensuous Am 1-1 thru 3-3	Antonick M	78	114	Michael Bruce Associates		H	$500
Corvette Sensuous Am 83-1 thru 85-3	Antonick M	83+	114	Michael Bruce Associates		H	$500
Corvette Sports Car of America	Antonick M	80	114	Michael Bruce Associates		H	$60
Corvettes for Road	Rasmussen H	84	114	MBI	Survivors	H	$40
Corvettes Technically Speaking	Harrison M C	77	114	M & H Engineering		S	$125
Cosworth	Wells K	87	297	Kimberley		S	$30
Cougar Source Book	Bonsall T E	83	166	Bookman Dan	Source Book	S	$30
Crescent Color Gd to Classic Cars	Roberts P	80	401	Hamlyn/Crown/Crescent		H	$10
Cruel Sport	Daley R	63	297	Prentice/Studio V/Crown		H	$90
Cult of Big Rigs	Ewens G/Ellis M	77	306	Quarto/Book Sales/Chrtwl		H	$20
Cult of Harley-Davidson	Foster G	82	607	Osprey Publications	Osprey Colour	S	$30
Custom Body Era	Pfau H	70	501	Barnes/Castle		H	$100
Custom Cars 1954 Annual (Trend 109)	Behme R L	53	422	Trend	Trend Book	S	$20
Custom Motorcycles St Bikes on Show	Morland A	83	601	Osprey	Colour Lib	S	$30
Customizing Vans	Beedie M	78	307	Blaketon Hall/Arco		H	$20
Cycle Jumpers	Spiegel M	73	601	Scholastic/Berkley		S	$10
DAF - World Trucks No 5	Kennett P	79	303	PSL	World Trucks	H	$30
Daimler & Lanchester Owners' Comp	Whyte R I	81	105	DLOC		S	$20
Daimler 1896 to 1946 50 Years of...	Nixon S J C	46	105	Foulis		H	$70
Daimler Dart & V8 250 1959-69	Clarke R M	82	105	Brooklands	Brooklands	S	$30
Daimler Tradition	Smith B E	72	105	Transport Bookman		H	$90
Danhausens World Modelcar Book '79		78	702	Danhausen		S	$30
Danhausens World Modelcar Book '85	Lang H P/Lang P G	84	702	Danhausen		S	$20
Danhausens World Modelcar Book '86	Lang H P/Lang P G	85	702	Danhausen		S	$20
Daredevils of Speedway	Olney R R	66	205	Grosset & Dunlap		H	$30
Das Buch Von Volkswagen 1938-1988	Vetten H	88	150	Volkswagen AG		H	$50
Das Maybach-Register	Metternich M G W	81	124	Sieger Verlag		H	$70
Das Werk Opel	Kroth K A	30S	124	Max Schroder		H	$40
Data Book of Tires 1930-41 US Cars		50S	405	Clymer		S	$20
Datsun 240Z & 260Z 1970-1977	Clarke R M	80	167	Brooklands	Brooklands	S	$30
Datsun 280ZX		78	126	Nissan Motor Co		S	$30
Datsun Automobiles from Japan	Schrader H	76	167	Schrader		H	$40
Datsun Z-Cars (Consumer Guide)	Consumer Gd	81	167	Pub Intl/Castle	Consumer Guide	H	$30
David Brown's	Donnelly	60	103 904	Collins		H	$125
Dawn of Motoring How Car Came Brit	Johnson E	86	130 401	Mercedes U K		H	$40
Day I Died	Kahn M	74	205	Gentry/Wren		H	$40
Daytona 500 1985 Yearbook	Breslauer K C	85	204	Auto Racing Memories		S	$30
Daytona U.S.A.	Neeley W	79	206	Aztex		H	$50
De Dion Bouton	Perier J	78	120	Auto. Club de France		S	$60
De Dion Bouton (Ballantine)	Bird A	71	120	Ballantine Books	Ballantine #6	S	$20
De Lorean Stainless Steel Illusion	Lamm J	83	168	Newport Press		H	$100
De Tomaso Automobiles	Wyss W A	81	118	Osprey		H	$90
De Tomaso Pantera Autohistory	Norbye J P	80	118	Osprey	Autohistory	H	$50
Deals on Wheels HT Buy, Care for...	Page G	83	401	Page		S	$10
Decline and Fall Am Auto Industry	Yates B	83	419	Empire		H	$30
DeLorean	DeLorean J Z	85	168	Zondervan		H	$40
DeLorean Tapes	Eddy P	84	168	Collins		S	$30
Delage (French)	Dollfus A	84	120	EPA	Toute L'Hist	S	$30
Delahaye	Rousseau J	50	120	L'Anthologie Automobile		S	$90
Delahaye Sport et Prestige	Jolly F	81	120	Editions Presse Audio.		H	$80
Dennis - World Trucks No 6	Kennett P	79	303	PSL	World Trucks	H	$30
Der Mercedes-Benz 190 Portrait.....	Simsa P	86	130	Econ Verlag		H	$90
Derek Bell My Racing Life (Spcl ed)	Bell D/Henry A	88	205 136	PSL		L	$150

Title	Author	Pub date	Subjects		Publisher	Series	Bind	Price
Design & Development of Indy Car	Huntington R	81	299		HP Books		S	$40
Design and Behaviour of Racing Car	Moss S/Pomeroy L	63	202		Kimber		H	$70
Design of Racing Sports Cars	Campbell C	73+	202		Chapman & Hall/Bentley		H	$50
Designers Great Autos & Men who...	Setright L J K	76	502		Follett		H	$30
Designing and Building Special Cars	Jute A	85	405		David & Charles		H	$50
Designing and Building Sports Car	Lockwood N	60	405		Scientific/Foulis		H	$40
Designing Tomorrow's Cars	Korff W H	80	502		M-C Publ		H	$50
Designs of Raymond Loewy		75	502		Smithsonian		S	$40
Destination Monte	Harper P	64	209		Stanley Paul		H	$40
Detroit is my Home Town	Bingay M W	46	401		Bobbs-Merrill		H	$30
Deutsche Autos 1920-1945	Oswald W	82	408		Motorbuch		H	$80
Deutsche Autos 1945-1975	Oswald W	83	408		Motorbuch		H	$80
Deutsche Krader im Kriege	Knittel V S		606		Podzun-Pallas-Verlag	Waffen-Arsenal	S	$20
Development of Eng Traction Engines	Clark R H	60	903		Goose		H	$60
Devil Behind Them	Bentley J	58	205		Prentice-Hall		H	$40
Devil Wagon in God's Country	Berger M L	79	419		Archon		H	$30
Diamond Jub Brighton Run(7" record)	Baxter R	50S	401		Schofield Productions	Sound Stories		$30
Diamond Jubilee Manx Grand Prix		83	603		TT Special		S	$20
Dicing With Death	Lewis P	61	298		Daily Mirror		S	$40
Dick Seaman Racing Champ/Motorist	Chula	41+	205		Foulis/Clymer		X	$40
Die Bugattis Automobile Mobil......	Conway H G/v Fersen H H..	83	107		Christians Verlag		H	$125
Die Geschichte der Feuers. bis 1945	Ewald G		302		Motorbuch Verlag		H	$50
Die Geschichte der Marken R-R/Bentl	Rosfeldt K	81	139		Verlag Karl Brinkman		H	$100
Diesel Car Book	Barlow R	81	405		Grove Press		S	$20
Diesel Cars Benefits Risks.........		82	405		National Academy Press		S	$30
Diesel Man & Engine	Grosser M	78	404	405	Atheneum		H	$40
Diesels from Woodshed	Cummins C L	70	404		SAE		S	$20
Dinkey Toys & Modelled Miniatures		81	702		Richardson M & S	Hornby Comp....	H	$80
Dino The Little Ferrari	Nye D	79	121		Barnes/Osprey		H	$60
Directory of Classic Spts-Rac Cars	Lawrence M	87	297		Aston		S	$40
Discussion of Alt Spts Cr Concepts	Knight R J/Randle J N	77	405	127	SAE		S	$30
DKW Auto Union Guide	Ayling K	61	124		Sports Car Press/Crown	Mod Sports Car	S	$30
DMC Evaluator Vol 1/2 Lesney 1-75	Harrington P B	82	702		DMC Publications		S	$20
DMC Evaluator Vol 2/1 Corgi/Spot-on	Harrington P B	81	702		Railway City Pub		S	$20
DMG 1890-1915 (German)		15	130		Daimler-Motoren-Gesell...		H	$900
Do Your Own Car Spraying	Revere P	77	405		W Foulsham		H	$20
Doble Steam Cars Buses, Lorries...	Walton J	65+	158		Light Steam Power		H	$100
Dodge Cars 1924-38	Clarke R M	78	115		Brooklands	Brooklands	S	$20
Dodge Military Vehicles Coll. 1	Clarke R M	84	115	301 308	Brooklands	Brooklands	S	$30
Dodge Story	McPherson T A	75	115		Crestline	Crestline	H	$100
Dodges Auto Family Fortune & Misfor	Pitrone J M/Elwart J P	81	115	404	Icarus Press		H	$50
Don't Get Taken Every Time	Sutton R	82+	401		Viking Penguin		X	$20
Donald Campbell CBE	Knowles A	69	205	211	Allen & Unwin/Barnes		H	$30
Dossier Auto GTO Ferrari	Pascal D	84	121		EPA		S	$20
Dossiers Chlgq Renault V4 1919-1923	Hatry G/Le Maitre C	80	120		Editions Lafourcade		H	$100
Dossiers Chlgq Renault V5 1924-33	Hatry G/Le Maitre C	81	120		Editions Lafourcade		H	$150
Douglas (Carrick)	Carrick P	82	606		PSL	World Motor Cy	H	$30
Down the Grid	Mills W	65	297		Ian Allen		H	$20
Drag Racing Chassis Manual	Alston C	85	202		Alston Industries		H	$80
Drag Racing Yesterday and Today	Parks W	66	201		Trident		H	$50
Dragging and Driving (juv)	MacPherson T	60	201		Putnam		H	$10
Dream Cars (Trend Book 107)	Horsley F	53	502		Trend	Trend Book	X	$20
Dream Cars Design Studies & Proto..	Frostick M	80	401	502	Dalton Watson	Dalton Watson	H	$60
Dream Cars Past & Present	Vose K	89	401		Image Bank/Mallard		H	$50
Dream Machine Gold Age Am Aut 46-65	Flint J	76	403		Quadrangle/NY Times Book		H	$40
Dream Machines Vans & Pickups(juv)	Stambler I	80	301		Putnam		H	$20
Dream Maker Rise & Fall of DeLorean	Fallon I/Srodes J	83	168		Putnam		H	$40
Dream Maker William C Durant GM	Weisberger B A	79	160		Little Brown		H	$30
Dreamboats & Milestones Cars of 50s	Halla C	81	403		Tab		S	$20
Drive It! Compl Bk L C Karting	Smith M/Calvert R	85	214		Haynes		H	$20
Drive It! Compl Bk of Formula 2	Wood T	84	297		Haynes		H	$20
Drive It! Compl Bk of Formula Ford	Bingham P	84	122		Haynes		H	$30
Drive It! Compl Bk of Rallying	Turner S/Mason T	78+	209		Haynes		H	$20
Driven American Four-Wheeled Love..	Mandel L	77	419		Stein and Day		H	$30
Drivers in Action	Klemantaski L/Frostick M	55	298		Bodley		H	$70
Driving Ambition Alan Jones	Jones A/Botsford K	81	205		Atheneum		H	$30
Driving in Competition(Johnson)	Johnson A	71+	203		Bond-Parkhurst/Haessner		H	$30
Driving Passion Psychology of Car	Marsh P/Collett P	86	419		Faber & Faber		H	$30
Driving with Car Control	Bondurant B	80	203		SRA		H	$30
Ducati Singles	Walker M	85+	606		Osprey	Coll Lib	H	$50
Duesenberg (Steinwedel/Newport)	Steinwedel L W/Newport J	70+	116		Chilton/Nelson/Norton		H	$40
Duesenberg J Owners Manual(reprint)		51	116		Clymer		S	$20
Duesenberg Worlds Finest Motorcar		79	116		Royco Enterprises		S	$20
Dusty Heroes	Sawyer J	78	299		Hungness		H	$200
Dynamics of US Automobile Industry	Edwards C E	65	419		Univ of SC		H	$40
Early American Car Advertisements	Bowers Q D	66	503		Vestal/Crown/Bonanza		H	$30
Early Automobiles (juvenile)	Rachlis E	61+	424		Western Publishing		S	$10

Title	Author	Pub date	Subjects		Publisher	Series	Bind	Price
Early Cars (Sedgwick)	Sedgwick M	62	401		Weidenfeld		H	$20
Early Days of Automobile in America	Janeway E	56	424		Random	Landmark	H	$20
Earlyriders Motorcycling thru Years	Kimzey L	78	601		Paisano		S	$20
Economy Car Blitz	Wherry J H	56	412		Associated Booksellers		H	$30
Ecurie Ecosse Scotlands Racing Team	Murray D	62	127		S Paul/MBC		H	$80
Eddie Called Me Boss	Sommers D	79	205		Warren		H	$40
Edsel Affair	Warnock C G	80	158		Pro West		H	$60
Effetto Alfa (includes record)(Eng)	Nencini F	80S	101		Alfa Romeo		S	$150
Eighteen-ninety-three Auto..	Berkebile D H	64	158		Smithsonian		S	$40
Eighty Jahre Camera und Automobil	Beer H	63	510		Terhag-Verlag		H	$125
Eighty-five Jahre Berliner Auto....	Stuhlemmer R	82	401		Dalton Watson	Dalton Watson	H	$40
ELC2 The MG K3 Magnette	Nye D	81	131		Horseless Carriages	Sports Car P...	S	$50
El Automovil en el Uruguay 1900-30	Tatlock A C	81	401		Ediciones Banda Oriental		S	$30
El Camino Source Book	Lehwald E A	83	111		Bookman	Source Book	S	$30
Eldorado Classic Source Book	Bonsall T E	84	110		Bookman Dan	Source Boo	S	$30
Electric Car Alternative to the...	Naidu G M/Tesar G/Udell G	74	417		Pub Sciences Group		S	$20
Electric Car Book	Whitener B	81	417		Love Street Books		S	$20
Electric Vehicles Des/Build Yr Own	Hackleman M	77+	417		Earthmind/Peace Press		S	$30
Electroplating for the Amateur	Warburton L	50+	405		Argus		S	$30
Eleven Hundred Companion	Ullyett K	67	131	105	S Paul		H	$30
Elite Cars Exciting Look Exp.......	Consumer Gd	80	401		Publications Intl	Consumer Gd	S	$10
Elite Cars Fastest and Finest	Consumer Gd	87	401		Publications Intl	Consumer Gd	H	$20
Emergency and High Speed Driv Tec..	Clark J M	76	203		Gulf		H	$30
Emergency Service Vehicles of UK	Sturman C	80	303		Ian Allan		H	$20
Enciclopedia Ferrari (Italian)	D'Argenzio R	85	121		Casa Editrice		S	$30
Ency of American Automobile(Ldvgsn)	Ludvigsen K E/Wise D B	74+	403		Orbis/Chartwell		H	$30
Ency of American Automobiles	Georgano G N	68+	403		Rainbird/Dutton		H	$40
Ency of American Cars 1930-1942	Moloney J H	77	403		Crestline	Crestline	H	$60
Ency of American Cars 1930-1980	Langworth R M	84	403		Publications Intl		H	$50
Ency of American Cars 1940-1970	Langworth R M/Consumer Gd	80	403		Publications Intl		H	$40
Ency of American Supercars	Ackerson R C	81	403		Bookman		S	$30
Ency of Auto Racing Greats	Cutter R	73	297		Prentice		H	$90
Ency of Automobiles (Angelucci)	Angelucci E	67	412		Odhams		H	$40
Ency of Eur Spts & GT Cars from 61	Robson G	80	412		Haynes		H	$70
Ency of Motor Racing	Pritchard A/Davey K	69	297		Robert Hale/McKay		H	$40
Ency of Motor Sport	Georgano G N	71	297		Rainbird/Ebury/Viking		H	$150
Ency of Motorcar	Drackett P	79+	401		Mandarin/Octopus/Crown		H	$40
Ency of Motorcycling	Bishop G	80	601		Putnam/Bison		H	$30
Ency of Sports Cars	Nichols R	86	401		Bookthrift			$
Ency of Sportscars	Georgano G N	85	412		Bison		H	$30
Ency of Worlds Classic Cars	Robson G	77	401		Salamander/Chartwell		H	$30
End of the Line Autoworkers........	Feldman R/Betzold M	88	419		Weidenfeld		H	$40
End of the Road Vanishing Architect	Margolies J	77	506		Penguin		S	$30
Endless Quest for Speed 1-portfolio	Davis S C H/Crosby G	46	504		Autocar		S	$150
Endless Quest for Speed 2-portfolio	Davis S C H/Crosby G	46	504		Autocar		S	$150
Enduro	Jones T F	70	602		Chilton		S	$10
Engine Design V2	Giles J G	68	405		Iliffe	Auto Tech	X	$10
Engines Were Rolls-Royce	Harker R	79	139		Macmillan		H	$100
Enzo Ferrari 50 Years of Motoring	Casucci P	80	121	121	Mondadori/Crown/Greenwich		H	$60
Enzo Ferrari Le Mythe	Pascal D	80S	121		Ch Massin		H	$40
Enzo Ferrari Memoirs (Hamilton)	Ferrari E	63+	121		Hamilton		H	$125
Enzo Ferrari Memoirs (MBC)	Ferrari E	63	121		Motoraces Book Club		H	$50
Enzo Ferrari Pilota	Moretti V	87	121		Edizioni di Autocritica		H	$60
Enzo Ferrari Story Autobiography	Ferrari E	63	121		Macmillan/Hamish Hamilton		H	$180
Ephemera of Travel & Transport	Anderson/Swinglehurst	81	507		New Cavendish Books		H	$40
ERF - World Trucks No 1	Kennett P	78	303		PSL/Aztex	World Trucks	H	$30
Escort Mk 1 2 & 3 Dev & Comp Hist	Walton J	85	156		Haynes		H	$40
Esquires American Autos and Makers	Wilkie D J	63	403		Esquire/Harper & Row		H	$20
Essential Tec for Profess Driver	Grill L	87	306		IAP		S	$20
Ettore Bugatti	Bradley W F	48	107		MRP		H	$90
European Automobiles of 50s and 60s	Martinez A/Nory J L	82	401		EPA/Vilo		H	$40
European Classic Cars Survivors	Rasmussen H	75	401		Picturama	Survivors	H	$60
European Sports Cars of 50's	Rasmussen H	78	401		Picturama	Survivors	H	$60
European Trucks On the Road in.....	Jacobs D	83	303		Osprey	Osprey Col Ser	S	$30
Evel Knievel on Tour	Saltman S/Green M	77	610		Dell		S	$20
Everyones Color Bk of Classic Cars	Roberts P	80	401		Hamlyn		H	$10
Evolution of Racing Car	Pomeroy L	66	298		Kimber		H	$80
Exciting World of Jackie Stewart	Connery/Davis/Dymock...	74	205		Collins		H	$30
Excuse My Dust	Partridge B	43	419		Whittlesey House		H	$40
Exotic Cars (Brown)	Brown S	85	401		Gallery/Smith/Multimedia		H	$20
Exotic Cars (Nichols)	Nichols R	85	401		Bison		H	$30
F 3000	Barbe S	88	298		L'Equipe		H	$60
F W Lanchester Life of Engineer	Kingsford P W	60	105		Arnold		H	$125
Fabulous Cars of 1920s & 1930s(Juv)	Knudson R L	81	401		Lerner		H	$20
Fabulous Firebird	Lamm M	79	138		Lamm-Morada		H	$50
Fabulous Hoosier (Carl G Fisher)	Fisher J	47	205		McBride		H	$40
Fabulous Porsche 917	Hinsdale P	76	136		Haessner		S	$100

Title	Author	Pub date	Subjects	Publisher	Series	Bind	Price
Facel Vega 1959-1964(French)		81	120	EPA	Les Archives...	S	$40
Facel Vega Excellence......(French)	Daninos J		120	EPA	Grand Tourisme	H	$40
Facts About Grand Prix Team Tyrrell	Gill B	77	298	Whizzard G		H	$40
Fairground and Circus Transport	Vanderveen B H	73	306	Warne	Olyslager Lib	H	$20
Famous Auto Museums 2 Museo...Turin	Fujimoto A	79	401	San'ei Shobo Pub		H	$40
Famous Auto Races Rallies	Lessner E	56	297	Hanover House		H	$40
Famous Custom & Show Cars	Barris G/Scagnetti J	73	422	Dutton		H	$40
Famous GM Cars GM Family Album	Stern P V/Brindle M	62	160 504	GM		S	$20
Famous Marques of Britan	Wood J	83+	406	Mandarin/Octopus/etc		H	$60
Famous Motor Races	Walkerley R	63	298	Barker		H	$30
Famous Old Cars	Bowman H W	57+	401	Fawcett/Arco	Arco Auto Lib	X	$30
Famous Racing Cars	Hodges D	62	297	Temple		H	$20
Famous Racing Cars Fifty of the....	Nye D	89	297	Guild Pub		H	$60
Fangio	Fangio J M/Giambertone M	63	205	Landsborough/Trust		S	$30
Fangio (from the film)	Jenkinson D	73	205	Beachplex/Joseph		H	$80
Fangio Racing Driver	Merlin O	59	205	Desclee Brouwer/Bat/Bent		H	$60
Farina (Italian)Brochure		?	501	HPRacing Line		S	$20
Farm Tractor (Appleyard)	Appleyard J	87	901 504	David & Charles		H	$40
Farm Tractors	Baldwin N	77+	904	Old Motor/Warne	Kaleidoscope	H	$20
Fast and Furious	Garrett R	69	297	Arco		H	$30
Fast as White Lightning	Chapin K	81	299	The Dial Press		H	$20
Fast Company Men Machines Am Racing	Miller J	72	299	Follett		H	$30
Fast Green Car	Butterworth W E	65+	207	Norton/Grosset/Tempo		X	$20
Fast Guys Rich Guys and Idiots	Moses S	86	297	September Press		H	$60
Fast Lane Summer N American Rd Rac	Mandell L	81	299	Squarebooks		H	$40
Fast One (novel)	Daley R	78	207	Crown		H	$20
Fast Ones	Miller P	64	297	Arco		H	$30
Faster Racers Diary	Stewart J/Manso	72	205	Farrar/Straus/Giroux		X	$30
Faster Than Sound Quest LS Record	Shapiro H	75	211	Barnes		H	$40
Fastest Men In World On Wheels	Houlgate D	71	211	World		H	$70
Fastest Men on Earth	Clifton P	64	211	Day		H	$40
Fastest on Earth	Eyston G E T	39+	211	Clymer		X	$40
Faza/Car Graphic Abarth Guide	Cosentino A S	84	151	Nigensha		H	$180
Ferodo Story 1897-1957	Ferodo	57	418	Ferodo		H	$30
Ferrari (Ballantine/Foulis Mini)	Setright L J K	71+	121	Ballantine/Foulis		X	$30
Ferrari (Exeter)		83	121	Col Lib/Exeter/S&S		H	$10
Ferrari (Foreword by Niki Lauda)	Eaton G	82	121	Col Lib/Crescent	Colour Library	H	$20
Ferrari (Laban)	Laban B	84	121	Multimedia/Smith/Gallery		H	$20
Ferrari (Rogliatti)	Rogliatti R	73	121	LEA/Crowell/Hamlyn		H	$100
Ferrari (Tanner) 1E	Tanner H	59	121	Foulis/Bentley		H	$125
Ferrari (Tanner) 2E	Tanner H	64	121	Foulis/Bentley		H	$90
Ferrari (Tanner) 3E	Tanner H	68	121	Bentley		H	$80
Ferrari (Tanner) 4E	Tanner H	74	121	Foulis		H	$70
Ferrari (Tanner) 5E	Tanner H/Nye D	79	121	Haynes		H	$70
Ferrari 126 C3 (Italian)	Chiavegato C	83	121	Forte Editore		H	$70
Ferrari 126 C4	Chiavegato C	84	121	Forte Editore		H	$70
Ferrari 25 Years of Formula One	Barnes J W	74	121	John W. Barnes Jr.		H	$40
Ferrari 250 GTO Autohistory	Clarke D	83	121	Osprey	Autohistory	H	$40
Ferrari 250 GTO Super Profile	Harvey C	82	121	Haynes	Super Profile	H	$30
Ferrari 250LM	Massini M/Box R de la	83	121	Osprey		H	$70
Ferrari 275 330GT 330GTC Parts Book		70S	121	Carbooks		S	$40
Ferrari 275GTB & GTS Autohistory	Webb I	81	121	Osprey	Autohistory	H	$50
Ferrari 275GTB 275GTS..... (French)	Pourret J G	84	121	Publications Intl		H	$100
Ferrari 308 & Mondial Autohistory	Willoughby G	82	121	Osprey	Autohistory	X	$50
Ferrari 365 GTB/4 Dayt World S/C#1	Nye D	84	121	Albion Scott/Moto-Art		H	$50
Ferrari 365 GTB/4 Daytona	Braden P/Roush G	82	121	Newport/Osprey		H	$80
Ferrari 410 Superamerica Series III	Ridgley D W	83	121	Ridgley		S	$50
Ferrari 512 V-12 Competition Cars	Lampe M	82	121	Manfred Lampe		H	$300
Ferrari 80 2E (Italian)	Ferrari E	80	121	Enzo Ferrari		H	$500
Ferrari 80 3E (Italian)	Ferrari E	81	121	Enzo Ferrari		H	$250
Ferrari Album 2	Thompson J	81	121	Color Market		S	$30
Ferrari Album 3	Thompson J	82	121	Color Market		S	$30
Ferrari Automobili 1947-1953	Millanta C/Orsini/Zagari	85	121	Editoriale Olimpia		H	$150
Ferrari and Maserati in Action	Tanner H	57	121 172	Hamish Hamilton		H	$200
Ferrari au Mans (French)	Pascal D	84	121	EPA		H	$70
Ferrari Berlinetta Boxer Autohist.	Nichols M	79	121	Osprey	Autohistory	H	$60
Ferrari Berlinetta Classic Line 1	Groh P	80S	121	Verlag Classic Line		H	$300
Ferrari Brochures & Sales Lit	Merritt R	77	121	Barnes		S	$150
Ferrari Cabriolets & Spyders AH	Thompson J	85	121	Osprey	Autohistory	H	$40
Ferrari Cars 1957-1962	Clarke R M	79	121	Brooklands	Brooklands	S	$30
Ferrari Cars 1962-1966	Clarke R M	79	121	Brooklands	Brooklands	S	$30
Ferrari Cars 1966-1969	Clarke R M	79	121	Brooklands	Brooklands	S	$30
Ferrari Cars 1969-1973	Clarke R M	80	121	Brooklands	Brooklands	S	$30
Ferrari Cars 1977-1981	Clarke R M	82	121	Brooklands	Brooklands	S	$30
Ferrari Collection No 1 1960-1970	Clarke R M	81	121	Brooklands	Brooklands	S	$20
Ferrari Days (Modena 83)	Stefanini A	83	121	Editore NiuItaly		H	$90
Ferrari Dino 206GT etc Autohistory	Webb I	80	121	Osprey	Autohistory	H	$50

Title	Author	Pub date	Subjects	Publisher	Series	Bind	Price
Ferrari Early Berli/Comp Coupes	Batchelor D	74	121	MBI/DB/Haessner		S	$70
Ferrari Early Spy & Comp Rdstrs	Batchelor D	75	121	Dean Batchelor/Haessner		S	$60
Ferrari Faszination Auf Radern	Becker H/Klutmann M	83	121	Auto Becker		H	$250
Ferrari Formula 1 Cars 1948-1976	Thompson J	76	121	Aztex Corp.		H	$100
Ferrari Gran Turismo/Comp B'lin't's	Batchelor D	77	121	Haessner		S	$125
Ferrari Grand Prix Cars	Henry A	84	121	Hazleton/Osprey		H	$50
Ferrari GTO (Art & Car)	Lewandowski J	87	121	Sudwest	Art & Car	H	$600
Ferrari GTO Anniversary	Pourret J G	87	121	ACLA		H	$60
Ferrari Guide to Cars from 1959		74+	121	Maranallo Concessionaires		S	$20
Ferrari I Love GTO	Pasquero F/Varisco F	83	121	Mondadori/Liberia dell		H	$60
Ferrari in Bedroom (fiction)	Shepherd J	72	121	Dodd Mead		H	$20
Ferrari Le 4 Cilindri Sport	Munaron G	87	121	La Mille Miglia Editrice		H	$400
Ferrari Library	Moe D	83	121	MMC		S	$30
Ferrari Man Machines	Grayson S	75	121	Automobile Quarterly		H	$60
Ferrari Miniatures au 1/43 1962-83	Lastu J M/Lastu D	80S	121 702	Editions Adepte		H	$70
Ferrari Mondiale (1975)		75	121	Fratelli Fabbri Editori		S	$30
Ferrari Oper Maint Serv HB 1948-63	Merritt R	75	121	Barnes		S	$150
Ferrari Own Club 25 Yrs Honoring...	Schroeder M/Schroeder S	86	121	Ferrari Owners Club		H	$50
Ferrari Own Club Monterey 1984	Schroeder M/Schroeder S	85	121	Ferrari Owners Club		H	$50
Ferrari Owners Handbook	Tanner H	59	121	Clymer		S	$180
Ferrari Owners Survival Manual		77+	121	FAF Motorcars		S	$30
Ferrari Pocket History	Orsini L	80	121	Automobilia/Liberia dell	Complete Book	S	$20
Ferrari Register (V1)	Marvin R B	83	121	Ferrari Data Bank		S	$100
Ferrari Register V2	Marvin R B	85	121	Ferrari Data Bank		H	$100
Ferrari Serial Numbers Part 1	Raab H A	88	121	Raab		S	$40
Ferrari Sports and GT Cars	Fitzgerald/Merritt/Th'psn	68+	121	Bond/Norton/CBS/PSL		H	$125
Ferrari Sports Racing & Prototype..	Prunet A	83	121	EPA/Norton/Haynes	Ferrari Legend	H	$125
Ferrari Spts/Rac Rd Cars(Cons Gd) H	Eaton G	82	121	Publications Intl	Consumers Gd	H	$50
Ferrari Spts/Rac Rd Cars(Cons Gd) S	Consumer Gd	83	121	Publications Intl	Consumer Gd	S	$20
Ferrari Story #01	Rogliatti G	84	121	Stamperia Artistica		S	$30
Ferrari Story #03	Rogliatti G	85	121	Stamperia Artistica		S	$30
Ferrari Story #06	Rogliatti G	86	121	Stamperia Artistica		S	$30
Ferrari Story #08	Rogliatti G	86	121	Stamperia Artistica		S	$30
Ferrari Testa Rossa V-12	Finn J E	79	121	Newport/Osprey		H	$125
Ferrari Testarossa	Murani P/Pasini S/Orsini	85+	121	Automobilia		H	$90
Ferrari Tipo 166 Original Sports...	Anselmi A T	85	121	Libreria dell Auto/Haynes		H	$60
Ferrari Tuning Tips Maint Tech	Roush G L/Apen J R	75+	121	FAF Motorcars		S	$40
Ferrari Turbo	Thompson J	82	121	Osprey		H	$40
Ferrari Type 195 Sport (profile)	Dethlefsen D	77	121	Dethlefsen		S	$30
Ferrari Type 212 (profile)	Dethlefsen D	76	121	Dethlefsen		S	$30
Ferrari V-12 Sports Cars 1946-56	Pritchard A	70	121	Leventhal/Arco	Arco Famous Car	H	$40
Ferrari Yearbook 1949 (Italian)		50	121	Ferrari		S	$3000
Ferrari Yearbook 1949 (reprint)		69	121	Richard F. Merritt		S	$125
Ferrari Yearbook 1950 (Italian)		51	121	Ferrari		S	$3000
Ferrari Yearbook 1951 (Italian)		52	121	Ferrari		S	$3000
Ferrari Yearbook 1952 (Italian)		53	121	Ferrari		S	$2500
Ferrari Yearbook 1953 (Italian)		54	121	Ferrari		S	$2000
Ferrari Yearbook 1954 (Italian)		56	121	Ferrari		S	$2000
Ferrari Yearbook 1955 (Italian)		56	121	Ferrari		S	$1250
Ferrari Yearbook 1956 (Italian)		56	121	Ferrari		S	$1000
Ferrari Yearbook 1957 (Italian)		58	121	Ferrari		S	$1500
Ferrari Yearbook 1957 (reprint)		77	121	C Dedolph		S	$100
Ferrari Yearbook 1958 (Italian)		59	121	Ferrari		S	$1500
Ferrari Yearbook 1959 (Italian)		60	121	Ferrari		S	$1500
Ferrari Yearbook 1960 (Italian)		61	121	Ferrari		S	$1250
Ferrari Yearbook 1960 (reprint)		77	121	C Dedolph		S	$90
Ferrari Yearbook 1961 (Italian)		62	121	Ferrari		S	$1250
Ferrari Yearbook 1962 (Italian)		63	121	Ferrari		S	$1250
Ferrari Yearbook 1963 (Italian)		64	121	Ferrari		S	$1000
Ferrari Yearbook 1963 (reprint)		78	121	C Dedolph		S	$90
Ferrari Yearbook 1964 (Italian)		64	121	Ferrari		S	$800
Ferrari Yearbook 1965 (Italian)		65	121	Ferrari		S	$600
Ferrari Yearbook 1966(Italian)46-66		66	121	Ferrari		S	$800
Ferrari Yearbook 1966(reprint)46-66		77	121			S	$90
Ferrari Yearbook 1967 (Italian)		67	121	Ferrari		S	$600
Ferrari Yearbook 1968-69-70(Italian		70	121	Ferrari		S	$400
Ferrari's Drivers	Fenu M	80	121	Kimber		H	$30
Ferraris for Road	Rasmussen H	80	121	MBI	Survivors	H	$40
Ferrarissima #01 (Original Ed)	Madaro G	84	121	Automobilia		H	$125
Ferrarissima #02 (Original Ed)	Madaro G	85	121	Automobilia		H	$125
Ferrarissima #03 (Original Ed)	Madaro G	85	121	Automobilia		H	$125
Ferrarissima #04 (Original Ed)	Madaro G	86	121	Automobilia		H	$125
FIA Yr Bk of Automobile 1969		69	204	PSL		S	$30
FIA Yr Bk of Automobile Sport 1971		71	204	PSL		S	$20
FIA Yr Bk of Automobile Sport 1972		72	204	PSL		S	$20
FIA Yr Bk of Automobile Sport 1973		73	204	PSL		S	$20
FIA Yr Bk of Automobile Sport 1974		74	204	PSL		S	$20

Title	Author	Pub date	Subjects		Publisher	Series	Bind	Price
FIA Yr Bk of Automobile Sport 1975		75	204		PSL		S	$20
FIA Yr Bk of Automobile Sport 1976		76	204		PSL		S	$20
FIA Yr Bk of Automobile Sport 1977		77	204		PSL		S	$20
Fiat	Sedgwick M	74	152		Arco		H	$60
Fiat (Pocket History)	Bernabo F	81	152		Automobilia	Comp History	S	$20
Fiat (Shimwell)	Shimwell R	77	152		Luscombe	Great Cars	H	$40
Fiat A Fifty Years Record		51	152		Arnoldo Mondadori		H	$70
Fiat Sports Cars From 1945 to X1/9	Robson G	84	152		Osprey		H	$70
Fiat World Trucks No 9	Kennett P	80	303		PSL	World Trucks	H	$30
Fiat X1/9 1972-1980	Clarke R M	81	152		Brooklands	Brooklands	S	$30
Fiat X1/9 Autohistory	Walton J	82	152		Osprey		H	$40
Fiberglass Repairs	Petrick P J	76	405		Cornell Maritime		S	$20
Fiero Facts Book		83	138		Fiero Owners Club of Amer		S	$30
Fiesta Concept of Economical Veh	Aigner J/Franz F	78	169		SAE		S	$20
Fifty Anni 1912-1962 (Italian)	ANFIA	62	409	501	ANFIA(Italian Auto Ind)		H	$200
Fifty Famous Motor Races (Specl ed)	Henry A	88	297		PSL		L	$150
Fifty Year of Am Auto Design 30-80	Nesbitt D	85	502		Publications Intl		H	$10
Fifty Years of American Automobiles	Consumer Gd	89	403		Pub Intl/Crown/Beekman		H	$80
Fifty Years of Brooklands	Gardner C	56	206		Heinemann		H	$50
Fifty Years of Le Mans Racing	Autocar	73	206		IPC Business Press	Autocar Special	S	$30
Fifty Years of Lincoln Mercury	Dammann G H	71	166	161	Crestline	Crestline	H	$40
Fifty Years of Motorbuses 1924-1974	Leicester City Transport	74			Leicester City Transport		S	$20
Fifty Years on Tracks	Caterpillar Staff	54	906		Caterpillar Tractor Co		H	$80
Fifty Years Traction Avant Citroen	Sabates F	85	153		Edition N7		S	$50
Fighting Fire With Fire	Peckham J M	72	302		Haessner		H	$50
Fill'er Up Archit History Gas Stat	Vieyra D I	79	401		Macmillan/Collier		S	$50
Fill'er Up! Story 50 Years Motoring	Partridge B	52	401		McGraw		H	$20
Finding the Groove	Higdon H	73	299		Putnam		H	$30
Fins & Chrome American Autos of 50s	DeWaard E J	82	403		Bison		H	$30
Fins & Fifties Cars Chrome Culture	Key M/Thacker T	87	403		Osprey		H	$50
Fire Apparatus Pict Hist LA Fire D	Klass G	74	302		Ruccione		S	$50
Fire Crash Vehicles from 1950	Vanderveen B H	76	302		Warne	Olyslager	H	$30
Fire Engines & Fire-Fighting	Burgess-Wise D	77	302		Mandarin/Octopus/Lngmdw		H	$20
Fire Engines Firefighters	Ditzel P C	76	302		Rutledge/Crown		H	$30
Fire Engines in Color	Ingram A/Bishop D	73	302		Blandford/Macmillan		H	$20
Fire Engines of Europe	Creighton J	80	302		Ian Henry	Transport	H	$20
Fire Engines of United Kingdom	Creighton J	81	302		Ian Henry	Transport	H	$20
Fire Engines of World	Mallet J	81	302		Vilo		H	$50
Fire Fighting Apparatus 100 Yrs Am	Da Costa P	64	302		Floyd Clymer		S	$40
Fire Rigs Fighting Fires	Sytsma J F	82	302		Sytsma, John F		H	$70
Fire Story of Fire Engine	Goodenough S	78	302		Orbis/Book Sales/Chartwel		H	$30
Fire-Fighting Vehicles 1840-1950	Vanderveen B H	76	302		Warne	Olyslager	H	$30
Firebird (Carlyon)	Carlyon R	84	138		Gallery/Smith		H	$20
Firestone Story	Lief A	51	418		Whittlesey/McGraw		H	$30
First AMC(motorcycle) Racing Scene	Main-Smith B	80	603		BMS		S	$20
First and Fastest	Hough R	63	297		George Allen and Unwin		H	$20
First Henry Ford Study in..........	Jardim A	70	415		MIT		H	$50
First Knocker Norton Scene	Main-Smith B	79	606		BMS		S	$10
First Porsche Parade in Japan		80S	136		Neko		H	$40
First Velocette Scene	Main-Smith B	77	606		BMS		S	$20
Fit for Chase Cars & Movies	Lee R	69	509		Barnes/Castle		H	$30
Five Hundred Miles to Go Story Indy	Bloemker A	61	208		Coward-Mcann		H	$40
Five Hundred Souvenir Book	Hungness C/Fox J	80	208		Hungness		S	$10
Fix Your Chevrolet V8&6 1966-1975	Toboldt B	75	111		Goodheart-Willcox		H	$20
Fix Your Ford V-8's&6's 1932-1952	Toboldt B	52	122		Goodheart-Willcox		H	$20
Flat Out	Eyston G E T	33+	211		John Miles		H	$60
Flivver King	Sinclair U	69	415		Phaedra		H	$30
Floyd Clymer Alb Hist Stm Trac Eng	Clymer F	49	903		Clymer/Bonanza		H	$20
Floyd Clymer Catalog 1909 Cars	Clymer F	58	403		Clymer		S	$30
Floyd Clymer Catalog 1912 Cars	Clymer F	55	403		Clymer		S	$30
Floyd Clymer Catalog 1914 Cars	Clymer F	58	403		Clymer		S	$30
Floyd Clymer Catalog 1918 Cars	Clymer F	50S	403		Clymer		S	$30
Floyd Clymer Catalog 1921 Cars	Clymer F	58	403		Clymer		S	$30
Floyd Clymer Catalog 1924 Cars	Clymer F	58	403		Clymer		S	$30
Floyd Clymer Catalog 1927 Cars	Clymer F	55	403		Clymer		S	$30
Floyd Clymer Catalog 1929 Cars	Clymer F	50S	403		Clymer		S	$30
Floyd Clymer Catalog 1950 Autos	Clymer F	50	403		Clymer		S	$30
Floyd Clymer Catalog Brit Cars 1951	Lukins A H	51	406		George Ronald/Clymer		S	$20
Floyd Clymer Catalog Brit Mtrcycles	Ashby J B/Angier D J	51	606		Clymer		S	$30
Floyd Clymer Hist Motor Scrap Bk#1H	Clymer F	44	401		Clymer		H	$30
Floyd Clymer Hist Motor Scrap Bk#1S	Clymer F	44	401		Clymer		S	$30
Floyd Clymer Hist Motor Scrap Bk#2	Clymer F	44	401		Clymer		X	$30
Floyd Clymer Hist Motor Scrap Bk#3	Clymer F	46	401		Clymer		X	$30
Floyd Clymer Hist Motor Scrap Bk#4	Clymer F	47	401		Clymer		H	$30
Floyd Clymer Hist Motor Scrap Bk#5	Clymer F	48	401		Clymer		H	$30
Floyd Clymer Hist Motor Scrap Bk#6	Clymer F	50	401		Clymer		H	$30
Floyd Clymer Hist Motor Scrap Bk#7	Clymer F	54	401		Clymer		H	$30

Title	Author	Pub date	Subjects			Publisher	Series	Bind	Price
Floyd Clymer Hist Motor Scrap Bk#8	Clymer F	50S	401			Clymer		S	$30
Floyd Clymer Hist S/B 1899	Clymer F	55	401			Clymer		S	$30
Floyd Clymer Hist S/B For Mtcyl V1	Clymer F	55	606			Clymer		S	$40
Floyd Clymer Hist S/B Ford Mod T	Clymer F		122			Clymer		S	$30
Floyd Clymer Hist S/B Steam V1	Clymer F	45	414			Clymer/Bonanaza/Clymer		H	$40
Floyd Clymer Hist S/B Vol 1 Foreign	Clymer F	55	414			Clymer		S	$20
Flying Lady (RROC) Complete thru 86			139			RROC		S	$200
Flying on Four Wheels Frank Costin	Ortenburger D	86	202	205	129	PSL		H	$70
Flying on Ground	Fittipaldi E/Hayward E	73	205			Kimber		H	$50
Follow Circus	Hoy R	69	207			Pacific		H	$20
For Practice Only	Klemantaski L/Frostick M	59	298			Bodley		H	$60
Ford & Fordson Tractors	Williams M	85	904			Blandford		H	$50
Ford 1903 to 1984 (Consumer Guide)	Lewis D L/McCarville.....	83	122			Pub Intl/Beekman/Crown		H	$30
Ford Agency Pictorial History	Dominguez H	81	122			MBI		S	$30
Ford at Fifty 1903-1953		53	122			Simon & Schuster		H	$30
Ford Bk of Styling	Laas W	63	122	502		Ford Motor Co		S	$40
Ford Book of Competition Motoring	Clark J/Brinton A	65	169	297		S Paul		H	$30
Ford Cobra Guide	Carroll W	64	109			Sports Car Press	Mod SportsCar	S	$40
Ford Competition Cars	Frostick M/Gill B	76+	169			Haynes		H	$40
Ford Cortina Mk 1 62-66 Autohistory	Wood J	84	156			Osprey	Autohistory	H	$40
Ford Decline and Rebirth 1933-1962	Nevins A/Hill F E	62	122			Scribners	Nevins Triology	H	$40
Ford Dust and Glory Racing History	Levine L	68	169			Macmillan		H	$250
Ford Dynasty American Story	Brough J	77	415			Doubleday		H	$30
Ford Escort Drawing Bd to Race Trk		68	156			Speed & Sports		S	$20
Ford Expansion & Challenge 1915-33	Nevins A/Hill F E	57	122			Scribners	Nevins Triology	H	$70
Ford Formula One Racing Cars	Geary L	82	156			Ian Henry	Transport	H	$20
Ford GT 40 SAE Papers		79	122			SAE		S	$60
Ford GT 40 Sports Cars Profile #1	Archibald S	84	122			Sapphire		S	$20
Ford GT40 Anglo-Am Comp Classic	Hodges D	84	122			MRP		H	$80
Ford GT40 Prototypes and Sports Crs	Hodges D	70	122			Leventhal/Arco		H	$50
Ford Ideals Mr Ford's Page	Ford H	22	415			Dearborn Pub Co		H	$20
Ford in Thirties	Woudenberg P R	76	122			Petersen		S	$20
Ford Methods and Ford Shops	Arnold H L/Faurote F L	15	122			Engineering Magazine		H	$150
Ford Military Vehicles	Geary L	83	303	308		Ian Henry Pub	Transport Ser	H	$30
Ford Models V-8 B & A Cars	Page V W	33	122			Norman W Henley		H	$30
Ford Motor Cars - 1912 Catalog			122			Floyd Clymer		S	$10
Ford Mustang 1967-1973	Clarke R M	82	122			Brooklands	Brooklands	S	$30
Ford Panel Vans	Cole L	80	156			Ian Henry	Transport Ser	H	$20
Ford Performance Cars 1963-1973			122			Special Interest Cars		S	$20
Ford Performance Handbook (Hot Rod)	Brock R/Hot Rod Editors	62	122			Petersen	Hot Rod	S	$30
Ford Performance Years V1	Schorr M L	83	122			Quicksilver	Quicksilver	S	$20
Ford Popular	Turner	84	156			Osprey		H	$50
Ford Ranchero 1957-1979 Photofacts	Siuru B/Holder B	84	122			MBI	CMB Photofacts	S	$40
Ford Retractable 1957-59 Photofacts	Magayne J H	83	122			MBI	CMB Photofacts	S	$50
Ford Road 75th Anniv Ford Motor Co	Sorensen L	78	122			Silverado		H	$50
Ford RS Escorts 1968-80	Clarke R M	82	156			Brooklands	Brooklands	S	$30
Ford Small-Block HT High Perf Eng..	Schorr M L	76	122			Performance Pub		S	$20
Ford Specials	Stephens P J	60	156			Foulis/Scientific		H	$40
Ford Spotters Guide 1920-1980	Burness T	81	122			MBI		S	$30
Ford Street Performance Handbook	Schorr M L	85	122			Quicksilver	Quicksilver	S	$30
Ford That Beat Ferrari History GT40	Jones G/Allen J	85	169			Kimberley's		H	$180
Ford Times Man Company	Nevins A/Hill F E	54	122			Scribners	Nevins Triology	H	$60
Ford Treasury of Station Wag Living	Reck F M/Moss W	57	122			Simon & Schuster		H	$20
Ford Trucks Transport Since 45	Ingram A	78	303			MRP		H	$40
Ford Unconventional Biog Men/Times	Herndon B	69	415			Weybridge		H	$30
Ford vs Ferrari (Zuma/US edition)	Pritchard A	84	122	121		Zuma		H	$70
Ford vs Ferrari 1E	Pritchard A	68	169	121		Pelham Books		H	$100
Fords American Epic	Collier P/Horowitz D	87	415			Summit		H	$20
Foreign Racing Motorcycles	Bacon R	79	603			Haynes		H	$40
Forest Domain of Pierce-Arrow	Meyer J C	84	170			South Cal Region PA Soc		H	$30
Forget Gas Pumps Make Your Own Fuel	Wortham J/Whitener B	79	417			Love Street Books		S	$20
Formula 1 86/87 World C/S Y/B 01	Braillon D	86	204			ACLA		H	$100
Formula 1 87-88 World C/S Y/B 02	Braillon D	87	204			ACLA		H	$80
Formula 1 Racing Modern Era	Rosinski J	74	297			Madison/Grosset/Denoel		H	$40
Formula 1(Gude art)	Gude F	84	504			Gude		H	$80
Formula 2	Grant G	53	298			Foulis		H	$40
Formula 3 Record of 500cc Racing	May C A N	51	298			Foulis		H	$50
Formula Car Technology	Holmes H/Alexander D	80	202			Steve Smith		S	$30
Formula Ferrari(Italian)	Chiavegato C	84	121			Forte Editore		S	$50
Formula Ford Book	Brittan N	77	297	169		PSL		H	$40
Formula Junior	Blunsden J	61	298			MRP		H	$70
Formula Junior Guide	Morrow H	61	297			Sports Car Press	Mod Sports Car	S	$90
Formula One 74(only book in series)	Lyons P/Gilligan V	74	204			Oxman		H	$40
Formula One Cars & Drivers (Turner)	Turner M/Roebuck N	83	297	504		Temple		H	$150
Formula One G P Car (12" record)	Pomeroy L	50S	297			Schofield Productions	Sound Stories		$50
Formula One Grand Prix Rac Since 46	Pritchard A	66	298			Allen & Unwin		H	$50
Formula One Record Bk 1961 - 65	Thompson/Rabagliati/Sheld	74	297			Leslie Frewin Publishers		H	$150

Title	Author	Pub date	Subjects		Publisher	Series	Bind	Price
Formula One Ultimate in Rac Cars	Taylor R	74	213		Western	Golden Wheels	H	$10
Formula One YB 1987 (FOCA)		87	204		Grid		H	$90
Formula One YB 1988 (FIA) #2	Constanduros B	87	204		Grid		H	$90
Forty Years of Design with Fiat	Giacosa D	79	152		Automobilia		H	$100
Four Wheel Drive Handbook	Crow J T/Warren C A	70	311	309	Bond-Parkhust		S	$20
Four Wheel Drive Story	Troyer H	54	311		McGraw-Hill		H	$80
Four Wheeled-Morgan Vol 1 Flat Rad	Hill K	77	164		MRP		H	$100
Four-4-2 64-86 Data Bk/Price Guide	Zavitz R P	85	162		Bookman		S	$30
Four-4-2 Vol II Source Book	North P	85	162		Bookman Dan	Source Book	S	$30
Four-Wheel Drives Racing's Formula	Henry A	75	297		Macmillan	Donington MM	H	$30
Foyt	Libby B	74	205		Hawthorn		H	$40
Francis Beart Single Purpose	Clew J	78	610		Haynes		H	$40
Francois Cevert Contract with Death	Halle J C	75	205		Flammarion/Kimber		H	$70
Freiheit auf zwei Radern BMW	Lingnau G	82	606		ECON		H	$80
French Cars from 1920-1925	Dumont P	78	407		Warne		H	$50
French Grand Prix	Hodges D	67	206		Temple	Classic Mtr Rac	H	$40
French Grand Prix 1906-1914(S/B #7)	Karslake K	49	206		MRP		S	$50
French Vintage Cars	Bolster J	64	407		Autosport/Batsford		H	$60
Freude am Fahren BMW Charakter.....	Simsa P	83	106		ECON		H	$60
From Bugatti to Bougainvillea	Sutherland R D	82	107	297	Sutherland		S	$20
From Chain Drive to Turbo AFN Story	Jenkinson D	84	105		PSL		H	$100
From Cockpit	McLaren B	63+	205		Muller/MBC		H	$60
From Cyclecar to Microcar	Worthington-Williams M	81	406		Dalton Watson		H	$50
From Engines to Autos 5 Pioneers	Diesel E	60	404		Regnery		H	$40
From Indianapolis/Brands to Le Mans	Tommasi T	74	297		Derbi Books		H	$40
From Last to First Neil Bonnett....	Webb N C	79	205		Strode		H	$40
From Motorcycle to Superbike Hist..	Thompson E/Cadell L	86	601		New Orchard		H	$30
From Veteran to Vintage	Karslake K/Pomeroy L	56	401		Temple		H	$150
Frontenac Cylinder Head (Catalog)		29	299		Floyd Clymer		S	$10
Full Chat	Pope N B	52	610		MRP		H	$100
Full Throttle	Birkin H	32+	205		Foulis		H	$30
Fun of Old Cars Coll & Rest Ant....	Stubenrauch B	67	401		Dodd Mead		H	$40
Future for Automotive Technology	Seiffert U/Walzer P	84	405	150	Pinter		H	$40
Future of the Automobile Rpt of MIT	Altshuler A et al	84	419		MIT		X	$20
Galloping Gertrude by Motorcar 1908	Loeper J J	80	419		Atheneum		H	$20
Gas Food and Lodging	Baeder J	82	401	510	Cross River/Abbeville		H	$50
Gas Guts and Glory Great Moments...	Ayling K	70	297		Abelard-Schuman		H	$20
Gas Turbine Engine Design..........	Norbye J P	75	202		Chilton		H	$40
Gasoline Age	Glasscock C B	37	419		Bobbs-Merrill		H	$40
Gasoline Automotive Advntrs C Bates	Houston J D	73+	416		Capra		H	$20
Gears & Transmissions V4	Giles J G	69	405		Iliffe	Auto Tech	H	$20
Gentlemen Start Your Engines	Shaw W	55	205		Coward-McCann		H	$40
George Eaton Five Minutes to Green	Orr F	70	205		Longman		S	$30
George Roesch & Invincible Talbot	Blight A	70	105		Grenville		H	$70
German Automobile Coachwork	Benter C/Schrader H	76	501		Schrader		H	$125
German Fire Engines Since 1945	Orth H P	81	302		efb-Verlag		H	$60
German Grand Prix	Posthumus C	66	206		Temple	Classic Mtr Rac	H	$50
German High-Performance Cars	Sloniger J/von Fersen H	65	408		Batsford/Bentley		H	$50
German Racing Cars and Drivers	Molter G	50	298		Clymer		S	$50
Get a Horse! Story of Auto America	Musselman M M	50	401		Lippincott		H	$20
Getting Started in Model-Building	Lozier H	71	704		Hawthorn		H	$30
Getting Started in Motorsport	Turner S/Mason T	85	297		Haynes		H	$20
Ghia Ford's Carrozzeria	Burgess-Wise D	85	169	501	Osprey		H	$60
Giant Dumptrucks	Baldwin N	84	306		Warne		H	$40
Giants of Small Heath(BSA)	Ryerson B	80	606		Haynes		H	$40
Gilles Villeneuve (French)	Henry A	88	205		EPA	Toute L'Hist	S	$20
Gilles Vivo (Italian)	De Agostini C	83	205		Conti Editore		H	$70
Ginetta G15 Super Profile	Rose J	86	105		Haynes	Super Profile	H	$20
Gioachino Colombo Le Origini del...	Moretti V	85	121		Sansoni Autocritica		H	$80
Glory Road	Watson D	73	297		Stadia		S	$10
GMC 6x6 & DUKW Universal Truck	Boniface/Jeudy	78	301		MBI		H	$60
Go Formula Ford HT Start Single....	Smith B	69	297		Foulis		H	$30
Gods Own Junkyard...America Ldscp	Blake P	64	419		Holt, Reinhart & Winston		H	$30
Going for Broke Chrysler Story	Moritz M/Seaman B	81	112		Doubleday		H	$40
Golden Age of American Racing Car	Borgeson G	66	297		Norton/Crown/Bonanza		H	$125
Golden Age of Fours	Hodgdon T A	76+	601		Bagnall		S	$40
Golden Age of Luxury Car	Hildebrand G	80	401		Dover		S	$20
Golden Age of Motoring	Fondin J	82	401		Edita		H	$50
Golden Age of Sports Cars	Steinwedel L W	72	401		Chilton		H	$20
Golden Anniv Lincoln MC 1921-1971	Kimes B R	70	161		AQ		X	$50
Golden Book of Automobile Stamps	Bond N K	52	424		Simon & Schuster		S	$20
Golden Oldies Classic Bike Tests	Nicks M	81	601		PSL		H	$40
Golden Wheels	Wagner R	86	401		Western Reserve/Zubal		H	$40
Golden Years of Trucking	Goodman J O	77	306		Ontario Trucking Assoc		H	$50
Good of it All	Round T E	57	212		Round		H	$20
Goodwood Private View Photos 49-56	Read C/Read R	85	206		Nelson & Saunders		S	$40
Gordon Bennett Races	Montagu	53+	206		Cassell/MBC		H	$70

Title	Author	Pub date	Subjects		Publisher	Series	Bind	Price
Gottlieb Daimler Karl Benz(leaflet)	Nallinger F	?	130		Im Propylaen-Verlag		S	$40
Gottlieb Daimler Maybach und Benz	Schildberger F	75	130		Sonderdruck.............		S	$30
Graf Berghe von Trips (Wolfgang)	Harster H/Fodisch J	88	205		Nurburgring Rennsportmu..		S	$20
Graham	Hill G/Ewart	76	205		St. Martin's		H	$20
Graham Hill (Italian)	Tommasi T	69	205		L'Editrice dell'Automobil		H	$30
Graham Hill's Car Racing Guide	Hill G	71	205		Sterling		H	$20
Grand Delusions Cosmic...(DeLorean)	Levin H	83	168		Viking Penguin		H	$40
Grand National Autobiog R Petty	Petty R/Neelt B	71	205		Regnery		H	$30
Grand Prix (Lyndon)	Lyndon B	35	298		John Miles		H	$250
Grand Prix 1906-72	Setright LJK	73	297		Norton		H	$125
Grand Prix and Sports Cars(drawing)	Hays R	64	504	297	Arco		H	$50
Grand Prix at Glen (juvenile)	Jackson R B	65	206		Walck		H	$20
Grand Prix Bugatti	Conway H G	68+	107		Foulis/Haynes/Bentley		H	$100
Grand Prix Car 1906-1939	Pomeroy L	49	297		MRP/Temple		H	$600
Grand Prix Car 1954/1966	Setright L J K	68	297		Norton		H	$150
Grand Prix Car Vol I	Pomeroy L	54	297		MRP/Temple		H	$400
Grand Prix Car Vol II	Pomeroy L	54	297		MRP/Temple		H	$400
Grand Prix Cars	Jenkinson D	59	297		Sports Car Press		H	$30
Grand Prix Cars Drivers Circuits	Hodges D/Nye D/Roebuck N	81	297		Joseph/St. Martin/Outlet		H	$70
Grand Prix Champions	Heglar M S	73	297		Bond Parkhurst/R & T		H	$20
Grand Prix Championship(1950-1970)	Pritchard A	71	297		Grosset & Dunlap		H	$30
Grand Prix Chmpshp Courses & Drvs	Borgeson G	68	297		Norton		H	$30
Grand Prix Classic Src Bk (Pontiac)	Sass D	85	138		Bookman Dan	Source Book	S	$20
Grand Prix Complete Bk F1 Racing	Hayward E	71	297		Dodd Mead		H	$20
Grand Prix D'Europe 1958(7" record)	Bolster J	50S	206		Schofield Productions	Sound Stories		$20
Grand Prix Driver (juvenile)	Butterworth W E	69	213	207	Norton		H	$20
Grand Prix Driver (Lang)	Lang H	53	205	130	Foulis		H	$70
Grand Prix Ferrari	Pritchard A	74	121		Hale		H	$50
Grand Prix Gift Book (juvenile)		67	298	213	Young World Prod (UK)		H	$30
Grand Prix Guide 71 Marlboro	Reust F	72	204		Kreuzer		S	$30
Grand Prix Guide 73 Marlboro	Reust F	73	204		SIL		S	$30
Grand Prix Guide 74	Reust F	73	204		SIL		H	$30
Grand Prix Intl Spec Iss Ferrari 86	Renvoize P P	86	121		GPI/GELT		S	$30
Grand Prix Mercedes Type W125 1937	Jenkinson D	70	130		Arco	Famous Car	H	$30
Grand Prix of Canada	Donaldson G	84	206		Avon		S	$30
Grand Prix Racing (Williams - juv)	Williams P J	67	213		Scholastic		S	$10
Grand Prix Racing 1906-1914	Mathieson T A S O	65	298		Connoisseur Automobile		H	$180
Grand Prix Racing Facts & Figures	Monkhouse G L/King-Farlow	50+	297		Foulis		H	$50
Grand Prix Rpt Auto Union(German)	Kirchberg P	84	124		transpress VEB Verlag		H	$40
Grand Prix Tyrrells	Nye D	75	298		Macmillan	Donington MM	H	$40
Grand Prix Wld Chmpshp 59	Stanley L T	60	204		Barnes	GP Wld Chmpshp	H	$90
Grand Prix Wld Chmpshp 60(GP Year)	Stanley L T	61	204		Barnes	GP Wld Chmpshp	H	$90
Grand Prix Wld Chmpshp 61	Stanley L T	62	204		Barnes	GP Wld Chmpshp	H	$90
Grand Prix Wld Chmpshp 62	Stanley L T	63	204		Barnes	GP Wld Chmpshp	H	$90
Grand Prix Wld Chmpshp 63	Stanley L T	64	204		Barnes	GP Wld Chmpshp	H	$90
Grand Prix Wld Chmpshp 64	Stanley L T	65	204		Macdonald/Doubleday	GP Wld Chmpshp	H	$70
Grand Prix Wld Chmpshp 65	Stanley L T	66	204		Macdonald	GP Wld Chmpshp	H	$125
Grand Prix Wld Chmpshp 66	Stanley L T	67	204		Macdonald	GP Wld Chmpshp	H	$80
Grand Prix Wld Chmpshp 67	Stanley L T	68	204		Macdonald	GP Wld Chmpshp	H	$150
Grand Prix Wld Chmpshp 68(GP #10)	Stanley L T	69	204		Allen/McKay	GP Wld Chmpshp	H	$60
Grand Prix Wld Chmpshp 69(GP #11)	Stanley L T	70	204		McKay	GP Wld Chmpshp	H	$60
Grand Prix World Formula One C/S 85	Roebuck N/Townsend	85	204		GS Publications		H	$70
Grand Prix Year (1970)	Simon T	71	297		Coward McCann		H	$30
Grand Tour 1982-83 (Harrahs Coll)		82	401		Graphics Etc		S	$20
Grands Prix 1934-1939	Walkerley R	48+	297		MRP		H	$70
Grease Machines	Consumer Gd	78	422		Pub Intl/Crown/Beekman		H	$20
Great American Automobiles	Bentley J	57	403		Prentice Hall		H	$20
Great American Automotive Story	Automotive Industries	76	401		Chilton		H	$20
Great American Autos from 1890-1930	Brooks L	72	401		Scholastic		S	$20
Great American Cars	Wood J	85	401		Multimedia/Smith/Gallery		H	$20
Great American Convertible (Lngwth)	Langworth R M	88	403		Pub Intl/Beekman House	Consumer Gd	H	$40
Great American Convertible (Wieder)	Wieder R/Hall G	77	403		Baron Wolman/Doublday		S	$30
Great American Dream Machines	Hirsch J	85	403		Macmillan/Random		X	$50
Great American Fire Engines	Mallet J	84	302		EPA/Outlet/Crescent		H	$30
Great American Race 1984		84	401		Greatrace Ltd		S	$30
Great American Race Drivers	Libby B	70	205		Cowles Book		H	$30
Great American Woodies & Wagons	Narus D J	77	403		Crestline	Crestline	H	$100
Great Auto Races	Helck P	75	297	504	Abrams		H	$300
Great Auto Races (Hough)	Hough R ed	61	297		Harper		H	$40
Great Auto Trivia Book	Frumkin	85	401		Crown/Outlet		S	$20
Great Automobile Club (juvenile)	O'Leary M/Haslam J	68	416		Constable/Longmans		H	$20
Great Automobile Designs	Mclellan J	74	502		Arco		H	$40
Great British Bikes	Ward I/Caddell L	76	606		Orbis			$40
Great British Drivers	Davis S C H	57	205		Hamish Hamilton		H	$40
Great British Motorcycles of 50s	Currie B	80	606		Hamlyn		H	$30
Great Camero	Lamm M	78+	111		Lamm-Morada Publ. Inc.		H	$30
Great Car Collections of the World	Eves E/Burger D	86	401		Multimedia/Smith/Gallery		H	$30

Title	Author	Pub date	Subjects		Publisher	Series	Title Bind	Index Price
Great Cars	Stein R	67	401		Grosset & Dunlap/Ridge		H	$30
Great Cars (New English Library)	Howell M	71	401		New English Library		H	$10
Great Cars From Ford	Langworth R M/Consumer Gd	82	122		Publications Intl		S	$20
Great Cars in Profile (V4 Misc Pfs)	Harding A	71	401		Profile Publications		S	$30
Great Cars of All Time	Robbin I	60	401		Grosset		H	$30
Great Cars of Fifties	Consumer Gd	85	403		Publications Intl		H	$20
Great Cars of Forties	Consumer Gd	85	403		Publications Intl		H	$20
Great Cars of Golden Age	Brazendale K	79	401		Geografico/Orbis/Crescent		H	$30
Great Cars of Sixties	Consumer Gd	85	403		Publications Intl		H	$20
Great Classics Auto Eng in Gold Age	Seiff I	82+	401		Hoffman/Orbis/Smith/Gall		H	$40
Great Collectors Cars	Rogliatti G	73	401		Mondadori/Grosset		H	$40
Great Drivers (Mase)	Mase A	81	205	510	Libro Port		H	$125
Great German Cars	Roberts P	85	408		Multimedia/Smith/Gallery		H	$20
Great Manifold Bolt-On Edelbrock	McFarland J	82	202		Edelbrock		S	$30
Great Marques Alfa Romeo	Owen D	85+	101		Octopus/Book Sales/Chtwl		H	$20
Great Marques BMW	Walton J	83	106		Octopus		H	$30
Great Marques Jaguar	Harvey C	82	127		Mandarin/Octopus		H	$30
Great Marques Mercedes-Benz	Bell R	80	130		Octopus		H	$30
Great Marques of America	Wood J	86	403		Mandarin/Octopus		H	$30
Great Marques Poster Book Jaguar	Harvey C	85	127		Octopus/Woodbury/Dalton		S	$20
Great Marques Poster Book MG	Harvey C	85	131		Octopus/Woodbury/Dalton		S	$20
Great Marques Rolls-Royce	Wood J	82	139		Mandarin/Octopus		H	$30
Great Moments in Auto Racing	Stambler I	68	297		Four Winds		X	$30
Great Motor Sport of Thirties	Dugdale J	77	298		Gentry/Two Continents		H	$60
Great Motorcycles Hist 22 Famous...	Wood G/Renstrom R C	72	606		Bond Parkhurst		S	$20
Great Old Cars Where are they Now?	Yost S K	60	401		Wayside		S	$20
Great Racing Cars & Drivers (Engel)	Engel L K	79	205		Arco		H	$40
Great Racing Cars & Drivers (Fox)	Fox C	72	297		Ridge/Grosset/Madison Sq		H	$40
Great Racing Cars (Sullivan)	Sullivan G	87	213		Dodd Mead		H	$20
Great Racing Cars of Donington Coll	Nye D/Goddard G	74	297		Macmillan		H	$60
Great Racing Drivers	Hodges D	66	205		Newnes/Arco		H	$60
Great Racing Drivers (Nye)	Nye D	77	205		Hamlyn		H	$30
Great Road Races 1894-1914	Villard H S	72	212		Barker		H	$40
Great Trucks (Consumer Gd)	Kuipers J F J	83	306		Publications Intl	Consumer Gd	H	$20
Great Way to Go Auto in Canada	Collins R	69	413		Collins/Ryerson		H	$50
Greatest Cars	Stein R	79	401		Ridge/Simon Schuster/WHS		H	$40
Green Fields Fairer Lanes	Moreland F W	69	415		Five Star		H	$50
Green Helmet	Cleary J	57	207		Fontana		X	$30
Greyhound Story Hibbing Everywhere	Schisgall O	85			Ferguson/Doubleday		H	$30
Griffith Borgeson Hot Rods(Fawcett)	Borgeson G	59	201		Fawcett	Fawcett	S	$20
Group 7 Wld's Most Pwfl Rac Cars	Ludvigsen K E	71+	297		World/Arco		H	$90
GT Granturismo Story 1 Ferr Testa..		87	121		GT Granturismo e Comp....		S	$20
GT40 Individual Hist & Race Record	Spain R	86	156		Osprey		H	$180
GTO A Source Book	Bonsall T E	83	138		Bookman	Source Book	S	$30
Guide to American Sports Car Racing	Stone W S	60+	297		Hanover/Doubleday		H	$40
Guide to Competition Driving	O'Shea P	57	203		Sports Car Press		S	$30
Guide to Corvette Speed	Ludvigsen K E	69	114		Sports Car Press	Mod Sports	S	$30
Guide to Ferrari Cars Since 1959		74+	121		Maranello Concessionaires		S	$20
Guide to Model Car Racing	Stambler I	67	701		Norton		H	$20
Guide to Racing Cars	Yates B	63	297		Sterling/Crown/Bonanza		H	$20
Guide to Rallying	Reid L	57	209		Sports Car Press		S	$10
Guide to Transport Museums of GB	Garvey J	82	412		Pelham		S	$30
Guide to Used Sports Cars	Christy J	57	401		Sports Car Press	Mod Sports Car	S	$20
Guiness Bk of Car	Harding A/Allport W/etc	87	401		Guiness		H	$40
Guiness Bk of Formula One	Morrison I	89	297		Guiness		H	$50
Gurneys Eagles	Ludvigsen K E	76	299		MBI		H	$125
Gypsy on 18 Wheels Truckers Tale	Krueger R	75	301		Praeger		S	$20
H Miller Racing Cars & Engines-1927		51	299		Floyd Clymer		S	$10
Hail to Jeep (original)	Wade Wells A	46	117		Harper		H	$80
Half Tracks	Vanderveen B H	70S	308		Warne	Olyslager	H	$40
Half-Safe Across Atlantic by Jeep	Carlin B	55	117	212	Deutsch		H	$40
Hammer Down Heavy Truckers Romance.	Lesberg S/Goldberg N	77	301		Peebles		X	$10
Handbook High Performance Driving	Kenyon L	75	203		Dodd, Mead		H	$30
Handbook of Automobiles 1915-1916	Ass of Lic Auto Mfgs	70	403		Dover		S	$30
Handbook of Automobiles 1925-1926	Ass of Lic Auto Mfgs	73	403		Dover		S	$30
Handbook of Gasoline Autos 1904-06	Ass of Lic Auto Mfgs	69	403		Dover		S	$30
Handbook of Gasoline Autos 1908	Barnes K W	63	403		Bell		H	$20
Handbook of Grand Prix Cars	Tanner H	63	297		Floyd Clymer		S	$30
Handbook of Motocross (juv)	Murray J	78	602		Putnam		H	$10
Happy Wheels Appr. Metropolitan	Rieman K	80	158		Sterner Stuff		S	$40
Hard Driving	Holbrook G	76	299		Pageant-Poseidon		H	$20
Hard Driving My Yrs with DeLorean	Haddad W	85	168		Random		H	$40
Harley Davidson (Ballantine)	Hendry M D	72	607		Ballantine	Ballantine #12	S	$30
Harley Earl & Dream Machine	Bayley S	83	404		Knopf		H	$50
Harley-Davidson Cult Lives On	Foster G	84	607		Osprey	Osprey Colour	S	$30
Harley-Davidson in Nederland	Drie H v	83	607		Big-Twin		H	$50
Harrahs Auto Coll (cat)		74	401		Harrah's		S	$10

Title	Author	Pub date	Subjects	Publisher	Series	Bind	Price
Harrahs Auto Coll Annotation (cat)		65	401	Harrah's		S	$10
Harrahs Auto Coll Roster (cat)		60S	401	Harrah's		S	$10
Harrahs Auto Coll Special Edition		75	401	Harrah's		S	$20
Harrahs Auto Coll(Batchelor)	Batchelor D/Lamm M	84	401	GP Publishing		H	$80
Harry Ferguson Inventor and Pioneer	Fraser C	72	404 901	Murray		H	$70
Harry Ferguson Life of (juv)	Wymer N	61	404 901	Phoenix	Liv Biog	H	$50
Hauling Heavyweights Moving Extra..	Tuck B	86	306	PSL		S	$30
Haynes First 25 Years	Clew J	85	418	Haynes		H	$30
Healey (Autocar)	Garnier P	83	104	Temple/Hamlyn		H	$50
Healey Handsome Brute	Harvey C	78	104	Oxford Ill/St Martins		H	$80
Healey Specials	Healey G	80	104	Gentry/Haynes		H	$50
Healeys and Austin-Healeys	Browning P/Needham L	70	104	Foulis/MBI		H	$80
Heavenly Bodies Pirelli Calendar		75	510	Harmony Books/Pan		S	$100
Heavy Haulage	Hawthorne R	70S	303	Steaming		S	$10
Heavy Truck	Park C	82	306	Osprey		H	$50
Hells Angels Strange & Terrible	Thompson H S	66	601	Random/Ballantine		X	$40
Henry Ford & Grass-roots America	Wik R M	72	415	Univ of Mich		X	$40
Henry Ford (Burlingame)	Burlingame R	54	415	Knopf/Quadrangle		X	$10
Henry Ford and Benjamin B Lovett A	Twork E O	82	415	Harlo		H	$30
Henry Ford and Greenfield Village	Simonds W A	38	415	Stokes		H	$30
Henry Ford Engineer (juv)	Neyhart L A	50	415	Houghton Mifflin		H	$30
Henry Ford Highlights of His Life	Edison Institute	54	415	Henry Ford Museum		S	$10
Henry Ford His Life His Work His...	Simonds W A	43	415	Bobbs Merrill		H	$30
Henrys Wonderful Model T 1908-1927	Clymer F	55	122	Clymer/McGraw/Bonanza		H	$40
Herbert Austin	Church Roy	79	105	Europa Publ		H	$30
Herbie Goes Bananas	Claro J	80	150	Scholastic		S	$10
Herbie Rides Again	Cebulash M	74	150	Scholastic		S	$10
Heroes of Stock Car Racing	Libby B	75	205	Random	Sports Library	H	$20
Herr Uber 1000 PS	Neubauer A	59	130 205	HDV		H	$40
Hershey P.A.		71	401	Directional Advertising		S	$20
High Gear	Jones E	55	416	Bantam		S	$20
High Performance Cars 1958-1959	Grant G/Bolster J	57	410	Autosport		S	$20
High Performance Cars 1961-1962	Grant G/Bolster J	61	410	Autosport		S	$20
High Performance Cars 1965-1966	Grant G/Bolster J	65	410	Autosport		S	$20
High Performance Driving	Peterson P	74	203	Simon & Schuster		H	$20
High Performance Escorts Mk 1 68-74	Clarke R M	84	156	Brooklands	Brooklands	S	$30
High Performance Escorts Mk 2 75-80	Clarke R M	84	156	Brooklands	Brooklands	H	$30
High Speed Driving	Haynes J H		203	Haynes		S	$20
High Speed Internal Combustion Eng	Ricardo H	23+	405	Blackie/Interscience		H	$250
High Speed Low Cost 140mph Mini	Staniforth A	69	171	PSL		H	$40
High Speed Two Stroke Petrol Engine	Smith P H	65	405	Foulis/Autobooks		H	$60
Highlights of Hist 25 Yrs w/ Motor	Motor	29	401	Motor(US)		H	$80
Hillman Minx Guide	Page S F	63	104	Sports Car Press		H	$20
Hist of British Dinkey Toys 1934-64	Gibson C	66+	702	MAP/Mikansue		S	$20
Hist of Comm. Vehicles of World	Kuipers J F J	72	306	Oakwood Press		H	$40
Hist of Electric Model Roads.......	Greenslade R W	80S	701	Leisure-Time		S	$70
Hist of Fire-Fighting & Equip...	Ingram A	78	302	New Eng Lib/Book Sls/Chtw		H	$20
Hist of French Dinkey Toys	Roulet J M	78	702	editions Adepte		H	$50
Hist of Geelong Speed Trials 56-85	Grant G	86	206	Grant		H	$40
Hist of Hudson	Butler D	82	163	Crestline	Crestline	H	$60
Hist of Lamborghini	Box R de la R/Crump R	74+	128	Transport Bookmen		H	$60
Hist of London Taxicab	Georgano G N	72	306	David & Charles		H	$40
Hist of Manx Grand Prix		60	603	Shell		S	$40
Hist of Mercedes-Benz Mot Veh & Eng	Schildberger F	72	130	Daimler-Benz		H	$125
Hist of Motor Car	Matteucci M	70	401	Crown		H	$20
Hist of Motor Racing	Boddy W/Laban B	77+	297	Macdonald/Orbis/Smith		H	$40
Hist of Motorized Vehcls 1769-1946	Kidner R W	49	401	Clymer		S	$30
Hist of Racing Car	Lurani G	72	297	Crowell		H	$40
Hist of Rolls-Royce Motor Cars Vol1	Morton C W	64	139	Foulis		H	$150
Hist of Sports Cars	Georgano G N	70	401	Rainbird/Dutton		H	$50
Hist of Studebaker Corp 1852-23	Erskine A R	24	145	Studebaker		H	$100
Hist of Vint Mtcycl Club Aust (NSW)		78	601	VMCC of Aust		H	$30
Hist of Worlds Classic Cars	Hough R/Frostick M	63	401	Allen & Unwin		H	$60
Hist of Worlds Motorcycles	Hough R/Setright L J K	66	601	Harper & Row		H	$40
Hist of Worlds Racing Cars	Hough R/Frostick M	65	297	Harper & Row		H	$40
Hist of Worlds Sports Cars	Hough R	61	401	Harper		H	$40
Hist on Road Vintage Car Miscellany	Anderson J R L	58	401	Hamish Hamilton		H	$40
Histoire De L'Automobile En France	Saka P/Menu J/Dauliac J-P	82	407	Fernand Nathan		H	$50
Histoire del Automobile Belge (Fr)	Kupelian Y/J	70S	402	Paul Legrain		H	$80
Historia del Automovil en Espana	Ciuro J	70	402	CEAC		H	$40
Historic American Roads	Rose A C/Rakeman C	76	401 419	Crown		H	$20
Historic Commercial Vehicles	Mack R F	72	306	Turntable		S	$10
Historic Motor Racing	Pritchard A	69	297	Grosset & Dunlap		H	$20
Historic Racing Car Models	Ross F	76	702	Lothrop		H	$30
Historical Facts International Veh	IHC		158	IHC		S	$20
Historical Persp. of Farm Machinery		80	901	Soc.of Automotive Engrs		S	$40
Holden First 25 Years		73	173	Holden		S	$20

Title	Author	Pub date	Subjects	Publisher	Series	Bind	Price
Holdens Vs Fords	Harding M	85	402	View Productions		H	$50
Holly 5200 Carburetor Handbook	Urich M	82	202	H P Books		S	$20
Honda (Myers)	Myers C	84	606	Arco		H	$20
Honda (Woollett)	Woollett M	83	606	Temple/Newnes/Hamlyn		H	$40
Honda Early Classic Motorcycles	Bacon R	85	606	Osprey	Osprey Coll Lib	H	$50
Honda F1 1964-1968 (Japanese)	Car Graphic	84	126 298	Nigensha Publishing		H	$200
Honda Man & His Machines	Sanders S	75	126	Little Brown		H	$30
Honda Motor Men Management etc	Sakiya T	82	126	Kodansha		H	$40
Hors Ligne Special Ferrari/1985	Kroon R	85	121	Hors Ligne		S	$40
Horseless Carriage Days	Maxim H P	36+	401	Harper & Bros/Dover		X	$40
Horseless Carriage(Rolt)	Rolt L T C	50	297	Constable		H	$40
Hot Rod Bodywork & Painting 1988	Cogan R	88	405	Petersen		S	$10
Hot Rod Chassis Construction	Hot Rod	67	202	Petersen/Signet/NAL		S	$10
Hot Rod Corvette No 02	Kelley L	78	114	Petersen		S	$10
Hot Rod Engines	Hot Rod	67	202	Petersen/Signet/NAL		S	$10
Hot Rod Handbook (Fawcett)	Hochman L	58	201	Fawcett	Fawcett	S	$10
Hot Rod Magazine Yearbook #1 1961	Martin W H/Hot Rod Eds	61	201	Petersen	Hot Rod	S	$40
Hot Rod Magazine Yearbook #2 1962		62	201	Hot Rod Magazine	Hot Rod	H	$30
Hot Rod Pictorial	Orr V	49	201	Clymer		S	$30
Hot Rod Pictorial (Hot Rod)	Greene B/Hot Rod	67	201	Petersen	Hot Rod	S	$30
Hot Rod Technical Library	Francisco D etc	61+	201	Spotliet/Trend/Hot Rod		H	$20
Hot Seat Complete Manual of Rally..	Fellows S	84	209	MRP		H	$20
Hounds of Road History Greyhound	Jackson C	84		Bowling Green U/Kendall		H	$50
House of Goodyear	Allen H	49	418	Corday		H	$70
How & Where of 8-litre Bentleys	Sedgwick S	72	139	BDC		S	$40
How Many Are Left Autos of the 40s		81	412	Automotive Info Clearing		S	$30
How Many Are Left Autos of the 50s		81+	412	Automotive Info Clearing		S	$30
HT Avoid Speeding Tickets Fst Dr HB	Reynolds M	86+	203	New Freedom		S	$30
HT Build Cust/Design Plastic Models	Gordon T L	82	704	Tab		S	$20
HT Build Racing Car	Domark K J	49	202	Clymer		S	$40
HT Build Street Rod		85	422	Brooklands/Petersen		S	$30
HT Convert to Electric Car	Lucas T/Riess F	80	417	Michelman/Crown		H	$30
HT Go Saloon Car Racing	Brittan N	67	297	PSL		H	$20
HT Hop Up Chevrolet & GMC 6 cy Eng	Huntington R	51	111	Clymer		S	$20
HT Hotrod & Race Your Datsun	Waar B	84	167	Steve Smith		S	$40
HT Hotrod Your 2.0-liter OHC Ford	Vizard D	84	169	Fountain/HP		S	$40
HT Hotrod Your Buick V6	Sessions R	86	108	HP		X	$30
HT Import European Car	Duguay J	85	401	Williamson		S	$30
HT Modify Datsun 510/610/240Z......	Fisher B/WaarB	73	167	HP		S	$30
HT Modify Ford SOHC Engines	Vizard D	84	169	Fountain		S	$30
HT Modify Your Mini	Vizard D	87	171	Fountain Press		S	$40
HT Modify Your Nissan/Datsun OHC En	Honsowetz F	86	167	HP		S	$30
HT Prepare Car For Rallying	Sauer G	86	209	Ford Motorsport		S	$30
HT Rebuild Your Honda Car Engine	Wilson T	85	126	HP		S	$20
HT Rebuild Yr 1.3,1.6, 2.0 OHC Ford	Vizard D	80	169	HP		S	$40
HT Repair Your Foreign Car	O'Kane D	68	405	Doubleday		H	$30
HT Restore Antique & Classic Cars	Uskali G/Johnson C	54	405	Popular Mechanics		H	$40
HT Restore w/ Metal Joining Techs	Fairweather T	88	405	Osprey	Osprey Rest Gd	H	$30
HT Ride Observed Trials	Shipman C	73	602	HP		S	$30
HT Succeed in Bigtime Trucking	Boyle D H	77	301	Ten Speed Press		S	$20
HT Tune Your Car(Petersen's)	Murray S	75+	405	Petersen		H	$20
HT Watch Motor Racing	Moss S	75	297	Gentry		H	$30
Hudson & Railton Cars 1936-1940	Clarke R M	76	163 105	Brooklands	Brooklands	S	$30
Hudson Postwar Years	Langworth R M	77	163	MBI	Postwar Years	H	$60
Hunt v Lauda Grand Prix Season 1976	Benson D	76	205	Daily Express		S	$20
Hurst Source Book	North P	85	162 201	Bookman	Source Book	S	$30
Hyphen in Rolls-Royce	Oldham W J	67	139	Foulis		H	$40
Il Museo dell'Automobile Torino	Biscaretti di Ruffia R	66	401	Auto Club d'Italia		H	$60
Il Quadrifoglio #2 Alfa Romeo 10-85		85	101	Alfa Romeo		S	$30
Il Tridente Storia della Maserati	Boschi S	64	172	Poligrafici il Borgo		H	$180
Ill Ency of Military Vehicles	Hogg I V/Weeks J	80	308	Quarto/New Burlington		H	$40
Ill Ency of Motorcycles	Tragatsch E	77+	601	Quarto/Chartwell/Hamlyn		H	$40
Ill Ency of Trucks Buses	Miller D	82+	306	Quarto/Hamlyn		H	$50
Ill Hist of Trucks and Buses	Miller D	82	306	Quarto/A&W/Galahad		H	$10
Ill History of Automobiles	Wise D B	80	401	Quarto/A&W		H	$10
Ill History of Bentley Car	Bentley W O	64	139	Allen & Unwin/Bentley		H	$100
Ill History of Indianapolis 500	Fox J C	67+	208	World/Hungness		H	$150
Ill History of Rallying	Robson G	81	209	Osprey		H	$40
Ill History of Road Transport	Burgess-Wise D/Miller D	86	401	Quarto/New Burlington		H	$30
Ill Motor Cars of World	Olyslager P	71	401	Grosset & Dunlap		H	$20
IMSA '84 Yearbook	Van der Feen D	84	204	IMSA		S	$30
IMSA '86 Yearbook	Van der Feen D	86	204	Intl Mtr Spts Association		S	$30
IMSA '87 Yearbook		88	204	Paul Oxman Publishing		S	$30
IMSA '88 Yearbook	Burns G	89	204	IMSA		S	$30
Imago 15 (Italian)		71	506	Pininfarina S.p.A.			$70
Immortal 2.9 Alfa-Romeo 8C 2900 A/B	Moore S	86	101	Parkside		H	$150
Imported Car Spotter's Guide	Burness T	79	401	MBI		S	$40

Title	Author	Pub date	Subjects		Publisher	Series	Bind	Price
INUFA Katalog 1972		72	306		Vogt-Schild		S	$60
INUFA Katalog 1973		73	306		Vogt-Schild		S	$60
INUFA Katalog 1975		75	306		Vogt-Schild		S	$60
INUFA Katalog 1983		83	306		Vogt-Schild		S	$50
INUFA Katalog 1984		84	306		Vogt-Schild		S	$50
In First Gear French Auto Ind to 14	Laux J M	76	407		Liverpool U		H	$40
In Good Shape	Bayley S	79	502		Van Nostrand		S	$30
In Track of Speed	Moss S	57+	205		Frederick Muller		H	$40
Incompleat Corvair Story	Newell D	79	113		Bob Terkelson		S	$40
Incredible A J Foyt	Engel L K	70	205		Arco		H	$30
Index Rolls-Royce/Bent Periodicals	Clarke T C		139		Transport Bookman		S	$20
Indianapolis 1946 Yearbook supp'm't	Clymer F	46	208		Clymer		S	$30
Indianapolis 1947 Yearbook	Clymer F	47	208		Clymer		S	$40
Indianapolis 1948 Yearbook supp'm't	Clymer F	48	208		Clymer		S	$50
Indianapolis 1949 Yearbook	Clymer F	49	208		Clymer		X	$30
Indianapolis 1950 Yearbook	Clymer F	50	208		Clymer		S	$90
Indianapolis 1951 Yearbook	Clymer F	51	208		Clymer		S	$90
Indianapolis 1952 Yearbook	Clymer F	52	208		Clymer		S	$125
Indianapolis 1953 Yearbook	Clymer F	53	208		Clymer		S	$90
Indianapolis 1954 Yearbook	Clymer F	54	208		Clymer		S	$90
Indianapolis 1955 Yearbook	Clymer F	55	208		Clymer		S	$90
Indianapolis 1956 Yearbook	Clymer F	57	208		Clymer		S	$100
Indianapolis 1957 Yearbook	Clymer F	58	208		Clymer		X	$90
Indianapolis 1958 Yearbook	Clymer F	59	208		Clymer		S	$150
Indianapolis 1959 Yearbook	Clymer F	59	208		Clymer		X	$100
Indianapolis 1960 Yearbook	Clymer F		208		Clymer			$180
Indianapolis 1961 Yearbook	Clymer F	62	208		Clymer		S	$100
Indianapolis 1962 Yearbooks	Ritch O C	62	208		Clymer		S	$50
Indianapolis 1963 Yearbook	Ritch O C	63	208		Clymer		X	$80
Indianapolis 1964 Yearbook	Clymer F	64	208		Clymer		S	$50
Indianapolis 1965 Yearbook	Clymer F	65	208		Clymer		X	$50
Indianapolis 1966 Yearbook	Clymer F	66	208		Clymer		X	$50
Indianapolis 1967 Yearbook	Clymer F	67	208		Clymer		X	$50
Indianapolis 1968 Yearbook	Davidson D	68	208		Clymer		S	$50
Indianapolis 1969-1972 Yearbook	Mahoney J	80	208		Hungness		H	$200
Indianapolis 1973 Yearbook	Hungness C	73	208		Hungness		X	$100
Indianapolis 1974 Yearbook	Hungness C	74	208		Hungness		X	$30
Indianapolis 1975 Yearbook	Hungness C	75	208		Hungness		X	$30
Indianapolis 1976 Yearbook	Hungness C	76	208		Hungness		X	$30
Indianapolis 1977 Yearbook	Hungness C	77	208		Hungness		X	$30
Indianapolis 1978 Yearbook	Hungness C	78	208		Hungness		S	$30
Indianapolis 1979 Yearbook	Hungness C	79	208		Hungness		X	$30
Indianapolis 1983 Yearbook	Hungness C	83	208		Hungness		X	$40
Indianapolis 1984 Yearbook	Hungness C	84	208		Hungness		X	$30
Indianapolis 1985 Yearbook	Hungness C	85	208		Hungness		X	$30
Indianapolis 500 (Fox)	Fox J C	67	208		World		H	$125
Indianapolis 500(Devaney)	Devaney J & B	76	208		Rand McNally		H	$60
Indianapolis 500(Engel)	Engel L K	70	208		Four Winds		H	$30
Indianapolis 500(Yates)	Yates B	56+	213	208	Harper		H	$30
Indianapolis Race History		46	208		Floyd Clymer		X	$60
Indianapolis Records	Hess A	59	211	105	Stuart & Richards		H	$30
Indomitable Tin Goose	Pearson C	60	158		MBI/Abelard		H	$70
Industrial Design	Loewy R	79	502	145	Overlook		H	$125
Industrial Design(Spec sig ltd ed)	Loewy R	79	502	145	Overlook Press		H	$500
Indy 500 American Inst Under Fire	Dorson R	74	208		Bond/Parkhurst		H	$40
Indy 500 Mechanic	Brawner C/Scalzo J	75	208		Chilton		H	$40
Indy Race and Ritual	Reed T	80	208		Presidio		S	$20
Innovations			502		US Steel		H	$100
Inside 100 Great Cars	Hodges D	88	401		M Cavendish/Orbis/Foulis		H	$40
Inside Story of Fastest Fords	Ludvigsen K E	69	122		Style Auto		H	$80
Insiders Guide to Indy Car Racing	Amabile R	89	299		Am Cars		S	$20
Insolent Chariots	Keats J	58+	419		Lippincott/Fawcett/Crest		X	$30
Internal Combustion Eng Analysis...	Obert E F/Jennings B H	44+	405		International Textbook		H	$60
Internal-Combustion Engine	Taylor C F/Taylor E S	38+	405		International Textbook		H	$40
International - World Trucks #11	Kennett P	81	301		PSL	World Trucks	H	$40
International GP Bk of Motor Racing	Frewin M	65	297		Leslie Frewin		H	$30
International Motor Cycle Rac Book	Macauley T	71	603		Souvenir		H	$30
International Motor Racing (Nye)	Nye D	73	297		Macmillan/Crowell	Leisureguides	H	$10
International Motor Racing Bk #2	Drackett P	68	204		Souvenir		H	$20
International Motor Racing Bk #3	Drackett P	69	204		Souvenir		H	$20
International Motor Racing Bk #4	Drackett P	70	204		Souvenir Press		H	$20
International Motor Racing Bk(#1)	Drackett P	67	204		Souvenir Press		H	$30
Interstaters (Australian Trucking)	Johnson M B	83	306		Savvas/Truckin Life		H	$40
Introduction to Mini		84	171		Mini City		S	$30
Invention of Automobile	Nixon S J C	36	130		Country Life		H	$30
Investigation Dev German GP Cars 34	British Intelligence	47	130	298	HM Stationery Office		S	$400
Investigation of Ralph Nader	Whiteside T	72	401		Arbor		H	$30

Title	Author	Pub date	Subjects		Publisher	Series	Bind	Price
Investors Ill Gd to Am Conv 1946-76	Webb C	79	403		Barnes		H	$50
ISDT'73 Olympics of Motorcycling	Schneiders R	73	602		Chilton		H	$20
Is Bug Dead? Great Beetle Ad.......	Dalrymple M	82	150	503	Stewart Tabori Chang		S	$30
Isle of Man TT '60 Pt 1(12" record)	Walker G	50	603		Schofield Productions	Sound Stories		$40
Isle of Man TT '60 Pt 2(12" record)	Walker G	50S	603		Schofield Productions	Sound Stories		$40
Isle of Man TT 1959(12" record)	Walker G	50S	603		Schofield Productions	Sound Stories		$40
Isotta Fraschini (Anselmi)	Anselmi A T	77	118		G. Milani/MBI/Albion		H	$180
Isotta Fraschini 8C Monterosa Cat		50S	118		Clymer		S	$30
Isotta-Fraschini(Ballantine)	Nicholson T R	71	118		Ballantine	Ballantine #3	S	$20
Italian Cars Neko Pictorial 2		83	409		Neko	Neko	S	$30
Italian High-Performance Cars	Pritchard A/Davey K	67	409		Allen & Unwin/Bentley		H	$60
Italian Motorcycles	Parker T	84	606		Osprey	Osprey Col Lib	S	$30
Italian Motorcycles Guide	Ayton C J	85	606		Temple/Newnes/Hamlyn		H	$20
Its Been An Exciting Ride	Echlin J/Gilson C	89	418		Echlin		H	$20
J H Lartigue Et Les Autos	Lartigue J H	74	510		Chene		H	$150
Jack Brabhams Motor Racing Book	Brabham J	60+	205		Muller		H	$30
Jackie Stewart (Italian)	Tommasi T	71	205		Auto.Club d Italia		S	$40
Jackie Stewart World Champ(Signed)	Stewart J/Dymock E	70	205		Regnery/Pelham		H	$100
Jackie Stewart World Champion	Stewart J/Dymock E	70	205		Regnery		H	$20
Jackie Stewart World Driving Champ.	Engel L K	70	205		Arco		H	$20
Jackie Stewarts Owner Driver Book	Stewart J	73	405		Dodd Mead		H	$20
Jackie Stewarts Princ(autographed)	Stewart J	86	205	203	Hazleton/MBI		H	$100
Jacques-Henri Lartigue(English)	Lartigue J-H	86	510		Centre National/Pantheon		S	$20
Jaguar (Ballantine)	Montagu	71	127		Ballantine	Ballantine #10	S	$30
Jaguar (Exeter)	Kowal B	83+	127		Exeter/Bookthrift/S&S		H	$10
Jaguar (Foulis)	Montagu	75+	127		Foulis/Haynes	Minimarque	H	$30
Jaguar (Pocket History)	Frostick M	80	127		Automobilia	Complete Book	S	$20
Jaguar 1979 (Japanese)			127		Neko		S	$30
Jaguar Biography	Montagu	61	127		Cassell/Norton		H	$50
Jaguar Cars 1948-1951	Clarke R M	71	127		Brooklands	Brooklands	S	$30
Jaguar Cars 1951-1953	Clarke R M	71	127		Brooklands	Brooklands	S	$30
Jaguar Cars 1954-1955	Clarke R M	71	127		Brooklands	Brooklands	S	$30
Jaguar Cars 1955-1957	Clarke R M	72	127		Brooklands	Brooklands	S	$30
Jaguar Cars 1957-1961	Clarke R M	72	127		Brooklands	Brooklands	S	$30
Jaguar Cars Practical Guide........	Vandiest C L	61	127		Pearson		H	$40
Jaguar Companion	Ullyett K	59	127		Stanley Paul	Companion	H	$40
Jaguar Complete Ill History	Porter P	84	127		Warne/Haynes		H	$50
Jaguar D Type & XKSS Autohistory	Robson G	83	127		Osprey	Autohistory	H	$40
Jaguar Defin Hist SEE Jaguar Hist			127					$
Jaguar Drivers Yearbook 1977(first)	Skilleter P	78	127		Magpie		H	$50
Jaguar Drivers Yearbook 1978	Skilleter P	79	127		Magpie		H	$50
Jaguar Drivers Yearbook 1979-80	Skilleter P	80	127		Magpie		H	$50
Jaguar Drivers Yearbook 1980-81	Skilleter P	81	127		Magpie		H	$40
Jaguar E Type 1961-66	Clarke R M	75	127		Brooklands	Brooklands	S	$30
Jaguar E Type Autohistory	Jenkinson D	82	127		Osprey	Autohistory	H	$40
Jaguar Guide	Bentley J	57	127		Sports Car Press	Mod Sports Car	S	$30
Jaguar History Great British Car	Whyte A	80+	127		PSL/Sterling		H	$60
Jaguar Il Fascino di......(Italian)	Casucci P	79	127				S	$100
Jaguar Lord Montagu of Beaulieu	Montagu	67	127		Barnes		H	$40
Jaguar Mk II Auto-Classic #2	Schrader H	80S	127		Albion Scott	Auto-Classic	S	$20
Jaguar Motor Racing & Manufacturer	Berry R	78	127		Aztex		S	$20
Jaguar Since 1945	Busenkell	82	127		Norton		H	$40
Jaguar Sports (Autocar)	Garnier P	75	127		Hamlyn		H	$40
Jaguar Sports Cars 1957-1960	Clarke R M	72	127		Brooklands	Brooklands	S	$30
Jaguar SS Cars 1931-1937	Clarke R M	70	127		Brooklands	Brooklands	S	$40
Jaguar SS Cars 1937-1947	Clarke R M	70	127		Brooklands	Brooklands	S	$40
Jaguar SS90 & SS100 Super Profile	Whyte A	84	127		Haynes	Super Profile	H	$20
Jaguar Story	Wherry J H	67	127		Chilton	Sebring	H	$30
Jaguar Tradition	Frostick M	73	127		Dalton Watson	Dalton Watson	H	$60
Jaguar Tradition of Sports Cars	Viart B	85	127		EPA/MBI/Haynes		H	$80
Jaguar Under Southern Cross	Hughes L	80	127		Bronle Motor Books		H	$150
Jaguar V12 Engine Des/Background	Hassan W	79	127		TASS of AUEW		S	$30
Jaguar XJ12 1972-80	Clarke R M	81	127		Brooklands	Brooklands	H	$30
Jaguar XJ40 Evolution of Species	Whyte A	87	127		PSL		H	$50
Jaguar XJ40 Project (IME Paper)		86	127		Inst Mech Engineers		S	$50
Jaguar XJ6 1968-72	Clarke R M	81	127		Brooklands	Brooklands	H	$30
Jaguar XJ6 Series II 1973-1979	Clarke R M	85	127		Brooklands	Brooklands	S	$30
Jaguar XJS	Fletcher R	83	127		Cadogan/Haynes	High Performanc	H	$40
Jaguar XJS 1975-80	Clarke R M	81	127		Brooklands	Brooklands	H	$30
Jaguar XK in Australia	Elmgreen J/Mcgrath T	85	127		JTZ		H	$250
Jaguar XK-E Source Book	Sass D	84	127		Bookman	Source Boo	S	$30
Jaguar XKE Collection No 1 1961-74	Clarke R M	81	127		Brooklands	Brooklands	S	$20
Jaguars for Road	Rasmussen H	85	127		MBI	Survivor S	H	$100
Jaguars in Competition	Harvey C	79	127		Osprey		H	$50
James Flood Book of Early Motoring	Paynting H H	68	402		James Flood		H	$150
James Hunt	Lyons P	75	205		Augustus Books		S	$10
James Hunt Against All Odds	Young E S	77	205		Hamlyn		H	$30

Title	Author	Pub date	Subjects			Publisher	Series	Bind	Price
Janet Guthrie First Woman at Indy	Olney R R	78	205			Harvey House		H	$30
Japanese Motor Cycles(Hamlyn Guide)	Ayton C J	82	606			Hamlyn		H	$20
Javelin Source Book	Campbell S	83	102			Bookman Pub	Source Book	S	$30
Jeep (Clayton)	Clayton M	82	117			David & Charles		H	$40
Jeep Collection No 1 1942-1954	Clarke R M	83	117			Brooklands	Brooklands	S	$20
Jeep(Olyslager)	Vanderveen B H	70	117			Warne	Olyslager	H	$30
Jeepney	Torres E	79	306			GCF Books		H	$40
Jensen Cars 1946-1967	Clarke R M	80	105			Brooklands	Brooklands	S	$30
Jensen Cars 1967-1979	Clarke R M	80	105			Brooklands	Brooklands	S	$30
Jensen Healey 1972-1976	Clarke R M	80	105			Brooklands	Brooklands	S	$30
Jensen Healey Stories	Browning P/Blunsden J	74	105			MRP		H	$70
Jensen Interceptor 1966-1976	Clarke R M	80	105			Brooklands	Brooklands	S	$30
Jim Clark at Wheel H	Clark J	64	205			Arthur Barker/Coward		H	$60
Jim Clark at Wheel S	Clark J	66	205			Pocket Books		S	$20
Jim Clark Portrait of Great Driver	Gauld G	68	205			Arco/Hamlyn		H	$40
Jim Clark Remembered	Gauld G	75+	205			PSL/Arco		H	$40
Jim Clark Story	Gavin B	67	205			Frewin		H	$60
Jimmy Murphy and White Dusbg (juv)	Briggs R/Carter B	68	116	205	504	Hamilton		H	$50
Jo Siffert	Deschenaux J	72	205			Kimber		H	$50
Jochen Rindt Story of Wld Champion	Pruller H	70	205			Kimber		H	$70
Jody An Autobiography	Scheckter J	76	205			Keartland/Haynes		H	$50
John Cobb Story	Davis S C H		205	211		Foulis		H	$50
John Cooper Grand Prix Carpetbagger	Cooper J/Bentley J	77	205			Haynes/Doubleday		H	$40
John Deere Tractors		76	907			John Deere		S	$30
John Studebaker American Dream	Corle E	48	145			Dutton		H	$40
Jokeswagen Book	Preston C	66	150			Bernard Geis/Random		H	$20
Jowett Jupiter Car that Leaped.....	Nankivell E	81	105			Batsford		H	$50
Juan Manuel Fangio	Molter G	56	205			Foulis		H	$50
Jupiters Travels H	Simon T	79	212	601		Doubleday		X	$30
Just For Record Thrust 2	Ackroyd J	84	211			CHW Roles		H	$40
Kaingaroa Super Trucks	Lowe	83	306			Lodestar Press		S	$20
Kaiser-Frazer Cars Clymer Test Rpt	Clymer F	47	158			Clymer		S	$40
Kaleidoscope of Farm Tractors	Baldwin N	77	904			Old Motor		H	$40
Kaleidoscope of Lorries & Vans	Baldwin N	79	303			Marshall Harris		H	$40
Kaleidoscope of Motor Cycling	Howard D	77	601			Old Motor Magazine		H	$40
Kaleidoscope of Steam Wagons	Whitehead R A	79	306			Marshall Harris		H	$40
Kandy-Kolored Tangerine-Flake......	Wolfe T	66	416			Cape/Pan		S	$30
Karting Fun on Four Wheels	Radlauer E	67	214			Bowmar		S	$10
Karting Guide	Patchen M	61	214			Sports Car Press	Mod Sports Car	S	$20
Keke Autobiography	Rosberg K/Botsford K	85	205			Hutchinson		H	$40
Keke Rosberg (Constanduros)	Constanduros B	84	205			Kimberley's		S	$10
Ken Purdys Book of Automobiles	Purdy K W	72	401			Playboy		X	$20
Kenny Roberts	Coleman B	82	610			Weidenfeld		H	$60
Kimberley Driver Prfl 02 Derek Bell	Constanduros B	85	205			Kimberley's		S	$20
Kimberley Driver Prfl 03 Villeneuve	Henry A	80S	205			Kimberley		S	$20
Kimberley GP Team Gd 01 Williams	Constanduros B	82	298			Kimberley's		S	$20
Kimberley GP Team Gd 02 Brabham	Constanduros B	82	298			Kimberley's		S	$20
Kimberley GP Team Gd 03 Ferrari	Constanduros B	83	121			Kimberley's		S	$30
Kimberley GP Team Gd 04 Renault	Constanduros B	83	120			Kimberley's		S	$20
Kimberley GP Team Gd 05 McLaren	Constanduros B	80S	298			Kimberley's		S	$20
Kimberley GP Team Gd 06 Lotus	Constanduros B	83	129			Kimberley's		S	$20
Kimberley GP Team Gd 07 Tyrell	Hamilton M	83	298			Kimberley's		S	$20
Kimberley GP Team Gd 08 Alfa Romeo	Constanduros B	83	101			Kimberley's		S	$20
Kimberley GP Team Gd 11 Williams	Constanduros B	84	298			Kimberley's		S	$20
Kimberley GP Team Gd 12 Brabham	Constanduros B	80S	298			Kimberley's		S	$20
Kimberley GP Team Gd 13 Ferrari	Henry A	84	121			Kimberley's		S	$30
Kimberley GP Team Gd 14 McLaren	Constaduros B		298			Kimberley's		S	$20
Kimberley Rally Team Gd 01 Audi	Buhlmann K	84	124			Kimberley's		S	$10
King of Dragsters (Garlits)	Garlits D/Yates B	67+	201	205		Chilton		H	$30
King of Road (Petty)	Petty R	77	205			Rutledge/Macmillan		H	$40
King Richard I Richard Petty	Petty R/Neely W	86	205			Macmillan		H	$40
King Richard Richard Petty Story	Libby B/Petty R	77	205			Doubleday		H	$30
Kings of Road (S)	Purdy K W	61	401			Bantam		S	$20
Kings of Road (H)	Purdy K W	49+	401			Little/Hutchinson/Bnza		H	$40
Kit Car Catalog 1985		85	423			Homebuilt Publications		S	$20
Klassische Wagen I	Von Fersen H	71	401			Hallwag		H	$40
Klassische Wagen II	Hediger F	74	401			Hallwag		H	$40
Know Thy Beast Vincent	Stevens E M G	72+	606			Vincent Pub		H	$60
Knudson Biography	Beasley N	47	160	404		Whittlesey/McGraw Hill		H	$40
Kraftfahrzeuge der Feuerwehr.......	Oswald W/Gihl M	77	302			Motorbuch Verlag		H	$50
KSS Velocette Super Profile	Clew J	84	606			Haynes	Super Profile	H	$20
Kurtis-Kraft Story	Hitze E	74	158			Interstate Printers		S	$100
L A Freeway Appreciative Essay	Brodsly D	81	419	401		Univ of California		H	$20
L'Album de la DS	Borge J/Viasnoff N	83	153			EPA		H	$70
L'Art et L'Automobile	Poulain H	73	504			Les Clefs du Temps		H	$300
L'Automobile (Buffet)	Buffet B	85	504			Maurice Garnier		H	$90
L'epopee Matra Sports 64-74(French)	Roux R J	77	298			Bias		H	$60

Title	Author	Pub date	Subjects	Publisher	Series	Bind	Price
L'Indimenticabile 82 della Ferrari	Rossi A	82	121	FOR-VEM		S	$30
La 2CV	Borge J/Viasnoff N	77	153	Veyrier/Balland		H	$40
La Belle Chauffeusse	Wiegersma F	81	506	VOC Angel Books		H	$50
La Carrozzeria Italiana (English)	Rancati G	77	501	Enrico Yamazaki		S	$70
La DS Citroen	Puiboube D	86	153	Editions Atlas	Les Voitures...	H	$30
La Favolosa Lancia	Centenari M	76	157	Editoriale Domus		H	$90
La Favolosa Targa Florio (Italian)	Canestrini G	66	206	LEA		H	$200
La Ferrari in tuta	Borsari G	80	121	Auto Sprint		S	$50
La France et L'Automobile	Bishop C W	71	407	Editions Genin		S	$30
La Lancia 70 Years of Excellence	Weernink W	79	157	MRP		H	$80
La Scommessa di Gianni Lancia(Ital)	Moretti V	86	157	Edizioni di Autocritica		H	$70
La Storia Della Mille Miglia	Lurani G	79	206	Instituto Geografico.....		H	$80
Lagonda History of Marque	Davey K/May	78	105	David & Charles		H	$100
Lamborghini (Bonsall)	Bonsall T E	88	128	Bookman/Smith/Gallery		H	$20
Lamborghini (Borel)	Borel J M	82	128	Lamborghini/Grafiche T		H	$125
Lamborghini Cars from Sant' Agata	Box R de la R/Crump R	81	128	Osprey		H	$70
Lamborghini Countach (Borel)	Borel J M	85	128	Casa Editrice		H	$125
Lamborghini Countach World S/C #2	Coulter J	85	128	Albion Scott/Moto-Art	World Super Car	H	$50
Lamborghini Guide 1963-73		63	128	Transport Bookman		S	$20
Lamborghini Miura	Coltrin P/Marchet J-F	82	128	Osprey		H	$90
Lamborghini Traume auf vier Radern	Box R de la R	86	128	Serag		H	$150
Lanchester Motor Cars A History	Bird A/Hutton-Stott F	65	105	Cassell		H	$70
Lancia (Autocar)	Garnier P	81	157	Hamlyn		H	$50
Lancia Aurelia GT (Italian)	Bernabo F	83	157	Libreria dell'Automobile	auto classiche	H	$60
Lancia Fulvia & Flavia Coll Guide	Weernink W	84	157	MRP	Coll Guide	H	$50
Lancia Stratos 1972-1985	Clarke R M	85	157	Brooklands	Brooklands	S	$30
Lancia Stratos Super Profile	Robson G	83	157	Haynes	Super Profile	H	$30
Lancia the Shield and Flag	Trow N	80	157	David & Charles		H	$60
Land Speed Record	Posthumus C/Tremayne D	71+	211	Osprey/Crown		H	$60
Land Speed Record Breakers	Knudson R L	81	211	Lerner		H	$30
Land Transport Tomorrow	Wells G	70	419	Clifton Books		H	$20
Landscape with Machines	Rolt L T C	71+	404	Sutton		X	$20
Larry Reid's New Rally Tables	Reid L	71	209	Sports Car Press	Mod Sports Car	S	$20
Last American Convertibles	Hirsch J/Weith W	79	401	Collier		S	$20
Last Billionaire Henry Ford	Richards W C	48	415	Scribner		H	$30
Last Hero see BLUEBIRD & DEAD LAKE			211				$
Last of Great Road Races	Mutch R	75	603	Transport Bookman		S	$30
Last Season Life of Bruce McLaren	Beeching J	72	205	Walter R Haessner		H	$50
Le Auto D'oro Evoluzione della.....	Rapi F L/Santovetti F	68	504	LEA/Auto Club d'Italia		H	$200
Le Auto dei Papi/Pontiffs' Cars	Moretti V	81	401	Edizioni di Autocritica		H	$90
Le Auto-Giocattolo Italiane 1890-60	Rampini P	87	703	Rampini		H	$125
Le Ferrari (large format)	Rogliatti G	66	121	L'Editrice del Auto......		H	$250
Le Grandi Alfa Romeo (Italian)	Fusi L	69	101	L'Editrice dell'Automobil		H	$500
Le Grandi Automobili 01		82	410	Automobilia		S	$30
Le Grandi Automobili 02		82	410	Automobilia		S	$30
Le Grandi Automobili 03		83	410	Automobilia		S	$30
Le Grandi Automobili 04		83	410	Automobilia		S	$30
Le Grandi Automobili 05		83	410	Automobilia		S	$30
Le Grandi Automobili 06		83	410	Automobilia		S	$30
Le Grandi Automobili 07		84	410	Automobilia		S	$30
Le Grandi Automobili 08		84	410	Automobilia		S	$30
Le Grandi Automobili 09		84	410	Automobilia			$30
Le Grandi Automobili 10		84	410	Automobilia		S	$30
Le Grandi Automobili 11		85	410	Automobilia		S	$30
Le Grandi Automobili 12		85	410	Automobilia		S	$30
Le Grandi Automobili 13		85	410	Automobilia		S	$30
Le Grandi Automobili 14		85	410	Automobilia		S	$30
Le Grandi Automobili 15		86	410	Automobilia		S	$30
Le Grandi Automobili 16	Alfieri B	86	410	Automobilia		S	$40
Le Grandi Automobili 17	Alfieri B	86	410	Automobilia		S	$30
Le Grandi Automobili 18	Alfieri B	87	410	Automobilia		S	$50
Le Grandi Fiat	Anselmi A T	67	152	Auto Club d'Italia		H	$100
Le Mans '59 (Moss)	Moss S	59	206	Cassell/Hanover		H	$80
Le Mans (Bamsey)	Bamsey I	87	206	Miura/Batsford	Wld Grt Mtr Cmp	H	$80
Le Mans (Clausager)	Clausager A D	82	206	Barker		H	$60
Le Mans (Klemantaski)	Klemantaski L/Frostick M	60	206	Macmillan		H	$180
Le Mans 1923-39 (French)	Potherat J	72	206	Ed. del'automobiliste		H	$60
Le Mans 24 (Fiction)	Petitclerc D B	71	206 207	Harcourt Brace/Playboy		X	$30
Le Mans 24 Heures Du Mans 1(84 Eng)	McKay P/Naismith B	84	206	Garry Sparke		H	$40
Le Mans 24-Hour Race	Hodges D	63	206	Temple Press Books	Classic Mtr Rac	H	$40
Le Mans 24-Hour Race 1949-73	Moity C	74	206	Edita		H	$150
Le Mans 24-Hours Race 1978	Moity C	79	206	Pub Intl/Edita		H	$80
Le Mans 24-Hours Race 1979	Thibault/Guichard	80	206	Publications Intl		H	$90
Le Mans Starring Steve McQueen	Donaldson E	71	206 509	Aurora		S	$20
Le Mans Story	Fraichard G	54	206	Bodley		H	$50
Le Mans Twice Around Clock(juv'n'l)	Gibson M	62	206	Putnam		H	$30
Le Origini del Mito	Colombo G	85	121	Sansoni/Autocritica		H	$80

Title	Author	Pub date	Subjects	Publisher	Series	Bind	Price
Le Piu Belle Vetture D'Epoca	Rogliatti G	70	401	LEA		H	$60
Le Vetture Alfa Romeo Dal 1910	Fusi L	65+	101	Editrice Adiemme		H	$90
Le Zagato Fulvia Sport Junior Z	Marchiano M	86	157 101	Libreria dell Automobile		H	$70
Lead Sleds Chopped & Low '35 - '54	Key M	84	422	Osprey		S	$40
Leader of the Pack Barry Sheene	Beacham I	83+	610	Macdonald/Q Anne/Futura		S	$20
Legend of Henry Ford	Sward K	48	415	Rinehart		H	$30
Legend of Lincoln	Kimes B R/Paddock L C	85	161	Automobile Quarterly		S	$20
Legend of Lotus Seven	Ortenberger D	81	129	Newport/Osprey		H	$100
Legendary Hispano Suiza	Green J	77	120	Dalton Watson	Dalton Watson	H	$100
Legion Ascot Speedway 1920s-1930s	Lucero J R	82	206	Orecul Pub.		H	$90
Les 180 220 300 Mercedes	Puiboube D	85	130	Editions Atlas	Voitures Annees	H	$40
Les 24 Heures du Mans (Labric)	Labric R/Ham G	49	206 504			S	$1500
Les 24 Heures du Mans 1980	Moity C	80	206	Publications Intl		H	$80
Les 24 Heures du Mans 1981	Moity C	81	206	Publications Intl		H	$80
Les Automobiles Delage(French)	Rousseau J	78	120	Editions Lariviere		H	$150
Les Dinkey Toys et Dinkey Supertoys	Roulet J M	84	702	EPA		H	$90
Les Fabuleuses Ferrari(French)	Bellu S	83	121	EPA	Les Fabuleux	H	$30
Les Poids Lourds (French)	Borge J/Viasnoff N	75	303	Balland		H	$50
Les Prestigieuses Citroen	Sabates F	86	153	Editions CH Massin		H	$50
Les Voitures de Grande Serie...50	Sabates F	87	407	Editions CH Massin		H	$30
Les Voitures de Police/Gangsters	Borge J/Viasnoff N	78	401	Balland		S	$30
Les Voitures de Pompiers	Borge J/Viasnoff N	76	302	Balland		S	$30
Les Voitures Francaises Annees 50	Bellu R	83	407	Delville		H	$125
Les Voitures Francaises de 1920-25	Dumont P	77	407	EPA		H	$40
Lesney Matchbox I-75 Ser. Diecasts	Hammond M A	72	702	Reedminster		H	$40
Lessico Della Carrozzeria	Valentini F	79	501	Automobilia		H	$40
Lets Call It Fiesta	Seidler E	76	169	Edita		S	$20
Leyland Bus	Jack	84	303	Transport Publishing Co.		H	$70
Leyland World Trucks No 14	Kennett P	83	303	PSL	World Trucks	H	$30
License Plate Book	Murray T C	78+	507	Murray		S	$30
Liebe Zu Ihm (5 lang)		60	136	Porsche		H	$500
Life at Limit	Hill G	69	205	Coward-McCann/Kimber		H	$40
Life of American Workman Chrysler	Chrysler W P/Sparkes B	37+	112	Curtis/Dodd Mead		H	$40
Life of Automobile (trnltd fr Russ)	Ehrenburg I	29+	416	Urizen		H	$30
Life of Ted Horn	Catlin R	49	205	Clymer		S	$30
Life Story of Juan Manuel Fangio	Hansen R	56	205	Edita		S	$40
Life With Speed King (Campbell)	Villa L	79	205 211	Marshall Harris	Kaleidoscope	H	$40
Lifes Bits & Pieces	Hoel J C (Pappy)	73	601 610	J C Hoel		S	$30
Light Car Technical History	Caunter C F	70	401	Her Majestys Stat Office		S	$30
Light Vans & Trucks 1919-39	Ingram A/Baldwin N	77	307	Almark		H	$20
Lightning Conductor Discov America	Willamson C N/A M	00S	212	Country Life Press		H	$40
Lightning Conductor Strange Adven..	Williamson C N/A M	02+	212	Methuen/Henry Holt		H	$40
Lightweight Bikes	Woollett M	81	601	Batsford	Batsford PB	S	$10
Like Father Like Son M & D Campbell	Drackett P	69	205 211	Clifton		H	$30
Lincoln & Continental Postwar Years	Woundenberg P R	80	161	MBI	Marques Amer	H	$60
Lincoln (Ballantine)	Hendry M D	71	161	Ballantine	Minimarque #8	S	$20
Lincoln Car Graphic Lib (Japanese)	Kobayashi S	71	161	Car Graphic/Nigensha	Car Grap Lib 47	S	$40
Lincoln Continental	Ritch O C	63	161	Clymer/MBI		S	$40
Lincoln Motorcar 60 Yrs Excellence	Bonsall T E	81	161	Bookman Dan		H	$125
Lionel Martin Biography	Demaus A B	80	103	Transport Bookman		H	$40
Liska Portfolio(1953 copyright)	Liska H	53	130 504	Daimler-Benz AG		H	$
Liska Portfolio(1954 copyright)	Liska H	54	130 504	Daimler-Benz AG		H	$
Liska Portfolio(1955 copyright)	Liska H	55	130 504	Daimler-Benz AG		H	$250
Living Tradition Rolls-Royce	Buckley J R	58	139	Rolls-Royce		H	$50
Locomobile Steam Cars Sls Brochure		50S	158	Floyd Clymer		S	$20
London Motor Bus Its Origins & Dev	Bruce J G/Curtis C H	73		London Transport		H	$20
London Motor Show 1930	Dalton L	70	401	Dalton Watson	Dalton Watson	H	$40
London RT Bus (Wagstaff)	Wagstaff J S	73		Oakwood	Locomotion Pprs	S	$10
London Taxi	Georgano G N	85	306	Shire	Shire Album	S	$10
London to Calcutta 1938	Wright O D/White E L D	88	212	Little Hills		H	$40
Long Drive An Accont London-Sydney	Stathatos J	78	209	Pelham/Atheneum		H	$40
Longest Auto Race	Schuster G/Mahoney T	66	212	John Day Co. Inc.		H	$50
Looking Back	Alexander J	82	298 510	At Speed Press		H	$80
Lorries Trucks Vans since 1928	Bishop D/Ingram A	75	306	Blandford		H	$20
Lost Causes of Motoring	Montagu	60+	401	Cassell		H	$70
Lost Causes of Motrg Europe Vol 1	Montagu	71	401	Cassell/Barnes		H	$50
Lost Causes of Motrg Europe Vol 2	Montagu	71	401	Cassell/Barnes		H	$40
Lotus 49	Hodges D	70	129	Arco/Leventhal	Famous Car	H	$50
Lotus Comp Surv Sports GT & Touring	Harvey C	80	129	Osprey		H	$50
Lotus Complete Story	Harvey C	85	129	Foulis/Haynes		H	$30
Lotus Cortina 1963-1970	Clarke R M	84	129 156	Brooklands	Brooklands	S	$30
Lotus Elan Autohistory	Ward I	84	129	Osprey	Autohistory	H	$40
Lotus Elan Collection No 1 1962-74	Clarke R M	81	129	Brooklands	Brooklands	S	$20
Lotus Elan Collection No 2 1963-72	Clarke R M	83	129	Brooklands	Brooklands	S	$20
Lotus Elite & Eclat 1974-1981	Clarke R M	82	129	Brooklands	Brooklands	S	$30
Lotus Esprit 1975-1981	Clarke R M	82	129	Brooklands	Brooklands	S	$40
Lotus Esprit Autohistory	Walton J	82+	129	Osprey	Autohistory	H	$40

Title	Author	Pub date	Subjects		Publisher	Series	Bind	Price
Lotus Seven 1957-1980	Clarke R M	81	129		Brooklands	Brooklands	S	$30
Lotus Seven Collection No 1 1957-82	Clarke R M	82	129		Brooklands	Brooklands	S	$20
Lotus Sports Racing Cars Design....	Pritchard A	87	129		PSL/Sterling		H	$40
Lotus Story (French)	Camus P	78	129		SIPE		S	$30
Lotus Story of the Marque	Smith I H	58	129		MRP		H	$40
Louis Chevrolet Memorial		75	111		Indianapolis Speedway		S	$10
Louis Renault	Rhodes A	69	120		Cassell		H	$30
Love Bug (from the movie)	Buford G/Cebulash M	69	150	509	Scholastic		S	$10
Lucas 1st 100 Years V2 Successors	Nockolds H	78	418		David & Charles		H	$70
Lucien Bianchi Mes Rallyes	Bianchi L	69	209		Flammarion		S	$50
Lucky All My Life	Clew J	79	404		Haynes		H	$40
Lucky Lott Hell Driver	Robinson D	85	205		Boston Mills		S	$20
Luigi Colani Design 1		86	502		Inova-Verlag		S	$50
Luigi Colani Designing Tomorrow	Fujimoto A	78	502		Car Styling		H	$80
MAN World Trucks No 04	Kennett P	78	303		PSL/Aztex	World Trucks	H	$30
Mack	Montville J	73	301		Haessner		H	$70
Mack Living Legend of Highway	Montville J	79	301		Aztex		X	$60
Mad Motorists Great Peking-Paris...	Andrews A	65	212		Lippincott		H	$30
Magic of a Name	Nockolds R	45+	139		Foulis		H	$40
Magic of a Name(Color ed)	Nockolds R	49	139		Foulis		H	$100
Magic of MG	Allison M	72	131		Dalton Watson	Dalton Watson	H	$70
Magirus World Trucks No 13	Kennett P	83	303		PSL	World Trucks	H	$30
Magnificent Mercedes	Robson G	81	130		Bsghl/Haynes/Morrow/Otlet		H	$50
Make Money Owning Your Car	Olson J R	76	401		MBI		X	$30
Making Model Trucks	Scarborough G	80	702		PSL		H	$30
Making of Winner Porsche 917	Pihera L	72	136		Lippincott		H	$50
Mammoth Trucks Modern Day Heavy....	Tuck B	85	306		Osprey	Osprey Col Lib	S	$30
Man & Motor 20th Cent Love Affair	Jewell D	67	401		Walker		H	$30
Man & the Automobile 20th Century..	Jackson J	79	419		McGraw/Harrow House		H	$30
Man and Motor Cars(auto safety etc)	Black S	66	401		Norton		H	$20
Man with Two Shadows Story Ascari	Desmond K	81	205		Proteus/Scribner		H	$30
Manifold Pressures Motoring........	Brockbank R	58	504		Temple		H	$30
Manual for Old Car Rest. & Colls.	Pulfer H	60S	401		Harry Pulfer		S	$20
Marathon in Dust	Ireland I	70	209		Kimber		H	$40
Mario Andretti World Champion	Roebuck N	79	205		Hamlyn		H	$40
Mario Andretti World Driving Champ	Engel L K	70	205		Arco		S	$20
Mark Lincolns Classic Source Bk	Bonsall T E	83	161		Bookman Dan	Source Book	S	$30
Marklin 1895-1914 Great Toys	Parry-Crooke C	83	703		Denys Ingram		H	$125
Marlboro Salute 75th Anniv Indy 500	Davidson D	86	208		Marlboro		H	$30
Marmon 34 Sales Brochure		51	158		Floyd Clymer		S	$10
Martini Racing Story 68-82 (French)		83	298		Editions Daniel Briand		H	$80
Maryland Automobile History 1900-42	Seal R R	85	403		Adams		H	$40
Maserati (Pocket History)	Cancellieri G	81	172		LEA	Complete Book	S	$20
Maserati 250 F Classic GP Car	Jenkinson D	75	172		Macmillan		H	$50
Maserati 3011 Story of a Racing Car	Jenkinson D	87	172		Aries		H	$90
Maserati A6 Sales Catalog		50S	172		Floyd Clymer		S	$20
Maserati Birdcage	Finn J E	80	172		Osprey		H	$100
Maserati Catalogue Rais. 1926-1984	Cancellieri G	84	172		Automobilia		H	$400
Maserati etc Car Grap Lib(Japanese)	Takashima S	70S	172	128 118	Car Graphic/Nigensha	Car Grap Lib 30	S	$40
Maserati Geschichte Technik........	Lewandowski J	82	172		Motorbuch Verlag		H	$70
Maserati History	Pritchard A	76	172		David & Charles		H	$30
Maserati Owners Handbook	Tanner H	60S	172		Clymer		S	$80
Maserati Postwar Sportsrac'g Cars	Finn J E	77	172		Barnes		X	$150
Maserati Road Cars	Crump R/de la Rive Box R	79	172		Barnes/Osprey		H	$90
Master Catalog of Trucks	AIC	80	301		Automotive Info Clearing		S	$20
Master of Precision Henry Leyland	Leland W/Millbrook	66	404		Wayne University Press		H	$80
Matchless Once Lgst Br M/Cycle Mfr	Hartley P	81	606		Osprey			$
Maybach (German/English)	Metternich M G W	73+	124		Uhle & Kleimann		H	$125
Mazda Rotary Sports		79	126		NEKO		H	$80
McLaren Man Cars & Team	Young E S	71	298		Bond/Parkhurst		H	$70
Mechanism of Car	Judge A W	25+	405		Bentley	Motor Manuals	H	$20
Men and Rubber Story of Business	Firestone H S/Crowther S	26	418		Doubleday		H	$60
Men at Speed	Rudeen K	61	297		Holt		H	$20
Men Money & Motors	MacManus/Beasley	29	401		Harper		H	$30
Men of Thunder Fabled Daredevils...	Nolan W F	64	205		Bantam		S	$20
Mercedes & MB Racing Car Gd 1901-55	Posthumus C	78	130		Transport Bookman		S	$20
Mercedes (Coombe/Exeter/Col Lib)		84+	130		Col Lib/Exeter/Coombe		H	$10
Mercedes 190SL Auto Classic #3	Knittel S	80S	130		Podzun-Pallas	Auto-Classic	S	$20
Mercedes 300SL Auto Classic #5	Knittel S	83	130		Podzun-Pallas	Auto Classic	S	$20
Mercedes 350/450SL & SLC 1971-1980	Clarke R M	85	130		Brooklands	Brooklands	S	$30
Mercedes for Road 1946-1974	Rasmussen H	83	130		MBI	Survivors	H	$50
Mercedes Pioneer of an Industry	Ulmann A E	53	130		Carroll Press		S	$50
Mercedes-Benz (Bladon)	Bladon S	84	130		Gallery/Smith/Multimedia		H	$20
Mercedes-Benz (Davis)	Davis S C H	56	130		Muller		H	$60
Mercedes-Benz 1886-1986 (2 volumes)	Lewandowski J	86	130		Edita		H	$350
Mercedes-Benz 300SL (Art & Car Ed)	Lewandowski J	88	130		Sudwest	Art & Car	H	$400
Mercedes-Benz Book	Boesen/G Victor/W	81	130		Doubleday		H	$50

Title	Author	Pub date	Subjects	Publisher	Series	Bind	Price
Mercedes-Benz CIII Experim'tal Cars	Frere P	81	130	Edita		H	$60
Mercedes-Benz Comp Cars 1950-1957	Clarke R M	79	130	Brooklands	Brooklands	S	$30
Mercedes-Benz Companion	Ullyett K	66	130	Stanley Paul		H	$40
Mercedes-Benz First Hundred Years	Langworth R M	84	130	Publications Int/Beekman	Consumer Gd	H	$40
Mercedes-Benz Guide	Ludvigsen K E	59	130	Sports Car Press		S	$40
Mercedes-Benz Klassische (juvenile)	Seidel W E	85	130 424	Podszun		H	$20
Mercedes-Benz Postwar (Japanese)		70S	130	Car Grap L	Car Graphic	S	$30
Mercedes-Benz Prewar (Japanese)		70S	130	Car Graphic Library	Car Grap L	S	$30
Mercedes-Benz Racing Cars	Ludvigsen K E	71	130	Bond/Parkhurst		H	$150
Mercedes-Benz Roadsters Autohistory	Setright L J K	79	130	Osprey	Autohistory	H	$40
Mercedes-Benz S Sales Catalog		51	130	Clymer		S	$30
Mercedes-Benz S-Class & 190 16E	Howard G	84	130	Cadogan/Arco	High Performanc	H	$40
Mercedes-Benz SL & SLC Autohistory	Setright L J K	79+	130	Osprey	Autohistory	H	$40
Mercedes-Benz Story	Steinwedel L W	69	130	Chilton	Sebring	H	$50
Mercedes-Benz V8s Autohistory	McComb F W	80	130	Osprey	Autohistory	H	$50
Mercedes-Benz Vom 190E zum 560SEC	Hofner H	86	130	BLV		H	$125
Mercedes-Benz Vom 28/95PS zum SSKL	Schrader H	82	130	BLV	M-B Automobile	H	$90
Mercedes-Benz Vom 600 zum 450 SEL	Hofner H	84	130	BLV	M-B Automobile	H	$80
Mercedes-Konstruktionen in funf....	Siebertz P	51	130	Daimler-Benz		S	$300
Mercer Series 5 Sales Cat reprint		51	158	Floyd Clymer		S	$10
Mercer Series 6 Sales Cat reprint		51	158	Clymer		S	$10
Mercury & Edsel 1939-69 ID Guide	Bonsall T E	82	166	Bookman Dan	I D Guide	S	$30
Mercury Cougar 1967-1973 Photofacts	Halla C	84	166	MBI	CMB Photofacts	S	$30
Mercury Muscle Cars 1966-1971	Clarke R M	84	166	Brooklands	Brooklands	S	$30
Merry Old Mobiles on Parade	Sibley H	51	401	Goodheart-Willcox		S	$10
Messerschmitt Kabinenroller	Ziegler R	80S	124	Freunde		S	$70
Metz 25 - Sales Brochure			158	Floyd Clymer		S	$10
Mexican Road Race 1950	Goodman R	50	206	Clymer		S	$50
Mexico or Bust (World Cup Rally 70)	Kahn M	70	209	Harrap		H	$30
MG A B & C	Harvey C	80	131	Oxford Ill/Haynes		H	$60
MG (Shire-McComb)	McComb F W	85	131	Shire	Shire Album 152	S	$10
MG 1911 to 1978	Filby P	79	131	Haynes	Mini Marque	H	$20
MG Art of Abingdon	McLellan J	82	131	MRP		H	$70
MG Book of Car	Clausager A D	82	131	Gallery/Smith/Winchmore		H	$20
MG by McComb	McComb F W	78+	131	Osprey		H	$50
MG Cars	Davidson C P	58	131	Pearson/Arco	Car Maintenance	H	$20
MG Cars 1929-1934	Clarke R M	69	131	Brooklands	Brooklands	S	$30
MG Cars 1935-1940	Clarke R M	69	131	Brooklands	Brooklands	S	$30
MG Cars 1940-1947	Clarke R M	68	131	Brooklands	Brooklands	S	$30
MG Cars 1948-1951	Clarke R M	69	131	Brooklands	Brooklands	S	$30
MG Cars 1955-1957	Clarke R M	69	131	Brooklands	Brooklands	S	$20
MG Cars 1957-1959	Clarke R M	69	131	Brooklands	Brooklands	S	$20
MG Cars Early Years	Clarke R M	69	131	Brooklands	Brooklands	S	$40
MG Cars in the Thirties	Clarke R M	62	131	Brooklands	Brooklands	S	$30
MG Experience	Jacobs D	76	131	Transport Bookman		H	$40
MG Guide	Christy J	58	131	Sports Car Press		S	$20
MG International 1977	Knudson R L	77	131	MRP		H	$30
MG Mania Insomnia Crew	Stone H W/Knudson R	83	131	New England T Register		S	$50
MG MGB GT 1965-1980	Clarke R M	80	131	Brooklands	Brooklands	S	$30
MG Sports 4 cyl TB from Abingdon	Autocar	80S	131	Autocar		S	$20
MG Sports Car America Loved First	Knudson R L	75	131	Motorcars Unlimited		H	$50
MG Sports Car Supreme	Wherry J H	82	131	Barnes		H	$40
MG Sports Cars (Autocar)	Garnier P	74+	131	Hamlyn/St Martins		H	$40
MG Story	Wherry J H	67	131	Chilton		H	$40
MG TC 1945-1949	Clarke R M	84	131	Brooklands	Brooklands	S	$30
MG TD 1949-1953	Clarke R M	84	131	Brooklands	Brooklands	S	$30
MG TF 1953-1955	Clarke R M	84	131	Brooklands	Brooklands	S	$30
MG Workshop Manual	Blower W E	52	131	MRP/Bentley		H	$40
MGA Autohistory	McComb F W	83	131	Osprey	Autohistory	H	$40
MGA Collection #1 1955-1982	Clarke R M	84	131	Brooklands	Brooklands	S	$20
MGB Autohistory	McComb F W	82	131	Osprey	Autohistory	H	$40
MGB GT 1965-1980	Clarke R M	85	131	Brooklands	Brooklands	S	$30
MGB Handbook/Comphnsv Owners Manual	Turner S/Organ J	68	131	Foulis/Bentley		H	$40
Miata Mazda MX-5 (2 volume set)	Yamaguchi J K/Thompson J	89	126	Dai Nippon/St Martins		H	$60
Midget Motors and Karting	McFarland K/Sparks J C	61	214	Dutton		H	$20
Mighty Jaguar Sports Car	Nye D	80S	127	Speed - Sporting Cars		S	$30
Mighty Mercedes	Frostick M	71	130	Dalton Watson	Dalton Watson	H	$60
Mighty MGs Twin Cam MGC MGB GT V8..	Robson G	82	131	David & Charles		H	$70
Mike the Bike Again	Macauley T	80	610	Cassell		H	$30
Military Motorcycles	Ansell D	85	601	Batsford		H	$70
Military Motorcycles of World War 2	Bacon R	85	601	Osprey	Osprey Coll Lib	H	$50
Military Traction Engines & Lorries	Kidner R W	75	308	Oakwood	Locomotion Pprs	S	$10
Military Transport of World War I	Ellis C/Bishop D	70	308	Blandford/Macmillan		H	$20
Military Transport of World War II	Ellis C/Bishop D	71	308	Blandford/Macmillan		H	$20
Mille Miglia (Italian)	Canestrini G	67	206	Auto Club d'Italia		H	$300
Mille Miglia (Lawrence)	Lawrence M	88	206	Miura/Batsford	Wld Grt Mtr Cmp	H	$80
Mille Miglia 1927-57 (English)	Lurani G	81	206	Edita		H	$125

Title	Author	Pub date	Subjects		Publisher	Series	Bind	Price
Mille Miglia 1984	Auto Club of Brescia	84	206		La Mille Miglia Editrice		H	$150
Miller Dynasty	Dees M L	81	158		Barnes		H	$450
Miller Racing Engine Catalog 1927		51	158		Clymer		S	$10
Million Miles Ago	Shilton N	82	610		Haynes		H	$40
Million Miles of Racing	Davison G S/Heath P	50	603		T T Special		H	$70
Mini-Cooper 1961-1971	Clarke R M	81	171		Brooklands	Brooklands	S	$30
Minic Lines Bros Tinplate Vehicles	Richardson S	81	703		Mikansue		S	$30
Mobilgas Economy Run 1951	Clymer F	51	209		Clymer		S	$20
Mobilgas Economy Run 1952	Clymer F	52	209		Clymer		S	$20
Mobilgas Economy Run 1953	Clymer F	53	209		Clymer		S	$20
Mobilgas Economy Run 1954	Clymer F	54	209		Clymer		S	$20
Model Car Building	Neumann B	71	702		Putnam	Here is yr Hobb	H	$20
Model Car Collecting	Jewell F B	63	704		Temple		H	$20
Model Car Racing	Schleicher R	79	701		Chilton		H	$30
Model Car Racing (R/C & Tabletop)	Schleicher R	79	701		Chilton		S	$30
Model Cars (Consumer Gd)	Consumer Gd	78	704		Pub Intl/Harper/Beekman	Consumer Gd	X	$20
Model Cars of Gerald Wingrove	Wingrove G	79	702		New Cavendish/Methuen		H	$125
Model Cars of Japan	Nakajima N	77	702		Hoikusha	Color Books	S	$30
Model Cars of World	Nakajima N	77	702		Hoikusha	ColorBooks #34	S	$30
Model Cars You Threw Away	Dooks C R	78	702		Transport Bookmen		S	$10
Model Road Racing Handbook	Schleicher R	67	701		Van Nostrand		H	$40
Model Stationary Engines Design....	Muncaster H	12	704		Tee		S	$20
Model T Ford in Speed Sport	Pulfer H	56	122		Dan R Post		S	$50
Modern Buses and Coaches (juv)	Morrissey C B	52			Temple		H	$20
Modern Classics Grt Crs Pstwr Era	Taylor R	78+	401		Scribners/Beekman		H	$40
Modern Electrical Equip for Autos	Judge A W	62	405		Bentley	Motor Manuals	H	$10
Modern Motorcars (juvenile)	Hunt K C	52	424		Temple		H	$20
Modern Motorcycle Mechanics	Nicholson J B	42+	609		Nicholson		H	$40
Modern Sports Car	McCahill T	54	401		Prentice		H	$20
Modern Steam Car and Its Background	Derr T S	45	414		Clymer		S	$20
Moggie The Purch, Maint & Enjoy....	Musgrove C	80	164		Quills		H	$80
Moments That Made Racing History	Walkerley R	59	297		Temple/Sports Car Press		H	$20
Monaco Grand Prix	Hodges D	64	206		Temple	Classic Mtr Rac	H	$50
Monaco Grand Prix 1959(12" record)	Lloyd N	50S	206		Schofield Productions	Sound Stories		$40
Monarch Illus Gd to Basic Car Care	Pettis A	77	401		Simon & Schuster		S	$10
Money-Wise Guide to Sports Cars	Bohr P	82	401		Harcourt,Brace,Jnovch		S	$20
Monster Trucks Car Crushers........	Bargo M	86	301		MBI		H	$30
Montagu Motor Museum		59	401		Cassell		S	$20
Monte Carlo Classic Source Book	Lehwald E A	85	111		Bookman	Source Book	S	$20
Monte Carlo Rally	Lowry R	50S	209		Foulis		H	$30
Monte Carlo Rally (Castrol) 1954	Davis S C H/Walkerley R	54	209		Castrol		S	$30
Monte Carlo Rally (Robson)	Robson G	89	209		Miura/Batsford	Wld Grt Mtr Cmp	H	$80
Monteverdi (German)	Gloor G/Wagner C L	80	173		Automobile Monteverdi		H	$300
Month at Brickyard	Kleinfield S	77	208		Holt		H	$40
Montlhery Story of Paris Autodrome	Boddy W	61	206		Cassell		H	$80
Monza 1922-72 50 Years of History		72	206		Autodromo di Monza		H	$60
Mopar 273 318 etc Perf Gd & Catalog	Yale S	75	132		Phase III		S	$10
Mopar Big-Block HT High Perf Eng...	Schorr M L	76	132		Performance Pub		S	$20
Mopar Oval Track Modifications	Shepard L S	83	132		Mopar		S	$40
Mopar Oval Track Performance Book	Chrysler Corporation	83	132		Chrysler Corporation		S	$40
Mopar Performance Years V1 Dodge...	Schorr M L	82	132		Quicksilver	Quicksilver	S	$20
Mopar Performance Years V2	Schorr M L	84	132		Quicksilver	Quicksilver	S	$20
Mopar Performance Years V3	Schorr M L	84	132		Quicksilver	Quicksilver	S	$20
Mopar Street Performance Handbook	Schorr M L	85	132		Quicksilver	Quicksilver	S	$20
More Healeys Frog-eyes Sprites.....	Healey G	78	104		Gentry Books		H	$60
More Mini Tuning	Trickey C	68+	171		Speed Sport	Speed Sport	S	$30
More Morgan Pictorial History of...	Bowden G H	76	164		Gentry		H	$40
More Sketches by Casque	Davis S C H	30S	298	504	Iliffe		H	$80
More Than Courage (juvenile fict)	Baudouy M	61	601		Harcourt Brace		S	$20
More Than You Promise	Smallzried/Roberts	42	404	145	Harper		H	$60
More Wheelspin Post-war Comp Mtrng	May C A N	48	298		Foulis		H	$40
Moretti (Italian)	Ruberi M	89	118		Ruberi		S	$50
Morgan (French)	McComb F W	85	164		EPA	Toute L'Hist...	S	$20
Morgan 3 Whlr H/B Ford Engine Mdls	Birks T	81	164		Morgan 3 Wheeler Club		S	$20
Morgan 3-Wheeler 1930-52	Clarke R M	80	164		Brooklands	Brooklands	S	$40
Morgan Cars 1936-1960	Clarke R M	79	164		Brooklands	Brooklands	S	$30
Morgan Cars 1960-1970	Clarke R M	79	164		Brooklands	Brooklands	S	$30
Morgan Cars 1969-1979	Clarke R M	80	164		Brooklands	Brooklands	S	$30
Morgan First and Last of Real......	Bowden G H	72+	164		Gentry/Haynes		H	$70
Morgan Four Wheeler Workshop Manual	Dowdeswell J		164		Dowdeswell		S	$40
Morgan History of Famous Car			164		Morgan		S	$20
Morgan Sweeps Board 3-Wheeler..	Alderson J D	78+	164		Gentry/Haynes		H	$50
Morgans in Colonies	Sheally J H	78	164		Jordan & Co/MBI		H	$70
Morgans Pride of British	Sheally J H	82	164		Tab		H	$60
Morris Cars First 35 Years	Edwards H	78	105		Morris Register		S	$30
Morris Minor 1948-1970	Clarke R M	80	105		Brooklands	Brooklands	S	$30
Morris Minor Collection No 1	Clarke R M	82	105		Brooklands	Brooklands	S	$20

Title	Author	Pub date	Subjects		Publisher	Series	Bind	Price
Morris Minor Purchase & Restoration	Bateman R	81	105		Bateman		S	$10
Morris Minor Ser MM Super Profile	Newall R	84	105		Haynes		H	$20
Morris Minor Worlds Supreme........	Skilleter P	81	105		Osprey		H	$50
Morris Motor Cars 1913-1983	Edwards H	83	105		Moorland		H	$60
Most Unique Machine Michigan.......	May G S	75	401		Eerdmans		H	$30
Moto Guzzi Genius & Sport	Colombo M	83	606		Automobilia		H	$40
Moto Guzzi Twins	Walker M	86	606		Osprey	Osprey Coll Lib	H	$50
Moto MM Alla ricerca della.........	Ruffini E/Tozzi G	88	606		Nada		H	$125
Moto Oggi (Italian)	Colombo M/Patrignani R	71	601		L'Editrice dell Auto		S	$20
Motocourse 1976-1977	Carter C	77	608		Hazleton		H	$250
Motocourse 1977-1978	Carter C	78	608		Hazleton		H	$300
Motocourse 1978-1979	Coleman B	79	608		Hazleton		H	$350
Motocourse 1979-1980	Coleman B	80	608		Hazleton		H	$180
Motocourse 1980-1981	Clifford P	80	608		Hazleton		H	$125
Motocourse 1981-1982	Clifford P	81	608		Hazleton		H	$70
Motocourse 1982-1983	Clifford P	82	608		Hazleton		H	$70
Motocourse 1983-1984	Clifford P	83	608		Hazleton		H	$150
Motocourse 1984-1985	Clifford P	84	608		Hazleton		H	$60
Motor Badges & Figureheads	Jewell B	78	507		Midas		X	$50
Motor Car 1765-1914	Bird A	60	401		Batsford		H	$30
Motor Car 1946-56	Sedgwick M	79	401		Batsford		H	$70
Motor Car Bosch Book of	Day J	75+	405		Berkeley/St Martins		H	$20
Motor Car Illustrated Intl History	Wise D B	77+	401		Orbis		H	$30
Motor Car Index 1928-1939		64	412		Autobooks		H	$50
Motor Car Industry in Coventry.....	Thoms D/Donnelly T	85	419		St Martins		H	$30
Motor Car Lovers Companion	Hough R	65	401		Harper & Row		H	$20
Motor Cars 1770-1940	Porazik J	81	401		Slovart/Smith/Galley	Handbook Guide	H	$10
Motor Cycle Cavalcade Hist of MC	Ixion	50+	601		Iliffe/SRP		H	$40
Motor Cycle Index 1913-1924		64	601		Fletcher/Autobooks		H	$40
Motor Cycle Racing	Carrick P	69	604		Hamlyn		H	$20
Motor Cycle Year 1975-1976(Moto Yr)	Howdle P	75	608		Edita		H	$60
Motor Cycles Technical History	Caunter C F	56	601		HM Stationery Office		S	$20
Motor Cycling in 1930s	Currie B	81	601		Hamlyn		H	$30
Motor Engineers Pocket Book	Coker/Hemmings	52	405		George Newnes		H	$30
Motor Memories Saga Whirling Gears	Lewis E	47	401		Alved/Clymer		H	$30
Motor Modelling	Hays R	61	702		Arco		H	$20
Motor Museums of Europe	Stobbs W	83	401		Barker/Weidenfeld		H	$50
Motor Racing (Davis)	Davis S C H	32	139	205	Iliffe		H	$80
Motor Racing (Lonsdale - Davis)	Davis S C H	57	297		Seeley		H	$60
Motor Racing (Lonsdale - Howe)	Howe E	44	297		Seeley		H	$60
Motor Racing 1946	Gibson J E	48	204		MRP		S	$70
Motor Racing 1947	Gibson J E	49	204		MRP		S	$80
Motor Racing and Record Breaking	Eyston G E T/Lyndon B	35	297		Batsford		H	$100
Motor Racing Camera 1894-1916	Georgano G N	76	297		David & Charles		H	$30
Motor Racing Circuits of Europe	Klemantaski L	58	298		Batsford		H	$60
Motor Racing Drivers Past & Present	Sallon	56	298	504	Shell-Mex		S	$40
Motor Racing Facts & Figures	Walkerley R	61+	297		Batsford/Bentley		H	$50
Motor Racing Grand Prix Greats	Gill B	72	205		Drake		H	$20
Motor Racing International Way No 1	Brittan N	70	204		Kaye & Ward		H	$20
Motor Racing International Way No 2	Brittan N	71	204		Kaye & Ward		H	$20
Motor Racing in Safety Human Factor	Henderson M	68	297		PSL		H	$40
Motor Racing Management	Wyer J	56	103	297	Bodley Head		H	$40
Motor Racing Mavericks	Nye D	74	297		Batsford		H	$40
Motor Racing Sketchbook	Demand C	50S	297	504	Foulis		H	$125
Motor Racing Today Innes Ireland	Ireland I	61	298		Barker		H	$50
Motor Racing with Mercedes-Benz	Monkhouse G L	45	130		Foulis/Clymer		X	$60
Motor Racing Year (1969-Pritchard)	Pritchard A	70	204		MRP		H	$40
Motor Racing Year 1963-4	Blunsden J/Brinton A	63	204		Knightsbridge		H	$30
Motor Racing Year 1964-5	Blunsden J/Brinton A	64	204		Knightsbridge		H	$30
Motor Racing Year 1965-6	Blunsden J/Brinton A	65	204		Knightsbridge		H	$30
Motor Racing Year 1966-7	Motor Racing staff	66	204		Knightsbridge		H	$30
Motor Racing Year 1967-8	Motor Racing staff	67	204		Knightsbridge		H	$30
Motor Racing Year 1968-9	Motor Racing staff	68	204		Knightsbridge		H	$30
Motor Racing Year 1970	Blunsden J	70	204		MRP		H	$30
Motor Racing Year 1971	Blunsden J	70	204		MRP		H	$30
Motor Racing Year 1972	Blunsden J	71	204		MRP		H	$40
Motor Racing Year 1973	Blunsden J	72	204		MRP		H	$30
Motor Racing Year 1975	Blunsden J	76	204		MRP		S	$30
Motor Racing Year No 2 (1970)	Pritchard A	71	204		Pelham		H	$30
Motor Road Test Annual 1969		69	410		Hamlyn		S	$30
Motor Road Test Annual 1970		70	410		Hamlyn		S	$30
Motor Road Test Annual 1971		71	410		IPC		S	$30
Motor Road Test Annual 1972		72	410		IPC		S	$30
Motor Road Test Annual 1973		73	410		IPC		S	$30
Motor Road Test Annual 1974		74	410		IPC		S	$30
Motor Road Test Annual 1975		75	410		IPC		S	$30
Motor Road Test Annual 1979	Motor	79	410		IPC		S	$20

Title	Author	Pub date	Subjects	Publisher	Series	Bind	Price
Motor Road Test Annual 1985		85	410	Specialist & Professional		S	$40
Motor Road Test Annual 1986		86	410	Prospect		S	$50
Motor Road Test Annual 1987		87	410	Prospect		S	$50
Motor Sport Yearbook 1972 J Player	Gill B	72	204	Q Anne		S	$20
Motor Sport Yearbook 1973 J Player	Gill B	73	204	Q Anne/Collier Books		S	$20
Motor Sport Yearbook 1974	Gill B	73	204	Brickfield/Collier		S	$20
Motor Sport Yearbook 1975 J Player	Gill B	75	204	Brickfield/Queen Anne		S	$20
Motor Sport Yearbook 1976	Gill B	76	204	Queen Anne Press		S	$20
Motor Sports Car Road Tests 1E		61	401	Temple		S	$10
Motor Sports Car Road Tests 2E		65	401	Temple		S	$10
Motor Sports Pictorial History	Flower R	75	297	Putnam		H	$50
Motor Tramp	Heygate J	35	131	Cape		H	$70
Motor Trend Presents 100 Yrs ofAuto		86	401	Motor Trend		S	$30
Motor Trend World Auto. Yr.Bk. 1966		66	410	Motor Trend		H	$20
Motor Trend World Auto. Yr.Bk. 1967	Potter J E	67	410	Petersen		S	$20
Motor Trucks of America	Wren J A/Wren G J	79	301	Univ of Michigan		S	$30
Motor Wagons (long dist truck hist)	Russell P J	71	301	Pioneer Club Akron Ohio		H	$40
Motor Year Book 1949 (first)	Pomeroy L	49	410	Temple		H	$90
Motor Year Book 1950	Pomeroy L	50	410	Temple		H	$40
Motor Year Book 1951	Pomeroy L	51	410	Temple		H	$30
Motor Year Book 1952	Pomeroy L	52	410	Temple		H	$30
Motor Year Book 1953	Pomeroy L	53	410	Temple		H	$30
Motor Year Book 1954	Pomeroy L	54	410	Temple		H	$30
Motor Year Book 1955	Pomeroy L	55	410	Temple		H	$30
Motor Year Book 1956	Pomeroy L	56	410	Temple		H	$50
Motor Year Book 1957 (last)	Pomeroy L	57	410	Temple		H	$30
Motor-Cars Today	Harrison J	39+	405	Oxford		H	$20
Motor-Mania	Cutting R	69	404	Rand		H	$20
Motoraces of Grand Prix Racing	Monkhouse G L	47	298	Clymer		X	$30
Motorcars of Golden Past	Purdy K W	65	401	Little Brown		H	$90
Motorcycle (Lacombe)	Lacombe C	74	601	Denoel/Guiness/Grosset		H	$30
Motorcycle Ace Dick Mann Story	Mann D/Scalzo J	72	610	Regnery		H	$30
Motorcycle Book (Fawcett 123)	Bowman P	51	601	Fawcett	Fawcett	S	$10
Motorcycle Books Critical Survey	Congdon K	87	601	Scarecrow Press		H	$30
Motorcycle Comp Off Rd Riding & Rac	Patrignani R/Perelli C	74	604	Istituto Geografico/Orbis		H	$20
Motorcycle Dictionary/Terminology	Kosbab W H	84	601	Career		S	$20
Motorcycle Drag Racing Complete Gd	Griffin M	82	602	SA		S	$20
Motorcycle Engineering	Irving P E	73	609	Clymer/Speedsport		S	$40
Motorcycle Making of Harley (juvnl)	Jaspersohn W	84	607	Little Brown		H	$30
Motorcycle Racing in America	Spence J/Brown G	74	602	O'Hara		S	$20
Motorcycle Reminiscences	Ixion	22	601	Iliffe		B	$150
Motorcycle Road Craft Police.......		78	601	Her Majesty's Stat Office		S	$20
Motorcycle Sport Book	Wineland L/Hot Rod Eds	70S	602	Petersen	Hot Rod	S	$20
Motorcycle Tuning for Performance	Shipman C	73	609	HP		S	$30
Motorcycle World	Schilling P	74	601	Ridge/Random		H	$50
Motorcycles In Competition(Fawcett)	Bowman H W	52	604	Fawcett	Fawcett	S	$30
Motorcycles to 1945	Vanderveen B H	75	601	Warne	Olyslager	H	$30
Motorcyclists Encyclopedia	Miller R	72	601	BMS		S	$20
Motoring & Mighty	Garrett R	71	401	Stanley		H	$30
Motoring Annual (1957)	Douglas A	57	410	Ian Allen		H	$30
Motoring History	Rolt L T C	64	401	Studio Vista/Dutton		S	$30
Motoring Is My Business	Bolster J	58	205	Autosport		H	$40
Motoring Mascots of World 1E	Williams W C	77	507	MBI		H	$60
Motoring My Way	Sedgwick S	76	404	Batsford		H	$40
Motoring Sport	Stuck H/ Berggaller E	35	297	Foulis		H	$125
Motorists Weekend Book	Frostick M/Harding A	60	401	Batsford/Bentley		H	$30
Motorroller Mobil (scooters etc)	Kubisch U	85	401	606	Elefanten Press		S	$40
Motorsport On Two Wheels	Renstrom R C	60S	603	Bond Parkhurst		S	$30
Mountain Movers	Tuck B	84	306	PSL		H	$30
Move It! Ill Hist Heavy Haulage Veh	Tuck B	87	306	PSL		S	$30
Moving Forward	Ford H/Crowther	31	415	William Heinemann Ltd.		H	$125
Moving Heaven and Earth Le Tourneau	Ackland D F	49	904	Marshall Morgan & Scott		H	$50
Mr Clutch Story of George W Borg	Casey R J	48	404	Bobbs-Merrill		H	$30
Mr Monaco Graham Hill Remembered	Rudlin T	83	205	PSL		H	$40
Mudge Pond Express	Posey S	76	205	Putnam		H	$50
Muscle Buicks!	Bonsall T E	85	108	Bookman Publishing		S	$20
Muscle Car Mania Ad Coll 1964-1974	Frumkin M	81	503	MBI		S	$30
Muscle Cars	McGovren J	84	403	Quintet/Apple/Chartwell		H	$30
Muscle Cars (Consumer Gd)	Hall P	81	403	Publications Intl	Consumer Gd	H	$20
Muscle Cars (Nichols)	Nichols R	85	403	Brompton		H	$20
Muscle Cars Compared 1966-1970	Clarke R M	83	403	Brooklands	Brooklands	S	$30
Muscle Cars Compared Book 2 1965-71	Clarke R M	84	403	Brooklands	Brooklands	S	$30
Muscle Chevys!	Bonsall T E	85	111	Bookman Publishing		S	$20
Muscle Dodges!	Bonsall T E	85	115	Bookman Pub		S	$20
Muscle Mopars	Bonsall T E	85	132	Bookman Dan		S	$20
Museo Dell'Automobile CatalogoGen'l	Biscaretti diRuffia,C	62	401	Museo Dell'Auto.		H	$20
Mustang (Carlyon)	Carlyon R	84	122	Winchmore/Haynes		H	$30

Title	Author	Pub date	Subjects		Publisher	Series	Bind	Price
Mustang (Wright)	Wright N	85	122		Multimedia/Gallery/Smith		H	$20
Mustang Car That Started Ponycar...	Langworth R M	79	122		Publications Intl	Consumer Guide	H	$20
Mustang Complete Guide (Car Life)	Shattuck D	65	122		Bond Publishing		S	$20
Mustang Performance Years	Schorr M L	82	122		Quicksilver	Quicksilver SC	S	$20
My Days with Diesel	Cummins C L	67	404		Chilton		H	$60
My Father (Bio of William Durant)	Durant M	29	404		G P Putnam's Sons		L	$400
My Father Mr. Mercedes	Jellinek-Mercedes G	61	130		Chilton/Foulis		H	$30
My Forty Years With Ford	Sorensen C E	56	415		Norton		H	$40
My Greatest Race	Ball A	74	205		J Clark Fnd/Tempo/Dutton		X	$20
My Life and My Cars	Bentley W O	58+	139		Barnes		H	$60
My Life and Work	Ford H	22+	415		Garden City/Dbldy/Hnmnn		H	$40
My Mistress Death	Spafford R	56	207		Fawcett		S	$10
My Philosophy of Industry	Ford H	29	415		Coward MC		H	$50
My Twenty Years of Racing	Fangio J M/Giambertone M	61	205		Temple		H	$60
My Years With Ferrari	Lauda N	78	205	121	MBI		H	$50
My Years with General Motors	Sloan A P Jr	63	160		Doubleday		X	$30
My Years with Toyota	Kato S	81	126		Toyota		H	$40
NASCAR 25 Years of Racing Thrills	Spiegel M	74	299		Scholastic		S	$10
Nardi	Varisco F	87	118		Libreria dell'Auto		H	$50
Nash Family Album	Conde J	54	158		Nash		S	$30
Nelson Piquet Story of 83 Champshp.	Van Kempen R	80S	205		Kimberley's	Driver's Guides	S	$20
New 1984 Corvette(Consumer Guide)	Consumer Gd	83	114		Pub Intl		S	$10
New Automobiles of the Future	Stambler I	78	424		Putnam		H	$20
New BMW Guide	Wakefield R	79	106		Tab	Mod Sports Car	S	$20
New Comp Bk Coll Cars see COMP BK..	Langworth R M	87	401		Publications Intl		H	$
New Deals Chrysler Revival.........	Reich R B/Donahue J D	85	112		Times		H	$30
New Encyclopaedia Motorcars 1885 on	Georgano G N	68+	401		Dutton/Crescent		H	$70
New Fiat Guide	Norbye J P	69	152		Sports Car Press/Crown	Mod Sports Car	S	$20
New Ford Mustang(Press info reprint		64	122		Ford Motor Co		S	$20
New Fordson Album	Condie A T	85	904		Trent Valley		S	$40
New Formula One Turbo Age	Lauda N	82	202		Verlag Orac/MBI/Kimber		H	$60
New Guide to Rallying	Reid L	69	209		Sports Car Press	Mod Sports Car	S	$10
New Henry Ford	Benson A L	23	415		Funk & Wagnalls		H	$50
New Matadors	Baumann H H	65	297	510	Bond		H	$70
New Mazda Guide	Hollander M F	84	126		Tab		S	$30
New Mercedes-Benz Guide	Oldham J	77	130		Tab	Mod Sports Car	X	$40
New Porsche Guide	Sloniger J	68	136		Sports Car Press	Mod Sports Car	S	$20
New Stutz Fire Apparatus Co	Birchfield R	78	302		Birchfield		H	$60
New York Times Comp Gd Auto Racing	Radosta J S	71	297		Quadrangle		H	$20
New York to Paris 1908 (Thomas)	Thomas Motor Co	51	212	298	Clymer		S	$20
Niki Lauda (Italian)	Barili D	81	205		Edispo srl		H	$90
Nineteen 04 HB of Gasoline Autos		69	158		Chelsea House		H	$30
Nineteen 09-1912 Sears Mot Bug Cat	Sears	73	158		Digest		S	$10
Nineteen 84 Paper Corvette	Rose A	84	114		Dolphin/Doubleday		S	$30
Nineteen-57 Cars	Consumer Gd	80	403		Publications Intl	Consumer Guide	S	$20
Nineteen-60 Manx Grand Prix		60	603		Shell		S	$10
Nissan/Datsun History Nissan in US	Rae J B	82	167		McGraw		H	$40
No Excuses	Van Damm S	57	209	205	Putnam		H	$30
No Time to Loose Bill Ivy	Peck A	72	610		MRP		H	$30
Norton Story	Holliday B	72	606		PSL		X	$40
Norton(Ballantine)	Howard D	72	606		Ballantine	Ballantine	S	$30
Nostalgia My Life and Gas Engine	Rahn C A	75	404		Dennison		S	$10
Nuvolari	Lurani G	59	205		Morrow/Cassell		H	$125
Nuvolari (SCP)	Lurani G	63	205		Sports Car Press	Mod Sports Car	S	$20
Observer's Army Vehicles Directory	Vanderveen B H	74	308		Warne		H	$30
Observers Book Commercial Veh(1966)	Manwaring L A	66	306		Warne		H	$20
Observers Book Commercial Veh(1974)	Baldwin N	74	306		Warne		H	$20
Observers Book of Automobiles 1955	Parsons R T	55	410		Warne		H	$70
Observers Book of Automobiles 1956	Parsons R T	56	410		Warne		H	$60
Observers Book of Automobiles 1957	Manwaring L A	57	410		Warne		H	$40
Observers Book of Automobiles 1958	Manwaring L A	58	410		Warne		H	$40
Observers Book of Automobiles 1967	Manwaring L A	67	410		Warne		H	$20
Observers Book of Autos 09E 1963	Manwaring L A	63	410		Warne		H	$10
Observers Book of Autos 11E 1965	Manwaring L A	65	410		Warne		H	$10
Observers Book of Autos 21E 1978	Voller D/Alexander C	78	410		Warne		H	$10
Observers Book of Motor Sport	Macbeth G	75+	297		Warne		H	$10
Observers Fighting Veh Dir WW II	Vanderveen B H	69	308		Warne		H	$40
Of Men and Cars Tales of Men Raced	Christy J	60	297		Ziff-Davis		H	$20
Off Highway & Construction Trucks	Ingram A/Peck C	80	306		Blandford		H	$40
Off Road Handbook/Back Country Tips	Waar B	75	311		HP		S	$20
Off-Road Book (technical)	Schorr M L	79	311		Perf Pub		S	$10
Off-Road Fun Cars	Scholfield M/Hot Rod Eds	70	311		Petersen	Hot Rod	S	$20
Old Car Book (Fawcett 207)	Bentley J	53	401		Fawcett	Fawcett	S	$10
Old Car Value Guide	Craft Q	68	401		Quentin Craft	SemiAnnual	S	$30
Old Car Value Guide Vol 3-1	Craft Q	71	401		Quentin Craft	Semi Annual	S	$20
Old Car Value Guide Vol. 2-4	Craft Q	70	401		Quentin Craft	SemiAnnual	S	$20
Old Car Value Guide Vol. 3-2	Craft Q	72	401		Quentin Craft	SemiAnnual	S	$20

Title	Author	Pub date	Subjects		Publisher	Series	Bind	Price
Old Car Value Guide Vol. 4-1	Craft Q	73	401		Quentin Craft	SemiAnnual	S	$20
Old Cars World Over	Nagle E	58	401		Arco		H	$30
Old Greyhound Photo Portfolio	Redden R				Redden Archives		S	$50
Old Lorries Shire Album 138	Woodhams J	85	303		Shire Pub	Shire Album	S	$10
Oldsmobile (French)	Baillon A	87	162		EPA	Toute L'Hist.	S	$20
Oldsmobile 1904 SalesBrochure			162		Floyd Clymer		S	$10
Oldsmobile First Seventy-Five Years	Kimes B R/Langworth R M	72	162		AQ		X	$40
Oldsmobile Performance Years	Schorr M L	83	162		Quicksilver	Quicksilver	S	$20
Oldsmobile Postwar Years	Norbye J P	81	162		MBI	Marques America	H	$50
Oldtime Automobile(Fawcett 134)	Bentley J	51	401		Fawcett	Fawcett	S	$10
Oldtime Steam Cars (H)	Bentley J	53+	414		Fawcett/Arco		X	$30
Oldtimers (Art book - German text)	Buergle K/Simsa P	61	504		Motor-Presse-Verlag		H	$40
Oliver Advertising History	King A C	81	901		King		S	$20
Olympian Cars	Carson R B	76	401		Knopf		H	$125
Omnibus of Speed	Beaumont W/Nolan C	58+	297		G P Putnam's Sons/S Paul		H	$20
On A Clear Day YCS General Motors	DeLorean J Z/Wright J P	79	160		Wright/Avon		X	$30
On Starting Grid	Frere P	56	297	205	Batsford		H	$40
One Hundred 32 Unusual Cars Indy	Engel L K	70	208		Arco		H	$60
One Hundred of Worlds Finest Autos	Ritch O C	60	401		Clymer		S	$30
One Hundred Years Motorcycles	Clarke M	88	601		Mondadori/Portland		H	$40
One Hundred Yrs Am Fire Fight Ap(H)	Da Costa P	64	302		Clymer/Bonanza/Crown		X	$20
One Hundred Yrs of Auto 1886-1986	Ruiz M	84	401		Gallery/Smith/Mondadori		H	$40
One Hundred Yrs on Road	Flower R/Jones M W	81	419		McGraw		H	$50
One Hundred Yrs Porsche Mirrored...	Schrader H	76	136		Porsche		H	$90
Opel GT Coupe Auto-Classic #4	Knittel S	80S	124		Albion Scott	Auto-Classic	S	$20
Opel Wheels to the World		75	124		AQ		H	$40
Open Fords	Sorensen L	77	122		Silverado	Fordiana	H	$125
Original Lotus Elite	Ortenburger D	77	129		Newport Press		S	$50
Other Bentley Boys	Nagle E	64	139		Harrap		H	$50
Other Side of Hill	Hill B	78	205		Hutchinson/Stanley Paul		H	$20
Our First 50 Years 1905-55	Johnston R	55	105		Nuffield/BMC		H	$70
Out of Control (novel)	Gerber D	74	207		Prentice		H	$20
Over the Road History of Intercity	Meier A E/Hoschek	75			Motor Bus Society		H	$60
Overland by Auto in 1913	Copeland E M	81	212		Indiana Historical Soc		S	$30
Overtype Steam Road Waggon	Kelly M A	71	303		Goose		H	$40
Owen Magnetic'15-'16 Mod.SalesBroch			158		Floyd Clymer		S	$10
Packard 1942-1962	Dawes N T	75	159		Barnes		H	$70
Packard Cars 1920-1942	Clarke R M	77	159		Brooklands	Brooklands	S	$40
Packard Complete Story	Scott M G H	85	159		Tab		H	$60
Packard Eight Owners H/B 1929			159		Floyd Clymer		S	$10
Packard Guide	Marvin R B	87	159		Packard Data Bank		S	$60
Packard Hist of MC & Co (leather)	Kimes B R	78	159		AQ		L	$125
Packard Service Letters	Abbott R		159		Abbott		S	$40
Packard Story Car & Company	Turnquist R E	65	159		Barnes		H	$50
Pantera & Mangusta 1969-1974	Clarke R M	80	118		Brooklands	Brooklands	S	$40
Pantera 1970-1973	Clarke R M	80	118		Brooklands	Brooklands	S	$40
Panteras for Road	Rasmussen H	82	118		MBI	Survivors	H	$60
Parnelli Story of Auto Racing	Libby B	69	205		E P Dutton		H	$40
Parry Thomas Designer Driver	Tours H	59	205		Batsford		H	$50
Passenger Cars 1863-1904	Nicholson T R	70	401		Macmillian		H	$20
Passenger Cars 1905-12	Nicholson T R	71	401		Macmillan		H	$20
Passenger Cars 1913-23	Nicholson T R	72	401		Macmillian		H	$20
Passenger Cars 1924-1942	Sedgwick M	75	401		Blandford		H	$20
Passion for Cars	Gibbs A	74	401		David & Charles/Scribners		H	$20
Past Joys(toys)	Botto K	78	703		Chronicle		S	$40
Pastmasters Of Speed	May D	58	610		Temple		H	$60
PCV Autobiography of Philip Vincent	Vincent P C	76	610		Vincent		H	$40
Peak of Performance Pikes Peak.....	Young R	82	206		Ron Young		S	$40
Pebble Beach Matter of Style	Devlin R T	80	206		Newport Press		H	$150
Peking to Paris	Barzini L	72	212		Library Press		H	$50
Perf Cars Germany SEE GERMAN HIGH..			408					$
Performance Tuning Sunbeam Tiger	Chittenden G	67	105		Clymer		S	$50
Perpetuating Porsche Paranoia	Pietruska R	81	136		R P Design		S	$20
Petersens Basic Atmtv Tools........	Whitt D	74	405		Petersen		S	$10
Petersens Basic Atmtv Trblshooting	Caldwell B	77	405		Petersen		S	$10
Petersens Basic Chassis Susp Bra H	Hot Rod	71	202		Petersen/Denison		H	$30
Petersens Basic Clutches Trans	Hot Rod	71+	202		Petersen/Denison		X	$30
Petersens Basic Engine Hot Rodding	Schofield M/Hot Rod Eds	72	201		Petersen	Hot Rod	S	$30
Petersens Basic HT Tune Your Car	Murray C	79	405		Petersen		S	$10
Petersens Basic Ignit/Elec Systems	Murray S	77	405		Petersen		S	$10
Petersens Big Book of Auto Repair	Murray S	76+	405		Petersen		H	$30
Petersens Comp Bk Pickups & Vans	Murray S	72	306		Petersen		S	$20
Petersens Compl Bk Datsun	Hall A	75	167		Petersen		S	$20
Petersens Compl Bk Eng Swapping 4E	Murray S	75	405		Petersen/Hot Rod		S	$20
Petersens Compl Bk Engines 02E	Christy J/Hot Rod Editors	66	202		Petersen	Hot Rod	S	$20
Petersens Compl Bk Engines 06E	Hot Rod	70	202		Petersen		S	$20
Petersens Compl Bk Engines 08E	Schofield M	72	202		Petersen		S	$20

Title	Author	Pub date	Subjects	Publisher	Series	Bind	Price
Petersens Compl Bk Engines 10E	Murray S	74	202	Petersen		S	$20
Petersens Compl Bk Japanese Import	Murray S	72	167 126	Petersen		S	$20
Petersens Compl Bk Pinto	Murray S/Hall A	77	122	Petersen		S	$10
Petersens Compl Bk Plym Dodge Chrys	Murray S	73	132	Petersen		S	$30
Petersens Compl Bk Toyota	Hall A	75	126	Petersen		S	$20
Petersens Compl Bk Vega			111	Petersen		S	$10
Petersens Compl Chevrolet Book 3E	Murray S	73	111	Petersen		S	$20
Petersens Compl Chevrolet Book 4E	Murray S	75	111	Petersen		S	$30
Petersens Compl Ford Book 1E	Murray S	70	122	Petersen		S	$30
Petersens Compl Ford Book 2E	Murray S	72	122	Petersen		S	$20
Petersens Compl Ford Book 3E	Murray S	73	122	Petersen		S	$20
Petersens Compl Ford Book 4E	Murray S	76	122	Petersen		S	$20
Petersens Compl Volkswagen Book 3E	Murray S	73	150	Petersen		S	$20
Petersens History Drag Racing		81	201	Petersen		S	$40
Petersens World of Wheels	Tanner H	71	401	Petersen		S	$20
Peugeot Guide	Sloniger J	61	120	Sports Car Press	Mod Sports Car	S	$30
Peugeot Toute L'Histoire	Dumont P	82	120	EPA	Auto Histoire	S	$20
Phil Hill Yankee Champion	Nolan W F	62	205	Putnam		H	$125
Photo Formula-I Best Auto Yr 53-78		79	297 510	Edita		H	$150
Pickup & Van Spotter's Gd 1945-1982	Burness T	82	301	MBI		S	$30
Pickup Parade Light Truck Handbook	Kelley K	67+	301	Auto Book Press/Sincere		X	$30
Pictorial Hist Chrysler Corp. Cars		66+	112	Chrysler Corp.		S	$30
Pictorial Hist of Automobile (P.R.)	Roberts P	77	401	Ottenheimer/Grosset		H	$30
Pictorial Hist of Automobile(Motor)	Stern P V	53	401	Hearst/Viking		H	$50
Pictorial Hist of Car	Roberts P	78	401	Mandarin/Octopus		H	$30
Pictorial Hist of Trucks	Gibbins E/Ewens G	78	306	Orbis/Book Sales/Chartwel		H	$20
Pictorial Survey Rac Cars 1919-39	Mathieson T A S O	63	298	MRP		H	$125
Pierce-Arrow 1919 Sales Catalog			170	Floyd Clymer		S	$10
Pierce-Arrow (Ballantine)	Hendry M D	71	170	Ballantine Books	Ballantine #4	S	$30
Pierce-Arrow (Ralston)	Ralston M	80	170	Barnes		H	$50
Pierce-Arrow Golden Age	Ralston M	84	170	Ralston		H	$60
Pikes Peak Race to Clouds	Madow M	79	206	Marc Madow		S	$30
Piloti che gente 1E	Ferrari E	83	121	Enzo Ferrari		H	$250
Piloti che gente 1E(English)	Ferrari E	83	121	Enzo Ferrari		H	$200
Piloti che gente 4E	Ferrari E	87	121	Enzo Ferrari		H	$700
Pinin Farina Master Coachbuilder	Frostick M	77	501	Dalton Watson	Dalton Watson	H	$100
Pininfarina #06 Yearbook (Italian)	Colombo G	65	501	Pininfarina		S	$100
Pininfarina #09 Yearbook (Italian)	Colombo G	68	501	Pininfarina S.p.A		H	$100
Pininfarina #11 Yearbook (Italian)		71	501	Pininfarina		S	$180
Pininfarina #12 Yearbook (Italian)	Bernabo F	73	501	Pininfarina		S	$100
Pininfarina Architect of Cars	Frostick M	78	501	Dalton Watson	Dalton Watson	H	$70
Pininfarina Cinquantanni(English)	Pininfarina	80	501	Edizioni Pininfarina		H	$150
Pininfarina Nato Con L'Automobile	Caballo E	68	501	Della Palazzi		H	$80
Pininfarina Prestige & Trad.1930-80	Merlin D	80	501	Edita S.A.		H	$100
Pioneers in Industry Fairbanks M...	Fairbanks M	45	418 905	Fairbanks		H	$60
Pit & Paddock Bckgrnd MR 1894-1978	Frostick M	80	298	Moorland		H	$30
Pit Stop (cartoons)	Groves R	53	297	Autosport		S	$20
Playboy Book of Sports Car Repair	Darack A	80	405	Wideview		S	$10
Playboy Gd Rally Rac Spts Cr Drivg	Neeley W	81	203	Playboy		H	$20
Plymouth and DeSoto Story	Butler D	78	137 158	Crestline	Crestline	H	$100
Plymouth Barracuda 1964-1974	Clarke R M	85	137	Brooklands	Brooklands	S	$30
Pontiac 1926-1966 ID Guide	Bonsall T E	82	138	Bookman	ID Guide	S	$20
Pontiac Complete History 1926-1986	Bonsall T E	85	138	Bookman Publishing		H	$60
Pontiac Firebird 1967-73	Clarke R M	82	138	Brooklands	Brooklands	S	$30
Pontiac GTO Americas Premier S/C	Schorr M L	78	138	Performance Publications		S	$20
Pontiac Performance Handbook	Martin W H/Hot Rod Eds	63	138	Petersen	Hot Rod	S	$30
Pontiac Performance Years	Schorr M L	82	138	Quicksilver	Quicksilver	S	$20
Pontiac Postwar Years	Norbye J P	79	138	MBI		H	$40
Pontiac Show Cars Experimentals....	Sass D	86	138	Bookman		S	$20
Pontiac Trans-Am High Perf Handbook	Schorr M L	81	138	Quicksilver	Supercar	S	$20
Popular Mechanics Auto Album	Throm E L/Crenshaw J S	52	401	Popular Mechanics		X	$20
Porsche (Cotton)	Cotton M	82	136	Col Lib/Crown/Crescent		H	$20
Porsche (in Japanese) V5		71	136	Car Graphic Library	Car Grap L	S	$30
Porsche (Kobayashi)	Kobayashi S	73	136	MBI		S	$40
Porsche (Pritchard)	Pritchard A	69	136	Pelham		H	$30
Porsche 1978(Japanese)	Inouye T	78	136	Neko		S	$30
Porsche 1979 (Japanese)	Inouye T	79	136	Neko	Neko	S	$30
Porsche 1980 (Japanese)	Inouye T	80	136	Neko	Neko	S	$30
Porsche 356 Auto Classic #1	Schrader H	82	136	Podzun-Pallas/Albion	Auto Classic	S	$30
Porsche 356 Autohistory	Jenkinson D	81	136	Osprey	Autohistory	H	$40
Porsche 4 Cyl 4 Cam Spts & Rac Cars	Sloniger J	77	136	Batchelor/MBI		S	$60
Porsche 911 (Consumer Guide)	Consumer Gd	87	136	Publications Intl	Consumer Guide	H	$20
Porsche 911 (Harvey)	Harvey C	80	136	Haynes/Oxford Ill	Classic Car	H	$60
Porsche 911 Collection No 1 1965-75	Clarke R M	81	136	Brooklands	Brooklands	S	$20
Porsche 911 Collection No 2 1974-81	Clarke R M	82	136	Brooklands	Brooklands	S	$20
Porsche 911/912 Source Book	Miller S	84	136	Bookman	Source Boo	S	$30
Porsche 914 1969-1975	Clarke R M	80	136	Brooklands	Brooklands	S	$30

Title	Author	Pub date	Subjects		Publisher	Series	Bind	Price
Porsche 917 Kimberley Rac S/C Gd 1	Cotton M	87	136		Kimberley		S	$30
Porsche 924 1975-1981	Clarke R M	82	136		Brooklands	Brooklands	S	$30
Porsche 928 Collection #1	Clarke R M	82	136		Brooklands	Brooklands	S	$20
Porsche 935 Supercars in Profile #2	Archibald S	85	136		Sapphire	Sprcrs in Prfl	S	$20
Porsche 959: Art & Car Edition	Lewandowski J	86	136		Sudwest	Art & Car	H	$800
Porsche and Volkswagen Companion	Ullyett K	62	136	150	S Paul/Autobooks		H	$30
Porsche Book Definitive Ill History	Boschen L	77	136		Stephens/Arco		H	$80
Porsche Cars 1952-1956	Clarke R M	79	136		Brookalnds	Brooklands	S	$30
Porsche Cars 1957-1960	Clarke R M	79	136		Brooklands	Brooklands	S	$30
Porsche Cars 1960-1964	Clarke R M	79	136		Brooklands	Brooklands	S	$30
Porsche Cars 1964-1968	Clarke R M	79	136		Brooklands	Brooklands	S	$30
Porsche Cars 1968-1972	Clarke R M	79	136		Brooklands	Brooklands	S	$30
Porsche Cars 1972-1975	Clarke R M	80	136		Brooklands	Brooklands	S	$30
Porsche Complete Story	Harvey C	83	136		Haynes	Mini Marque	H	$30
Porsche Double World Champs.1900-77	Von Frankenberg R	78	136		Haynes		H	$40
Porsche Engineers Talk Shop		79?	136		Porsche		S	$40
Porsche Factory Tour Summer 1960		60	136		Spyder Entr., Inc.		S	$40
Porsche Family Tree		78	136		Porsche		S	$10
Porsche Guide	Solinger	58	136		Sports Car Press		S	$30
Porsche Man & His Cars	Von Frankenberg R	61+	136		Bentley		H	$50
Porsche Neko(Japanese)		82	136		Neko	Neko	S	$30
Porsche Panorama 1st 25 Years	Barrett F	82	136		Porsche Club of America		H	$80
Porsche Past & Present	Jenkinson D	83	136		Gentry		H	$40
Porsche Racing Cars of 70s	Frere P	80	136		Stephens/Arco		H	$50
Porsche SAE Papers		79	136		Amer. Soc. of Auto Engrs		S	$30
Porsche Sport 73	Rusz J	73	136		Bond Parkhst/CBS/Haessner		S	$30
Porsche Sport 74/75	Rusz J	75	136		Ruszkiewicz/CBS/Haessner		S	$50
Porsche Sport 76/77	Rusz J	77	136		Ruszkiewicz/CBS		S	$30
Porsche Story	Weitmann J	68	136		Arco		H	$50
Porsche Tradition of Greatness (H)	Langworth R M	83	136		Publications Int	Consumer Guide	H	$40
Porsche Tradition of Greatness (S)	Langworth R M	84	136		Publications Intl	Consumer Gd	S	$10
Porsche Turbo Collection #1 1975-80	Clarke R M	81	136		Brooklands	Brooklands	S	$20
Porsche Year 1982	Miller S	82	136		Carrera International		X	$60
Porsches at Le Mans	Pascal D	84	136	206	Haynes		H	$100
Porsches for Road	Rasmussen H	81	136		MBI	Survivors	H	$50
Post-war Brit Thorougbreds Purc/Res	Hudson B	72	406		Foulis		H	$30
Post-war Brit Thoroughbreds 1955-60	Hudson B	81	406		Haynes		H	$40
Poster Book of Antique Auto Ads	Garrett H	74	503		Citadel/Lyle Stewart		S	$40
Postwar British Cars	Greenwood G	48	406		Clymer		H	$30
Postwar British Motorcycles	Ayton C J	82	606		Hamlyn		H	$30
Postwar MG & Morgan	Blakemore/Rasmussen	79	131	164	Picturama	Survivor S	H	$50
Power Basics of Auto Racing	Presto K/Bryce J	86	203		Hope		S	$20
Power Behind Aston Martin	Courtney G	78	103		Oxford Ill		H	$40
Power to Go Story of Auto Industry	Denison M	56	419		Doubleday		H	$20
Power to Win(Ford Cosworth)	Blunsden J	83	202	156	MRP		H	$80
Powered by Jaguar Cooper HWM.......	Nye D	80	127	105	MRP		H	$40
PPG Indy Car World Series 1981('80)	Kirby G	81	204		Competition Images		S	$20
Preserved Lorries	Jenkinson K A	77	306		Ian Allen		H	$30
Preserving Commercial Vehicles	Jenkinson K A	82	309		PSL		H	$30
Presidents on Wheels	Collins H R	71	401		Acropolis/Bonanza		H	$40
Pride of Bentleys	Adams J	78	139		NAL/Chartwell		H	$60
Pride of Road Pict St Tract....	Lane M R	76	903		New English Library		H	$50
Private Entrant Racing Rob Walker	Cooper-Evans M	65	298		Cassell/MBC		H	$50
Private Motor Car Collections of GB	Hugo P	73	401		Dalton Watson	Dalton Watson	H	$50
Prize Posters	Rennert J	85	503		Poster Auctions/G Smith		H	$60
Production Figures for US Cars	Heasley J	77	403		MBI		S	$20
Professional Amateur C Kettering	Boyd T A	57	404		Dutton		H	$40
Profile No 01 Mercedes 1908 &1914GP	Bird A	66	130		Profile Publications		S	$30
Profile No 02 Rolls Royce Phantom I	Oliver G A	66	139		Profile Publications		S	$30
Profile No 03 Hispano-Suiza V-12	Boddy W	66	120		Profile Publications		S	$30
Profile No 04 Jaguar XK Series	Appleton J	66	127		Profile Publications		S	$30
Profile No 05 Lanchester 38&40 H.P.	Bird A	66	105		Profile Publications		S	$20
Profile No 06 Duesenberg J & SJ	Nicholson T R	66	116		Profile Publications		S	$30
Profile No 07 Bentley 3 1/2 & 4 1/4	Oliver G A	66	139		Profile Publications		S	$30
Profile No 08 Vanwall GP Car	Jenkinson D	66	298		Profile Publications		S	$20
Profile No 09 Auburn Straight-eight	Betts Jr C	66	116		Profile Publications		S	$30
Profile No 10 Bugatti Type 35 GP	Eaton G	66	107		Profile Publications		S	$30
Profile No 11 Alvis Speed 20,25,etc	Nicholson T R	66	105		Profile Publications		S	$20
Profile No 12 Ferrari Tipo 625&555	Davey K/Pritchard A	66	121		Profile Publications		S	$30
Profile No 13 Ford Model T 1908-27	Bird A	66	122		Profile Publications		S	$10
Profile No 14 Alfa Romeo Type RL	Hull P/Fusi L	66	101		Profile Publications		S	$10
Profile No 15 MG Magnette K3	McComb F W	66	131		Profile Publications		S	$30
Profile No 16 Jowett Javelin&Jupitr	Tubbs D	66	105		Profile Publications		S	$10
Profile No 17 Napier 40/50 1919-24	Barker R	66	105		Profile Publications		S	$10
Profile No 18 1926-27 1 1/2 Delage	Posthumus C	66	120		Profile Publications		S	$30
Profile No 19 4.5 S-Type Invicta	Buckley J R	66	105		Profile Publications		S	$30
Profile No 20 Frazer-Nash 1948-53	Jenkinson D	66	105		Profile Publications		S	$10

Title Index

Title	Author	Pub date	Subjects	Publisher	Series	Bind	Price
Race Report 2 (Renn Report) 1968-69	Guba E	69	204	Hanns Reich Verlag		H	$100
Race Report 3 (Renn Report) 1969-70	Guba E	70	204	Motorbuch Vertag		H	$100
Race Report 4 (Renn Report) 1970-71	Guba E	71	204	Motorbuch Vertag		H	$125
Race Report 5 (Mtr Spt Ann)1971-72	Guba E	72	204	Motorbuch Verlag/Grenvill		H	$80
Racedrivers	Muller B	63	205 510	Motor-Presse-Verlag		H	$150
Racer	Ruesch H	53	207	Ballantine		S	$10
Racer Story of Gary Nixon	Scalzo J	70	610	Parkhurst/Curtis		X	$40
Racers & Drivers Fastest Men/Cars..	Yates B	68	205	Bobbs Merrill		H	$30
Racers and Drivers Reader	Harding A	72	297	Batsford/Arco		H	$20
Racers Inside Story of Williams	Nye D	82	298	Barker		H	$50
Races That Shook World H	Walkerley R		297	Sports Car Press/Temple	Mod Sports Car	H	$30
Races That Shook World S	Walkerley R	59	297	Arco/Mod Sports Car Press		S	$20
Racing & Sports Car Chassis Design	Costin M/Phipps D	61+	202	Batsford/Bentley		H	$40
Racing & Tuning Production Mtcycles	Knight R	70	604	Speed & Sports		S	$30
Racing All My Life Derek Minter	Minter D	65	610	Barker		H	$40
Racing a Sports Car	Mortimer C	51	298	Foulis		H	$50
Racing Bugs Formula V & Super V	Olney R R/Grable R	74	150 297	Putnam		H	$30
Racing Car Development & Design	Clutton C/Posthumus C/DJ	56	202	Batsford		X	$50
Racing Car Drivers Wld (Caracciola)	Caracciola R	61	205	Farrar		H	$60
Racing Car Explained (juv)	Pomeroy L	63	202	Temple		H	$30
Racing Car Oddities	Nye D	75	297	Arco		H	$40
Racing Car Pocketbook	Jenkinson D	62	297	Batsford		H	$20
Racing Car Review 1947 (first)	Jenkinson D	47	204	Grenville		H	$50
Racing Car Review 1950	Jenkinson D	50S	204	Grenville		H	$40
Racing Car Review 1951	Jenkinson D	50S	204	Grenville		H	$40
Racing Cars & Hist of Mtr Sport	Roberts P	73	297	Octopus		H	$20
Racing Cars & Rec Break 1898-1921	Nicholson T R	71	297	Blandford/Macmillan		H	$20
Racing Cars (Batsford Bk/in Color)	Bensted-Smith R	62+	297	Batsford/Viking		H	$20
Racing Cars (Guba)	Guba E/Nye D	69	298	Race Report/Fountain		S	$40
Racing Cars (Nelson)	Groves R	50S	213 504	Nelson		H	$30
Racing Cars (Nye)	Nye D	80	297	Grisewood/Booktft/Exeter		H	$10
Racing Cars (Rand McNally)	Casucci P	80	297	Mondadori/Rand McNally	R-M Col Ill Gds	S	$20
Racing Cars Racing Cars Racing Cars	Hough R	66	297	Hamlyn		H	$20
Racing Cars Seventy Yrs of Record B		72	297	Golden Press		H	$10
Racing Cars Today	Walkerley R	62	298	Barker		H	$30
Racing Coopers	Owen A	59+	298	Cassell/MBC		H	$90
Racing Driver Theory/Pract Fast....	Jenkinson D	58	203	Batsford/Bentley		X	$40
Racing Fords	Tanner H	68	169	Meredith		H	$150
Racing Game (Davison)	Davison G S	56	603	Clymer		S	$20
Racing History of Bentley	Berthon D	56+	139	Bodley Head/Autobooks		H	$300
Racing Mechanic 7 Yrs Ferr (Cuoghi)	Walton J	80+	297 121	Osprey		H	$50
Racing Motor Cycle	Willoughby V	80	603	Hamlyn		H	$40
Racing Motorist	Davis S C H	49	298	Iliffe		H	$30
Racing Porsches	Frere P	71+	136	Arco/Motorbuch/Stephens		H	$50
Racing Porsches Matsuda Collection	Matsuda Y	82	136	Matsuda		H	$125
Racing Sports Cars	Klemantaski L/Frostick M	56	298	Macmillan/Bodley		H	$60
Racing Sprint Cars (juvenile)	Stambler I	79	299 213	Putnam		H	$30
Racing Stock	Silber M	76	299	Doubleday		S	$20
Racing Stutz(Ballantine)	Howell M	72	158	Ballantine	Ballantine #2	S	$30
Racing Through Century	Davison G S		603	TT Special		H	$50
Racing to Win Wood Bros Style	Engel L K	74	299	Arco		H	$40
Racing Voiturettes	Karslake K	50	298	MRP		H	$150
Racing Wheels	Kenyon J W	41	603 416	Nelson		H	$40
Racing with David Brown Aston Vol 1	Wyer J/Nixon C	80	103	Transport Bookman		H	$80
Racing with David Brown Aston Vol 2	Nixon C	80	103	Transport Bookman		H	$80
Racing Yamaha KT100-S Engine	Genibrel J L	86	603	Steve Smith		S	$30
Racing Year	Davison G S	50	603	T T Special		H	$60
Raid Ferrari D'Epoca Modena 81(Eng)	Stefanini A	81	121	Cons Centro Creativo		H	$90
Rallies and Trials	Davis S C H	51	209	Iliffe & Sons, Ltd		H	$30
Rally 1932-1986	Hamilton M	87	209	Partridge		H	$70
Rally Book	Hebb D	73	209	Hawthorn		S	$20
Rally Handbook	Hudson-Evans R	72	209	Batsford		H	$20
Rally Navigation	Holmes M	75+	209	Haynes		H	$30
Rally-Go-Round	Garrett R	70	209	Stanley Paul		H	$20
Rallycourse 1982-83	Greasley M	82	209	Hazleton		H	$90
Rallycourse 1984-85	Greasley M	84	209	Hazleton		H	$90
Rallycourse 1985-86	Greasley M	85	209	Hazleton		H	$90
Rallycourse 1986-87	Greasley M	86	209	Hazleton		H	$100
Rallying 78	Holmes M/Bishop H	78	209	Haynes		H	$40
Rallying To Win Complete Guide To..	Calvin J	74	209	Bond Parkhurst/Haessner		H	$30
Rallying to Monte Carlo	Couper M	56+	209	Ian Allan Ltd/SBC		H	$20
Rallyworld 1987-88	Foubister P	87	209	Tudor		S	$50
Rallyworld 1988-89	Foubister P	88	209	Tudor		S	$50
Rambler Family Album	Conde J	61	102	American Motors		S	$30
Ranchero Source Book	Ackerson R C	83	122	Bookman	Source Book	S	$30
Range Rover Companion	Bladon S	84	105	Kimberley's		H	$40
Range Rover/Land-Rover	Robson G	79	105	David & Charles		H	$40

Title	Author	Pub date	Subjects		Publisher	Series	Bind	Price
Rayfield 1914 Sales Catalog reprint			158		Clymer		S	$10
Real Steel An Investor's and.......	Neville B	75+	401		Running Press		S	$20
Record Breakers	Villa L/Gray T	69	211		Hamlyn/Transatlantic		H	$70
Record of Motor Racing 1894-1908	Rose G	49	297		MRP/Autobooks		H	$200
Red Car (MG, juvenile)	Stanford D	54	131	207	Scholastic		S	$40
Registration Plates of World	Parker N A	78	507		Europlate		S	$30
Relics of the Road #1 GMC Gems	Rice G	71+	301		Hastings House	Relics of Road	H	$70
Relics of the Road #2 Keen Kenworth	Rice G	73	301		Hastings	Relics of Road	H	$70
Relics of the Road #3 International	Rice G	75	301		Hastings	Relics of Road	H	$70
Remember Those Great VW Ads	Abott D	82	503	150	European Illustration		H	$100
Renault (Loup)	Loup S	57	120		Dumont/Bodley Head		H	$40
Renault 1898-1965	Richard Y	65	120		Pierre Tisne		H	$60
Renault Cars & Charisma	McLintock J D	83	120		PSL		H	$50
Renault Challenge	Seidler E	81	120		Edita		S	$30
Renault Dauphine Cars	Coker A J	63	120		Pearson	Car Maint	H	$20
Renault Guide	Sloniger J	60	120		Sports Car Press	Mod Sports Car	S	$30
Renault Leading French MC Mfctrer		68	120		Renault		H	$50
Resa Kungligt(Swedish)	Nordberg N	76	173		Raben & Sjogren		H	$30
Restoration of Antique&Classic Cars	Wheatley R	64+	405		Bentley		H	$30
Restoration Vintage & Thorbrd Cars	Wheatley R/Morgan B	57+	405		Batsford		H	$30
Restoring Convertibles Rags to.....	Mills B	77	405		MBI		S	$30
Review/Preview 85/86	Bonsall T E	85	401		Bookman Dan		S	$20
Ricart Pegaso La Pasion del Auto...	Mosquera C/Coma-Cros E	88	173		Arcris Ediciones		H	$200
Rickenbacker Autobiography	Rickenbacker E V	68	205		Prentice/Hutchinson		H	$40
Ride It Comp Bk Flat Track Racing	Foster G	78	601		Haynes		H	$20
Riding Machines For Kids	Baldwin E/Baldwin S	84	703		Chilton	Chilton Hobby	S	$30
Riley Cars 1940-1945	Clarke R M	72	105		Brooklands	Brooklands	S	$30
Riley Cars 1945-1950	Clarke R M	72	105		Brooklands	Brooklands	S	$30
Riley Cars 1950-1955	Clarke R M	73	105		Brooklands	Brooklands	S	$30
Riley Prod/Comp Hist pre-1939	Birmingham A T	65+	105		Foulis		H	$70
Risk Life Risk Limb	Cooper-Evans M	68	205		Pelham		H	$40
Riviera Classic Source Book	Zavitz R P	84	108		Bookman Publishing	Source Boo	S	$30
Road & T Exotic Cars:5	Bryant T L	87	401		CBS		S	$10
Road & T Ferrari	Bryant T L	87	121		CBS		S	$20
Road & T Gd to Nissan 300ZX	Paddock L C	89	167		Diamandis		S	$20
Road & T Gd to Toyota MR2	Batchelor D/Duncan T	85	126		CBS		S	$20
Road & T Guide Sports & GT 1982	Wakefield R	81	410		CBS		S	$20
Road & T Guide Sports & GT 1983	Wakefield R	82	410		CBS		S	$20
Road & T Guide Sports & GT 1984	Wakefield R	83	410		CBS		S	$20
Road & T Ill Auto Dictionary	Dinkel J	77	405		Norton		H	$20
Road & T on Merc Spts/GT 70-80	Clarke R M	82	130		Brooklands	Brooklands	S	$30
Road & T Road Test/BG Ann 1982	Simanatis D	82	410		CBS		S	$20
Road & T Road Test/BG Ann 1983	Bryant T L	83	410		CBS		S	$20
Road & T Road Test/BG Ann 1984	Simanatis D	84	410		CBS		S	$20
Road & T Road Test/BG Ann 1985	Clendenin D	85	410		CBS		S	$20
Road and Car in American Life	Rae J B	71	419		MIT Press		H	$30
Road is Yours Story of Auto & Men	Cleveland R M	51	401		Greystone		H	$20
Road Movies Comp Gd Cinema on Whls	Williams M	82	509		Proteus/Scribner		S	$30
Road Race	Jones C	77	297		McKay		H	$40
Road Race Round World NY to Paris	Jackson R B	65	212	213	Walck		S	$20
Road Racer	Butterworth W E	67+	207		Norton/Grosset/Tempo		X	$20
Road Racing Annual 1976('75 season)	Lyons P/Knepper/Gilligan	75	204		Oxman		S	$80
Road Racing Annual 1977	Lyons P	77	204		Oxman		S	$40
Road Racing Annual 1978	Lyons P	78	204		Oxman		H	$50
Road Racing at Watkins Glen	Valent H	58	206		Watkins Glen C of C		H	$200
Road Racing in America	Engel L K	71	299		Dodd Mead		H	$30
Road Runner V2 Source Book	North P	85	137		Bookman Dan	Source Book	S	$30
Road Vehicle Aerodynamics	Scibor-Rylski A J	75+	202		Pentech		H	$70
Roadcraft Police Drivers Manual		60	203		HMSO		S	$10
Roadtests Republished V1 1930-40		74	601		BMS		S	$20
Roadtests Republished V3 1960-65		75	601		BMS		S	$20
Roar In City (Long Beach GP)	McCollister J E	75	206		Performance Marketing		H	$40
Roaring Road Best Auto Rac Stories	Werstein I ed	57	297		Automotive Periodicals		S	$10
Roaring Twenties Album of Early....	Posthumus C	80	297		Blandford		H	$40
Rocket Powered Racing Vehicles.....	Humphreys B J/Malewicki	74	211		Rockets		S	$50
Rolling Homes	Lidz J	79	306		A&W Visual Library		S	$20
Rolling Sculpture Designer & Work	Buehrig G M	75	116	502	Haessner		H	$125
Rolls Man of Speed	Meynell L	53	139		Bodley Head		H	$50
Rolls of Rolls-Royce	Montagu	67	139		Cassell/MBC		H	$50
Rolls on Rocks	Gray R	71	139		Compton Press		H	$30
Rolls-Royce & Bentley Cars-Brief Gd	Adams J B M	72	139		Adams		S	$20
Rolls-Royce & Great Victory		72	139		Bronte-Hill		H	$40
Rolls-Royce (Autocar) Story of Best	Garnier P	77	139		Autocar		X	$30
Rolls-Royce (Ballantine)	Setright L J K	71	139		Ballantine	Ballantine #7	S	$30
Rolls-Royce (Bishop)	Bishop G	82	139		Col Lib/Crescent/Crown		H	$20
Rolls-Royce (Borge/French)	Borge J/Viasnoff N	80	139		Henri Veyrier		H	$50
Rolls-Royce (Exeter)		83	139		Exeter/Col Lib/Bookthrift		H	$20

Title	Author	Pub date	Subjects	Publisher	Series	Bind	Price
Rolls-Royce (Pocket History)	Frostick M	80	139	Automobilia	Complete Book	S	$20
Rolls-Royce (Shire-Wood)	Wood J	87	139	Shire	Shire Album 198	S	$10
Rolls-Royce 40/50hp Ghosts Phntms..	Oldham W J	74	139	Haynes		H	$100
Rolls-Royce 75 Yrs Motoring Exclnc	Eves E	79	139	Orbis/Chartwell/Book Sale		H	$40
Rolls-Royce Alpine Compendium......	Leefe C	73	139	Transport Bookmen		H	$50
Rolls-Royce An Album....British R-R	Post D R	53	139	Post		X	$90
Rolls-Royce and Bent 25-65 Brief Gd	Adams J B M	60S	139	Adams & Oliver		S	$30
Rolls-Royce Cars 1930-1935	Clarke R M	69	139	Brooklands	Brooklands	S	$40
Rolls-Royce Cars 1935-1940	Clarke R M	70	139	Brooklands	Brooklands	S	$40
Rolls-Royce Cars 1940-1950	Clarke R M	70	139	Brooklands	Brooklands	S	$40
Rolls-Royce Catalogue 1910/1911	Rolls-Royce	73	139	EP/Crown/Bonanza		H	$30
Rolls-Royce Companion	Ullyett K	69	139	Stanley Paul & Co.		H	$50
Rolls-Royce Complete Works	Fox M/Smith S	84	139	Faber & Faber		S	$20
Rolls-Royce Corniche Super Profile	Harvey C	84	139	Haynes	Super Profile	H	$20
Rolls-Royce Elegance Continues	Dalton L	71+	139	Dalton Watson	Dalton Watson	H	$180
Rolls-Royce Formative Yrs 1906-1939	Harvey-Bailey A	81+	139	Rolls-Royce Heritage Trst	Historical	S	$20
Rolls-Royce Growth of Firm	Lloyd I	78	139	Macmillan		H	$60
Rolls-Royce History of Car	Bennett M	73+	139	Haynes		H	$50
Rolls-Royce Humour	Schrauzer G N	78	139	RROC		H	$40
Rolls-Royce in America	De Campi J W	75	139	Dalton Watson	Dalton Watson	H	$60
Rolls-Royce in Thirties	Clarke R M	60	139	Brooklands	Brooklands	S	$40
Rolls-Royce Living Legend	Post D R	58	139	Post		H	$70
Rolls-Royce Manual 1925-1939	Haynes J H	64	139	Haynes		S	$40
Rolls-Royce Memories (reprint)	Buist H M	26	139	Cambridge Univ P/RROC		H	$40
Rolls-Royce Men (juvenile)	Rowland J	69	139	Roy		H	$30
Rolls-Royce Merlin at War	Lloyd I	78	139	Macmillan		H	$60
Rolls-Royce Motor Car	Bird A/Hallows I	64+	139	Batsford/St. Martin/Crown		H	$80
Rolls-Royce Phantom II Continental	Gentile R	80	139	Dalton Walton	Dalton Watson	H	$80
Rolls-Royce Phantoms	Tubbs D	64	139	Hamish Hamilton		H	$50
Rolls-Royce Prewar (Japanese)		70S	139	Car Graphic Library	Car Graphic	S	$30
Rolls-Royce Sil Wraith SC reprint			139	Clymer		S	$10
Rolls-Royce Silver Cld Autohistory	Robson G	80	139	Osprey	Autohistory	H	$50
Rolls-Royce Silver Shadow Autohist.	Bolster J	79	139	Osprey	Autohistory	H	$50
Rolls-Royce Silver Spirit Autohist.	Robson G	85	139	Osprey	Autohistory	H	$40
Rolls-Royce Twenty to Wraith	Harvey-Bailey A	86	139	Sir Henry Royce Mem Found		S	$30
Rolls-Royce Years of Endeavour	Lloyd I	78	139	Macmillan		H	$60
Romance of Firefighting	Holzman R S	56	302	Harper		H	$70
Romance of Renault	Seidler E	73	120	Edita		H	$70
Ronnie Peterson SuperSwede/GP Driv	Henry A	75+	205	Haynes		X	$40
Rotary Engine	Yamamoto K	81	405	Sankaido/Toyo Kogyo/Mazdq		H	$50
Rotary Piston Machines	Wankel F	65	405	Deutsche Verlag/Iliffe		H	$60
Rothmans GP Motorcycle YB 1986-87	Harris N	86	608	Queen Anne		S	$40
Round World in a Motorcar	Scarfoglio A	09	212	Mitchell Kennerley		H	$250
Rover	Oliver G A	71	105	Cassell		H	$60
Rover 2000 + 2200 1963-1977	Clarke R M	84	105	Brooklands	Brooklands	S	$30
Rover 3/3.5 litre 1958-1973	Clarke R M	84	105	Brooklands	Brooklands	S	$30
Rover 3500 1968-1977	Clarke R M	86	105	Brooklands	Brooklands	S	$30
Rover Memories	Hough R/Frostick M	66	105	Allen & Unwin		H	$80
Rover Story A Century of Success	Robson G	77	105	PSL		H	$40
Rowe Motor History 1908-1925	Summar D J	75	301	Lancaster C Hist Soc	Journal of LCHS	S	$10
Roy Salvadori Racing Driver	Salvadori R/Pritchard A	85	205	PSL		H	$40
Royal Daimlers	Smith B E	76	105	Transport Bookman		H	$60
Royal Enfield Motor Cycles	Booker C A E	48+	606	Pearson		H	$40
Royal Enfield Postwar Models	Bacon R	82	606	Osprey	Osprey Coll Lib	H	$50
Royalty on Road	Montagu/Frostick	80	401	Collins		H	$50
Rule of Road Intl Gd Hist/Practice	Kincaid P	86	401	Greenwood		H	$20
Runabouts and Roadsters............	Stubenrauch B	73	401	Dodd Mead		H	$40
RX-7 New Mazda RX-7 and Mazda Rot..	Yamaguchi J K	85	126	Dai Nippon/St Martins		H	$60
Saab Guide	Ayling K	61	173	Sports Car Press/Crown	Mod Sports Car	S	$30
Saab Innovator	Chatterton M	80	173	David & Charles		H	$50
Saab Turbo Autohistory	Robson G	83	173	Osprey	Autohistory	H	$40
Saab Way	Sjögren G	84	173	Saab		S	$60
Safari Fever	Brittan N	72	209	MRP		H	$20
Safety Last	Eyston G E T	75	205	Vincent		H	$40
Safety Last An Indictment Auto Ind.	O'Connell J/Myers A	66	419	Random		H	$30
Saga of Roaring Road	Wagner F J	49	205	Floyd Clymer		S	$40
Salmson Story	Draper C	74	120	David & Charles		H	$30
Salt of the Earth (Ab Jenkins)	Jenkins A	39+	205 211	Clymer		X	$50
Sammy Miller on Trials	Miller S	69+	601	Parkhurst		H	$30
Sands of Speed (Babs)	Williams G	73	211	Davies		H	$40
Scalextric Cars & Equipment........	Gillham R	81+	701	Haynes/Foulis		H	$50
Scammell - World Trucks No 8	Kennett P	79	303	PSL	World Trucks	H	$30
Scammell Vehicles	Vanderveen B H	71	303	Warne	Olyslager	H	$30
Scania World Trucks No 2	Kennett P	78	303	PSL/Aztex	World Trucks	H	$30
Schlumpf Automobile Coll(3 lang)	Schrader H	79	401	Schrader/BLV		X	$150
Schlumpf Obsession	Jenkinson D/Verstappen P	77	401	Doubleday/Hamlyn		H	$125
Schweizer Autos	Schmid E	78	402	Edita		H	$60

Title	Author	Pub date	Subjects		Publisher	Series	Bind	Price
Source Book of Fire Engines	Miller D	83	302		Ward Lock Ltd		S	$20
Source Book of Rolls-Royce	Barrass E	83	139		Ward Lock		H	$20
Sox and Martin Bk of Drag Racing	Sox R/Martin B/Neeley B	74	201		Regnery		H	$80
Special Interest Am Cars(1930-1960)	Murray S	76	403		Petersen	Petersen	S	$20
Special Rac Cars & Hot Rods of Wld	Elfrink H	50	297		Clymer		S	$20
Specialist Brit Spts/Rac Crs 50s60s	Pritchard A	86	406		Osprey		H	$60
Specialist Sports Cars Brit Small..	Filby P	74	406		David & Charles		H	$40
Specification Book US Cars 20-29	Naul G M	78	403		MBI		S	$30
Specification Book US Cars 30-69	Naul G M	80	403		MBI		S	$30
Speed and How To Obtain It	Harwood J E G	25+	609		Iiffe Books/Clymer		X	$40
Speed Camera (How-to)	Tompkins E S	46	297	510	Foulis		H	$40
Speed Hill-Climb	May C A N	62	298		Foulis		H	$40
Speed Indy Car Racing	Jezierski C	85	299		Abrams		H	$50
Speed John Surtees Own Story	Surtees J	63+	610	205	Arthur Barker/MBC		H	$50
Speed Merchants	Keyser M	73	297		Rutledge/Prentice-Hall		H	$50
Speed on Salt Hist Bonneville......	Eyston G E T/Bradley W F	36+	211		Batsford/Clymer		H	$50
Speed Triumphant	Fisson P	51	298		Putnam		H	$50
Speed Tuning & Trouble Shooting	Martin W H/Hot Rod Eds	63	202		Petersen	Hot Rod	S	$20
Speed Was My Life	Neubauer A	58	205		Clarkson Potter/Barrie		H	$70
Speed with Style	Revson P/Mandel L	74	205		Doubleday/Kimber		H	$50
Speedbikes	Woollett M	83	601		Arco		H	$20
Speedway Driver History	Werking N P	48	208		Clymer		S	$40
Spirit Celebrating 75 Yrs of R-R...	Dallison K	79	139	504	Spirit Group		H	$300
Spirit of America Winning	Breedlove C/Neeley B	71	211		Regnery		H	$40
Split Seconds My Racing Years	Mays R	51	205		Foulis		H	$60
Sport and Racing Cars	Yates R F/Yates B W	54	297		Harper & Row		H	$30
Sport Cars and Hot Rods(Fawcett 109	Horsley F	50	401		Fawcett	Fawcett	S	$10
Sporting Car Club'S.AustralianMtHis		77	401		SCCSA	Motoring Hist#1	S	$30
Sports and Classic Cars	Borgeson G/Jaderquist E	55	401		Prentice-Hall/Bonanza		H	$40
Sports Car & Competition Driving	Frere P	63	203		Batsford/Bentley		H	$40
Sports Car Album (Fawcett 181)	Freeman J W	53	401		Fawcett	Fawcett	X	$20
Sports Car Bodywork	Locke B W	54+	202		Bentley		H	$50
Sports Car Championship	Pritchard A	72	297		Hale		H	$50
Sports Car Development and Design	Stanford J	57	401		Batsford		H	$30
Sports Car Engine Factors in Perf..	Calculus	49	202		Clymer		S	$40
Sports Car Engine Its Tuning & Mod	Campbell C	64+	202		Bentley		H	$20
Sports Car Pocketbook	Boddy W	61	401		Batsford		H	$10
Sports Car Rallies Trials Gymkhanas	Hebb D/Peck A	56	209		Channel		H	$30
Sports Cars (Batsford Bk/in Color)	Barker R	62	401		Batsford/Viking	Batsford/Col Bk	H	$10
Sports Cars (Freeman)	Freeman J W	55	401		Random		H	$40
Sports Cars (Hutton)	Hutton R	73	401		Hamlyn		H	$10
Sports Cars (Nye)	Nye D	80+	401		Grisewood/Bookthft/Exeter		H	$10
Sports Cars (poster book)	Bamber J/Davies G/Ward M	85	401	503	Outlet/Newnes/Viscount		S	$30
Sports Cars 1928-1939	Nicholson T R	69	401		Blandford/Macmillan		H	$20
Sports Cars Book Two 1907-1927	Nicholson T R	70	401		Blandford/Macmillan		H	$20
Sports Cars Facts and Pictures	Conley A L	54	401		Greenberg		H	$40
Sports Cars History and Development	Georgano G N	87	401		Johnston/Book Sls/Chtwl		H	$30
Sports Cars In Competition	Bowman H W	52	297		Fawcett		S	$20
Sports Cars in Action	Bond J R	54	401		Holt		H	$50
Sports Cars of Future	MacMinn S	59	401		Sports Car Press	Mod Sports Cars	S	$10
Sports Cars of World (Halmi)	Halmi R	58	401		Sports Car Press		H	$20
Sports Cars of World (Stein)	Stein R	52	401		Scribner		H	$50
Sports Cars of World(Petersen 1971)	Kovacik B	71	401		Petersen		S	$10
Sports Cars of World(Petersen 1972)	Bishop A	72	401		Petersen		S	$10
Sports Cars on Road and Track	Hutton R	73	297		Hamlyn		H	$20
Sports Cars Today	Walkerley R	62	401		Arthur Barker Ltd		H	$10
Sportscar Specials (Trend 178)	Rolofson B	60	401		Trend	Trend Book	S	$20
Sportsmanlike Driving	AAA	47+	203		American Automobile Assn		H	$30
Sportwagen in Deutschland	Von Fersen H	68	408		Motorbuch Verlag		H	$50
Spot-On Diecast Models by Tri-ang	Thompson G	83	702		Haynes		H	$30
Spyder California Ferrari of.....	Carrick G M	76	121		John W.Barnes		S	$40
Stainless Steel Carrot	Wilkinson S	73	299		Houghton		H	$20
Standard Car 1903-1963 Ill Hist	Davy J R	67	105		Sherbourne Press		H	$60
Stanley Steam Cars 1917 Sales Cat			158		Floyd Clymer		S	$10
Stanley Steamers Q & A 1920			158		Floyd Clymer		S	$10
Star Cars	Cartier E	86	297		Quartet		S	$20
Stars and their Cars	Barris G	73	509		Laufer		S	$10
Starting from Scratch (cartoons)	Groves R	54	297		Autosport		S	$20
Starting Grid to Chequered Flag	Frere P	62	205		Batsford		S	$20
Station Wagon Its Saga and Develop.	Briggs B	75	403		Vantage Press		H	$40
Steam Cars 1770-1970	Montagu/Bird A	71	414		Cassell/St Martins		H	$100
Steam Cars 1910 Sales Cat			158		Floyd Clymer		S	$10
Steam Lorry	Kidner R W	48+	303		Oakwood	Locomotion Pprs	S	$10
Steam on Road	Wise D B	73	414		Hamlyn		H	$20
Steam Scene V1	Blenkinsop R J	76	903		Steam Eng Pub		S	$30
Steam Scene V2	Blenkinsop R J	76	903		Steam Eng Pub		S	$30
Steam Scene V3	Blenkinsop R J	77	903		Steam Eng Pub		S	$30

Title	Author	Pub date	Subjects	Publisher	Series	Bind	Price
Steam Scene V4	Blenkinsop R J	77	903	Steam Eng Pub		S	$30
Steam Scene V5	Blenkinsop R J	78	903	Stem Eng Pub		S	$30
Steam-Powered Automobile An Answer.	Jamison A	70	414	Indiana		H	$30
Stirling Moss	Raymond R	53	205	MRP		H	$50
Stirling Moss's Book of Motor Sport	Mineau W	55	297	Cassell		H	$40
Stock Car Driving Tecniques	Parsons B/Smith S	73	203	Steve Smith		S	$20
Stock Car Racer (juv fict)	Jackson C	57	213	Follett		H	$30
Stock Car Racing at Daytona Beach	Breslauer K C	86	206	Auto Racing Memories		S	$10
Stock Car Racing Grnd Nat Comp(juv)	Jackson R B	68	299	Walck		H	$20
Stock Car Racing USA	Engel L K	73	299	Dodd, Mead		H	$30
Storia della Formula 1(Italian)4Vol	Poltronieri M		297	Edzioni Equipe		H	$300
Stories of Road & Track	Crow J T	70	401	Bond Parkhurst		H	$30
Story of American Automobile	Anderson R E	50	419	Public Affairs		H	$30
Story of Automobile	Barber H L	17	401	Munson		H	$40
Story of Black Beauty	Davies R A	81	139	Carlton		H	$40
Story of BMW Motorcycles	Croucher R	82	606	PSL		H	$40
Story of Brooklands Vol 3	Boddy W	50	206	Grenville		H	$50
Story of BSA Motor Cycles	Holliday B	78	606	PSL		H	$40
Story of Car	Hodges D/Wise D B	74	401	Hamlyn		H	$20
Story of Fisher Body		65+	418 401	General Motors		S	$10
Story of Ford GP Engine Design &Dev	Blunsden J/Phipps D	71	156	Bentley		H	$30
Story of Ford in Canada			122	Ford of Canada		H	$30
Story of Formula I 1954-1960	Jenkinson D	60	297	Tee & Whiten/Grenville		H	$50
Story of George Romney	Mahoney T	60	102	Harper		H	$30
Story of Honda Motor Cycles	Carrick P	76	606	PSL		H	$50
Story of Hudson Motor Car 1909-1957	Wood E V	73	163	Triangle Press		S	$20
Story of Kawasaki Motor Cycles	Carrick P	78	606	PSL		H	$40
Story of London Bus	Day J R	73		London Transport		H	$20
Story of Lotus 1947-1960 Birth Leg	Smith I H	70+	129	MRP		H	$70
Story of Lotus 1961-1971	Nye D	72	129	MRP/Bentley		H	$80
Story of Manx	Davison G S	48	606	TT Special		H	$60
Story of Panther Motor Cycles	Jones B	83	606	PSL/Thorsons		H	$50
Story of Royal Enfield Motor Cycles	Hartley P	81	606	PSL		H	$40
Story of Rudge Motorcycles	Hartley P	85	606	PSL		H	$40
Story of Stanley Steamer H	Woodbury G	50	158	Norton		H	$70
Story of Stanley Steamer S	Woodbury G	67	158	Clymer		S	$60
Story of Triumph Motorcycles	Louis H/Currie B	75+	606	PSL		H	$50
Story of Triumph Sports Cars	Robson G	73	146	MRP		H	$60
Story of TT	Davison G S	47	603	TT Special		H	$50
Story of Ulster	Davison G S	49	603	TT Special		H	$60
Story of Velocette	Beresford G	50S	606	T T Special		H	$40
Streamlined Cars in Germany	Kieselbach R J F	82	408	W. Kohlhammer GmbH		H	$100
Streamling & Car Aerodynamics	Norbye J P	77	202	Tab	Mod Spts Car	S	$20
Street Bikes Superbikes/Tourers....	Taylor R	74	601	Golden Press	Golden Wheels	H	$10
Street Machines 49 and on Custom...	Morland A	84	201	Osprey		S	$30
Street Rod (Felsen - fiction)	Felsen H G	53+	201	Random/Bantam		X	$20
Street Rodding Gallery	Hall C/O'Toole L	87	201	Graffiti		S	$20
Street Rods Pre-48 American Rods	Morland A	83	422	Osprey	Osprey Color	S	$30
Stromlinienbusse in Deshld(English)	Kieselbach R J F	83		Kohlhammer edition		H	$100
Stropus Gd to Auto Rac Timing/Score	Stropus J V	75	297	Sports Car Press	Mod Sports Car	S	$20
Studebaker Cars 1923-1939	Clarke R M	80	145	Brooklands	Brooklands	S	$30
Studebaker Complete Story	Cannon W A/Fox F K	81	145	Tab		H	$125
Studebaker Last Years 1952-66 (Ads)	Mayborn M	73	145	Highland		S	$20
Studebaker Postwar Years	Langworth R M	79	145	MBI		H	$60
Studebaker Second 50 Yrs 02-52 (Ads)	Mayborn M	73	145	Highland Enterprises		S	$20
Study of Four-Stroke Mtrcycl Engine	Brokaw P M	70	609	Bagnall		S	$20
Stutz 11 Days 7 Hours 15 Minutes	Sturm W F		158	Floyd Clymer		S	$20
Stutz Fire Engine Co Indianapolis	Birchfield R	70S	302	Birchfield		H	$180
Stutz Series E Sales Catalog 1913		50S	158	Clymer		S	$20
Style Auto - 01 (Italian)	Cinti F	63	508	Edistyle		H	$70
Style Auto - 02 (Italian)	Cinti F	63	508	Style Auto		H	$50
Style Auto - 03 (Italian)	Cinti F	64	508	Style Auto		H	$50
Style Auto - 04 (English)	Bellia G	64	508	Style Auto		X	$50
Style Auto - 05 (English)		64	508	Style Auto		X	$30
Style Auto - 06 (English)	Bellia G	65	508	Style Auto		H	$50
Style Auto - 07 (English)	Bellia G	65	508	Style Auto		X	$50
Style Auto - 08 (English)	Bellia G	65	508	Style Auto		S	$50
Style Auto - 09 (English)	Dinarich M	65	508	Style Auto		S	$50
Style Auto - 10 (English)	Bellia G		508	Style Auto		S	$50
Style Auto - 11 (English)	Bellia G		508	Style Auto		S	$50
Style Auto - 12 (English)	Bellia G		508	Style Auto		X	$50
Style Auto - 13 (English)	Dinarich M	67	508	Style Auto		H	$50
Style Auto - 14 (English)			508	Style Auto		X	$30
Style Auto - 15 (English)			508	Style Auto		X	$50
Style Auto - 16 (English)	Dinarich M	68	508	Style Auto		S	$50
Style Auto - 17 (English)	Dinarich M	68	508	Style Auto		H	$50
Style Auto - 18 (English)			508	Style Auto		X	$50

Title	Author	Pub date	Subjects	Publisher	Series	Bind	Price
Style Auto - 19 (English)			508	Style Auto		X	$50
Style Auto - 20 (English)	Dinarich M	69	508	Style Auto		H	$60
Style Auto - 21 (English)	Dinarich M	69	508	Style Auto		H	$40
Style Auto - 22 (English)		69	508	Style Auto		S	$30
Style Auto - 23 (English)			508	Style Auto		X	$30
Style Auto - 24 (English)			508	Style Auto		X	$30
Style Auto - 25 (English)			508	Style Auto		X	$30
Style Auto - 26 (English)			508	Style Auto		X	$30
Style Auto - 27 (English)			508	Style Auto			$30
Style Auto - 28 (English)		70	508	Style Auto			$30
Style Auto - 29 (English)	Dinarich M	71	508	Style Auto		H	$30
Style Auto - 30 (English)			508	Style Auto		X	$30
Style Auto - 31 (English)			508	Style Auto		X	$30
Style Auto - 32 (English)			508	Style Auto		X	$30
Style Auto - 33 (English)			508	Style Auto		X	$30
Style Auto - 34/35 (English)			508	Style Auto		X	$30
Style Auto - 36 (English)			508	Style Auto		X	$30
Style Auto - 37 (English) (last)	Dinarich M	78	508	Style Auto		H	$30
Styling Automobile Design	Von Mende H	79	502	Motorbuch Verlag		H	$30
Styling The Look of Things	PR Staff of GM	55	502 160	General Motors		S	$40
Such Sweet Thunder Sty Ford GP Eng	Blunsden J/Phipps D	71	156 298	MRP		H	$40
Summer of Triumph Life of Caruthers	Higdon H	77	205	Putnam		H	$30
Sunbeam Alpine & Tiger 1959-1967	Clarke R M	79	105	Brooklands	Brooklands	S	$30
Sunday Driver	Yates B	72	205	Farrar,Straus/Doubleday		X	$40
Super Catalog of Car Parts and Acc.	Hirsch J	74	412	Workman		X	$20
Super Fords	Wyss W A	79	122	Zuma Marketing		S	$30
Superbike Road Tests(M/C Weekly)	Sanderson G	82	601	Hamlyn		H	$30
Superbiking	Ditchburn B	83	601	Osprey		S	$20
Supercars of Seventies	Sinek J	79	401	Hamlyn		H	$30
Supercars Worlds Finest (Sinek)	Sinek J	79	401	Hamlyn/Domus		H	$30
Supercars Worlds Finest (Walton)	Walton J/Caddell L	88	401	Macdonald/Longmeadow		H	$30
Supercharge	Norman E	69	202	Norman		S	$20
Supercharged Mercedes	Schrader H/Demand C	79	130	Edita		H	$100
Supercharging Cars and Motor Cycles	Brierley M	67	202 609	Lodgemeark		S	$30
Superfast Type 410 Superamerica	Dethlefsen D	78	121	Dethlefsen		S	$30
Superspeedway Story of NASCAR......	Benyo R	77	299	Mason/Charter/Reinhold		X	$40
Superstars of Auto Racing (juv)	Olney R R	75	205	Putnam		H	$30
Supertuning	Hot Rod	66	202	Petersen/Signet/NAL		S	$10
Suppressed Inventions & How They Wk	Brown M H	74+	405	Madison		S	$40
Suspension & Brakes Tuning Comp	Watkins M B	70	202	Speed Sport	Tuning Comp #3	S	$20
Suzuki	Clew J	80	606	Haynes		H	$30
Suzuki Two-Strokes	Bacon R	84	606	Osprey	Osprey Coll Lib	H	$50
T Series MG	Knudson R L	73	131	Motorcars Unlimited		X	$60
T T Tales & other stories	Davison G S	50	603	T T Special		H	$70
T T Thrills	Cade L	57	603	Frederick Muller Ltd.		H	$100
Talbot (French)	Renou M	85	120	EPA	Toute L'Hist	S	$30
Talbot Automobile (German)	Borge J/Viasnoff N	80	120	Schrader/Henri Veyrier		H	$70
Talbot Sunbeam-Lotus MRP Rally Lib	Robson G	85	120	MRP	Rally Library 3	S	$20
Tales of Master Mechanic	Bunn M	72	405	Popular Science		S	$30
Targa Florio Authentic History	Bradley W F	55	206	Foulis		H	$100
Targa Florio Seventy Epic Years....	Owen D	79	206	Haynes		H	$40
Taxi Project Realistic Solutions...	Ambasz E	76	401 306	Museum of Modern Art		S	$20
Taxicabs Photographic History	Warren P/Linskey M	76	401	Almark		H	$50
Tazio Vivo (Italian)	De Agostini C	87	205	Conti Editore		H	$70
Team Suzuki	Battersby R	82	606	Osprey		H	$60
Technique of Motor Racing (Hard)	Taruffi P	59	203	MRP/Bentley		H	$30
Ten Ans de Coupe Gordini Tome 2	Courtel C		120	Editions Michael Hommell		S	$30
Ten Ans de Courses (Montaut)	Montaut E	08?	504 297	Montaut Mabileau Editeurs		S	$3000
Ten Years of Motor Racing 1896-1906	Jarrott C	06+	298	Foulis		H	$80
Theme Lotus (prior to '86 editions)	Nye D	78+	129	MRP		H	$60
They Call Me Mr. 500	Granatelli A	69	205	Henry Regnery		H	$30
Think Small VW	Various	67	150	Volkswagen of America		H	$30
Third Generation Lotuses Coll Guide	Robson G	83	129	MRP	Coll Guide	H	$50
Third James Flood Bk of Early Motor	Paynting H H	76	402	James Flood Charity Trust	Early Motoring	H	$150
Thirty ans de Vehicules d'Incendie.	Horb A/Martineau J E	77	302	EPA	Coll Biblioth..	H	$50
Thirty Days in May Indy 500	Higdon H	71	208	Putnam		H	$30
Thirty-two Ford Deuce	Thacker T	84	122	Osprey		H	$60
This is a Studebaker Year Vol 6	Cannon W A	76	145	Cannon		S	$20
This Was Pioneer Motoring	Karolevitz R F	68	401	Superior		H	$40
This Was Trucking A Pictorial Hist	Karolevitz R F	66	306	Superior/Bonanza		H	$40
Thoroughbred & CC Gd Engine Rest...		85	405	Temple/Newnes/Hamlyn		H	$30
Those Bentley Days	Hillstead A F C	53	139	Faber		H	$70
Those Daring Young Men in their J..	Davies J/Annakin K/Searle	69	213 209	Putnam		H	$20
Those Elegant Rolls-Royce	Dalton L	67	139	Dalton Watson	Dalton Watson	H	$80
Those Incredible Indy Cars	Calvin J	73	208	Sports Car Press	Mod Sports Car	S	$30
Those Wonderful Old Automobiles	Clymer F	53	401	Clymer/Bonanza		H	$20
Three Pointed Star (12" record)	Lloyd N/Pomeroy L	50S	130	Schofield Productions	Sound Stories		$40

Title	Author	Pub date	Subjects		Publisher	Series	Bind	Price
Three Wheeler	Watts B	70	164		Morgan 3 Wheeler Club		S	$20
Three-56 Porsche Rest Gd Authent...	Johnson B	87	136		356 Registry		S	$40
Three-Pointed Star Story of MB	Scott-Moncrieff D	55+	130		Cassell/Norton/MBI/Haynes		H	$50
Thunderbird (French)	Baillon A	87	147		EPA	Toute L'Hist	S	$20
Thunderbird Ill V1 #1 Fall 1974	Taylor F	74	147		Thunderbird Publications		X	$50
Thunderbird Ill V1 #2 Winter 1975	Taylor F	75	147		Thunderbird Publications		X	$40
Thunderbird Ill V1 #3 Spring 1975	Taylor F	75	147		Thunderbird Publications		X	$40
Thunderbird Ill V1 #4 Summer 1975	Taylor F	75	147		Thunderbird Publications		X	$40
Thunderbird Ill V2 #1 Fall 1975	Taylor F	75	147		Thunderbird Publications		X	$40
Thunderbird Ill V2 #2 Winter 1976	Taylor F	76	147		Thunderbird Publications		X	$40
Thunderbird Ill V2 #3 Spring 1976	Taylor F	76	147		Thunderbird Publications		X	$40
Thunderbird Ill V2 #4 Summer 1976	Taylor F	76	147		Thunderbird Publications		X	$40
Thunderbird Odyssey Auto Design	Boyer W P	86	147		Taylor Publishing		X	$70
Thunderbird Story Personal Luxury	Langworth R M	80	147		MBI		H	$80
Tiger Alpine Rapier Sporting Cars..	Langworth R M	82	105		Osprey		H	$50
Tiger Exceptional Motorcar	Carroll W	78	105		Auto Book Press		S	$60
Tiger Making of Sports Car	Taylor M	79	105		Gentry/Haynes		H	$80
Times Review of Brit Mot Ind 1946	SMMT	46	401		Times/Clymer		S	$20
Tin Lizzie Story of Fab Model T....	Stern P V	55	122		Simon & Schuster		H	$30
Today and Tomorrow	Ford H	26	415		Doubleday/Heinemann		H	$40
Tokheim Pump Co 1901-1980	Lee B	80	507		Lee		S	$30
Top Fuelers Drag Racing Royalty	Stambler I	78	201	213	Putnam		H	$30
Top Up or Down? (Hist Leasing Ind)	Saunders H	72	418		Saunders		H	$30
Touch of Class 101 Great Marques...	Whyte A	85	401		Mandarin/Octopus/Lngmdw		H	$20
Touch Wood 1E	Hamilton D	60	205		MBC/Barrie&Rockliff		H	$100
Touring Superleggera Giant Among...	Anderloni C/Anselmi A	83	501		Edizioni di Autocritica		H	$125
Tourist Trophy 75 Story	Hanks F	75	603		TT Special		S	$20
Toutes les Citroen	Bellu R	79	153		Jean-Pierre Delville		H	$125
Toy Autos 1890-1939 (Ottenheimer)	Pressland D	84	703		Ingram/Harper & Row		H	$80
Toyota First 20 Years in USA		77	126		Toyota Motor Sales		H	$40
Toyota Motor Sports (Japanese)	Kumano M etc	88	126				S	$50
Toyota Twin Cam 1979 (Japanese)		79	126		Neko		S	$40
Toyota Twin Cam II (Japanese)	Inouye K	81	126		Neko	Neko	S	$40
Toys Meeting	Bossi M	83	703		IDEA3		S	$40
Track Tests Sports Cars	Bowler M	81	401		Hamlyn		H	$30
Traction Avant 7-11-15-22	De Serres O	84	153		EPA		H	$80
Traction Engines in Colour	Finch B J	80	903		Ian Allen		H	$50
Traction Engines in Review	Finch B J	71	903		Ian Allen		H	$50
Tractor Pioneer Life of H Ferguson	Fraser C	73	901		Ohio Univ Press		H	$50
Transport Museums (UK)	Simmons J	70	401		Allen & Unwin		H	$40
Transportation Tour of Museums	Simmons J	70	401		Barnes		H	$30
Travels with 2CV Epic Journey......	Earwaker N	88	153		Javelin		S	$30
Travels with Zenobia Paris to Alb..	Lane R W/Boylston H D	83	122	212	University of Missouri		H	$20
Treasury of Automobile	Stein R	61	401		Ridge/Crown		H	$20
Treasury of Early Am Autos 1877-25	Clymer F	50	403		McGraw		H	$20
Treasury of Foreign Cars	Clymer F	57	401		Clymer/Bonanza		H	$30
Treasury of Motorcycles of World	Clymer F	65	601		McGraw Hill/Bonanza		H	$30
Trend Book 1955 Mtr Trnd Auto Yr Bk	Carroll W	55	410		Trend	Trend Bk #118	S	$10
Trend Book 1957 Comp Gd Cars World	Bayless K M	57	410		Trend	Trend Book #142	S	$10
Trend Book 1958 Auto Gd Cars World	Bayless K M	58	410		Trend	Trend Book #167	S	$10
Trend Book 1959 Gd to Cars of World	Bayless K M	59	410		Trend	Trend Book #182	S	$10
Tribute to Turbo (Carrera)	Ludvigsen K E	75	136		Porsche		H	$
Trio at Top	Mahoney D	70	205		Robert Hale		H	$30
Triumph (Pocket History)	Frostick M	81	146		Libreria dell'Automobile	Comp Hist	S	$20
Triumph 2000 2.5 2500 1963-1977	Clarke R M	86	146		Brooklands	Brooklands	S	$30
Triumph Companion	Ullyett K	62	146		Stanley Paul/Autobooks		H	$40
Triumph Mtrcycl Mechanics Handbook	Richardson L D	75	609		Hi-Torque		S	$20
Triumph of an Idea Story of H Ford	Graves R H	34	415		Doubleday		H	$20
Triumph Singles	Bacon R	84	606		Osprey	Osprey Coll Lib	H	$40
Triumph Sports	Autocar	78+	146		Hamlyn/IPC		X	$40
Triumph Stag 1970-1980	Clarke R M	82	146		Brooklands	Brooklands	S	$30
Triumph Stag 70-84 Coll #1	Clarke R M	84	146		Brooklands	Brooklands	S	$30
Triumph TR Maintenance Mod & Tuning	Maclay J L S	67	146		Haynes		H	$30
Triumph TR2 & TR3 1952-1960	Clarke R M	79	146		Brooklands	Brooklands	S	$30
Triumph TR5/250 & TR6 Companion	Rossie S/Clarke I	84	146		Kimberley		H	$40
Triumph TR6 Collection No 1 1969-83	Clarke R M	84	146		Brooklands	Brooklands	S	$20
Triumph TR7 & TR8 1975-1981	Clarke R M	83	146		Brooklands	Brooklands	S	$30
Triumph Vitesse & Herald 1959-1971	Clarke R M	84	146		Brooklands	Brooklands	S	$30
Truck On Rebldg P/U & Other Advntrs	Jerome J	77	306		Houghton/Bodley Head		H	$20
Trucker A Portrait Am Cowboy	Stern J	75	301		McGraw		S	$20
Trucking Around World	Bergendahl S/Sjoberg S	84	306		Verlagshaus/Osprey		H	$60
Trucks & Trucking	Bradley E	79	306		Octopus/Treasure		H	$20
Trucks and Super-Trucks (juvenile)	Richards N/Richards P	80	301		Mus of Science/Doubleday		H	$10
Trucks Illustrated History 1896-20	Georgano G N/Demand C	78	306		Edita/Macdonald/Two Cont.		H	$50
Trucks of Every Sort (juvenile)	Robbins K	81	301		Crown		H	$20
Trucks of Sixties & Seventies	Baldwin N	81	306		Warne		H	$30
Trucks of World Highways	Ingram A	79	306		Blandford/New Orchard		H	$30

Title	Author	Pub date	Subjects		Publisher	Series	Bind	Price
Wankel Rotary Engine Intro & Guide	Dark H E	74	405		Indiana		H	$40
War Against Automobile	Bruce-Briggs B	75	419		Dutton		H	$20
Way to Win	Turner S	74	209		MRP		H	$30
We At Porsche Autobio Ferry Porsche	Bentley J	76	136		Haynes		H	$40
We Never Called Him Henry	Bennett H	51	415		Fawcett		X	$20
Weber Carburettors 2 Tuning & Maint	Passini J	73	405		Speedsport		S	$20
What Car is That?	Roberts P	80	401		Mandarin/Octopus		H	$10
What Henry Ford Is Doing	Bonville F	17+	415		Bureau of Information		S	$30
What Was McFarlan?	Marvin K/Arnheim A	67	158		Arnheim		S	$60
Whatever Became of Baby Austin	Underwood	65	158		Heritage		S	$125
Whatever Happ Brit M/Cycle Industry	Hopwood B	81	606		Haynes		S	$20
Whats it Like Out There?	Andretti M/Collins B	70	205		Henry Regnery		X	$30
Wheels and Wheeling Smithsonian....	Oliver S H/Berkebile D H	74	601		Smithsonian		S	$20
Wheels at Speed	Chula	46	298		Foulis		H	$40
Wheels for Nation	Donovan F	65	419		Crowell		H	$20
Wheels of London(boxed with access)	Marshall P	72	306		Sunday Times Magazine		H	$200
Wheels Round World	Hess A	51	212		Newman Neame		H	$20
Wheelspin Abroad Continental.......	May C A N	49	298		Foulis		H	$40
When Engines Roar	Nolan W F/Beaumont C	64	205		Bantam		S	$10
When the Flag Drops	Brabham J/Hayward E	71	205		Kimber/Coward McCann		H	$40
Where to go Really 4-Wheelin in Ca	Smith C	88	311		Cloud 9 Publications		S	$10
White Steam Car '07/'08 Sales Cat.			158		Floyd Clymer		S	$10
White Steam TouringCarSalesBulletin			158		Floyd Clymer		S	$10
Whos Who in Motor Cycling	Torrens	35	610		Esso		S	$40
Why Citroen	Chassin J P	77+	153		Northfield Industries		S	$40
Wild Cars	Hill M	74	422		Hamlyn		H	$20
Wild Mook 18 Big Rig (Japanese)	Imai K	70S	301		World Photo Press		S	$40
Wild Mook 23 (US Trucking-Japanese)	Imai K	78	301		World Photo Press		S	$40
Wild Mook 28 Fire Eng & F/F (Jap)	Imai K	79	302		World Photo Press		S	$40
Wild Mook 53 Ca Hwy Patrol (Jap)	Imai K	70S	401		World Photo Press		S	$40
Wild Roads Story Transcon. Motoring	Nicholson T R	69	212		Norton		H	$30
Wild Wheel	Garrett G	52	415		Pantheon		H	$20
William Fisk Harrah Life &.....	Mandel L	81	404		Doubleday		H	$30
William Morris Viscount Nuffield	Overy R J	76	105		Europa	Lib of Business	H	$30
Wonder Book of Motors		40S	401		Ward Lock		H	$50
Wonder Book of Motors 2E(?)		26?	401		Ward Lock		H	$70
Wonderful Wheels	Golding H	72	401		Angus & Robertson Aust		H	$10
Wonderful World of Automobile	Davis P	60+	401		Macgibbon & Kee/Crowell		H	$30
Wonderful World of Automobiles	Purdy K W	71	401		DBI Books		S	$20
Works Driver Autobiog of P Taruffi	Schroeder J J	64	205		Temple		H	$70
Works Minis	Taruffi P/Tubbs D B	71+	171		Haynes		S	$30
Works of George Arlington Moore	Browning P	74	405	404	Madison		S	$40
Works Team Rootes Comp Dept	Brown M H	64	105	209	Cassell		H	$50
World Automotive Industry	Frostick M	78	419		David & Charles		H	$40
World Cars '62(World Car Catalogue)	Bloomfield G	62	410		LEA		H	$180
World Cars '63(World Car Catalogue)	D'Angelo S	63	410		LEA		H	$180
World Cars '63-Italian	D'Angelo S	63	410		LEA		H	$80
World Cars '64(World Car Catalogue)	D'Angelo S	64	410		Auto Club Italy/Herald		H	$125
World Cars '65(World Car Catalogue)	D'Angelo S	65	410		Auto Club Italy/Herald		H	$125
World Cars '65-Italian		65	410		Auto Club d'Italia		H	$60
World Cars '66(World Car Catalogue)	D'Angelo S	66	410		Auto Club Italy/Herald		H	$125
World Cars '67(World Car Catalogue)	D'Angelo S	67	410		Auto Club Italy/Herald		H	$125
World Cars '67-Italian		67	410		Auto Club d'Italia		H	$60
World Cars '68(World Car Catalogue)	D'Angelo S	68	410		Auto Club Italy/Herald		H	$125
World Cars '69(World Car Catalogue)	D'Angelo S	69	410		Auto Club Italy/Herald		H	$125
World Cars '70(World Car Catalogue)		70	410		Auto Club Italy/Herald		H	$100
World Cars '71(World Car Catalogue)		71	410		Auto Club Italy/Herald		H	$90
World Cars '72		72	410		Auto Club Italy/Herald		H	$90
World Cars '73		73	410		Herald/Auto Club Italy		H	$90
World Cars '74		74	410		Auto Club Italy/Herald		H	$90
World Cars '75		75	410		Auto Club Italy/Herald		H	$90
World Cars '76		76	410		Auto Club Italy/Herald		H	$90
World Cars '77		77	410		Auto Club Italy/Herald		H	$90
World Cars '78	Losch A	78	410		Auto Club Italy		H	$90
World Cars '79	Losch A	79	410		Auto Club Italy/Herald		H	$70
World Cars '80	Losch A	80	410		Auto Club Italy/Herald		H	$50
World Cars '81	Losch A	81	410		Auto Club Italy/Herald		H	$70
World Cars '82	Losch A	82	410		Auto Club Italy/Herald		H	$50
World Cars '83	Losch A	83	410		Auto Club Italy/Herald		H	$50
World Cars '84	Losch A	84	410		Auto Club Italy/Herald		H	$30
World Cars '85 (last)	Losch A	85	410		Auto Club Italy/Herald		H	$30
World Champions From Farina/Stewart	Pritchard A	72	205		Macmillan		H	$30
World Championship (Grant)	Grant G	59	298		Autosport		H	$40
World Championship Motor Cycl Rac	Woollett M	73	604		Hamlyn		H	$40
World Motor Racing/Rallying H/B 70	Kahn M	70	209		Mayflower		S	$20
World of Automobile	Stein R	73	401		Ridge Press		H	$40
World of Automobiles (Comp set 22)	Ward I	74	401		Orbis/CBS/Quattroruote		H	$125

Title	Author	Pub date	Subjects	Publisher	Series	Bind	Price
World of Model Cars (Smeed)	Smeed V	80	704	Bison/Chartwell/Bk Sales		H	$30
World of Model Cars (Williams)	Williams G	76	704	G P Putnam's Sons		H	$30
World of Motorcycles (Comp Set 22)	Ward I	79	601	Orbis/CBS		H	$250
World of Racing Cars	Dymock E	72	297	Hamlyn		H	$10
World of Racing Endurance Racing	Wilkinson S	81	213	Childrens Press		H	$10
World Rallying 01	Holmes M/Bishop H	79	209	Osprey		H	$150
World Rallying 02 Rothmans 79-80	Holmes M/Bishop H	80	209	Osprey		H	$40
World Rallying 03 Rothmans 80-81	Holmes M/Bishop H	81	209	Osprey		H	$40
World Rallying 05 Rothmans 82-83	Holmes M/Bishop H	83	209	Rothmans		H	$40
World Rallying 06 Audi Sport 83-84	Holmes M	84	209	David Sutton Publications		H	$40
World Rallying 07 Audi Sport 84-85	Holmes M	85	209	David Sutton Publications		H	$40
World Rallying 10 Pirelli 87-88	Holmes M	88	209	Van/Blandford		H	$40
World Sports Car Championship	Posthumus C	61	297	MacGibbon		H	$40
World Understanding On Two Wheels	Pratt P R	80	601	Pratt		S	$20
Worlds Automobiles 1880-1958	Doyle G R	59	412	Temple		H	$40
Worlds Commercial Vcles1830-1964	Georgano G N	65	306	Temple		H	$20
Worlds Fastest Cars (Trend 120)	Horsley F	55	211	Trend	Trend Book	S	$10
Worlds Fastest Cars Ill Gd to......	McGovren J	85	412	Quintet/Book Sls/Chtwell		H	$20
Worlds Fastest Motorcycles	Scott M/Cutts J	86	601	Quintet/Chartwell		H	$20
Worlds Finest Motor Car(SC reprint)		70S	116	Duesenberg		S	$20
Worlds Great Race Drivers (Juv)	Orr F	72	205 213	Random House		H	$20
Worlds Land Speed Record	Boddy W	51+	211	MRP/Phoenix		X	$40
Worlds Largest Mtrng Spectacle	Nelson R	72	401	Directional		S	$10
Worlds Motor Museums	Nicholson T R	70	401	Lippincott		H	$60
Worlds Number One Flat-out.........	Bledsoe J	75	299	Doubleday		H	$30
Worlds Racing Cars 1E	Armstrong D	58	297	Macdonald/Hanover		H	$40
Worlds Racing Cars 2E	Twite M L	64	297	Macdonald/Doubleday		H	$30
Worlds Racing Cars 3E	Twite M L	66	297	Macdonald/Doubleday		H	$30
Worlds Veteran to Vintage Cars	Lloyd J	60	401	Macdonald/Hanover		H	$20
Wreck and Recovery	Thomas A	87	303	PSL		S	$30
Wreckers & Recovery Vehicles	Vanderveen B H	72+	306	Haynes/Warne	Olyslager	H	$30
X Cars Detroit's 1-of-a-kind Autos	Lent H B	71	403	Putnam		H	$40
XVme Grand Prix Monaco 57 (7" rec)	Moss S/Lloyd N	50S	206	Schofield Productions	Sound Stories		$30
Yamaha	Woollett M	84	606	Arco		S	$20
Yamaha Legend	Macauley T	79	606	St. Martins		H	$40
Yamaha Two-Stroke Twins	MacKellar C	85	606	Osprey	Osprey Coll Lib	H	$50
Year of Silver Arrows Wld C/S 89-90	Spurring Q	90	130	Q Editions		S	$20
Yesterdays Cars	Dexler P R	79	424	Lerner		H	$10
Young Henry Ford Picture Hist......	Olson S	63	415	Wayne		H	$30
Young Sportsmans Gd to Spts Car Rac	Janes H B	62	213	Nelson		H	$20
Yumping Yarns (F1 cartoons)	Bamber J	88	297 504	Tudor Journals		S	$20
Z Car Enthusiasts Guide (Datsun)	Millspaugh B	86	126	Millspaugh		S	$60
Z/28 Camaro No 1 Teams Cafe Racer	Schorr M L	78	111	Performance		S	$20
Zagato	Marchiano M	84	501	Automobilia		H	$180
Zagato (Italian)	Fagiuoli/Gerosa	69	501	Auto Club D'Italia		H	$180
Zagato Alfa Romeo ES 30 Zagato		80S	101	Grafica Milanese		S	$30
Zagato Aston Martin Vantage Zagato	Marchiano M/Bowler	86	103 501	Aston Martin		S	$30
Zen and Art of Motorcycle Maint....	Pirsig R M	74	601	Bantam		S	$10

Author	Title	Pub date	Subjects		Publisher	Series	Bind	Price
AAA	Sportsmanlike Driving	47+	203		American Automobile Assn		H	$30
AIC	Master Catalog of Trucks	80	301		Automotive Info Clearing		S	$20
AMOC	Aston Martin Register 1963	63	103		AMOC		S	$70
ANFIA	Fifty Anni 1912-1962 (Italian)	62	409	501	ANFIA(Italian Auto Ind)		H	$200
Abbey S	Book of the Austin Seven and Eight	35+	105		Pitman	Motorists Lib	S	$30
Abbott R	Packard Service Letters		159		Abbott		S	$40
Abott D	Remember Those Great VW Ads	82	503	150	European Illustration		H	$100
Ackerson R C	Ency of American Supercars	81	403		Bookman		S	$30
Ackerson R C	Ranchero Source Book	83	122		Bookman	Source Book	S	$30
Ackerson R C	Shelby Source Bk Cobras & Mustangs	84	109	122	Bookman	Source Book	S	$30
Ackland D F	Moving Heaven and Earth Le Tourneau	49	904		Marshall Morgan & Scott		H	$50
Ackroyd J	Just For Record Thrust 2	84	211		CHW Roles		H	$40
Adams J	Pride of Bentleys	78	139		NAL/Chartwell		H	$60
Adams J B M	Rolls-Royce & Bentley Cars-Brief Gd	72	139		Adams		S	$20
Adams J B M	Rolls-Royce and Bent 25-65 Brief Gd	60S	139		Adams & Oliver		S	$30
Aigner J/Franz F	Fiesta Concept of Economical Veh	78	169		SAE		S	$20
Alderson J D	Morgan Sweeps Board 3-Wheeler..	78+	164		Gentry/Haynes		H	$50
Alexander J	At Speed	72	297		R&T/Bond Parkhurst		H	$600
Alexander J	At Speed Special Limited edition	72	297		R&T/Bond Parkhurst		H	$1000
Alexander J	Looking Back	82	298	510	At Speed Press		H	$80
Alfieri B	Alfa Romeo 164	87	101		Automobilia		S	$90
Alfieri B	Le Grandi Automobili 17	86	410		Automobilia		S	$30
Alfieri B	Le Grandi Automobili 16	86	410		Automobilia		S	$40
Alfieri B	Le Grandi Automobili 18	87	410		Automobilia		S	$50
Allen H	House of Goodyear	49	418		Corday		H	$70
Allison M	Magic of MG	72	131		Dalton Watson	Dalton Watson	H	$70
Allred M	Automotive Window Engraving	86	405		Allred		S	$30
Alston C	Drag Racing Chassis Manual	85	202		Alston Industries		H	$80
Altshuler A et al	Future of the Automobile Rpt of MIT	84	419		MIT		X	$20
Amabile R	Insiders Guide to Indy Car Racing	89	299		Am Cars		S	$20
Ambasz E	Taxi Project Realistic Solutions...	76	401	306	Museum of Modern Art		S	$20
Amherst Villiers	Amherst Villiers Superchargers	30S	202		Eoin Young (reprint)		S	$30
Ammen C	Comp HB Sand Blasting	79	405		Tab		S	$20
Anderloni C/Anselmi A	Touring Superleggera Giant Among...	83	501		Edizioni di Autocritica		H	$125
Anderson J R L	Hist on Road Vintage Car Miscellany	58	401		Hamish Hamilton		H	$40
Anderson R E	Story of American Automobile	50	419		Public Affairs		H	$30
Anderson/Swinglehurst	Ephemera of Travel & Transport	81	507		New Cavendish Books		H	$40
Andretti M/Collins B	Whats it Like Out There?	70	205		Henry Regnery		X	$30
Andrews A	Mad Motorists Great Peking-Paris...	65	212		Lippincott		H	$30
Angelopolous A/Verlin B	Race	58	208		Bobbs-Merrill		H	$300
Angelucci E	Ency of Automobiles (Angelucci)	67	412		Odhams		H	$40
Ansell D	Military Motorcycles	85	601		Batsford		H	$70
Anselmi A T	Isotta Fraschini (Anselmi)	77	118		G. Milani/MBI/Albion		H	$180
Anselmi A T	Le Grandi Fiat	67	152		Auto Club d'Italia		H	$100
Anselmi A T	Carrozzeria Italiana Culturae......	78	501		Alfieri/Automobilia		H	$60
Anselmi A T	Carrozzeria italiana Advancing Art	80	501		Automobilia		H	$100
Anselmi A T	Ferrari Tipo 166 Original Sports...	85	121		Libreria dell Auto/Haynes		H	$60
Antonick M	Corvette Americas Only(leather)	78	114		Michael Bruce Associates		L	$150
Antonick M	Corvette Sensuous Am 1-1 thru 3-3	78	114		Michael Bruce Associates		H	$500
Antonick M	Corvette Sports Car of America	80	114		Michael Bruce Associates		H	$60
Antonick M	Corvette Americas Only	78	114		Michael Bruce Associates		H	$50
Antonick M	Corvette Sensuous Am 83-1 thru 85-3	83+	114		Michael Bruce Associates		H	$500
Antonick M	Secrets of Show Cars	81	401		Michael Bruce		S	$20
Appleton J	Cars in Profile 11 Jaguar D-Type	73	127		Profile Publications		S	$10
Appleton J	Profile No 04 Jaguar XK Series	66	127		Profile Publications		S	$30
Appleton J	Profile No 36 Jaguar C-type	66	127		Profile Publications		S	$30
Appleyard J	Farm Tractor (Appleyard)	87	901	504	David & Charles		H	$40
Archibald S	Ford GT 40 Sports Cars Profile #1	84	122		Sapphire		S	$20
Archibald S	Porsche 935 Supercars in Profile #2	85	136		Sapphire	Sprcrs in Prfl	S	$20
Armstrong D	Automobile Year 1967-68 #15	68	204		Edita S.A.		H	$150
Armstrong D	Automobile Year 1968-69 #16	69	204		Edita S.A.		H	$150
Armstrong D	Automobile Year 1969-70 #17	70	204		Edita S.A.		H	$180
Armstrong D	Automobile Year 1970-71 #18	71	204		Edita S.A.		H	$125
Armstrong D	Automobile Year 1971-72 #19	72	204		Edita S.A.		H	$150
Armstrong D	Automobile Year 1973-74 #21	74	204		Edita S.A.		H	$125
Armstrong D	Automobile Year 1975-76 #23	76	204		Edita S.A.		H	$100
Armstrong D	Automobile Year 1977-78 #25	78	204		Edita S.A.		H	$100
Armstrong D	Automobile Year 1978-79 #26	79	204		Edita S.A.		H	$80
Armstrong D	Automobile Year 1979-80 #27	80	204		Edita S.A./Norton		H	$80
Armstrong D	Automobile Year 1980-81 #28	81	204		Edita S.A.		H	$80
Armstrong D	Automobile Year 1974-75 #22	75	204		Edita S.A./Chilton		H	$150
Armstrong D	Profile No 38 O.M. 1920-31 6-cylndr	66	118		Profile Publications		S	$10
Armstrong D	Worlds Racing Cars 1E	58	297		Macdonald/Hanover		H	$40
Arnold H L/Faurote F L	Ford Methods and Ford Shops	15	122		Engineering Magazine		H	$150
Artzberger B	Corvair Hist & Restoration Guide	84	113		Aztex		S	$50
Ash D	Automobile Almanac 1977	77	410		Automobile Almanac		H	$10
Ash D	Automobile Almanac 1973	73	410		Automobile Almanac/Crowel		H	$20
Ash D	Automobile Almanac 1972	71	410		Automobile Almanac		S	$20

Author	Title	Pub date	Subjects		Publisher	Series	Bind	Price
Ash D	Automobile Almanac 1971	70	410		Morrow		H	$20
Ash D	Automobile Almanac 1967	67	410		Essandess/Simon Schuster		S	$30
Ash D	Automobile Almanac 1975	75	410		Automobile Almanac		H	$20
Ashby J B/Angier D J	Floyd Clymer Catalog Brit Mtrcycles	51	606		Clymer		S	$30
Aspden R	Classic MG	83	131		Bison/Bookthrift/Exeter		H	$20
Ass of Lic Auto Mfgs	Handbook of Gasoline Autos 1904-06	69	403		Dover		S	$30
Ass of Lic Auto Mfgs	Handbook of Automobiles 1925-1926	73	403		Dover		S	$30
Ass of Lic Auto Mfgs	Handbook of Automobiles 1915-1916	70	403		Dover		S	$30
Aurora Plastics Corp	Comp HB Model Car Racing	67	701		Prentice		H	$40
Auto Club of Brescia	Mille Miglia 1984	84	206		La Mille Miglia Editrice		H	$150
Auto Trade Journal	Auto in 1912	66	403		Iron Horse		S	$10
Autocar	MG Sports 4 cyl TB from Abingdon	80S	131		Autocar		S	$20
Autocar	British Car Owner's Handbook	51	406		Clymer		S	$20
Autocar	Triumph Sports	78+	146		Hamlyn/IPC		X	$40
Autocar	Fifty Years of Le Mans Racing	73	206		IPC Business Press	Autocar Special	S	$30
Automotive Industries	Great American Automotive Story	76	401		Chilton		H	$20
Ayling K	DKW Auto Union Guide	61	124		Sports Car Press/Crown	Mod Sports Car	S	$30
Ayling K	Saab Guide	61	173		Sports Car Press/Crown	Mod Sports Car	S	$30
Ayling K	Gas Guts and Glory Great Moments...	70	297		Abelard-Schuman		H	$20
Ayton C	Book of Bubblecars	64+	401		Pitmans		S	$50
Ayton C J	Japanese Motor Cycles(Hamlyn Guide)	82	606		Hamlyn		H	$20
Ayton C J	Italian Motorcycles Guide	85	606		Temple/Newnes/Hamlyn		H	$20
Ayton C J	Postwar British Motorcycles	82	606		Hamlyn		H	$30
Azema J	Solido Catalogue d'un Univers	83	702		EPA		H	$150
Bacon J H	American Steam-Car Pioneers	84	403	414	Newcomen		S	$40
Bacon R	Foreign Racing Motorcycles	79	603		Haynes		H	$40
Bacon R	Triumph Singles	84	606		Osprey	Osprey Coll Lib	H	$40
Bacon R	Military Motorcycles of World War 2	85	601		Osprey	Osprey Coll Lib	H	$50
Bacon R	Velocette Flat Twins	85	606		Osprey	Osprey Coll Lib	H	$50
Bacon R	Ariel Postwar Models	83+	606		Osprey	Osprey Coll Lib	H	$50
Bacon R	Honda Early Classic Motorcycles	85	606		Osprey	Osprey Coll Lib	H	$50
Bacon R	AJS and Matchless Postwar Models	83+	606		Osprey	Osprey Coll Lib	H	$50
Bacon R	Villiers Singles & Twins	83	606		Osprey	Osprey Coll Lib	H	$40
Bacon R	Suzuki Two-Strokes	84	606		Osprey	Osprey Coll Lib	H	$50
Bacon R	Royal Enfield Postwar Models	82	606		Osprey	Osprey Coll Lib	H	$50
Badre P/Martinez A	Classic Sports Cars	87	401		EPA/Bookthrift/Exeter		H	$20
Baeder J	Gas Food and Lodging	82	401	510	Cross River/Abbeville		H	$50
Baillon A	Oldsmobile (French)	87	162		EPA	Toute L'Hist.	S	$20
Baillon A	Thunderbird (French)	87	147		EPA	Toute L'Hist	S	$20
Baldwin E/Baldwin S	Riding Machines For Kids	84	703		Chilton	Chilton Hobby	S	$30
Baldwin N	Trucks of Sixties & Seventies	81	306		Warne		H	$30
Baldwin N	Kaleidoscope of Lorries & Vans	79	303		Marshall Harris		H	$40
Baldwin N	Kaleidoscope of Farm Tractors	77	904		Old Motor		H	$40
Baldwin N	Vintage Lorry Annual # 1	79	303		Marshall Harris		H	$40
Baldwin N	Farm Tractors	77+	904		Old Motor/Warne	Kaleidoscope	H	$20
Baldwin N	Giant Dumptrucks	84	306		Warne		H	$40
Baldwin N	Observers Book Commercial Veh(1974)	74	306		Warne		H	$20
Balestra N/De Agostini C	Cisitalia	80	118		Automobilia		H	$150
Ball A	My Greatest Race	74	205		J Clark Fnd/Tempo/Dutton		X	$20
Bamber J	Yumping Yarns (F1 cartoons)	88	297	504	Tudor Journals		S	$20
Bamber J/Davies G/Ward M	Sports Cars (poster book)	85	401	503	Outlet/Newnes/Viscount		S	$30
Bamsey I	Automobile Sport 82-83	82	204		Haynes		H	$40
Bamsey I	Automobile Sport 81-82	81	204		Iconplan		H	$50
Bamsey I	Le Mans (Bamsey)	87	206		Miura/Batsford	Wld Grt Mtr Cmp	H	$80
Barbe S	F 3000	88	298		L'Equipe		H	$60
Barber H L	Story of Automobile	17	401		Munson		H	$40
Bargo M	Monster Trucks Car Crushers........	86	301		MBI		H	$30
Barili D	Niki Lauda (Italian)	81	205		Edispo srl		H	$90
Barker R	Bugatti (Ballantine)	71	107		Ballantine Books	Ballantine #1	S	$20
Barker R	Sports Cars (Batsford Bk/in Color)	62	401		Batsford/Viking	Batsford/Col Bk	H	$10
Barker R	Profile No 17 Napier 40/50 1919-24	66	105		Profile Publications		S	$10
Barker R	Sonographic #01 Edwardian Monsters	77	401		Nigensha Car Graphic	Sonographic	H	$70
Barker R	Sonographic #04 American Classics	77	403		Nigensha Car Graphic	Sonographic	H	$70
Barker R/Harding A	Automobile Design Great Designers..	70	502		David & Charles		S	$40
Barlow R	Diesel Car Book	81	405		Grove Press		S	$20
Barnard C N	True's Automobile Yearbook #1 1952	52	410		Fawcett		S	$20
Barnard C N	True's Automobile Yearbook #2 1953	53	410		Fawcett		S	$20
Barnard C N	True's Automobile Yearbook #3 1954	54	410		Fawcett		S	$20
Barnard C N	True's Automobile Yearbook #5 1956	56	410		Fawcett		S	$20
Barnard C N	True's Automobile Yearbook #6 1957	57	410		Fawcett		S	$20
Barnes J W	Ferrari 25 Years of Formula One	74	121		John W. Barnes Jr.		H	$40
Barnes K W	Handbook of Gasoline Autos 1908	63	403		Bell		H	$20
Baron H	Automobile/1	64	401		Ridge/Pocket Books		S	$20
Barraclough R	Profile No 63 Morris Bullnose Cowly	67	105		Profile Publications		S	$10
Barrass E	Source Book of Rolls-Royce	83	139		Ward Lock		H	$20
Barrett F	Porsche Panorama 1st 25 Years	82	136		Porsche Club of America		H	$80
Barris G	Stars and their Cars	73	509		Laufer		S	$10
Barris G/Scagnetti J	Famous Custom & Show Cars	73	422		Dutton		H	$40

Author	Title	Pub date	Subjects		Publisher	Series	Bind	Price
Barris G/Scagnetti J	Cars of Stars	74	509		Jonathan David		H	$40
Barron J/Tubbs D B	Vintage Cars (Batsford/Viking)	60	401		Batsford	Batsford Col Bk	H	$10
Bartlett K/Shepherd J	Big Rev Kev (Australian driver)	83	205		Lansdowne		H	$40
Barzini L	Peking to Paris	72	212		Library Press		H	$50
Bastow D	W O Bentley Engineer	78	139		Haynes		H	$80
Batchelor D	Ferrari Gran Turismo/Comp B'lin't's	77	121		Haessner		S	$125
Batchelor D	Ferrari Early Berli/Comp Coupes	74	121		MBI/DB/Haessner		S	$70
Batchelor D	Ferrari Early Spy & Comp Rdstrs	75	121		Dean Batchelor/Haessner		S	$60
Batchelor D/Duncan T	Road & T Gd to Toyota MR2	85	126		CBS		S	$20
Batchelor D/Lamm M	Harrahs Auto Coll(Batchelor)	84	401		GP Publishing		H	$80
Bateman R	Morris Minor Purchase & Restoration	81	105		Bateman		S	$10
Battersby R	Team Suzuki	82	606		Osprey		H	$60
Baudouy M	More Than Courage (juvenile fict)	61	601		Harcourt Brace		S	$20
Baumann H H	New Matadors	65	297	510	Bond		H	$70
Baxter R	Diamond Jub Brighton Run(7" record)	50S	401		Schofield Productions	Sound Stories		$30
Bayless K M	Trend Book 1957 Comp Gd Cars World	57	410		Trend	Trend Book #142	S	$10
Bayless K M	Trend Book 1958 Auto Gd Cars World	58	410		Trend	Trend Book #167	S	$10
Bayless K M	Trend Book 1959 Gd to Cars of World	59	410		Trend	Trend Book #182	S	$10
Bayley J	Vintage Years at Brooklands (mtcyc)	68	603		Goose		H	$50
Bayley S	In Good Shape	79	502		Van Nostrand		S	$30
Bayley S	Harley Earl & Dream Machine	83	404		Knopf		H	$50
Beacham I	Leader of the Pack Barry Sheene	83+	610		Macdonald/Q Anne/Futura		S	$20
Beasley N	Knudson Biography	47	160	404	Whittlesey/McGraw Hill		H	$40
Beattie I	Comp Bk Automobile Body Des	77	502		Haynes		H	$30
Beaumont W/Nolan C	Omnibus of Speed	58+	297		G P Putnam's Sons/S Paul		H	$20
Becker H/Klutmann M	Ferrari Faszination Auf Radern	83	121		Auto Becker		H	$250
Beeching J	Last Season Life of Bruce McLaren	72	205		Walter R Haessner		H	$50
Beedie M	Customizing Vans	78	307		Blaketon Hall/Arco		H	$20
Beer H	Eighty Jahre Camera und Automobil	63	510		Terhag-Verlag		H	$125
Behme R L	Custom Cars 1954 Annual (Trend 109)	53	422		Trend	Trend Book	S	$20
Belasco W J	Americans on Road Autocamp to Motel	79	419		MIT		S	$20
Bell D	Cast Iron Wonder Chevrolets Fab Six	61	111		Clymer		S	$30
Bell D/Henry A	Derek Bell My Racing Life (Spcl ed)	88	205	136	PSL		L	$150
Bell R	Great Marques Mercedes-Benz	80	130		Octopus		H	$30
Bellia G	Style Auto - 04 (English)	64	508		Style Auto		X	$50
Bellia G	Style Auto - 07 (English)	65	508		Style Auto		X	$50
Bellia G	Style Auto - 10 (English)		508		Style Auto		S	$50
Bellia G	Style Auto - 11 (English)		508		Style Auto		S	$50
Bellia G	Style Auto - 12 (English)		508		Style Auto		X	$50
Bellia G	Style Auto - 06 (English)	65	508		Style Auto		H	$50
Bellia G	Style Auto - 08 (English)	65	508		Style Auto		S	$50
Bellu R	Toutes les Citroen	79	153		Jean-Pierre Delville		H	$125
Bellu R	Les Voitures Francaises Annees 50	83	407		Delville		H	$125
Bellu S	Les Fabuleuses Ferrari(French)	83	121		EPA	Les Fabuleux	H	$30
Bellu S	Blue Blood Hist GP Cars in France	79	298		Warne/EPA		H	$50
Bennett H	We Never Called Him Henry	51	415		Fawcett		X	$20
Bennett M	Rolls-Royce History of Car	73+	139		Haynes		H	$50
Benson A L	New Henry Ford	23	415		Funk & Wagnalls		H	$50
Benson D	Hunt v Lauda Grand Prix Season 1976	76	205		Daily Express		S	$20
Bensted-Smith R	Racing Cars (Batsford Bk/in Color)	62+	297		Batsford/Viking		S	$20
Benter C/Schrader H	German Automobile Coachwork	76	501		Schrader		H	$125
Bentley J	Jaguar Guide	57	127		Sports Car Press	Mod Sports Car	S	$30
Bentley J	We At Porsche Autobio Ferry Porsche	76	136		Haynes		H	$40
Bentley J	Oldtime Steam Cars (H)	53+	414		Fawcett/Arco		X	$30
Bentley J	American Automobiles 1925-1935	53	403		Fawcett		H	$30
Bentley J	Antique Automobiles 1896-1915	51	401		Fawcett		H	$30
Bentley J	Old Car Book (Fawcett 207)	53	401		Fawcett	Fawcett	S	$10
Bentley J	Antique Automobiles (Fawcett 168)	52	401		Fawcett	Fawcett	S	$10
Bentley J	Oldtime Automobile(Fawcett 134)	51	401		Fawcett	Fawcett	S	$10
Bentley J	Great American Automobiles	57	403		Prentice Hall		H	$20
Bentley J	Devil Behind Them	58	205		Prentice-Hall		H	$40
Bentley W O	Ill History of Bentley Car	64	139		Allen & Unwin/Bentley		H	$100
Bentley W O	My Life and My Cars	58+	139		Barnes		H	$60
Bentley W O	Cars in My Life	63	139		Macmillan		H	$60
Benyo R	Superspeedway Story of NASCAR......	77	299		Mason/Charter/Reinhold		X	$40
Beresford G	Story of Velocette	50S	606		T T Special		H	$40
Bergendahl S/Sjoberg S	Trucking Around World	84	306		Verlagshaus/Osprey		H	$60
Berger M L	Devil Wagon in God's Country	79	419		Archon		H	$30
Berkebile D H	Eighteen-ninety-three Duryea Auto..	64	158		Smithsonian		S	$40
Bernabo F	Lancia Aurelia GT (Italian)	83	157		Libreria dell'Automobile	auto classiche	H	$60
Bernabo F	Fiat (Pocket History)	81	152		Automobilia	Comp History	S	$20
Bernabo F	Pininfarina #12 Yearbook (Italian)	73	501		Pininfarina		S	$100
Bernabo F	Auto Da Corsa I Documentari	68	298		Instituto Geografico.....		H	$90
Berry R	Jaguar Motor Racing & Manufacturer	78	127		Aztex		S	$20
Berthon D	Racing History of Bentley	56+	139		Bodley Head/Autobooks		H	$300
Berthon D	Profile No 22 Bentley 6 1/2 Litre	66	139		Profile Publications		S	$30
Berthon D	Profile No 56 Bentley 1922-1929	67	139		Profile Publications		S	$20
Berthon D/Stamer A	Cars in Profile 09 4 1/2 Bentley	73	139		Profile Publications		S	$10

Author	Title	Pub date	Subjects	Publisher	Series	Bind	Price
Bertieri C	Comicar (automobile in comic strip)	75	504	Editori Milano		H	$250
Betts Jr C	Profile No 09 Auburn Straight-eight	66	116	Profile Publications		S	$30
Betts Jr C	Profile No 57 Duesenberg 1920-1927	67	116	Profile Publications		S	$10
Betts Jr C	American Vintage Cars	63	403	Sports Car Press/Crown	Mod Sports Car	S	$20
Bianchi L	Lucien Bianchi Mes Rallyes	69	209	Flammarion		S	$50
Bingay M W	Detroit is my Home Town	46	401	Bobbs-Merrill		H	$30
Bingham P	Drive It! Compl Bk of Formula Ford	84	122	Haynes		H	$30
Bira B	Blue Wings To Bangkok	54	205	Foulis		H	$50
Bira B	Bits and Pieces	42+	205	Foulis		X	$50
Birchfield R	Stutz Fire Engine Co Indianapolis	70S	302	Birchfield		H	$180
Birchfield R	New Stutz Fire Apparatus Co	78	302	Birchfield		H	$60
Bird A	De Dion Bouton (Ballantine)	71	120	Ballantine Books	Ballantine #6	S	$20
Bird A	Profile No 01 Mercedes 1908 &1914GP	66	130	Profile Publications		S	$30
Bird A	Profile No 05 Lanchester 38&40 H.P.	66	105	Profile Publications		S	$20
Bird A	Profile No 13 Ford Model T 1908-27	66	122	Profile Publications		S	$10
Bird A	Profile No 25 De Dion Single-cylndr	66	120	Profile Publications		S	$30
Bird A	Profile No 43 Wolseley 1900-1905	66	105	Profile Publications		S	$10
Bird A	Profile No 55 Stanley Steam Cars	67	158	Profile Publications		S	$10
Bird A	Profile No 91 Rolls-Royce Sil Ghost	67	139	Profile Publications		S	$20
Bird A	Antique Automobiles (Bird)	67+	401	Allen & Unwin/Treasure		H	$20
Bird A	Motor Car 1765-1914	60	401	Batsford		H	$30
Bird A/Hallows I	Rolls-Royce Motor Car	64+	139	Batsford/St. Martin/Crown		H	$80
Bird A/Hutton-Stott F	Lanchester Motor Cars A History	65	105	Cassell		H	$70
Bird A/Hutton-Stott F	Veteran Motor Car Pocketbook	63	401	Batsford		H	$10
Birkin H	Full Throttle	32+	205	Foulis		H	$30
Birks T	Morgan 3 Whlr H/B Ford Engine Mdls	81	164	Morgan 3 Wheeler Club		S	$20
Birmingham A T	Riley Prod/Comp Hist pre-1939	65+	105	Foulis		H	$70
Biscaretti di Ruffia R	Il Museo dell'Automobile Torino	66	401	Auto Club d'Italia		H	$60
Biscaretti diRuffia,C	Museo Dell'Automobile CatalogoGen'l	62	401	Museo Dell'Auto.		S	$20
Bishop A	Sports Cars of World(Petersen 1972)	72	401	Petersen		S	$10
Bishop C W	La France et L'Automobile	71	407	Editions Genin		S	$30
Bishop D/Ingram A	Lorries Trucks Vans since 1928	75	306	Blandford		H	$20
Bishop G	Ency of Motorcycling	80	601	Putnam/Bison		H	$30
Bishop G	Age of Automobile	77	401	Hamlyn		H	$20
Bishop G	Classic Cars (Bishop)	79	401	Hamlyn/Crown/Crescent		H	$30
Bishop G	Concise Dictionary of Motorsport	79	297	Bison/Mayflower		H	$20
Bishop G	Rolls-Royce (Bishop)	82	139	Col Lib/Crescent/Crown		H	$20
Black S	Man and Motor Cars(auto safety etc)	66	401	Norton		H	$20
Blacker K	Vintage Bus Annual #1	79		Marshall Harris		H	$40
Bladon S	Range Rover Companion	84	105	Kimberley's		H	$40
Bladon S	Mercedes-Benz (Bladon)	84	130	Gallery/Smith/Multimedia		H	$20
Bladon S	BMW (Bladon)	85	106	Multimedia/Smith/Gallery		H	$10
Blake P	Gods Own Junkyard...America Ldscp	64	419	Holt, Reinhart & Winston		H	$30
Blakemore/Rasmussen	Postwar MG & Morgan	79	131 164	Picturama	Survivor S	H	$50
Blanc J C	Afgan Trucks	76	306	Stonehill		S	$30
Bledsoe J	Worlds Number One Flat-out.........	75	299	Doubleday		H	$30
Blenkinsop R J	Steam Scene V5	78	903	Stem Eng Pub		S	$30
Blenkinsop R J	Steam Scene V4	77	903	Steam Eng Pub		S	$30
Blenkinsop R J	Steam Scene V3	77	903	Steam Eng Pub		S	$30
Blenkinsop R J	Steam Scene V2	76	903	Steam Eng Pub		S	$30
Blenkinsop R J	Steam Scene V1	76	903	Steam Eng Pub		S	$30
Blight A	George Roesch & Invincible Talbot	70	105	Grenville		H	$70
Bloemker A	Five Hundred Miles to Go Story Indy	61	208	Coward-Mcann		H	$40
Bloomfield G	World Automotive Industry	78	419	David & Charles		H	$40
Blower W E	MG Workshop Manual	52	131	MRP/Bentley		H	$40
Blunsden J	Motor Racing Year 1970	70	204	MRP		H	$30
Blunsden J	Power to Win(Ford Cosworth)	83	202 156	MRP		H	$80
Blunsden J	Formula Junior	61	298	MRP		H	$70
Blunsden J	Motor Racing Year 1972	71	204	MRP		H	$40
Blunsden J	Motor Racing Year 1975	76	204	MRP		S	$30
Blunsden J	Motor Racing Year 1973	72	204	MRP		H	$30
Blunsden J	Motor Racing Year 1971	70	204	MRP		H	$30
Blunsden J/Brinton A	Motor Racing Year 1965-6	65	204	Knightsbridge		H	$30
Blunsden J/Brinton A	Motor Racing Year 1963-4	63	204	Knightsbridge		H	$30
Blunsden J/Brinton A	Motor Racing Year 1964-5	64	204	Knightsbridge		H	$30
Blunsden J/Phipps D	Story of Ford GP Engine Design &Dev	71	156	Bentley		H	$30
Blunsden J/Phipps D	Such Sweet Thunder Sty Ford GP Eng	71	156 298	MRP		H	$40
Bochroch A	American Automobile Racing	74+	297	Penguin/Viking/PSL		X	$50
Bochroch A R	Americans at Le Mans	76	299 206	Aztex		H	$90
Bochroch A R	American Cars of 1970s	82	403	Warne/Haynes		H	$30
Boddy W	Story of Brooklands Vol 3	50	206	Grenville		H	$50
Boddy W	Volkswagen Beetle Autohistory	82	150	Osprey	Autohistory	H	$40
Boddy W	Continental Sports Cars	51	401	Foulis		H	$40
Boddy W	Vintage Years of Morgan 3 Wheeler		164	Grenville		S	$30
Boddy W	Sports Car Pocketbook	61	401	Batsford		H	$10
Boddy W	Profile No 03 Hispano-Suiza V-12	66	120	Profile Publications		S	$30
Boddy W	Profile No 28 Napier-Railton 1933	66	105	Profile Publications		S	$10
Boddy W	Profile No 40 Daimler Double-Sixes	66	105	Profile Publications		S	$10

Author	Title	Pub date	Subjects			Publisher	Series	Bind	Price
Bowman P	Motorcycle Book (Fawcett 123)	51	601			Fawcett	Fawcett	S	$10
Box R de la R	Lamborghini Traume auf vier Radern	86	128			Serag		H	$150
Box R de la R	Automotive Art of Bertone	84	501			Haynes		H	$50
Box R de la R/Crump R	Lamborghini Cars from Sant' Agata	81	128			Osprey		H	$70
Box R de la R/Crump R	Hist of Lamborghini	74+	128			Transport Bookmen		H	$60
Boyd M	BP Book of Motor Racing	60	297			Stanley Pauls		H	$30
Boyd T A	Professional Amateur C Kettering	57	404			Dutton		H	$40
Boyer W P	Thunderbird Odyssey Auto Design	86	147			Taylor Publishing		X	$70
Boyle D H	HT Succeed in Bigtime Trucking	77	301			Ten Speed Press		S	$20
Brabham J	Jack Brabhams Motor Racing Book	60+	205			Muller		H	$30
Brabham J/Hayward E	When the Flag Drops	71	205			Kimber/Coward McCann		H	$40
Braden P/Roush G	Ferrari 365 GTB/4 Daytona	82	121			Newport/Osprey		H	$80
Braden P/Schimdt G	Abarth Fiat/Simca/Porsche..........	83	151	152	136	Newport/Osprey		H	$70
Bradley E	Trucks & Trucking	79	306			Octopus/Treasure		H	$20
Bradley W F	Targa Florio Authentic History	55	206			Foulis		H	$100
Bradley W F	Ettore Bugatti	48	107			MRP		H	$90
Braillon D	Formula 1 86/87 World C/S Y/B 01	86	204			ACLA		H	$100
Braillon D	Formula 1 87-88 World C/S Y/B 02	87	204			ACLA		H	$80
Branch H/Smith W	Unreasonable American Francis Davis	68	404			Acropolis		H	$30
Brawner C/Scalzo J	Indy 500 Mechanic	75	208			Chilton		H	$40
Brazendale K	Great Cars of Golden Age	79	401			Geografico/Orbis/Crescent		H	$30
Brazendale K/Aceti E	Classic Cars 50 Yrs Wlds Finest....	79	401			Exeter/Bookthrift/Orbis		H	$30
Breedlove C/Neeley B	Spirit of America Winning	71	211			Regnery		H	$40
Breslauer K C	Stock Car Racing at Daytona Beach	86	206			Auto Racing Memories		S	$10
Breslauer K C	Daytona 500 1985 Yearbook	85	204			Auto Racing Memories		S	$30
Brierley M	Supercharging Cars and Motor Cycles	67	202	609		Lodgemeark		S	$30
Briggs B	Station Wagon Its Saga and Develop.	75	403			Vantage Press		H	$40
Briggs R/Carter B	Jimmy Murphy and White Dusbg (juv)	68	116	205	504	Hamilton		H	$50
Brigham G	Serial Numbers of First Fifty Years	74	403			Brigham Press		S	$40
Brigham G	Serial Number Book US Cars 1900-75	79	403			MBI		S	$70
Brigham R B	American Car of 1921 (Motor Age)	78	403			Brigham Press		S	$30
Brindle M	Twenty Silver Ghosts(large edition)	71	139			McGraw/Barrie & Jenkins		H	$250
Brindle M/May	Twenty Silver Ghosts(small edition)	78	139			Doubleday		H	$40
British Intelligence	Investigation Dev German GP Cars 34	47	130	298		HM Stationery Office		S	$400
Brittan N	Safari Fever	72	209			MRP		H	$20
Brittan N	Formula Ford Book	77	297	169		PSL		H	$40
Brittan N	Motor Racing International Way No 1	70	204			Kaye & Ward		H	$20
Brittan N	Motor Racing International Way No 2	71	204			Kaye & Ward		H	$20
Brittan N	HT Go Saloon Car Racing	67	297			PSL		H	$20
Broad R	Citroen (Great Cars Series)	75	153			Luscombe	Great Cars	H	$40
Brock R/Hot Rod Editors	Ford Performance Handbook (Hot Rod)	62	122			Petersen	Hot Rod	S	$30
Brockbank R	Manifold Pressures Motoring........	58	504			Temple		H	$30
Brockbank R/Collier R	Bees Under My Bonnet (humour)	55	504			MRP		H	$30
Brodsly D	L A Freeway Appreciative Essay	81	419	401		Univ of California		H	$20
Brokaw P M	Study of Four-Stroke Mtrcycl Engine	70	609			Bagnall		S	$20
Brom J L	Twenty Thou Miles Afri Jungle (DKW)	57+	212	124		Gollancz/Pop Bk Club		H	$30
Brooks L	Great American Autos from 1890-1930	72	401			Scholastic		S	$20
Brough J	Ford Dynasty American Story	77	415			Doubleday		H	$30
Brough L A	Autos on Water Grt Lks Auto Carrier	87	401			Chatham		S	$20
Brown E	Case Album	82	901			Condie		S	$20
Brown E T/Davies A C	Book of the Triumph (motorcycles)	39+	606			Pitman	Mtr Cycl Lib	S	$40
Brown G	Comp Bk Horse Racing/Auto Racing	80	297			NY Times/Arno/Bobbs	NY Times SB His	H	$30
Brown J	Collectors Cars	85	401			Cavendish/Booksales/Chtwl		H	$20
Brown M H	Brown's Alchohol Motor Fuel Cookb'k	79+	417			Desert Publ		S	$30
Brown M H	Suppressed Inventions & How They Wk	74+	405			Madison		S	$40
Brown M H	Works of George Arlington Moore	74	405	404		Madison		S	$40
Brown S	Exotic Cars (Brown)	85	401			Gallery/Smith/Multimedia		H	$20
Browning P	Works Minis	71+	171			Haynes		S	$30
Browning P	Castrol Rally Manual 2	72	209			PSL		H	$20
Browning P	Castrol Rally Manual (1)	71	209			PSL		H	$20
Browning P/Blunsden J	Jensen Healey Stories	74	105			MRP		H	$70
Browning P/Needham L	Healeys and Austin-Healeys	70	104			Foulis/MBI		H	$80
Bruce J G	Source Book of Buses	81				Ward Lock		H	$20
Bruce J G/Curtis C H	London Motor Bus Its Origins & Dev	73				London Transport		H	$20
Bruce M	Best of Corvette Restorer 1953-1967	80	114			M Bruce Assoc		S	$50
Bruce-Briggs B	War Against Automobile	75	419			Dutton		H	$20
Bryant T L	Road & T Exotic Cars:5	87	401			CBS		S	$10
Bryant T L	Road & T Road Test/BG Ann 1983	83	410			CBS		S	$20
Bryant T L	Road & T Ferrari	87	121			CBS		S	$20
Buckley J R	Cars of Connoiseur	60	401			Batsford/Macmillan		H	$40
Buckley J R	Profile No 34 Delage D8 1928-1937	66	120			Profile Publications		S	$30
Buckley J R	Profile No 53 Delahaye Type 135	67	120			Profile Publications		S	$30
Buckley J R	Profile No 19 4.5 S-Type Invicta	66	105			Profile Publications		S	$30
Buckley J R	Classic Cars (in Col/Batsford Bk)	64	401			Batsford/Viking	Batsford/Col Bk	H	$10
Buckley J R	Living Tradition Rolls-Royce	58	139			Rolls-Royce		H	$50
Buckley M	Classic and Sportscar MG File	87	131			Bay View/Temple/Hamlyn		H	$50
Buehr W	Automobiles Past and Present	68	424			Morrow		H	$10
Buehrig G M	Rolling Sculpture Designer & Work	75	116	502		Haessner		H	$125

Author	Title	Pub date	Subjects		Publisher	Series	Bind	Price
Buergle K/Simsa P	Oldtimers (Art book - German text)	61	504		Motor-Presse-Verlag		H	$40
Buffet B	L'Automobile (Buffet)	85	504		Maurice Garnier		H	$90
Buford G/Cebulash M	Love Bug (from the movie)	69	150	509	Scholastic		S	$10
Bugatti L	Bugatti Story(Bugatti)	67	107		Chilton		H	$50
Buhlmann K	Kimberley Rally Team Gd 01 Audi	84	124		Kimberley's		S	$10
Buist H M	Rolls-Royce Memories (reprint)	26	139		Cambridge Univ P/RROC		H	$40
Bull M A	Vintage Motor Cycling (New Zealand)	70	601		Hedley		H	$40
Bunn M	Tales of Master Mechanic	72	405		Popular Science		S	$30
Burgess J	Connoisseurs Choice-Racing/Spt/TrgC	79	401		Walker & Company		S	$20
Burgess R W/Clew J R	Always in the Picture Velocette	71	606		Goose		H	$50
Burgess Wise D	Classic American Automobiles	80	403		Albany/Galahad		H	$30
Burgess-Wise D	Fire Engines & Fire-Fighting	77	302		Mandarin/Octopus/Lngmdw		H	$20
Burgess-Wise D	Ghia Ford's Carrozzeria	85	169	501	Osprey		H	$60
Burgess-Wise D	Automobile Archaeology	81	507		PSL		H	$40
Burgess-Wise D/Boddy W	Automobile First Century	83	401		Orbis/Greenwich		H	$30
Burgess-Wise D/Miller D	Ill History of Road Transport	86	401		Quarto/New Burlington		H	$30
Burlingame R	Henry Ford (Burlingame)	54	415		Knopf/Quadrangle		X	$10
Burness T	American Car Spotter's Gd 1920-1939	75+	403		MBI	Spotter	S	$60
Burness T	Imported Car Spotter's Guide	79	401		MBI		S	$40
Burness T	Pickup & Van Spotter's Gd 1945-1982	82	301		MBI		S	$30
Burness T	Ford Spotters Guide 1920-1980	81	122		MBI		S	$30
Burness T	Chevy Spotter's Guide 1920-1980	81	111		MBI		S	$20
Burness T	American Car Spotter's Gd 1940-1965	78	403		MBI	Spotter	S	$40
Burness T	American Car Spotter's Gd 1966-1980	81	403		MBI	Spotter	S	$30
Burness T	Cars of Early Twenties	68	403		Chilton		H	$40
Burness T	American Truck Spotters Gd 1920-70	78	301		MBI	Spotter	S	$30
Burness T	Cars of Early Thirties	70	403		Chilton/Galahad		H	$40
Burness T	Auto Album	83	401		Houghton Mifflin		S	$10
Burns G	IMSA '88 Yearbook	89	204		IMSA		S	$30
Burns J P A/Hatch J H	Adelaide Grand Prix Impact of Event	86	206		Centre for SA Econ Stud's		S	$30
Burris R	Velocette Development History	82+	606		Haynes		S	$40
Busenkell	Jaguar Since 1945	82	127		Norton		H	$40
Bushey J	Building Fire Truck (juvenile)	81	302		Carolrhoda		H	$20
Butler D	Plymouth and DeSoto Story	78	137	158	Crestline	Crestline	H	$100
Butler D	Hist of Hudson	82	163		Crestline	Crestline	H	$60
Butler H J	Antique Auto Body Leather Work	82	405		Post	Vintage Craft	S	$20
Butterworth W E	Grand Prix Driver (juvenile)	69	213	207	Norton		H	$20
Butterworth W E	Road Racer	67+	207		Norton/Grosset/Tempo		X	$20
Butterworth W E	Fast Green Car	65+	207		Norton/Grosset/Tempo		X	$20
Buttfield N	So Great a Change Story of Holden	79	173		Ure Smith		S	$20
CART	CART 1989 Media Guide	89	204		CART Pub Relations		S	$20
Caballo E	Pininfarina Nato Con L'Automobile	68	501		Della Palazzi		H	$80
Caddell/Winfield	Book of Superbikes	81	601		HP Books		S	$30
Cade L	T T Thrills	57	603		Frederick Muller Ltd.		H	$100
Cadillac	Cadillac Participtn World War (I)	19	110	308	Cadillac		H	$125
Calculus	Sports Car Engine Factors in Perf..	49	202		Clymer		S	$40
Caldwell B	Petersens Basic Atmtv Trblshooting	77	405		Petersen		S	$10
Calvin J	Rallying To Win Complete Guide To..	74	209		Bond Parkhurst/Haessner		H	$30
Calvin J	Those Incredible Indy Cars	73	208		Sports Car Press	Mod Sports Car	S	$30
Campbell C	Design of Racing Sports Cars	73+	202		Chapman & Hall/Bentley		H	$50
Campbell C	Sports Car Engine Its Tuning & Mod	64+	202		Bentley		H	$20
Campbell M	Sir Malcolm Campbells Bk Motorists	37	298		Hillman-Curl/Clymer		X	$30
Campbell S	Javelin Source Book	83	102		Bookman Pub	Source Book	S	$30
Camus P	Lotus Story (French)	78	129		SIPE		S	$30
Cancellieri G	Maserati (Pocket History)	81	172		LEA	Complete Book	S	$20
Cancellieri G	Maserati Catalogue Rais. 1926-1984	84	172		Automobilia		H	$400
Canestrini G	Mille Miglia (Italian)	67	206		Auto Club d'Italia		H	$300
Canestrini G	La Favolosa Targa Florio (Italian)	66	206		LEA		H	$200
Cannon W A	This is a Studebaker Year Vol 6	76	145		Cannon		S	$20
Cannon W A/Fox F K	Studebaker Complete Story	81	145		Tab		H	$125
Car Graphic	Honda F1 1964-1968 (Japanese)	84	126	298	Nigensha Publishing		H	$200
Caracciola R	Caracciola Mercedes Grand Prix Ace	55	130	205	Foulis		H	$70
Caracciola R	Racing Car Drivers Wld (Caracciola)	61	205		Farrar		H	$60
Carlin B	Half-Safe Across Atlantic by Jeep	55	117	212	Deutsch		H	$40
Carlyon R	Firebird (Carlyon)	84	138		Gallery/Smith		H	$20
Carlyon R	Mustang (Carlyon)	84	122		Winchmore/Haynes		H	$30
Carrick G M	Spyder California Ferrari of.....	76	121		John W.Barnes		S	$40
Carrick P	Story of Kawasaki Motor Cycles	78	606		PSL		H	$40
Carrick P	Story of Honda Motor Cycles	76	606		PSL		H	$50
Carrick P	Douglas (Carrick)	82	606		PSL	World Motor Cy	H	$30
Carrick P	Motor Cycle Racing	69	604		Hamlyn		H	$20
Carroll W	Ford Cobra Guide	64	109		Sports Car Press	Mod SportsCar	S	$40
Carroll W	Tiger Exceptional Motorcar	78	105		Auto Book Press		S	$60
Carroll W	Volkswagen Guide	58	150		Sports Car Press/Arco	Mod Sports Car	S	$30
Carroll W	Trend Book 1955 Mtr Trnd Auto Yr Bk	55	410		Trend	Trend Bk #118	S	$10
Carson R B	Olympian Cars	76	401		Knopf		H	$125
Carter C	Motocourse 1977-1978	78	608		Hazleton		H	$300
Carter C	Motocourse 1976-1977	77	608		Hazleton		H	$250

Author	Title	Pub date	Subjects		Publisher	Series	Bind	Price
Cartier E	Star Cars	86	297		Quartet		S	$20
Casey R J	Mr Clutch Story of George W Borg	48	404		Bobbs-Merrill		H	$30
Casucci P	Jaguar Il Fascino di......(Italian)	79	127				S	$100
Casucci P	Enzo Ferrari 50 Years of Motoring	80	121	121	Mondadori/Crown/Greenwich		H	$60
Casucci P	Racing Cars (Rand McNally)	80	297		Mondadori/Rand McNally	R-M Col Ill Gds	S	$20
Casucci P	Classic Cars (Rand McNally)	78	412		Mondadori/Rand McNally	R-M Col Ill Gds	S	$20
Caterpillar Staff	Fifty Years on Tracks	54	906		Caterpillar Tractor Co		H	$80
Cathcart A	Classic Motorcycle Racer Tests	84	604		Osprey	Osprey Coll Lib	H	$50
Catlin R	Life of Ted Horn	49	205		Clymer		S	$30
Caunter C F	Motor Cycles Technical History	56	601		HM Stationery Office		S	$20
Caunter C F	Light Car Technical History	70	401		Her Majestys Stat Office		S	$30
Cavara G	Sixty Vetture ai Raggi X	67	409	504	Auto Club d'Italia		S	$150
Cebulash M	Herbie Rides Again	74	150		Scholastic		S	$10
Centenari M	La Favolosa Lancia	76	157		Editoriale Domus		H	$90
Chambers M	Seven Year Twitch	62+	209		Foulis/MBC		H	$30
Chambers P	Catalog of British Cars 1949-1950	49	406		Clymer		S	$20
Chapin K	Fast as White Lightning	81	299		The Dial Press		H	$20
Chapman C	Seventy Years of Morgan Motoring	80	164		Morgan Clubs		S	$20
Chapman P	Canadian Motorsport Annual 1983-84	84	204		Wheelspin News		S	$30
Chapman P	Canadian Motorsport Annual 1981-82	82	204		Wheelspin News		S	$30
Chassin J P	Why Citroen	77+	153		Northfield Industries		S	$40
Chatterton M	Saab Innovator	80	173		David & Charles		H	$50
Chiavegato C	Formula Ferrari(Italian)	84	121		Forte Editore		S	$50
Chiavegato C	Ferrari 126 C4	84	121		Forte Editore		H	$70
Chiavegato C	Ferrari 126 C3 (Italian)	83	121		Forte Editore		H	$70
Chittenden G	Performance Tuning Sunbeam Tiger	67	105		Clymer		S	$50
Cholmondeley Tapper T P	Amateur Racing Driver	53	205		Foulis		H	$40
Christy J	MG Guide	58	131		Sports Car Press		S	$20
Christy J	Of Men and Cars Tales of Men Raced	60	297		Ziff-Davis		H	$20
Christy J	Guide to Used Sports Cars	57	401		Sports Car Press	Mod Sports Car	S	$20
Christy J/Hot Rod Editors	Petersens Compl Bk Engines 02E	66	202		Petersen	Hot Rod	S	$20
Chrysler	Chrysler Corp Story of American Co	55	112		Chrysler		S	$30
Chrysler Corporation	Mopar Oval Track Performance Book	83	132		Chrysler Corporation		S	$40
Chrysler W P/Sparkes B	Life of American Workman Chrysler	37+	112		Curtis/Dodd Mead		H	$40
Chula	Dick Seaman Racing Champ/Motorist	41+	205		Foulis/Clymer		X	$40
Chula	Wheels at Speed	46	298		Foulis		H	$40
Chula	Twain Have Met Eastern Prince......	57	205		Foulis		H	$50
Chula	Blue and Yellow 2 Seasons Rac Bira	47	205		Foulis		H	$40
Church Roy	Herbert Austin	79	105		Europa Publ		H	$30
Cimarosti A	Comp Hist Grand Prix Motor Racing	86+	298		Hallwag/Bateman/Crescent		H	$50
Cinti F	Style Auto - 01 (Italian)	63	508		Edistyle		H	$70
Cinti F	Style Auto - 02 (Italian)	63	508		Style Auto		H	$50
Cinti F	Style Auto - 03 (Italian)	64	508		Style Auto		H	$50
Ciuro J	Historia del Automovil en Espana	70	402		CEAC		H	$40
Clancy L B/Davies F	Believer Life Story of Mrs H Ford	60	415		Coward-McCann		H	$30
Clark J	Jim Clark at Wheel H	64	205		Arthur Barker/Coward		H	$60
Clark J	Jim Clark at Wheel S	66	205		Pocket Books		S	$20
Clark J M	Emergency and High Speed Driv Tec..	76	203		Gulf		H	$30
Clark J/Brinton A	Ford Book of Competition Motoring	65	169	297	S Paul		H	$30
Clark R	Sideways to Victory	76	209	205	MRP		H	$30
Clark R H	Development of Eng Traction Engines	60	903		Goose		H	$60
Clark R H	Brough Superior Rolls-Royce of MCs	64+	606		Goose/Haynes		H	$50
Clarke R M	Austin Seven Cars 1930-1935	71	105		Brooklands	Brooklands	S	$30
Clarke D	Ferrari 250 GTO Autohistory	83	121		Osprey	Autohistory	H	$40
Clarke M	One Hundred Years Motorcycles	88	601		Mondadori/Portland		H	$40
Clarke R M	Bentley Cars 1934-1939	70	139		Brooklands Books	Brooklands	S	$30
Clarke R M	Jaguar XJS 1975-80	81	127		Brooklands	Brooklands	H	$30
Clarke R M	Jaguar XJ6 1968-72	81	127		Brooklands	Brooklands	H	$30
Clarke R M	Jaguar XJ12 1972-80	81	127		Brooklands	Brooklands	H	$30
Clarke R M	Riley Cars 1950-1955	73	105		Brooklands	Brooklands	S	$30
Clarke R M	Bentley Cars 1940-1945	70	139		Brooklands	Brooklands	S	$30
Clarke R M	Porsche 914 1969-1975	80	136		Brooklands	Brooklands	S	$30
Clarke R M	Morgan 3-Wheeler 1930-52	80	164		Brooklands	Brooklands	S	$40
Clarke R M	Ferrari Collection No 1 1960-1970	81	121		Brooklands	Brooklands	S	$20
Clarke R M	Hudson & Railton Cars 1936-1940	76	163	105	Brooklands	Brooklands	S	$30
Clarke R M	MGB GT 1965-1980	85	131		Brooklands	Brooklands	S	$30
Clarke R M	Lotus Esprit 1975-1981	82	129		Brooklands	Brooklands	S	$40
Clarke R M	Porsche 924 1975-1981	82	136		Brooklands	Brooklands	S	$30
Clarke R M	Jaguar XKE Collection No 1 1961-74	81	127		Brooklands	Brooklands	S	$20
Clarke R M	Jaguar Cars 1957-1961	72	127		Brooklands	Brooklands	S	$30
Clarke R M	Austin A30 & A35 1951-1962	83	105		Brooklands	Brooklands	S	$30
Clarke R M	Austin Ten 1932-1939	74	105		Brooklands	Brooklands	S	$30
Clarke R M	High Performance Escorts Mk 1 68-74	84	156		Brooklands	Brooklands	S	$30
Clarke R M	High Performance Escorts Mk 2 75-80	84	156		Brooklands	Brooklands	H	$30
Clarke R M	Ford RS Escorts 1968-80	82	156		Brooklands	Brooklands	S	$30
Clarke R M	MG Cars 1955-1957	69	131		Brooklands	Brooklands	S	$20
Clarke R M	MG Cars 1957-1959	69	131		Brooklands	Brooklands	S	$20
Clarke R M	MG Cars 1929-1934	69	131		Brooklands	Brooklands	S	$30

Author	Title	Pub date	Subjects	Publisher	Series	Bind	Price
Clarke R M	Muscle Cars Compared Book 2 1965-71	84	403	Brooklands	Brooklands	S	$30
Clarke R M	Book of Morgan Three-Wheeler	50S	164	Brooklands	Brooklands	S	$40
Clarke R M	Cadillac in Sixties No 1	82	110	Brooklands	Brooklands	S	$20
Clarke R M	Jensen Healey 1972-1976	80	105	Brooklands	Brooklands	S	$30
Clarke R M	Muscle Cars Compared 1966-1970	83	403	Brooklands	Brooklands	S	$30
Clarke R M	Dodge Military Vehicles Coll. 1	84	115 301 308	Brooklands	Brooklands	S	$30
Clarke R M	Jaguar Sports Cars 1957-1960	72	127	Brooklands	Brooklands	S	$30
Clarke R M	Ferrari Cars 1977-1981	82	121	Brooklands	Brooklands	S	$30
Clarke R M	Mercedes-Benz Comp Cars 1950-1957	79	130	Brooklands	Brooklands	S	$30
Clarke R M	Morris Minor Collection No 1	82	105	Brooklands	Brooklands	S	$20
Clarke R M	Morris Minor 1948-1970	80	105	Brooklands	Brooklands	S	$30
Clarke R M	Jensen Cars 1946-1967	80	105	Brooklands	Brooklands	S	$30
Clarke R M	Jeep Collection No 1 1942-1954	83	117	Brooklands	Brooklands	S	$20
Clarke R M	Triumph TR7 & TR8 1975-1981	83	146	Brooklands	Brooklands	S	$30
Clarke R M	Road & T on Merc Spts/GT 70-80	82	130	Brooklands	Brooklands	S	$30
Clarke R M	Packard Cars 1920-1942	77	159	Brooklands	Brooklands	S	$40
Clarke R M	Chrysler Cars 1930-1939	80	112	Brooklands	Brooklands	S	$30
Clarke R M	Lancia Stratos 1972-1985	85	157	Brooklands	Brooklands	S	$30
Clarke R M	Pantera & Mangusta 1969-1974	80	118	Brooklands	Brooklands	S	$40
Clarke R M	Sunbeam Alpine & Tiger 1959-1967	79	105	Brooklands	Brooklands	S	$30
Clarke R M	Porsche Cars 1964-1968	79	136	Brooklands	Brooklands	S	$30
Clarke R M	Buick Cars 1929-39	75	108	Brooklands	Brooklands	S	$40
Clarke R M	Dodge Cars 1924-38	78	115	Brooklands	Brooklands	S	$20
Clarke R M	Rolls-Royce Cars 1940-1950	70	139	Brooklands	Brooklands	S	$40
Clarke R M	Alvis in Thirties	61	105	Brooklands	Brooklands	S	$30
Clarke R M	Porsche Turbo Collection #1 1975-80	81	136	Brooklands	Brooklands	S	$20
Clarke R M	Ferrari Cars 1962-1966	79	121	Brooklands	Brooklands	S	$30
Clarke R M	Ferrari Cars 1969-1973	80	121	Brooklands	Brooklands	S	$30
Clarke R M	Ferrari Cars 1966-1969	79	121	Brooklands	Brooklands	S	$30
Clarke R M	Ferrari Cars 1957-1962	79	121	Brooklands	Brooklands	S	$30
Clarke R M	VW Beetle 1956-1977	82	150	Brooklands	Brooklands	S	$30
Clarke R M	Ford Mustang 1967-1973	82	122	Brooklands	Brooklands	S	$30
Clarke R M	Daimler Dart & V8 250 1959-69	82	105	Brooklands	Brooklands	S	$30
Clarke R M	MG TC 1945-1949	84	131	Brooklands	Brooklands	S	$30
Clarke R M	Austin Healey 100 1952-1959	80	104	Brooklands	Brooklands	S	$30
Clarke R M	Jaguar E Type 1961-66	75	127	Brooklands	Brooklands	S	$30
Clarke R M	Porsche 911 Collection No 1 1965-75	81	136	Brooklands	Brooklands	S	$20
Clarke R M	Porsche 911 Collection No 2 1974-81	82	136	Brooklands	Brooklands	S	$20
Clarke R M	Porsche Cars 1972-1975	80	136	Brooklands	Brooklands	S	$30
Clarke R M	Triumph Vitesse & Herald 1959-1971	84	146	Brooklands	Brooklands	S	$30
Clarke R M	Triumph Stag 1970-1980	82	146	Brooklands	Brooklands	S	$30
Clarke R M	Triumph TR2 & TR3 1952-1960	79	146	Brooklands	Brooklands	S	$30
Clarke R M	Porsche Cars 1960-1964	79	136	Brooklands	Brooklands	S	$30
Clarke R M	Jaguar Cars 1955-1957	72	127	Brooklands	Brooklands	S	$30
Clarke R M	Jaguar Cars 1954-1955	71	127	Brooklands	Brooklands	S	$30
Clarke R M	Jaguar Cars 1951-1953	71	127	Brooklands	Brooklands	S	$30
Clarke R M	Jaguar Cars 1948-1951	71	127	Brooklands	Brooklands	S	$30
Clarke R M	Jaguar SS Cars 1937-1947	70	127	Brooklands	Brooklands	S	$40
Clarke R M	Jaguar SS Cars 1931-1937	70	127	Brooklands	Brooklands	S	$40
Clarke R M	Morgan Cars 1969-1979	80	164	Brooklands	Brooklands	S	$30
Clarke R M	Buick Riviera 1963-1978	85	108	Brooklands	Brooklands	S	$30
Clarke R M	Triumph Stag 70-84 Coll #1	84	146	Brooklands	Brooklands	S	$30
Clarke R M	Fiat X1/9 1972-1980	81	152	Brooklands	Brooklands	S	$30
Clarke R M	MG TD 1949-1953	84	131	Brooklands	Brooklands	S	$30
Clarke R M	MG TF 1953-1955	84	131	Brooklands	Brooklands	S	$30
Clarke R M	Pantera 1970-1973	80	118	Brooklands	Brooklands	S	$40
Clarke R M	Lotus Cortina 1963-1970	84	129 156	Brooklands	Brooklands	S	$30
Clarke R M	Porsche Cars 1968-1972	79	136	Brooklands	Brooklands	S	$30
Clarke R M	Plymouth Barracuda 1964-1974	85	137	Brooklands	Brooklands	S	$30
Clarke R M	Capri Muscle Cars 1969-1983	84	156	Brooklands	Brooklands	S	$30
Clarke R M	Lotus Elan Collection No 1 1962-74	81	129	Brooklands	Brooklands	S	$20
Clarke R M	Datsun 240Z & 260Z 1970-1977	80	167	Brooklands	Brooklands	S	$30
Clarke R M	Riley Cars 1940-1945	72	105	Brooklands	Brooklands	S	$30
Clarke R M	Riley Cars 1945-1950	72	105	Brooklands	Brooklands	S	$30
Clarke R M	Studebaker Cars 1923-1939	80	145	Brooklands	Brooklands	S	$30
Clarke R M	TVR 1960-1980	82	105	Brooklands	Brooklands	S	$30
Clarke R M	Porsche Cars 1957-1960	79	136	Brooklands	Brooklands	S	$30
Clarke R M	Porsche Cars 1952-1956	79	136	Brookalnds	Brooklands	S	$30
Clarke R M	MG MGB GT 1965-1980	80	131	Brooklands	Brooklands	S	$30
Clarke R M	Armstrong Siddeley Cars 1945-1960	72	105	Brooklands	Brooklands	S	$30
Clarke R M	MG Cars in the Thirties	62	131	Brooklands	Brooklands	S	$30
Clarke R M	Bentley Cars 1919-1929	69	139	Brooklands	Brooklands	S	$30
Clarke R M	Jaguar XJ6 Series II 1973-1979	85	127	Brooklands	Brooklands	S	$30
Clarke R M	Lotus Elite & Eclat 1974-1981	82	129	Brooklands	Brooklands	S	$30
Clarke R M	AC Cobra 1962-1969	80	109	Brooklands	Brooklands	S	$30
Clarke R M	Triumph 2000 2.5 2500 1963-1977	86	146	Brooklands	Brooklands	S	$30
Clarke R M	Pontiac Firebird 1967-73	82	138	Brooklands	Brooklands	S	$30
Clarke R M	Lotus Elan Collection No 2 1963-72	83	129	Brooklands	Brooklands	S	$20

Author	Title	Pub date	Subjects	Publisher	Series	Bind	Price
Clarke R M	Triumph TR6 Collection No 1 1969-83	84	146	Brooklands	Brooklands	S	$20
Clarke R M	MGA Collection #1 1955-1982	84	131	Brooklands	Brooklands	S	$20
Clarke R M	Austin Seven in Thirties	70	105	Brooklands	Brooklands	S	$30
Clarke R M	Bentley Cars 1929-1934	69	139	Brooklands	Brooklands	S	$30
Clarke R M	Bentley Cars 1945-1950	71	139	Brooklands	Brooklands	S	$30
Clarke R M	Corvette Cars 1955-1964	79	114	Brooklands	Brooklands	S	$30
Clarke R M	MG Cars 1935-1940	69	131	Brooklands	Brooklands	S	$30
Clarke R M	MG Cars 1940-1947	68	131	Brooklands	Brooklands	S	$30
Clarke R M	MG Cars 1948-1951	69	131	Brooklands	Brooklands	S	$30
Clarke R M	Morgan Cars 1960-1970	79	164	Brooklands	Brooklands	S	$30
Clarke R M	Rolls-Royce Cars 1930-1935	69	139	Brooklands	Brooklands	S	$40
Clarke R M	Rolls-Royce Cars 1935-1940	70	139	Brooklands	Brooklands	S	$40
Clarke R M	Singer Sports Cars 1933-1954	79	105	Brooklands	Brooklands	C	$30
Clarke R M	Rover 3/3.5 litre 1958-1973	84	105	Brooklands	Brooklands	S	$30
Clarke R M	Mercedes 350/450SL & SLC 1971-1980	85	130	Brooklands	Brooklands	S	$30
Clarke R M	Mercury Muscle Cars 1966-1971	84	166	Brooklands	Brooklands	S	$30
Clarke R M	Lotus Seven 1957-1980	81	129	Brooklands	Brooklands	S	$30
Clarke R M	Vintage Bentley Book	62	139	Brooklands	Brooklands	S	$40
Clarke R M	Jensen Cars 1967-1979	80	105	Brooklands	Brooklands	S	$30
Clarke R M	MG Cars Early Years	69	131	Brooklands	Brooklands	S	$40
Clarke R M	Jensen Interceptor 1966-1976	80	105	Brooklands	Brooklands	S	$30
Clarke R M	Morgan Cars 1936-1960	79	164	Brooklands	Brooklands	S	$30
Clarke R M	Rolls-Royce in Thirties	60	139	Brooklands	Brooklands	S	$40
Clarke R M	Chevrolet Camaro Coll No 1 1967-73	85	111	Brooklands	Brooklands	S	$20
Clarke R M	Rover 3500 1968-1977	86	105	Brooklands	Brooklands	S	$30
Clarke R M	Rover 2000 + 2200 1963-1977	84	105	Brooklands	Brooklands	S	$30
Clarke R M	Corvair 1959-1968	84	113	Brooklands	Brooklands	S	$30
Clarke R M	Porsche 928 Collection #1	82	136	Brooklands	Brooklands	S	$20
Clarke R M	Lotus Seven Collection No 1 1957-82	82	129	Brooklands	Brooklands	S	$20
Clarke R M	Mini-Cooper 1961-1971	81	171	Brooklands	Brooklands	S	$30
Clarke T C	Index Rolls-Royce/Bent Periodicals		139	Transport Bookman		S	$20
Claro J	Herbie Goes Bananas	80	150	Scholastic		S	$10
Clausager A D	Le Mans (Clausager)	82	206	Barker		H	$60
Clausager A D	MG Book of Car	82	131	Gallery/Smith/Winchmore		H	$20
Clavel B	Victory at Le Mans Hour by Hour....	71	206	Editions Laffont/Delacort		H	$50
Clayton M	Jeep (Clayton)	82	117	David & Charles		H	$40
Cleary J	Green Helmet	57	207	Fontana		X	$30
Clendenin D	Road & T Road Test/BG Ann 1985	85	410	CBS		S	$20
Cleveland R M	Road is Yours Story of Auto & Men	51	401	Greystone		H	$20
Clew J	Suzuki	80	606	Haynes		H	$30
Clew J	Best Twin Story of Douglas Mtcycl	74	606	Goose		H	$50
Clew J	Lucky All My Life	79	404	Haynes		H	$40
Clew J	Francis Beart Single Purpose	78	610	Haynes		H	$40
Clew J	KSS Velocette Super Profile	84	606	Haynes	Super Profile	H	$20
Clew J	Haynes First 25 Years	85	418	Haynes		H	$30
Clifford P	Motocourse 1981-1982	81	608	Hazleton		H	$70
Clifford P	Motocourse 1983-1984	83	608	Hazleton		H	$150
Clifford P	Motocourse 1980-1981	80	608	Hazleton		H	$125
Clifford P	Motocourse 1982-1983	82	608	Hazleton		H	$70
Clifford P	Motocourse 1984-1985	84	608	Hazleton		H	$60
Clifton P	Fastest Men on Earth	64	211	Day		H	$40
Clutton C	Profile No 61 Italias/Racing1907-08	67	118	Profile Publications		S	$20
Clutton C/Bird P/Harding	Vintage Motor Car Pocketbook	59	401	Batsford		H	$20
Clutton C/Posthumus C/DJ	Racing Car Development & Design	56	202	Batsford		X	$50
Clutton C/Stanford J	Vintage Motor Car	54+	401	Batsford		S	$10
Clymer F	Indianapolis 1953 Yearbook	53	208	Clymer		S	$90
Clymer F	Indianapolis 1958 Yearbook	59	208	Clymer		S	$150
Clymer F	Indianapolis 1960 Yearbook		208	Clymer			$180
Clymer F	Treasury of Motorcycles of World	65	601	McGraw Hill/Bonanza		H	$30
Clymer F	Treasury of Early Am Autos 1877-25	50	403	McGraw		H	$20
Clymer F	Cars of Stars & Movie Memories	54	509	Clymer		S	$30
Clymer F	Henrys Wonderful Model T 1908-1927	55	122	Clymer/McGraw/Bonanza		H	$40
Clymer F	Indianapolis 1951 Yearbook	51	208	Clymer		S	$90
Clymer F	Indianapolis 1950 Yearbook	50	208	Clymer		S	$90
Clymer F	Indianapolis 1946 Yearbook supp'm't	46	208	Clymer		S	$30
Clymer F	Indianapolis 1947 Yearbook	47	208	Clymer		S	$40
Clymer F	Indianapolis 1948 Yearbook supp'm't	48	208	Clymer		S	$50
Clymer F	Floyd Clymer Hist S/B 1899	55	401	Clymer		S	$30
Clymer F	Floyd Clymer Hist S/B Vol 1 Foreign	55	414	Clymer		S	$20
Clymer F	Kaiser-Frazer Cars Clymer Test Rpt	47	158	Clymer		S	$40
Clymer F	Floyd Clymer Catalog 1950 Autos	50	403	Clymer		S	$30
Clymer F	Indianapolis 1957 Yearbook	58	208	Clymer		X	$90
Clymer F	Indianapolis 1959 Yearbook	59	208	Clymer		X	$100
Clymer F	Floyd Clymer Hist S/B Steam V1	45	414	Clymer/Bonanaza/Clymer		H	$40
Clymer F	Treasury of Foreign Cars	57	401	Clymer/Bonanza		H	$30
Clymer F	Those Wonderful Old Automobiles	53	401	Clymer/Bonanza		H	$20
Clymer F	Indianapolis 1961 Yearbook	62	208	Clymer		S	$100
Clymer F	Indianapolis 1967 Yearbook	67	208	Clymer		X	$50

Author	Title	Pub date	Subjects		Publisher	Series	Bind	Price
Clymer F	Floyd Clymer Catalog 1929 Cars	50S	403		Clymer		S	$30
Clymer F	Floyd Clymer Hist S/B Ford Mod T		122		Clymer		S	$30
Clymer F	Floyd Clymer Hist Motor Scrap Bk#1S	44	401		Clymer		S	$50
Clymer F	Indianapolis 1964 Yearbook	64	208		Clymer		S	$50
Clymer F	Indianapolis 1965 Yearbook	65	208		Clymer		X	$50
Clymer F	Floyd Clymer Hist Motor Scrap Bk#1H	44	401		Clymer		H	$30
Clymer F	Floyd Clymer Hist Motor Scrap Bk#2	44	401		Clymer		X	$30
Clymer F	Floyd Clymer Hist Motor Scrap Bk#3	46	401		Clymer		X	$30
Clymer F	Floyd Clymer Hist Motor Scrap Bk#4	47	401		Clymer		H	$30
Clymer F	Floyd Clymer Hist Motor Scrap Bk#5	48	401		Clymer		H	$30
Clymer F	Floyd Clymer Hist Motor Scrap Bk#6	50	401		Clymer		H	$30
Clymer F	Floyd Clymer Hist Motor Scrap Bk#7	54	401		Clymer		H	$30
Clymer F	Indianapolis 1955 Yearbook	55	208		Clymer		S	$90
Clymer F	Indianapolis 1956 Yearbook	57	208		Clymer		S	$100
Clymer F	Indianapolis 1952 Yearbook	52	208		Clymer		S	$125
Clymer F	Indianapolis 1954 Yearbook	54	208		Clymer		S	$90
Clymer F	Indianapolis 1949 Yearbook	49	208		Clymer		X	$30
Clymer F	Floyd Clymer Hist Motor Scrap Bk#8	50S	401		Clymer		S	$30
Clymer F	Floyd Clymer Hist S/B For Mtcyl V1	55	606		Clymer		S	$40
Clymer F	Floyd Clymer Catalog 1909 Cars	58	403		Clymer		S	$30
Clymer F	Floyd Clymer Catalog 1918 Cars	50S	403		Clymer		S	$30
Clymer F	Comp Catalog Japanese Motor Veh	61	420		Clymer		S	$50
Clymer F	Mobilgas Economy Run 1951	51	209		Clymer		S	$20
Clymer F	Mobilgas Economy Run 1952	52	209		Clymer		S	$20
Clymer F	Mobilgas Economy Run 1953	53	209		Clymer		S	$20
Clymer F	Mobilgas Economy Run 1954	54	209		Clymer		S	$20
Clymer F	Floyd Clymer Catalog 1912 Cars	55	403		Clymer		S	$30
Clymer F	Indianapolis 1966 Yearbook	66	208		Clymer		X	$50
Clymer F	Floyd Clymer Catalog 1921 Cars	58	403		Clymer		S	$30
Clymer F	Floyd Clymer Catalog 1914 Cars	58	403		Clymer		S	$30
Clymer F	Floyd Clymer Catalog 1924 Cars	58	403		Clymer		S	$30
Clymer F	Floyd Clymer Catalog 1927 Cars	55	403		Clymer		S	$30
Clymer F	Floyd Clymer Alb Hist Stm Trac Eng	49	903		Clymer/Bonanza		H	$20
Cogan R	Hot Rod Bodywork & Painting 1988	88	405		Petersen		S	$10
Cohn D L	Combustion on Wheels	44	419		Houghton Mifflin		H	$20
Coker A J	Renault Dauphine Cars	63	120		Pearson	Car Maint	H	$20
Coker/Hemmings	Motor Engineers Pocket Book	52	405		George Newnes		H	$30
Cole L	Ford Panel Vans	80	156		Ian Henry	Transport Ser	H	$20
Coleman B	Corvette (Coleman)	83+	114		Wncmr/Smith/Gallery/CP		H	$20
Coleman B	Motocourse 1978-1979	79	608		Hazleton		H	$350
Coleman B	Motocourse 1979-1980	80	608		Hazleton		H	$180
Coleman B	Kenny Roberts	82	610		Weidenfeld		H	$60
Collier P/Horowitz D	Fords American Epic	87	415		Summit		H	$20
Collins H R	Presidents on Wheels	71	401		Acropolis/Bonanza		H	$40
Collins R	Great Way to Go Auto in Canada	69	413		Collins/Ryerson		H	$50
Colombo G	Pininfarina #09 Yearbook (Italian)	68	501		Pininfarina S.p.A		H	$100
Colombo G	Pininfarina #06 Yearbook (Italian)	65	501		Pininfarina		S	$100
Colombo G	Le Origini del Mito	85	121		Sansoni/Autocritica		H	$80
Colombo M	Moto Guzzi Genius & Sport	83	606		Automobilia		H	$40
Colombo M/Patrignani R	Moto Oggi (Italian)	71	601		L'Editrice dell Auto		S	$20
Coltrin P	Automotive Photog. of Peter Coltrin	78	297	510	Barnes		S	$40
Coltrin P/Marchet J-F	Lamborghini Miura	82	128		Osprey		H	$90
Conde J	American Motors Family Album	69+	102		American Motors Corp.		S	$30
Conde J	Cars That Hudson Built	80	163		Arnold-Porter		H	$60
Conde J	Rambler Family Album	61	102		American Motors		S	$30
Conde J	Nash Family Album	54	158		Nash		S	$30
Condie A T	New Fordson Album	85	904		Trent Valley		S	$40
Congdon K	Motorcycle Books Critical Survey	87	601		Scarecrow Press		H	$30
Conley A L	Sports Cars Facts and Pictures	54	401		Greenberg		H	$40
Connery/Davis/Dymock...	Exciting World of Jackie Stewart	74	205		Collins		H	$30
Constanduros B	Kimberley GP Team Gd 14 McLaren		298		Kimberley's		S	$20
Constanduros B	Kimberley GP Team Gd 02 Brabham	82	298		Kimberley's		S	$20
Constanduros B	Kimberley GP Team Gd 04 Renault	83	120		Kimberley's		S	$20
Constanduros B	Kimberley GP Team Gd 06 Lotus	83	129		Kimberley's		S	$20
Constanduros B	Kimberley GP Team Gd 08 Alfa Romeo	83	101		Kimberley's		S	$20
Constanduros B	Kimberley GP Team Gd 01 Williams	82	298		Kimberley's		S	$20
Constanduros B	Kimberley GP Team Gd 11 Williams	84	298		Kimberley's		S	$20
Constanduros B	Kimberley GP Team Gd 12 Brabham	80S	298		Kimberley's		S	$20
Constanduros B	Kimberley GP Team Gd 05 McLaren	80S	298		Kimberley's		S	$20
Constanduros B	Keke Rosberg (Constanduros)	84	205		Kimberley's		S	$10
Constanduros B	Kimberley GP Team Gd 03 Ferrari	83	121		Kimberley's		S	$30
Constanduros B	Formula One YB 1988 (FIA) #2	87	204		Grid		H	$90
Constanduros B	Kimberley Driver Prfl 02 Derek Bell	85	205		Kimberley's		S	$20
Consumer Gd	Great Cars of Fifties	85	403		Publications Intl		H	$20
Consumer Gd	Grease Machines	78	422		Pub Intl/Crown/Beekman		H	$20
Consumer Gd	Corvette Past Present Future	84	114		Publications Intl	Consumer Guide	H	$10
Consumer Gd	New 1984 Corvette(Consumer Guide)	83	114		Pub Intl		S	$10
Consumer Gd	Datsun Z-Cars (Consumer Guide)	81	167		Pub Intl/Castle	Consumer Guide	H	$30

Author	Title	Pub date	Subjects		Publisher	Series	Bind	Price
Consumer Gd	Elite Cars Fastest and Finest	87	401		Publications Intl	Consumer Gd	H	$20
Consumer Gd	American Sports Car (Consumer Gd)	79	403		Publications Intl/Crown		H	$20
Consumer Gd	Car Spotters Encyclopedia 1940-80	82	401		Publications Int		S	$40
Consumer Gd	Cars of 50s	78	403		Pub Int/Crown	Consumer Guide	X	$30
Consumer Gd	Great Cars of Forties	85	403		Publications Intl		H	$20
Consumer Gd	Great Cars of Sixties	85	403		Publications Intl		H	$20
Consumer Gd	Big Trucks (Consumer Gd)	77	306		Publications Intl/Crown		X	$20
Consumer Gd	Model Cars (Consumer Gd)	78	704		Pub Intl/Harper/Beekman		X	$20
Consumer Gd	Cars of 40s	79	403		Pub Intl/Crown/Beekman	Consumer Gd	X	$30
Consumer Gd	Elite Cars Exciting Look Exp.......	80	401		Publications Intl	Consumer Gd	S	$10
Consumer Gd	Cars of 30s	80	403		Publications Intl		H	$30
Consumer Gd	Competition Corvette	80	114		Publications Intl		S	$10
Consumer Gd	Chevrolet 1955-1957	87	111		Publications Intl/Crown		H	$20
Consumer Gd	Porsche 911 (Consumer Guide)	87	136		Publications Intl	Consumer Guide	H	$20
Consumer Gd	Nineteen-57 Cars	80	403		Publications Intl	Consumer Guide	S	$20
Consumer Gd	Ferrari Spts/Rac Rd Cars(Cons Gd) S	83	121		Publications Intl	Consumer Gd	S	$20
Consumer Gd	Cars of 60s	79	403		Pub Int/Crown/Beekman	Consumer Gd	X	$20
Consumer Gd	Camaro Full Story of Chevrolets....	83	111		Publications Intl	Consumer GGuide	S	$10
Consumer Gd	Corvette Americas Only True Spts Cr	78	114		Publications Intl/Mayflwr	Consumer Gd	H	$10
Consumer Gd	Fifty Years of American Automobiles	89	403		Pub Intl/Crown/Beekman		H	$80
Consumer Guide	Prototype Cars Cars That Never Were	81	401		Consumer Gd		S	$20
Conway H G	Grand Prix Bugatti	68+	107		Foulis/Haynes/Bentley		H	$100
Conway H G	Profile No 41 Type 57 Bugatti	66	107		Profile Publications		S	$20
Conway H G/Greilsamer J	Bugatti (Conway & Greilsamer)	78+	107		Editions Modelisme		H	$125
Conway H G/v Fersen H H..	Die Bugattis Automobile Mobil......	83	107		Christians Verlag		H	$125
Cook T	Vans and the Truckin' Life	77	307		Abrams		S	$20
Cooper J/Bentley J	John Cooper Grand Prix Carpetbagger	77	205		Haynes/Doubleday		H	$40
Cooper-Evans M	Risk Life Risk Limb	68	205		Pelham		H	$40
Cooper-Evans M	Private Entrant Racing Rob Walker	65	298		Cassell/MBC		H	$50
Copeland E M	Overland by Auto in 1913	81	212		Indiana Historical Soc		S	$30
Coram D	Aston Martin 1 1/2 International	73	103		Horseless Carriage	Sports Car Peop	S	$50
Coram D	Aston Martin Story of a Sports Car	57	103		MRP		H	$300
Coram D	Profile No 33 AstonMartin 1 1/2 Int	67	103		Profile Publications		S	$20
Corle E	John Studebaker American Dream	48	145		Dutton		H	$40
Corry F	Automobile Treasury of Ireland	79	401		Dalton Watson		H	$30
Corson R	Champions at Speed	79	205 213		Dodd Mead		H	$20
Cosentino A S	Faza/Car Graphic Abarth Guide	84	151		Nigensha		H	$180
Costin M/Phipps D	Racing & Sports Car Chassis Design	61+	202		Batsford/Bentley		H	$40
Cotton M	Porsche (Cotton)	82	136		Col Lib/Crown/Crescent		H	$20
Cotton M	Porsche 917 Kimberley Rac S/C Gd 1	87	136		Kimberley		S	$30
Cottrill P K	Automobile Ads List - Life 60-69	80	503		Rigel		S	$20
Coulter J	Lamborghini Countach World S/C #2	85	128		Albion Scott/Moto-Art	World Super Car	H	$50
Couper M	Rallying to Monte Carlo	56+	209		Ian Allan Ltd/SBC		H	$20
Courtel C	Ten Ans de Coupe Gordini Tome 2		120		Editions Michael Hommell		S	$30
Courtney G	Power Behind Aston Martin	78	103		Oxford Ill		H	$40
Crabb R	Birth of Giant Men & Incidents...	69	418		Chilton		H	$30
Craft Q	Old Car Value Guide	68	401		Quentin Craft	SemiAnnual	S	$30
Craft Q	Old Car Value Guide Vol. 2-4	70	401		Quentin Craft	SemiAnnual	S	$20
Craft Q	Old Car Value Guide Vol 3-1	71	401		Quentin Craft	Semi Annual	S	$20
Craft Q	Old Car Value Guide Vol. 3-2	72	401		Quentin Craft	Semi Annual	S	$20
Craft Q	Old Car Value Guide Vol. 4-1	73	401		Quentin Craft	SemiAnnual	S	$20
Crane L C	Vintage Racer No 07	81	204		General Racing Limited		S	$20
Crane L C	Vintage Racer No 12	83	204		General Racing		S	$20
Cray E	Chrome Colossus GM & Its Times	80	160		McGraw		H	$40
Creighton J	Comp Gd to Volvo 1800 Series	82	165		Dalton Watson		H	$40
Creighton J	Fire Engines of Europe	80	302		Ian Henry	Transport	H	$20
Creighton J	Fire Engines of United Kingdom	81	302		Ian Henry	Transport	H	$20
Creighton J	Volvo Cars & Commercial Vehicles	82	165		Ian Henry	Transport Ser	H	$30
Crombac G	Cars in Profile 10 Matra MS80	73	120 298		Profile Publications		S	$10
Croucher R	Story of BMW Motorcycles	82	606		PSL		H	$40
Crow C	City of Flint Grows Up	45	108		Harper		H	$30
Crow J T	Stories of Road & Track	70	401		Bond Parkhurst		H	$30
Crow J T	ARRC 1970 American Rd Rac Champions	71	204		Boojum Books		S	$20
Crow J T/Warren C A	Four Wheel Drive Handbook	70	311 309		Bond-Parkhust		S	$20
Crump R/de la Rive Box R	Maserati Road Cars	79	172		Barnes/Osprey		H	$90
Culpepper L	Collectors Cars (Culpepper)	79	401		Octopus		H	$20
Culshaw D/Hoffobin P	Comp Catalogue of British Cars	74	406		Walter Parrish/Morrow		H	$150
Cummins C L	My Days with Diesel	67	404		Chilton		H	$60
Cummins C L	Diesels from Woodshed	70	404		SAE		S	$20
Currie B	Motor Cycling in 1930s	81	601		Hamlyn		H	$30
Currie B	Great British Motorcycles of 50s	80	606		Hamlyn		H	$30
Cutter R	Ency of Auto Racing Greats	73	297		Prentice		H	$90
Cutting R	Motor-Mania	69	404		Rand		H	$20
D'Angelo S	World Cars '62(World Car Catalogue)	62	410		LEA		H	$180
D'Angelo S	World Cars '63(World Car Catalogue)	63	410		LEA		H	$180
D'Angelo S	World Cars '64(World Car Catalogue)	64	410		Auto Club Italy/Herald		H	$125
D'Angelo S	World Cars '66(World Car Catalogue)	66	410		Auto Club Italy/Herald		H	$125
D'Angelo S	World Cars '68(World Car Catalogue)	68	410		Auto Club Italy/Herald		H	$125

Author	Title	Pub date	Subjects		Publisher	Series	Bind	Price
D'Angelo S	World Cars '69(World Car Catalogue)	69	410		Auto Club Italy/Herald		H	$125
D'Angelo S	World Cars '65(World Car Catalogue)	65	410		Auto Club Italy/Herald		H	$125
D'Angelo S	World Cars '67(World Car Catalogue)	67	410		Auto Club Italy/Herald		H	$125
D'Angelo S	World Cars '63-Italian	63	410		LEA		H	$80
D'Argenzio R	Enciclopedia Ferrari (Italian)	85	121		Casa Editrice		S	$30
Da Costa P	Fire Fighting Apparatus 100 Yrs Am	64	302		Floyd Clymer		S	$40
Da Costa P	One Hundred Yrs Am Fire Fight Ap(H)	64	302		Clymer/Bonanza/Crown		X	$20
Da Costa P	Seagrave Fire Apparatus 1900-1930	78	302		Apache Press			$30
Dahlinger J C	Secret Life of Henry Ford	78	415		Bobbs-Merrill		H	$30
Daley R	Cars at Speed	61	297		Foulis/Collier/Lippincott		X	$30
Daley R	Cruel Sport	63	297		Prentice/Studio V/Crown		H	$90
Daley R	Fast One (novel)	78	207		Crown		H	$20
Dallison K	Spirit Celebrating 75 Yrs of R-R...	79	139	504	Spirit Group		H	$300
Dalrymple M	Is Bug Dead? Great Beetle Ad.......	82	150	503	Stewart Tabori Chang		S	$30
Dalton L	Those Elegant Rolls-Royce	67	139		Dalton Watson	Dalton Watson	H	$80
Dalton L	London Motor Show 1930	70	401		Dalton Watson	Dalton Watson	H	$40
Dalton L	Rolls-Royce Elegance Continues	71+	139		Dalton Watson	Dalton Watson	H	$180
Dalton L	Coachwork on Rolls-Royce 1906-1939	75	139		Dalton Watson	Dalton Watson	H	$100
Dammann G H	Fifty Years of Lincoln Mercury	71	166	161	Crestline	Crestline	H	$40
Dammann G H	Sixty Years of Chevrolet	72	111		Crestline	Crestline	H	$40
Dammann G H	Seventy Years of Chrysler	74	112		Crestline	Crestline	H	$80
Daniels J	Citroen SM Autohistory	81	153		Osprey	Autohistory	H	$50
Daniels J	British Leyland Truth About Cars	80	105		Osprey		H	$60
Daniels J	Colorful World of Motorsport	80	297		Octopus		H	$20
Daninos J	Facel Vega Excellence......(French)		120		EPA	Grand Tourisme	H	$40
Darack A	Playboy Book of Sports Car Repair	80	405		Wideview		S	$10
Dark H E	Auto Engines of Tomorrow	75	405		Indiana		H	$30
Dark H E	Wankel Rotary Engine Intro & Guide	74	405		Indiana		H	$40
Davey K/May	Lagonda History of Marque	78	105		David & Charles		H	$100
Davey K/Pritchard A	Profile No 12 Ferrari Tipo 625&555	66	121		Profile Publications		S	$30
Davey K/Pritchard A	Profile No 66 Cooper-Bristol F2	67	298		Profile Publications		S	$10
Davey K/Pritchard A	Profile No 84 Ferrari Tipo 340/375	67	121		Profile Publications		S	$30
Davidson C P	MG Cars	58	131		Pearson/Arco	Car Maintenance	H	$20
Davidson D	USAC 1972 Yearbook	72	204		USAC		S	$50
Davidson D	USAC 1972 Yearbook (Fawcett Ed)	72	204		Fawcett		S	$40
Davidson D	USAC 1976 (75 season) News Media Gd	76	204		USAC		S	$50
Davidson D	USAC 1977 (76 season) News Media Gd	77	204		USAC		S	$50
Davidson D	Marlboro Salute 75th Anniv Indy 500	86	208		Marlboro		H	$30
Davidson D	Indianapolis 1968 Yearbook	68	208		Clymer		S	$50
Davies J/Annakin K/Searle	Those Daring Young Men in their J..	69	213	209	Putnam		H	$20
Davies P	Tuning Datsuns	78	167		Speedsport		S	$20
Davies P	Tuning Four Cylinder Fords	71+	156		SpeedSport		S	$30
Davies R A	Story of Black Beauty	81	139		Carlton		H	$40
Davis D E	Car and Driver Racing Annual 66-67	67	204		Ziff-Davis		S	$30
Davis P	Wonderful Wheels	72	401		Angus & Robertson Aust		H	$10
Davis S C H	Rallies and Trials	51	209		Iliffe & Sons, Ltd		H	$30
Davis S C H	Motor Racing (Lonsdale - Davis)	57	297		Seeley		H	$60
Davis S C H	Racing Motorist	49	298		Iliffe		H	$30
Davis S C H	Mercedes-Benz (Davis)	56	130		Muller		H	$60
Davis S C H	Car Driving as Art	52	203		Iliffe		H	$20
Davis S C H	Atalanta	55	205		Foulis		H	$60
Davis S C H	Great British Drivers	57	205		Hamish Hamilton		H	$40
Davis S C H	Cars Cars Cars Cars	67	401		Hamlyn		H	$20
Davis S C H	John Cobb Story		205	211	Foulis		H	$50
Davis S C H	Motor Racing (Davis)	32	139	205	Iliffe		H	$80
Davis S C H	More Sketches by Casque	30S	298	504	Iliffe		H	$80
Davis S C H	Controlling Racing Car Team	51	298		Foulis		H	$30
Davis S C H/Crosby G	Endless Quest for Speed 1-portfolio	46	504		Autocar		S	$150
Davis S C H/Crosby G	Endless Quest for Speed 2-portfolio	46	504		Autocar		S	$150
Davis S C H/Walkerley R	Monte Carlo Rally (Castrol) 1954	54	209		Castrol		S	$30
Davison G S	T T Tales & other stories	50	603		T T Special		H	$70
Davison G S	Story of Manx	48	606		TT Special		H	$60
Davison G S	Story of Ulster	49	603		TT Special		H	$60
Davison G S	Racing Through Century		603		TT Special		H	$50
Davison G S	Racing Year	50	603		T T Special		H	$60
Davison G S	Story of TT	47	603		TT Special		H	$50
Davison G S	Racing Game (Davison)	56	603		Clymer		S	$20
Davison G S/Heath P	Million Miles of Racing	50	603		T T Special		H	$70
Davison G S/Heath P	Short Circuits!	51	603		T T Special		H	$70
Davy J R	Standard Car 1903-1963 Ill Hist	67	105		Sherbourne Press		H	$60
Dawes N T	Packard 1942-1962	75	159		Barnes		H	$70
Day D	Comp Bk Karting	61	214		Prentice-Hall		H	$30
Day J	Motor Car Bosch Book of	75+	405		Berkeley/St Martins		H	$20
Day J R	Story of London Bus	73			London Transport		H	$20
De Agostini C	Gilles Vivo (Italian)	83	205		Conti Editore		H	$70
De Agostini C	Tazio Vivo (Italian)	87	205		Conti Editore		H	$70
De Buron N	Bride and Bugatti(fiction)	58	107		Harvill/Norton		H	$40
De Campi J W	Rolls-Royce in America	75	139		Dalton Watson	Dalton Watson	H	$60

Author	Title	Pub date	Subjects		Publisher	Series	Bind	Price
De Paolo P	Wall Smacker	35	205		Thompson/De Paolo		H	$125
De Serres O	Traction Avant 7-11-15-22	84	153		EPA		H	$80
De la Plante A	Villeneuve	82	205		Macmillan/Gage		S	$40
DeLorean J Z	DeLorean	85	168		Zondervan		H	$40
DeLorean J Z/Wright J P	On A Clear Day YCS General Motors	79	160		Wright/Avon		X	$30
DeWaard E J	Fins & Chrome American Autos of 50s	82	403		Bison		H	$30
Dees M L	Miller Dynasty	81	158		Barnes		H	$450
Dejean P	Bugatti Carlo-Rembrandt-Ettore ...	82	107		Rizzoli Int. Pub.		H	$200
Demand C	Motor Racing Sketchbook	50S	297	504	Foulis		H	$125
Demand C/Rosemann E	Big Race	56	297	504	Bentley		H	$125
Demaus A B	Lionel Martin Biography	80	103		Transport Bookman		H	$40
Demaus A B	Victorian and Edwdn Cyclng/Motoring	77	401	510	Batsford		H	$30
Denison M	Power to Go Story of Auto Industry	56	419		Doubleday		H	$20
Derr T S	Modern Steam Car and Its Background	45	414		Clymer		S	$20
Deschenaux J	Jo Siffert	72	205		Kimber		H	$50
Desmond K	Man with Two Shadows Story Ascari	81	205		Proteus/Scribner		H	$30
Dethlefsen D	Superfast Type 410 Superamerica	78	121		Dethlefsen		S	$30
Dethlefsen D	Ferrari Type 212 (profile)	76	121		Dethlefsen		S	$30
Dethlefsen D	Ferrari Type 195 Sport (profile)	77	121		Dethlefsen		S	$30
Deutsch J G	Selling the Peoples Cadillac Edsel	76	158		Yale		H	$40
Devaney J & B	Indianapolis 500(Devaney)	76	208		Rand McNally		H	$60
Devlin R T	Pebble Beach Matter of Style	80	206		Newport Press		H	$150
Dexler P R	Yesterdays Cars	79	424		Lerner		H	$10
Di Ruffia C B	Auto 1954	53	410		Alfieri Editore/Tudor		H	$80
Di Ruffia C B	Auto 1953	52	410		Alfieri Editore		H	$80
Di Ruffia C B	Auto 1956	56	410		Alfieri Editore/Tudor		H	$80
Di Sirignano G	Car Mascots Enthusiasts Guide	77	507		Crescent		H	$80
Diesel E	From Engines to Autos 5 Pioneers	60	404		Regnery		H	$40
Dinarich M	Style Auto - 37 (English) (last)	78	508		Style Auto		H	$30
Dinarich M	Style Auto - 29 (English)	71	508		Style Auto		H	$30
Dinarich M	Style Auto - 16 (English)	68	508		Style Auto		S	$50
Dinarich M	Style Auto - 20 (English)	69	508		Style Auto		H	$60
Dinarich M	Style Auto - 09 (English)	65	508		Style Auto		S	$50
Dinarich M	Style Auto - 13 (English)	67	508		Style Auto		H	$50
Dinarich M	Style Auto - 17 (English)	68	508		Style Auto		H	$50
Dinarich M	Style Auto - 21 (English)	69	508		Style Auto		H	$40
Dinkel J	Road & T III Auto Dictionary	77	405		Norton		H	$20
Disney C	Shell Hist of African Safari Rally	66	209		E African Pub House		S	$60
Ditchburn B	Superbiking	83	601		Osprey		S	$20
Ditzel P C	Fire Engines Firefighters	76	302		Rutledge/Crown		H	$30
Ditzel P C	Comp Bk Fire Engines	82	302		Publications Intl	Consumer Gd	S	$10
Dobbins M F	Camaro 67-69 Fact Book	84	111		Dobbins		X	$40
Dollfus A	Delage (French)	84	120		EPA	Toute L'Hist	S	$30
Domark K J	HT Build Racing Car	49	202		Clymer		S	$40
Dominguez H	Ford Agency Pictorial History	81	122		MBI		S	$30
Donaldson E	Le Mans Starring Steve McQueen	71	206	509	Aurora		S	$20
Donaldson G	Grand Prix of Canada	84	206		Avon		S	$30
Donnelly	David Brown's	60	103	904	Collins		H	$125
Donohue M/Van Valkenburgh	Unfair Advantage	75	205		Dodd,Mead		H	$300
Donovan F	Wheels for Nation	65	419		Crowell		H	$20
Dooks C R	Model Cars You Threw Away	78	702		Transport Bookmen		S	$10
Dorson R	Indy 500 American Inst Under Fire	74	208		Bond/Parkhurst		H	$40
Douglas A	Motoring Annual (1957)	57	410		Ian Allen		H	$30
Dove S L	Buick Gran Sports GS Enthusiast....	89	108		Muscle Car Pubs		S	$40
Dowdeswell J	Morgan Four Wheeler Workshop Manual		164		Dowdeswell		S	$40
Doyle G R	Worlds Automobiles 1880-1958	59	412		Temple		H	$40
Drackett P	International Motor Racing Bk #4	70	204		Souvenir Press		H	$20
Drackett P	Classic Mercedes-Benz(Drackett)	83	130		Exeter/Bookthrift/Bison		H	$20
Drackett P	Ency of Motorcar	79+	401		Mandarin/Octopus/Crown		H	$40
Drackett P	Brabham Story of Racing Team	85	298		Weidenfeld/Barker		H	$50
Drackett P	All Color World of Cars	79	401		Mandarin/Octopus		H	$10
Drackett P	International Motor Racing Bk #3	69	204		Souvenir		H	$20
Drackett P	International Motor Racing Bk(#1)	67	204		Souvenir Press		H	$30
Drackett P	Like Father Like Son M & D Campbell	69	205	211	Clifton		H	$30
Drackett P	International Motor Racing Bk #2	68	204		Souvenir		H	$20
Draper C	Salmson Story	74	120		David & Charles		H	$30
Draper K G	Two Stroke Engine Design & Tuning	60+	609		Foulis/Autobooks		X	$40
Drie H v	Harley-Davidson in Nederland	83	607		Big-Twin		H	$50
Dudley J	British Road Racing (Dudley)	50	298		Ian Allen/Clymer		S	$30
Dugdale J	Great Motor Sport of Thirties	77	298		Gentry/Two Continents		H	$60
Duguay J	HT Import European Car	85	401		Williamson		S	$30
Dumble D B	Vintage Motorcycles in Australia	75	601		Vintage MC Club Victoria		S	$20
Dumble D B	Classic Motorcycles in Australia	77	601		Dumble		S	$20
Dumont P	French Cars from 1920-1925	78	407		Warne		H	$50
Dumont P	Peugeot Toute L'Histoire	82	120		EPA	Auto Histoire	S	$20
Dumont P	Citroen Great Marque of France	76	153		Interauto/MBI/EPA		H	$100
Dumont P	Bugatti Thoroughbreds From Molsheim	75	107		EPA/MBI/Albion Scott	Prestige.......	H	$125
Dumont P	Les Voitures Francaises de 1920-25	77	407		EPA		H	$40

Author	Title	Pub date	Subjects	Publisher	Series	Bind	Price
Dumont P/Barker R/Tubbs D	Automobiles and Automobiling	65	401 504	Viking/Bonanza/Edita		H	$60
Dunbar C S	Buses Trolleys & Trams	67		Hamlyn		H	$10
Durant M	My Father (Bio of William Durant)	29	404	G P Putnam's Sons		L	$400
Durnford H/Baechler G	Cars of Canada - Craven Foundation	73	413	McClelland & Stewart		H	$150
Dussek I	Profile No 58 H.R.G. 1935-1956	67	105	Profile Publications		S	$10
Dymock E	World of Racing Cars	72	297	Hamlyn		H	$10
Dymock E	Profile No 65 Plus Four Morgan	67	164	Profile Publications		S	$30
Eaglesfield B	Bugatti Book	54	107	MRP		H	$150
Early Ford V-8 Club	V-8 Album	85	122	Early Ford V-8 Club		H	$80
Earwaker N	Travels with 2CV Epic Journey......	88	153	Javelin		S	$30
Eaton G	Ferrari Spts/Rac Rd Cars(Cons Gd) H	82	121	Publications Intl	Consumers Gd	H	$50
Eaton G	Ferrari (Foreword by Niki Lauda)	82	121	Col Lib/Crescent	Colour Library	H	$20
Eaton G	Classic Ferrari (Eaton)	83	121	Exeter/Bison/Bookthrift		H	$20
Eaton G	Profile No 10 Bugatti Type 35 GP	66	107	Profile Publications		S	$30
Eaton Mfg	Chronicle of Auto Ind in Amer 93-46	46	418	Eaton Mfg		S	$40
Echlin J/Gilson C	Its Been An Exciting Ride	89	418	Echlin		H	$20
Eddy P	DeLorean Tapes	84	168	Collins		S	$30
Edison Institute	Henry Ford Highlights of His Life	54	415	Henry Ford Museum		S	$10
Edwards C E	Dynamics of US Automobile Industry	65	419	Univ of SC		H	$40
Edwards H	Morris Cars First 35 Years	78	105	Morris Register		S	$30
Edwards H	Morris Motor Cars 1913-1983	83	105	Moorland		H	$60
Ehrenburg I	Life of Automobile (trnltd fr Russ)	29+	416	Urizen		H	$30
Eisinger L	True's Automobile Yearbook #7 1958	58	410	Fawcett		S	$20
Eisinger L	True's Automobile Yearbook #8 1959	59	410	Fawcett		S	$20
Eisinger L	True's Automobile Yearbook #9 1960	60	410	Fawcett		S	$20
Elfrink H	Special Rac Cars & Hot Rods of Wld	50	297	Clymer		S	$20
Ellis C/Bishop D	Military Transport of World War II	71	308	Blandford/Macmillan		H	$20
Ellis C/Bishop D	Military Transport of World War I	70	308	Blandford/Macmillan		H	$20
Ellis J	Billboards to Buicks Advertising...	68	503 108	Abelard-Schuman		H	$50
Ellis S W	Smogless Days Advntur in 10 Stanley	71	158	Howell-North Books		H	$90
Elmgreen J/Mcgrath T	Jaguar XK in Australia	85	127	JTZ		H	$250
Engel G S	Book of Ford-Powered Perf Cars	67	122	Pocket Books		S	$20
Engel L K	Jackie Stewart World Driving Champ.	70	205	Arco		H	$20
Engel L K	Indianapolis 500(Engel)	70	208	Four Winds		H	$30
Engel L K	Mario Andretti World Driving Champ	70	205	Arco		S	$20
Engel L K	Incredible A J Foyt	70	205	Arco		H	$30
Engel L K	Great Racing Cars & Drivers (Engel)	79	205	Arco		H	$40
Engel L K	Racing to Win Wood Bros Style	74	299	Arco		H	$40
Engel L K	One Hundred 32 Unusual Cars Indy	70	208	Arco		H	$60
Engel L K	Stock Car Racing USA	73	299	Dodd, Mead		H	$30
Engel L K	Comp Bk Stock-Bod Drag Rac H	70	201	Four Winds		H	$30
Engel L K	Comp Bk NASCAR Stk Cr Rac	68	299	Four Winds/Scholastic		X	$30
Engel L K	Comp Bk Fuel & Gas Dragsters	68	201	Four Winds		H	$30
Engel L K	Road Racing in America	71	299	Dodd Mead		H	$30
Engel L K	Comp Bk Stock-Bod Drag Rac S	70	201	Scholastic		S	$10
Engel L K	Comp Motorcycle Book	74	601	Four Winds		H	$20
Engen G	Automotive Self Expression, Kit Car	76	423	Weigen		H	$30
Erskine A R	Hist of Studebaker Corp 1852-23	24	145	Studebaker		H	$100
Eves E	Autocourse 1960-61 Part One	60	204	Trafalgar/Victoria House		S	$180
Eves E	Rolls-Royce 75 Yrs Motoring Exclnc	79	139	Orbis/Chartwell/Book Sale		H	$40
Eves E/Burger D	Great Car Collections of the World	86	401	Multimedia/Smith/Gallery		H	$30
Ewald G	Die Geschichte der Feuers. bis 1945		302	Motorbuch Verlag		H	$50
Ewens G/Ellis M	Cult of Big Rigs	77	306	Quarto/Book Sales/Chrtwl		H	$20
Eyston G E T	Safety Last	75	205	Vincent		H	$40
Eyston G E T	Fastest on Earth	39+	211	Clymer		X	$40
Eyston G E T	Flat Out	33+	211	John Miles		H	$60
Eyston G E T/Bradley W F	Speed on Salt Hist Bonneville......	36+	211	Batsford/Clymer		H	$50
Eyston G E T/Lyndon B	Motor Racing and Record Breaking	35	297	Batsford		H	$100
Fagiuoli/Gerosa	Zagato (Italian)	69	501	Auto Club D'Italia		H	$180
Fairbanks M	Pioneers in Industry Fairbanks M...	45	418 905	Fairbanks		H	$60
Fairweather T	HT Restore w/ Metal Joining Techs	88	405	Osprey	Osprey Rest Gd	H	$30
Faith N	Wankel Curious/Engine Story........	75+	405	Stein and Day/Allen Unwin		H	$40
Falconer T	Chevrolet Corvette 68-82 Autohist..	83	114	Osprey		H	$40
Fallon I/Srodes J	Dream Maker Rise & Fall of DeLorean	83	168	Putnam		H	$40
Fangio J M/Giambertone M	My Twenty Years of Racing	61	205	Temple		H	$60
Fangio J M/Giambertone M	Fangio	63	205	Landsborough/Trust		S	$30
Feather A M	Aston Martin Coll Rd Tests 1921-42	74	103	Feather		H	$30
Feather A M	Aston Martin Coll Rd Tests 1948-59	79	103	Feather		S	$30
Feldman R/Betzold M	End of the Line Autoworkers........	88	419	Weidenfeld		H	$40
Fellows S	Hot Seat Complete Manual of Rally..	84	209	MRP		H	$20
Felsen H G	Street Rod (Felsen - fiction)	53+	201	Random/Bantam		X	$20
Fenner P R	Behind the Wheel Stories of..(juv)	64	213	Morrow		H	$20
Fenu M	Ferrari's Drivers	80	121	Kimber		H	$30
Ferodo	Ferodo Story 1897-1957	57	418	Ferodo		H	$30
Ferrari E	Piloti che gente 1E	83	121	Enzo Ferrari		H	$250
Ferrari E	Ferrari 80 3E (Italian)	81	121	Enzo Ferrari		H	$250
Ferrari E	Enzo Ferrari Story Autobiography	63	121	Macmillan/Hamish Hamilton		H	$180
Ferrari E	Enzo Ferrari Memoirs (Hamilton)	63+	121	Hamilton		H	$125

Author	Title	Pub date	Subjects		Publisher	Series	Bind	Price
Ferrari E	Piloti che gente 4E	87	121		Enzo Ferrari		H	$700
Ferrari E	Piloti che gente 1E(English)	83	121		Enzo Ferrari		H	$200
Ferrari E	Enzo Ferrari Memoirs (MBC)	63	121		Motoraces Book Club		H	$50
Ferrari E	Ferrari 80 2E (Italian)	80	121		Enzo Ferrari		H	$500
Fiat	Project X1/9 Cmpl Gd to Rac Prep...	79	152		Fiat Motors of NA		S	$30
Filby P	TVR Success Against the Odds	76	105		Wilton Gentry		H	$60
Filby P	MG 1911 to 1978	79	131		Haynes	Mini Marque	H	$20
Filby P	Specialist Sports Cars Brit Small..	74	406		David & Charles		H	$40
Finch B J	Traction Engines in Review	71	903		Ian Allen		H	$50
Finch B J	Traction Engines in Colour	80	903		Ian Allen		H	$50
Finn J E	Ferrari Testa Rossa V-12	79	121		Newport/Osprey		H	$125
Finn J E	Maserati Postwar Sportsrac'g Cars	77	172		Barnes		X	$150
Finn J E	Maserati Birdcage	80	172		Osprey		H	$100
Fiore T	Corvair Decade	80	113		Corvair Society		H	$50
Firestone H S/Crowther S	Men and Rubber Story of Business	26	418		Doubleday		H	$60
Fisher B	Chevrolet Speed Manual	54	111		Clymer		S	$30
Fisher B/Waar B	HT Modify Datsun 510/610/240Z......	73	167		HP		S	$30
Fisher J	Fabulous Hoosier (Carl G Fisher)	47	205		McBride		H	$40
Fisson P	Speed Triumphant	51	298		Putnam		H	$50
Fitch J/Nolan W F	Adventure on Wheels	59	205		Putnam		H	$100
Fittipaldi E/Hayward E	Flying on Ground	73	205		Kimber		H	$50
Fitzgerald/Merritt/Th'psn	Ferrari Sports and GT Cars	68+	121		Bond/Norton/CBS/PSL		H	$125
Fleming I	Chitty Chitty Bang Bang Magical Car	64	424		Random		H	$30
Fletcher R	Jaguar XJS	83	127		Cadogan/Haynes	High Performanc	H	$40
Flink J J	Car Culture (Flink)	75	419		MIT		X	$20
Flink J J	America Adopts the Auto 1895-1910	70	419		MIT		H	$40
Flint J	Dream Machine Gold Age Am Aut 46-65	76	403		Quadrangle/NY Times Book		H	$40
Flower R	Motor Sports Pictorial History	75	297		Putnam		H	$50
Flower R/Jones M W	One Hundred Yrs on Road	81	419		McGraw		H	$50
Foley S	Very Special Year Story Wld Chmpshp	73	206		J H Paull		S	$40
Fondin J	Golden Age of Motoring	82	401		Edita		H	$50
Forbes B C/Foster O D	Automotive Giants of America	26	404		Forbes		H	$30
Ford H	My Life and Work	22+	415		Garden City/Dbldy/Hnmnn		H	$40
Ford H	Today and Tomorrow	26	415		Doubleday/Heinemann		H	$40
Ford H	My Philosophy of Industry	29	415		Coward MC		H	$50
Ford H	Ford Ideals Mr Ford's Page	22	415		Dearborn Pub Co		H	$20
Ford H/Crowther	Moving Forward	31	415		William Heinemann Ltd.		H	$125
Ford Motor Company	Automotive News Ford 75th Ann Issue	78	169		Crain		S	$50
Foster G	Harley-Davidson Cult Lives On	84	607		Osprey	Osprey Colour	S	$30
Foster G	Cult of Harley-Davidson	82	607		Osprey Publications	Osprey Colour	S	$30
Foster G	Ride It Comp Bk Flat Track Racing	78	601		Haynes		H	$20
Foubister P	Rallyworld 1987-88	87	209		Tudor		S	$50
Foubister P	Rallyworld 1988-89	88	209		Tudor		S	$50
Fox J C	Ill History of Indianapolis 500	67+	208		World/Hungness		H	$150
Fox C	Great Racing Cars & Drivers (Fox)	72	297		Ridge/Grosset/Madison Sq		H	$40
Fox J C	Indianapolis 500 (Fox)	67	208		World		H	$125
Fox M/Smith S	Rolls-Royce Complete Works	84	139		Faber & Faber		S	$20
Foyt A J/Neeley W	AJ Life My Life as Americas.......H	83	205		Times Books		H	$40
Foyt A J/Neely W	AJ Life of Americas Greatest......S	83	205		Warner		S	$20
Fraichard G	Le Mans Story	54	206		Bodley		H	$50
Francisco D etc	Hot Rod Technical Library	61+	201		Spotliet/Trend/Hot Rod		H	$20
Franzini P/Delllanzo L	Quel Mondo Dipinto (Italian)	78	118		Editrice Lombarda		H	$70
Fraser C	Harry Ferguson Inventor and Pioneer	72	404	901	Murray		H	$70
Fraser C	Tractor Pioneer Life of H Ferguson	73	901		Ohio Univ Press		H	$50
Fredricks H A/Chambers A	Bricklin	77	173		Brunswick Press		H	$30
Freeman J W	Sports Cars (Freeman)	55	401		Random		H	$40
Freeman J W	Sports Car Album (Fawcett 181)	53	401		Fawcett	Fawcett	X	$20
Frere P	On Starting Grid	56	297	205	Batsford		H	$40
Frere P	Sports Car & Competition Driving	63	203		Batsford/Bentley		H	$40
Frere P	Porsche Racing Cars of 70s	80	136		Stephens/Arco		H	$50
Frere P	Mercedes-Benz CIII Experim'tal Cars	81	130		Edita		H	$60
Frere P	Cars in Profile 05 Porsche 917	73	136		Profile Publications		S	$20
Frere P	Racing Porsches	71+	136		Arco/Motorbuch/Stephens		H	$50
Frere P	Profile No 93 Ballots 1921-1932	67	120		Profile Publications		S	$10
Frere P	Cars in Profile 01 246 P4 Ferraris	72	121		Profile Publications		S	$10
Frere P	Starting Grid to Chequered Flag	62	205		Batsford		S	$20
Frewin M	International GP Bk of Motor Racing	65	297		Leslie Frewin		H	$30
Friedman D/Christy J	Carroll Shelbys Racing Cobra S	86	109		Newport/Petersen		S	$20
Frostick M	Works Team Rootes Comp Dept	64	105	209	Cassell		H	$50
Frostick M	Mighty Mercedes	71	130		Dalton Watson	Dalton Watson	H	$60
Frostick M	Dream Cars Design Studies & Proto..	80	401	502	Dalton Watson	Dalton Watson	H	$60
Frostick M	Rolls-Royce (Pocket History)	80	139		Automobilia	Complete Book	S	$20
Frostick M	Advertising and Motor-car	70	503		Lund Humphries		H	$90
Frostick M	Pinin Farina Master Coachbuilder	77	501		Dalton Watson	Dalton Watson	H	$100
Frostick M	Triumph (Pocket History)	81	146		Libreria dell'Automobile	Comp Hist	S	$20
Frostick M	Alfa Romeo Milano	74	101		Dalton Watson	Dalton Watson	H	$100
Frostick M	Aston Martin and Lagonda	77	103	105	Dalton Watson	Dalton Watson	H	$60
Frostick M	Jaguar Tradition	73	127		Dalton Watson	Dalton Watson	H	$60

Author	Title	Pub date	Subjects		Publisher	Series	Bind	Price
Frostick M	Pit & Paddock Bckgrnd MR 1894-1978	80	298		Moorland		H	$30
Frostick M	Pininfarina Architect of Cars	78	501		Dalton Watson	Dalton Watson	H	$70
Frostick M	V8	79	405		Beaulieu/Dalton Watson	Beaulieu Book	H	$20
Frostick M	Bentley Cricklewood to Crewe	80	139		Osprey		H	$70
Frostick M	Cars That Got Away Ideas Exper.....	68	401		Cassell		H	$60
Frostick M	Jaguar (Pocket History)	80	127		Automobilia	Complete Book	S	$20
Frostick M/Gill B	Ford Competition Cars	76+	169		Haynes		H	$40
Frostick M/Harding A	Motorists Weekend Book	60	401		Batsford/Bentley		H	$30
Frumkin	Great Auto Trivia Book	85	401		Crown/Outlet		S	$20
Frumkin M	Son of Muscle Car Mania Ads 1962-74	82	503		MBI		S	$30
Frumkin M	Muscle Car Mania Ad Coll 1964-1974	81	503		MBI		S	$30
Fry R	VW Beetle	80	150		David & Charles		H	$50
Fujimoto A	Car Styling No 19 - Bertone	77	508		San'ei Shobo		H	$60
Fujimoto A	Luigi Colani Designing Tomorrow	78	502		Car Styling		H	$80
Fujimoto A	Car Styling No 19	77	508		San'ei Shobo		H	$50
Fujimoto A	Car Styling No 46	84	508		San'ei Shobo		S	$50
Fujimoto A	Car Styling No 43	83	508		San'ei Shobo		X	$50
Fujimoto A	Car Styling No 50	85	508		San'ei Shobo		S	$50
Fujimoto A	Car Styling No 45	84	508		San'ei Shobo		X	$50
Fujimoto A	Car Styling No 44	83	508		San'ei Shobo		H	$50
Fujimoto A	Car Styling No 09	75	508		San'ei Shobo		H	$80
Fujimoto A	Car Styling No 17	77	508		San'ei Shobo		H	$60
Fujimoto A	Car Styling No 25	79	508		San'ei Shobo		H	$60
Fujimoto A	Car Styling No 26	79	508		San'ei Shobo		X	$60
Fujimoto A	Car Styling No 23	78	508		San'ei Shobo		X	$60
Fujimoto A	Car Styling No 49	85	508		San'ei Shobo		S	$50
Fujimoto A	Car Styling No 34	81	508		San'ei Shobo		H	$50
Fujimoto A	Car Styling No 35 1/2 - Giugiaro	81	508		San'ei Shobo		S	$70
Fujimoto A	Car Styling No 31 1/2 Porsche/Desg	80	508	136	San'ei Shobo		S	$70
Fujimoto A	Car Styling No 27	79	508		San'ei Shobo		X	$60
Fujimoto A	Car Styling No 28	79	508		San'ei Shobo		X	$60
Fujimoto A	Car Styling No 55	86	508		San'ei Shobo		S	$50
Fujimoto A	Car Styling No 06	73	508		San'ei Shobo		H	$80
Fujimoto A	Car Styling No 01	73	508		San'ei Shobo		H	$100
Fujimoto A	Car Styling No 02	73	508		San'ei Shobo		H	$100
Fujimoto A	Car Styling No 03	73	508		San'ei Shobo		H	$90
Fujimoto A	Car Styling No 04	73	508		San'ei Shobo		H	$90
Fujimoto A	Car Styling No 05	73	508		San'ei Shobo		H	$90
Fujimoto A	Car Styling No 07	74	508		San'ei Shobo		H	$80
Fujimoto A	Car Styling No 08	74	508		San'ei Shobo		H	$80
Fujimoto A	Car Styling No 10	75	508		San'ei Shobo		H	$80
Fujimoto A	Car Styling No 11	75	508		San'ei Shobo		H	$70
Fujimoto A	Car Styling No 12	75	508		San'ei Shobo		H	$70
Fujimoto A	Car Styling No 13	76	508		San'ei Shobo		H	$70
Fujimoto A	Car Styling No 14	76	508		San'ei Shobo		H	$70
Fujimoto A	Car Styling No 15	76	508		San'ei Shobo		H	$70
Fujimoto A	Car Styling No 16	76	508		San'ei Shobo		H	$60
Fujimoto A	Car Styling No 18	77	508		San'ei Shobo		H	$60
Fujimoto A	Car Styling No 20	77	508		San'ei Shobo		H	$60
Fujimoto A	Car Styling No 21	78	508		San'ei Shobo		H	$60
Fujimoto A	Car Styling No 22	78	508		San'ei Shobo		H	$60
Fujimoto A	Car Styling No 24	78	508		Beaulieu Shobo		H	$60
Fujimoto A	Car Styling No 29	80	508		San'ei Shobo		H	$60
Fujimoto A	Car Styling No 30	80	508		San'ei Shobo		H	$60
Fujimoto A	Car Styling No 31	80	508		San'ei Shobo		H	$60
Fujimoto A	Car Styling No 32	80	508		Haynes		H	$60
Fujimoto A	Car Styling No 33	81	508		Batsford		H	$60
Fujimoto A	Car Styling No 35	81	508		San'ei Shobo		H	$50
Fujimoto A	Car Styling No 36	81	508		San'ei Shobo		H	$50
Fujimoto A	Car Styling No 37	82	508		San'ei Shobo		H	$50
Fujimoto A	Car Styling No 38	82	508		San'ei Shobo		H	$50
Fujimoto A	Car Styling No 39	82	508		San'ei Shobo		H	$50
Fujimoto A	Car Styling No 40	82	508		San'ei Shobo		H	$50
Fujimoto A	Car Styling No 41	83	508		San'ei Shobo		H	$50
Fujimoto A	Car Styling No 42	83	508		San'ei Shobo		H	$50
Fujimoto A	Car Styling No 47	84	508		San'ei Shobo		S	$50
Fujimoto A	Car Styling No 48	84	508		San'ei Shobo		S	$50
Fujimoto A	Car Styling No 51	85	508		San'ei Shobo		S	$50
Fujimoto A	Car Styling No 52	85	508		San'ei Shobo		S	$50
Fujimoto A	Car Styling No 53	86	508		San'ei Shobo		S	$50
Fujimoto A	Car Styling No 54	86	508		San'ei Shobo		S	$50
Fujimoto A	Car Styling No 56	86	508		San'ei Shobo		S	$50
Fujimoto A	Car Styling No 57	87	508		San'ei Shobo		S	$50
Fujimoto A	Car Styling No 58	87	508		San'ei Shobo		S	$50
Fujimoto A	Car Styling No 59	87	508		San'ei Shobo		S	$50
Fujimoto A	Car Styling No 60	87	508		San'ei Shobo		S	$50
Fujimoto A	Car Styling No 61	87	508		San'ei Shobo		S	$50
Fujimoto A	Car Styling No 62	88	508		San'ei Shobo		S	$50

Author	Title	Pub date	Subjects		Publisher	Series	Bind	Price
Fujimoto A	Car Styling No 63	88	508		San'ei Shobo		S	$50
Fujimoto A	Car Styling No 64	88	508		San'ei Shobo		S	$50
Fujimoto A	Car Styling No 65	88	508		San'ei Shobo		S	$50
Fujimoto A	Car Styling No 66	88	508		San'ei Shobo		S	$50
Fujimoto A	Car Styling No 67	88	508		San'ei Shobo		S	$50
Fujimoto A	Car Styling No 68	89	508		San'ei Shobo		S	$50
Fujimoto A	Famous Auto Museums 2 Museo...Turin	79	401		San'ei Shobo Pub		H	$40
Fusi L	Le Grandi Alfa Romeo (Italian)	69	101		L'Editrice dell'Automobil		H	$500
Fusi L	Alfa Romeo All Cars Fr 1910/Tutte..	78+	101		Emmetigrafica		H	$200
Fusi L	Le Vetture Alfa Romeo Dal 1910	65+	101		Editrice Adiemme		H	$90
Fusi L	Alfa Romeo Tipo A Monoposto (Eng)	82	101		Emmetigrafica		H	$40
Fusi L/Slater R	Six C 1750 Alfa Romeo	68	101		MacDonald		H	$125
Gardiner G/O'Neill R	Collectors All Color Gd to Toy Cars	85	704		Salamander		H	$40
Gardner A T G	Car Racing 1953 (52 season)	53	204		Country & Sporting		S	$50
Gardner C	Fifty Years of Brooklands	56	206		Heinemann		H	$50
Garlits D/Hicks D E	Close Calls	84	205	201	Huntington House		S	$20
Garlits D/Yates B	King of Dragsters (Garlits)	67+	201	205	Chilton		H	$30
Garner P/Harvey M/Conway	Amazing Bugattis	79	107		Design Council/Barrons		S	$70
Garnier P	Art of Gordon Crosby	78	504		Hamlyn		H	$150
Garnier P	Sixteen on Grid	64	298		Cassell & Co		H	$40
Garnier P	Healey (Autocar)	83	104		Temple/Hamlyn		H	$50
Garnier P	Lancia (Autocar)	81	157		Hamlyn		H	$50
Garnier P	Jaguar Sports (Autocar)	75	127		Hamlyn		H	$40
Garnier P	Rolls-Royce (Autocar) Story of Best	77	139		Autocar		X	$30
Garnier P	Aston Martin (Autocar)	82	103		IPC/Hamlyn		H	$50
Garnier P	MG Sports Cars (Autocar)	74+	131		Hamlyn/St Martins		H	$40
Garnier P Editor	Aston Martin Britain's Mst Colorful	76	103		IPC Transport Press	Autocar	S	$40
Garrett G	Wild Wheel	52	415		Pantheon		H	$20
Garrett H	Poster Book of Antique Auto Ads	74	503		Citadel/Lyle Stewart		S	$40
Garrett R	Anatomy of Grand Prix Driver	70	297		Arthur Barker Ltd.		H	$20
Garrett R	Fast and Furious	69	297		Arco		H	$30
Garrett R	Motoring & Mighty	71	401		Stanley		H	$30
Garrett R	Rally-Go-Round	70	209		Stanley Paul		H	$20
Garton M	Tuning BMC Sports Cars	69	104	131	Speed Sport		S	$30
Garvey J	Guide to Transport Museums of GB	82	412		Pelham		S	$30
Gauld G	Jim Clark Portrait of Great Driver	68	205		Arco/Hamlyn		H	$40
Gauld G	Jim Clark Remembered	75+	205		PSL/Arco		H	$40
Gault W C	Checkered Flag (Gault - juvenile)	64	213		Dutton		H	$20
Gavin B	Autocourse 1963-64	64	204		Autocourse Publications		H	$200
Gavin B	Jim Clark Story	67	205		Frewin		H	$60
Geary L	Ford Military Vehicles	83	303	308	Ian Henry Pub	Transport Ser	H	$30
Geary L	Ford Formula One Racing Cars	82	156		Ian Henry	Transport	H	$20
Genibrel J L	Racing Yamaha KT100-S Engine	86	603		Steve Smith		S	$30
Gentile R	Rolls-Royce Phantom II Continental	80	139		Dalton Walton	Dalton Watson	H	$80
Georgano G N	Worlds Commercial Vcles1830-1964	65	306		Temple		H	$20
Georgano G N	New Encyclopaedia Motorcars 1885 on	68+	401		Dutton/Crescent		H	$70
Georgano G N	Classic Rolls-Royce	83	139		Exeter/Bison		H	$20
Georgano G N	Comp Ency Comm Vehicles	79	306		Krause		H	$80
Georgano G N	Ency of Motor Sport	71	297		Rainbird/Ebury/Viking		H	$150
Georgano G N	Hist of Sports Cars	70	401		Rainbird/Dutton		H	$50
Georgano G N	Ency of American Automobiles	68+	403		Rainbird/Dutton		H	$40
Georgano G N	Brooklands Pictorial History	78	206		Dalton Watson/Beaulieu		H	$30
Georgano G N	Comp Ency of M/C(see NEW ENC)	68+	401		Dutton		H	$50
Georgano G N	Motor Racing Camera 1894-1916	76	297		David & Charles		H	$30
Georgano G N	London Taxi	85	306		Shire	Shire Album	S	$10
Georgano G N	Cars 1886-1930	85	401		Nordbok/Beekman/Crown		H	$40
Georgano G N	Ency of Sportscars	85	412		Bison		H	$30
Georgano G N	Sports Cars History and Development	87	401		Johnston/Book Sls/Chtwl		H	$30
Georgano G N	Hist of London Taxicab	72	306		David & Charles		H	$40
Georgano G N/Demand C	Trucks Illustrated History 1896-20	78	306		Edita/Macdonald/Two Cont.		H	$50
Gerber D	Out of Control (novel)	74	207		Prentice		H	$20
Gershon D	Aston Martin 1963-1972	75	103		Oxford Illustrated		H	$40
Giacosa D	Forty Years of Design with Fiat	79	152		Automobilia		H	$100
Gibbins E/Ewens G	Pictorial Hist of Trucks	78	306		Orbis/Book Sales/Chartwel		H	$20
Gibbs A	Passion for Cars	74	401		David & Charles/Scribners		H	$20
Gibson C	Hist of British Dinkey Toys 1934-64	66+	702		MAP/Mikansue		S	$20
Gibson J E	Motor Racing 1947	49	204		MRP		S	$80
Gibson J E	Motor Racing 1946	48	204		MRP		S	$70
Gibson M	Le Mans Twice Around Clock(juv'n'l)	62	206		Putnam		H	$30
Giles J G	Body Construction & Design	71	405		Butterworth Group	AutoTech 6	H	$20
Giles J G	Carburation Lube & Eng Metallurgy	68	405		Iliffe Books	AutoTech	H	$10
Giles J G	Engine Design V2	68	405		Iliffe	Auto Tech	X	$10
Giles J G	Gears & Transmissions V4	69	405		Iliffe	Auto Tech	H	$20
Giles J G	Vehicle Equipment	69	405		Iliffe	AutoTech	S	$10
Giles J G	Vehicle Operation & Testing	69	405		Iliffe	Auto Tech V-7	H	$20
Gill B	Motor Racing Grand Prix Greats	72	205		Drake		H	$20
Gill B	Motor Sport Yearbook 1973 J Player	73	204		Q Anne/Collier Books		S	$20
Gill B	Motor Sport Yearbook 1974	73	204		Brickfield/Collier		S	$20

Author	Title	Pub date	Subjects	Publisher	Series	Bind	Price
Gill B	Motor Sport Yearbook 1976	76	204	Queen Anne Press		S	$20
Gill B	Motor Sport Yearbook 1975 J Player	75	204	Brickfield/Queen Anne		S	$20
Gill B	Motor Sport Yearbook 1972 J Player	72	204	Q Anne		S	$20
Gill B	Facts About Grand Prix Team Tyrrell	77	298	Whizzard G		H	$40
Gillham J	Buses & Coaches 1945-1965	76		Almark		H	$20
Gillham R	Scalextric Cars & Equipment........	81+	701	Haynes/Foulis		H	$50
Glasscock C B	Gasoline Age	37	419	Bobbs-Merrill		H	$40
Gloor G/Wagner C L	Monteverdi (German)	80	173	Automobile Monteverdi		H	$300
Golding H	Wonder Book of Motors 2E(?)	26?	401	Ward Lock		H	$70
Goode J	Australian Cars and Motoring	72	402	Lansdowne		H	$20
Goodenough S	Fire Story of Fire Engine	78	302	Orbis/Book Sales/Chartwel		H	$30
Goodman J O	Golden Years of Trucking	77	306	Ontario Trucking Assoc		H	$50
Goodman R	Mexican Road Race 1950	50	206	Clymer		S	$50
Gordon T L	HT Build Cust/Design Plastic Models	82	704	Tab		S	$20
Gorman R/Bond J R	Aluminum In Automobiles	59	405	Singer/Reynolds Metals Co		H	$40
Gotschke W	Walter Gotschke and M-B Racing Car*	80	504 130	Barnes/Rights Marketing		H	$400
Gottlieb R J	Classic Cars and Specials(Trend 135	56	401	Trend	Trend	S	$10
Grad F P etc	Automobile and Regulation of Impact	75	419	Oklahoma		H	$30
Granatelli A	They Call Me Mr. 500	69	205	Henry Regnery		H	$30
Grant G	Boys Book of Motor Sport	50S	213	Foulis		H	$50
Grant G	British Sports Cars(Grant)	47+	406	Foulis/Clymer		X	$30
Grant G	Hist of Geelong Speed Trials 56-85	86	206	Grant		H	$40
Grant G	AJS Hist of Great Motorcycle	69	606	PSL		H	$40
Grant G	Formula 2	53	298	Foulis		H	$40
Grant G	World Championship (Grant)	59	298	Autosport		H	$40
Grant G/Bolster J	High Performance Cars 1965-1966	65	410	Autosport		S	$20
Grant G/Bolster J	High Performance Cars 1961-1962	61	410	Autosport		S	$20
Grant G/Bolster J	High Performance Cars 1958-1959	57	410	Autosport		S	$20
Grant M	Veteran & Vintage Cars in Australia	72	401	Tuttle		H	$20
Granz P/Kirchberg P	Ahnen Unserer Autos	75	408	Transpress VEB		H	$40
Graves R H	Triumph of an Idea Story of H Ford	34	415	Doubleday		H	$20
Gray R	Rolls on Rocks	71	139	Compton Press		H	$30
Gray R D	Alloys and Automobiles E Haynes	79	404	Indiana Historical Soc		S	$30
Grayson S	Ferrari Man Machines	75	121	Automobile Quarterly		H	$60
Greasley M	Rallycourse 1986-87	86	209	Hazleton		H	$100
Greasley M	Rallycourse 1982-83	82	209	Hazleton		H	$90
Greasley M	Rallycourse 1985-86	85	209	Hazleton		H	$90
Greasley M	Rallycourse 1984-85	84	209	Hazleton		H	$90
Green E	Alfa Romeo (Green)	76	101	Evan Green Australia		H	$60
Green J	Bentley 50 Years of Marque	69+	139	Dalton Watson	Dalton Watson	H	$300
Green J	Legendary Hispano Suiza	77	120	Dalton Watson	Dalton Watson	H	$100
Greene B/Hot Rod	Hot Rod Pictorial (Hot Rod)	67	201	Petersen	Hot Rod	S	$30
Greene E	Small Foreign Car Guide	67	401	Arco		H	$20
Greenslade R W	Hist of Electric Model Roads.......	80S	701	Leisure-Time		S	$70
Greenwood G	Postwar British Cars	48	406	Clymer		H	$30
Gregoire J A	Twenty-four Hours at Le Mans(fict)	57	206 207	John Day		H	$40
Gregory K	Behind Scenes of Motor Racing	60	205	MacGibbon & Kee/MBC		H	$40
Greilsamer J/Azema B	Catalogue of Model Cars of World	67	702	Edita/Haessner/PSL		H	$125
Grice R	Vehicle Recovery Practical Gd	77	306	Butterworth		H	$30
Griffin M	Motorcycle Drag Racing Complete Gd	82	602	SA		S	$20
Griffith J	Built for Speed 24 Motorcycles	62	603	Temple		H	$40
Grill L	Essential Tec for Profess Driver	87	306	IAP		S	$20
Grimaldi U A	Alfar Romeo 75 Anniversario	80S	101	Edizioni Alfa Romeo		H	$100
Groh P	Ferrari Berlinetta Classic Line 1	80S	121	Verlag Classic Line		H	$300
Grosser M	Diesel Man & Engine	78	404 405	Atheneum		H	$40
Groves R	Starting from Scratch (cartoons)	54	297	Autosport		S	$20
Groves R	Pit Stop (cartoons)	53	297	Autosport		S	$20
Groves R	Racing Cars (Nelson)	50S	213 504	Nelson		H	$30
Guba E	Race Report 1 (Renn Report) 1967-68	68	204	Hanns Reich Verlag		H	$80
Guba E	Race Report 2 (Renn Report) 1968-69	69	204	Hanns Reich Verlag		H	$100
Guba E	Race Report 3 (Renn Report) 1969-70	70	204	Motorbuch Vertag		H	$100
Guba E	Race Report 4 (Renn Report) 1970-71	71	204	Motorbuch Vertag		H	$125
Guba E	Race Report 5 (Mtr Spt Ann)1971-72	72	204	Motorbuch Verlag/Grenvill		H	$80
Guba E/Nye D	Racing Cars (Guba)	69	298	Race Report/Fountain		S	$40
Gude F	Formula 1(Gude art)	84	504	Gude		H	$80
Guichard A	Automobile Year 1955-56 #3(Auto Rev	56	204	Edita S.A.		H	$250
Guichard A	Automobile Year 1956-57 #4	57	204	Edita S.A./Doubleday		H	$150
Guichard A	Automobile Year 1957-58 #5 (1958)	58	204	Edita S.A./Doubleday		H	$150
Guichard A	Automobile Year 1958-59 #6	59	204	Edita S.A./Doubleday		H	$150
Guichard A	Automobile Year 1959-60 #7	59	204	Edita S.A.		H	$150
Guichard A	Automobile Year 1960-61 #8	61	204	Edita S.A.		H	$150
Guichard A	Automobile Year 1953-54 #1(Auto Rev	53	204	Edita S.A.		S	$500
Guichard A	Automobile Year 1954-55 #2(Auto Rev	54	204	Edita S.A.		X	$800
Gunnell J	Convertibles Complete Story	84	401	Tab		S	$40
Gunnell J	Seventy-5 Years of Pontiac-Oakland	82	138	Crestline	Crestline	H	$100
Gunnell J	Chrysler 300 1955-1961 Photofacts	82	112	MBI	CMB Photofacts	S	$40
Gustin L R	Billy Durant Creator of GM	84	160	Craneshaw		H	$40
Haardt G/Audouin-Dubreuil	Black Journey - Africa with Citroen	27+	153 212	Cosmopolitan/Bles		H	$180

Author	Title	Pub date	Subjects	Publisher	Series	Bind	Price
Hackleman M	Electric Vehicles Des/Build Yr Own	77+	417	Earthmind/Peace Press		S	$30
Haddad W	Hard Driving My Yrs with DeLorean	85	168	Random		H	$40
Hafeli R	Verstummte Motoren (Schweizer GP)	69	206	Benteli Verlag		H	$150
Hailwood M/Walker M	Art of Motorcycle Racing	63+	604	Cassell		H	$90
Hall A	Petersens Compl Bk Datsun	75	167	Petersen		S	$20
Hall A	Petersens Compl Bk Toyota	75	126	Petersen		S	$20
Hall C/O'Toole L	Street Rodding Gallery	87	201	Graffiti		S	$20
Hall D K	Van People Great American..........	77	307	Crowell		S	$20
Hall P	Muscle Cars (Consumer Gd)	81	403	Publications Intl	Consumer Gd	H	$20
Halla C	Mercury Cougar 1967-1973 Photofacts	84	166	MBI	CMB Photofacts	S	$30
Halla C	Dreamboats & Milestones Cars of 50s	81	403	Tab		S	$20
Halle J C	Francois Cevert Contract with Death	75	205	Flammarion/Kimber		H	$70
Hallums E	Bugatti Quality of Work/Art	79	107	Mithra Press		S	$100
Halmi R	Sports Cars of World (Halmi)	58	401	Sports Car Press		H	$20
Hamilton D	Touch Wood 1E	60	205	MBC/Barrie&Rockliff		H	$100
Hamilton M	Autocourse 1986-87	86	204	Hazleton		H	$90
Hamilton M	Autocourse 1981-82	82	204	Hazleton		H	$125
Hamilton M	Autocourse 1980-81	80	204	Hazleton		H	$125
Hamilton M	Autocourse 1982-83	83	204	Hazleton		H	$180
Hamilton M	Autocourse 1979-80	80	204	Hazleton		H	$125
Hamilton M	Kimberley GP Team Gd 07 Tyrell	83	298	Kimberley's		S	$20
Hamilton M	Autocourse 1981-82(French)	81	204	Hazleton/Editions ACLA		H	$80
Hamilton M	Autocourse 1983-84	83	204	Hazleton		H	$80
Hamilton M	Autocourse 1984-85	84	204	Hazleton		H	$80
Hamilton M	Autocourse 1987-88	87	204	Hazleton		H	$90
Hamilton M	Autocourse 1985-86	85	204	Hazleton		H	$50
Hamilton M	Rally 1932-1986	87	209	Partridge		H	$70
Hammond M A	Lesney Matchbox I-75 Ser. Diecasts	72	702	Reedminster		H	$40
Hanks F	Tourist Trophy 75 Story	75	603	TT Special		S	$20
Hansen R	Life Story of Juan Manuel Fangio	56	205	Edita		S	$40
Harding A	Cars in Profile Coll. 1	73	401	Profile Pulications		H	$30
Harding A	Cars in Profile Coll. 2	74	401	Profile Publications	Cars in Profile	H	$30
Harding A	Classic Cars in Profile V1 1-24	67+	401	Profile/Doubleday		H	$70
Harding A	Classic Cars in Profile V2 25-48	67+	401	Profile/Doubleday		H	$70
Harding A	Classic Cars in Profile V4 73-96	68	401	Profile/Doubleday		H	$125
Harding A	Car Facts & Feats - Guinness	71+	412	Sterling/Guinness		H	$20
Harding A	Classic Cars in Profile V3 49-72	67	401	Profile/Doubleday		H	$70
Harding A	Great Cars in Profile (V4 Misc Pfs)	71	401	Profile Publications		S	$30
Harding A	Racers and Drivers Reader	72	297	Batsford/Arco		H	$20
Harding A	Classic Car Profiles V1 1-24/3V set	66	401	Profile Publications		H	$70
Harding A	Classic Car Profiles V2 25-60/3V st	67	401	Profile Publications		H	$125
Harding A	Classic Car Profiles V3 61-96/3V st	67	401	Profile Publications		H	$125
Harding A/Allport W/etc	Guiness Bk of Car	87	401	Guiness		H	$40
Harding M	Holdens Vs Fords	85	402	View Productions		H	$50
Harker R	Engines Were Rolls-Royce	79	139	Macmillan		H	$100
Harper P	Destination Monte	64	209	Stanley Paul		H	$40
Harper R	Vincent Vee Twins	82	606	Osprey	Osprey Coll Lib	H	$50
Harper R	Vincent HRD Story	75+	606	Vincent Publishing		H	$60
Harrington P B	DMC Evaluator Vol 1/2 Lesney 1-75	82	702	DMC Publications		S	$20
Harrington P B	DMC Evaluator Vol 2/1 Corgi/Spot-on	81	702	Railway City Pub		S	$20
Harris N	Rothmans GP Motorcycle YB 1986-87	86	608	Queen Anne		S	$40
Harrison J	Motor-Cars Today	39+	405	Oxford		H	$20
Harrison M C	Corvettes Technically Speaking	77	114	M & H Engineering		S	$125
Harster H/Fodisch J	Graf Berghe von Trips (Wolfgang)	88	205	Nurburgring Rennsportmu..		S	$20
Hartley J	Automobile Steering & Suspensn Q&A	77	405	Newnes		S	$20
Hartley P	Ariel Story	80	606	Argus Books Ltd		S	$30
Hartley P	Matchless Once Lgst Br M/Cycle Mfr	81	606	Osprey			$0
Hartley P	Brooklands Bikes in Twenties	80	604	Goose/Argus		S	$40
Hartley P	Story of Royal Enfield Motor Cycles	81	606	PSL		H	$40
Hartley P	Story of Rudge Motorcycles	85	606	PSL		H	$40
Harvey C	Healey Handsome Brute	78	104	Oxford Ill/St Martins		H	$80
Harvey C	Lotus Comp Surv Sports GT & Touring	80	129	Osprey		H	$50
Harvey C	Rolls-Royce Corniche Super Profile	84	139	Haynes	Super Profile	H	$20
Harvey C	Porsche Complete Story	83	136	Haynes	Mini Marque	H	$30
Harvey C	Lotus Complete Story	85	129	Foulis/Haynes		H	$30
Harvey C	Great Marques Poster Book Jaguar	85	127	Octopus/Woodbury/Dalton		S	$20
Harvey C	Great Marques Poster Book MG	85	131	Octopus/Woodbury/Dalton		S	$20
Harvey C	MG A B & C	80	131	Oxford Ill/Haynes		H	$60
Harvey C	Ferrari 250 GTO Super Profile	82	121	Haynes	Super Profile	H	$30
Harvey C	Great Marques Jaguar	82	127	Mandarin/Octopus		H	$30
Harvey C	Porsche 911 (Harvey)	80	136	Haynes/Oxford Ill	Classic Car	H	$60
Harvey C	Cars New Classics	81	401	Hennerwood/Octopus/Treasu		H	$20
Harvey C	Jaguars in Competition	79	127	Osprey		H	$50
Harvey-Bailey A	Rolls-Royce Formative Yrs 1906-1939	81+	139	Rolls-Royce Heritage Trst	Historical	S	$20
Harvey-Bailey A	Rolls-Royce Twenty to Wraith	86	139	Sir Henry Royce Mem Found		S	$30
Harwood J E G	Speed and How To Obtain It	25+	609	Iiffe Books/Clymer		X	$40
Hass E	Ahrens-Fox Rolls-Royce of F/E	82	302	Hass		X	$80
Hassan W	Jaguar V12 Engine Des/Background	79	127	TASS of AUEW		S	$30

Author	Title	Pub date	Subjects		Publisher	Series	Bind	Price
Hassan W/Robson G	Climax in Coventry My Life of Fine	75	404		MRP		H	$40
Hatry G/Le Maitre C	Dossiers Chlgq Renault V5 1924-33	81	120		Editions Lafourcade		H	$150
Hatry G/Le Maitre C	Dossiers Chlgq Renault V4 1919-1923	80	120		Editions Lafourcade		H	$100
Hawthorn M	Challenge Me Race	58+	205		William Kimber		H	$40
Hawthorn M	Champion Year My Battle Wld Title	59	205		Kimber		H	$40
Hawthorn M	Carlotti Takes the Wheel (juv fict)	59	213	207	Childrens Book Club		H	$50
Hawthorne R	Heavy Haulage	70S	303		Steaming		S	$10
Hay M	Bentley Vintage Years 1919-1931	86	139		Dalton Watson		H	$150
Haycraft W C	Book of Royal Enfield	35+	606		Pitman	Mtr Cycl Lib	X	$40
Haycraft W C	Book of P & M (motorcycles)	31+	606		Pitman	Mtr Cycl Lib	X	$40
Haycraft W C	Book of AJS	41+	606		Pitman	Mtr Cycl Lib	S	$40
Hayes E	Automobile Wooden Spoke Wheels		405		Oakcrest Machine Shop		S	$20
Haynes J H	Rolls-Royce Manual 1925-1939	64	139		Haynes		S	$40
Haynes J H	High Speed Driving		203		Haynes		S	$20
Hays R	Vanishing Litres	56	401		Macmillan		H	$40
Hays R	Grand Prix and Sports Cars(drawing)	64	504	297	Arco		H	$50
Hays R	Motor Modelling	61	702		Arco		H	$20
Hayward E	Grand Prix Complete Bk F1 Racing	71	297		Dodd Mead		H	$20
Hazan P	AC Cobra 260-289-427(French)	84	109		EPA	Grand Tourisme	H	$50
Healey D/Wisdom T	Austin Healey Guide	59	104		Sports Car Press	Mod Sports Car	S	$30
Healey D/Wisdom T/Boyd M	Austin Healey (Healey/Wisdom)	59	104		Cassell		H	$100
Healey G	More Healeys Frog-eyes Sprites.....	78	104		Gentry Books		H	$60
Healey G	Healey Specials	80	104		Gentry/Haynes		H	$50
Healey G	Austin Healey Story Big Healeys	77	104		Gentry/Haynes		H	$60
Heasley J	Production Figures for US Cars	77	403		MBI		S	$20
Hebb D	Comp Rally Book	79	209		Stein & Day		S	$20
Hebb D	Rally Book	73	209		Hawthorn		S	$20
Hebb D/Peck A	Sports Car Rallies Trials Gymkhanas	56	209		Channel		H	$30
Hediger F	Klassische Wagen II	74	401		Hallwag		H	$40
Heglar M S	Grand Prix Champions	73	297		Bond Parkhurst/R & T		H	$20
Helck P	Great Auto Races	75	297	504	Abrams		H	$300
Helck P	Checkered Flag (Helck)	61	504	297	Scribner/Castle		H	$200
Hendershot L	USAC 1970 Yearbook	70	204		USAC		S	$50
Henderson M	Motor Racing in Safety Human Factor	68	297		PSL		H	$40
Hendry M D	Pierce-Arrow (Ballantine)	71	170		Ballantine Books	Ballantine #4	S	$30
Hendry M D	Harley Davidson (Ballantine)	72	607		Ballantine	Ballantine #12	S	$30
Hendry M D	Lincoln (Ballantine)	71	161		Ballantine	Minimarque #8	S	$20
Henri-Labourdette J	Un Siecle de Carrosserie Francaise	72	501		Edita		H	$400
Henry A	Four-Wheel Drives Racing's Formula	75	297		Macmillan	Donington MM	H	$30
Henry A	Brabham Grand Prix Cars	85	298		Hazleton		H	$50
Henry A	Alain Prost (French)	87	205		EPA	Toute L'Hist	S	$20
Henry A	Gilles Villeneuve (French)	88	205		EPA	Toute L'Hist	S	$20
Henry A	Ferrari Grand Prix Cars	84	121		Hazleton/Osprey		H	$50
Henry A	Fifty Famous Motor Races (Specl ed)	88	297		PSL		L	$150
Henry A	Ronnie Peterson SuperSwede/GP Driv	75+	205		Haynes		X	$40
Henry A	Audi Quattro	84	124		Cadogan/Arco	High Perfor....	H	$30
Henry A	Kimberley GP Team Gd 13 Ferrari	84	121		Kimberley's		S	$30
Henry A	Kimberley Driver Prfl 03 Villeneuve	80S	205		Kimberley		S	$20
Henry A	Ayrton Senna Portrait of Champion	88	205		Hazleton		H	$40
Henry A	Autocourse 1989-90	89	204		Hazleton		H	$80
Henry A	Autocourse 1988-1989	88	204		Hazleton		H	$50
Herndon B	Ford Unconventional Biog Men/Times	69	415		Weybridge		H	$30
Hertz L H	Comp Bk Model Raceways & Rdways	64	701		Crown		H	$40
Hertz L H	Comp Bk Bldg/Coll Mod Autos	70	702		Crown		H	$40
Hess A	Wheels Round World	51	212		Newman Neame		H	$20
Hess A	Indianapolis Records	59	211	105	Stuart & Richards		H	$30
Heygate J	Motor Tramp	35	131		Cape		H	$70
Hicks R W	V-Twin Classic MtrCyc 1903-Present	85	601		Blandford		H	$40
Higdon H	Six Seconds To Glory Don Prudhomme	75	205	213	Putnam		H	$30
Higdon H	Summer of Triumph Life of Caruthers	77	205		Putnam		H	$30
Higdon H	Showdown at Daytona	76	206	213	Putnam		H	$20
Higdon H	Finding the Groove	73	299		Putnam		H	$30
Higdon H	Thirty Days in May Indy 500	71	208		Putnam		H	$30
Hildebrand G	Golden Age of Luxury Car	80	401		Dover		S	$20
Hill B	Other Side of Hill	78	205		Hutchinson/Stanley Paul		H	$20
Hill G	Life at Limit	69	205		Coward-McCann/Kimber		H	$40
Hill G	Graham Hill's Car Racing Guide	71	205		Sterling		H	$20
Hill G/Ewart	Graham	76	205		St. Martin's		H	$20
Hill K	Four Wheeled-Morgan Vol 1 Flat Rad	77	164		MRP		H	$100
Hill M	Wild Cars	74	422		Hamlyn		H	$20
Hillstead A F C	Those Bentley Days	53	139		Faber		H	$70
Hinsdale P	Fabulous Porsche 917	76	136		Haessner		S	$100
Hirsch J	Great American Dream Machines	85	403		Macmillan/Random		X	$50
Hirsch J	Super Catalog of Car Parts and Acc.	74	412		Workman		X	$20
Hirsch J/Weith W	Last American Convertibles	79	401		Collier		S	$20
Hitze E	Kurtis-Kraft Story	74	158		Interstate Printers		S	$100
Hochman L	Hot Rod Handbook (Fawcett)	58	201		Fawcett	Fawcett	S	$10
Hodgdon T A	Golden Age of Fours	76+	601		Bagnall		S	$40

Author	Title	Pub date	Subjects		Publisher	Series	Bind	Price
Hughes J	CART 1989-90 Men and Machines......	89	204		Autosport Intl		H	$60
Hughes L	Jaguar Under Southern Cross	80	127		Bronle Motor Books		H	$150
Hughes M	Classic and Sportscar Lotus File	87	129		Bay View/Temple/Hamlyn		H	$50
Hughes W J/Thomas J L	Sentinel V1 1875-1930	73	303		David & Charles		H	$40
Hugo P	Private Motor Car Collections of GB	73	401		Dalton Watson	Dalton Watson	H	$50
Hull P	Alfa Romeo (Ballantine)	71	101		Ballantine Books	Ballantine #2	S	$20
Hull P	Profile No 51 Alvis Front Wheel Dr.	67	105		Profile Publications		S	$10
Hull P	Cars in Profile 06 Alfa Monoposto..	73	101		Profile Publications		S	$10
Hull P/Fusi L	Profile No 14 Alfa Romeo Type RL	66	101		Profile Publications		S	$10
Hull P/Slater R	Alfa Romeo History	64+	101		Cassell/Transport/Pksd		H	$90
Humphreys B J/Malewicki	Rocket Powered Racing Vehicles.....	74	211		Rockets		S	$50
Hungness C	Indianapolis 1983 Yearbook	83	208		Hungness		X	$40
Hungness C	Indianapolis 1976 Yearbook	76	208		Hungness		X	$30
Hungness C	Indianapolis 1979 Yearbook	79	208		Hungness		X	$30
Hungness C	Indianapolis 1973 Yearbook	73	208		Hungness		X	$100
Hungness C	Indianapolis 1974 Yearbook	74	208		Hungness		X	$30
Hungness C	Indianapolis 1975 Yearbook	75	208		Hungness		X	$30
Hungness C	Indianapolis 1977 Yearbook	77	208		Hungness		X	$30
Hungness C	Indianapolis 1978 Yearbook	78	208		Hungness		S	$30
Hungness C	Indianapolis 1985 Yearbook	85	208		Hungness		X	$30
Hungness C	Indianapolis 1984 Yearbook	84	208		Hungness		X	$30
Hungness C/Fox J	Five Hundred Souvenir Book	80	208		Hungness		S	$10
Hunt K C	Modern Motorcars (juvenile)	52	424		Temple		H	$20
Hunter I	Aston Martin 1914-1940 Pict. Review	76	103		Transport Bookman		H	$40
Huntington R	Cord Front-Drive	57+	116		Clymer/MBI		X	$40
Huntington R	Souping Stock Engine	50	202		Clymer		S	$20
Huntington R	Design & Development of Indy Car	81	299		HP Books		S	$40
Huntington R	American Supercar Dev of...........	83	403		H P Books		S	$30
Huntington R	HT Hop Up Chevrolet & GMC 6 cy Eng	51	111		Clymer		S	$20
Hutton R	Sports Cars (Hutton)	73	401		Hamlyn		H	$10
Hutton R	Sports Cars on Road and Track	73	297		Hamlyn		H	$20
I Mech E Papers	Automobile Wheels and Tyres	83	405		I Mech E		S	$60
IHC	Historical Facts International Veh		158		IHC		S	$20
Imai K	Wild Mook 53 Ca Hwy Patrol (Jap)	70S	401		World Photo Press		S	$40
Imai K	Wild Mook 28 Fire Eng & F/F (Jap)	79	302		World Photo Press		S	$40
Imai K	Wild Mook 23 (US Trucking-Japanese)	78	301		World Photo Press		S	$40
Imai K	Wild Mook 18 Big Rig (Japanese)	70S	301		World Photo Press		S	$40
Ingram A	Trucks of World Highways	79	306		Blandford/New Orchard		H	$30
Ingram A	Hist of Fire-Fighting & Equip...	78	302		New Eng Lib/Book Sls/Chtw		H	$20
Ingram A	Ford Trucks Transport Since 45	78	303		MRP		H	$40
Ingram A/Baldwin N	Light Vans & Trucks 1919-39	77	307		Almark		H	$20
Ingram A/Bishop D	Fire Engines in Color	73	302		Blandford/Macmillan		H	$20
Ingram A/Peck C	Off Highway & Construction Trucks	80	306		Blandford		H	$40
Inomoto Y	Automobile Illustration (Japanese)	71	504		Nigensha		H	$200
Inouye K	BMW 1979(Japanese)	79	106		Neko	Neko	S	$30
Inouye K	Toyota Twin Cam II (Japanese)	81	126		Neko	Neko	S	$40
Inouye K	British Light Wt Spts 78 (Japanese)	78	105		Neko	Neko	S	$700
Inouye T	Porsche 1980 (Japanese)	80	136		Neko	Neko	S	$30
Inouye T	Porsche 1978(Japanese)	78	136		Neko		S	$30
Inouye T	Porsche 1979 (Japanese)	79	136		Neko	Neko	S	$30
Ireland I	All Arms and Elbows	67	205		Pelham Books		H	$80
Ireland I	Marathon in Dust	70	209		Kimber		H	$40
Ireland I	Motor Racing Today Innes Ireland	61	298		Barker		H	$50
Irving P E	Tuning for Speed	48+	609		Temple/Hamlyn/Clymer		X	$40
Irving P E	Motorcycle Engineering	73	609		Clymer/Speedsport		S	$40
Iskenderian E	Valve Timing for Maximum Output	62	202		Iskenderian		S	$20
Ixion	Motorcycle Reminiscences	22	601		Iliffe		B	$150
Ixion	Motor Cycle Cavalcade Hist of MC	50+	601		Iliffe/SRP		H	$40
Jack	Leyland Bus	84	303		Transport Publishing Co.		H	$70
Jackson R B	Stock Car Racing Grnd Nat Comp(juv)	68	299		Walck		H	$20
Jackson C	Hounds of Road History Greyhound	84			Bowling Green U/Kendall		H	$50
Jackson C	Stock Car Racer (juv fict)	57	213		Follett		H	$30
Jackson J	Man & the Automobile 20th Century..	79	419		McGraw/Harrow House		H	$30
Jackson R B	Road Race Round World NY to Paris	65	212	213	Walck		S	$20
Jackson R B	Grand Prix at Glen (juvenile)	65	206		Walck		H	$20
Jackson R B	Quarter-Mile Combat (juvenile)	75	201	213	Walck		H	$20
Jackson R B	Big Book of Old Cars (juvenile)	78	424		Walck/McKay		H	$10
Jackson W S	Profile No 88 Lincoln Continental	67	161		Profile Publications		S	$30
Jacobs D	American Trucks 2	82	301		Osprey	Col Lib	S	$30
Jacobs D	American Trucks Photographic Essay	80	301		Osprey	Osprey Col Lib	S	$30
Jacobs D	MG Experience	76	131		Transport Bookman		H	$40
Jacobs D	European Trucks On the Road in.....	83	303		Osprey	Osprey Col Ser	S	$30
Jacobson M A I	AA Book of Car	70	405		Drive Pub		H	$10
Jamison A	Steam-Powered Automobile An Answer.	70	414		Indiana		H	$30
Janes H B	Young Sportsmans Gd to Spts Car Rac	62	213		Nelson		H	$20
Janeway E	Early Days of Automobile in America	56	424		Random	Landmark	H	$20
Jardim A	First Henry Ford Study in..........	70	415		MIT		H	$50
Jarrott C	Ten Years of Motor Racing 1896-1906	06+	298		Foulis		H	$80

Author	Title	Pub date	Subjects		Publisher	Series	Bind	Price
Jaspersohn W	Motorcycle Making of Harley (juvnl)	84	607		Little Brown		H	$30
Jellinek-Mercedes G	My Father Mr. Mercedes	61	130		Chilton/Foulis		H	$30
Jenkins A	Salt of the Earth (Ab Jenkins)	39+	205	211	Clymer		X	$50
Jenkins B	Chevrolet Racing Engine	76	111		SA		S	$30
Jenkinson D	Automobile Year Bk of Sp Car Racing	82	297		Edita		H	$150
Jenkinson D	Grand Prix Mercedes Type W125 1937	70	130		Arco	Famous Car	H	$30
Jenkinson D	Fangio (from the film)	73	205		Beachplex/Joseph		H	$80
Jenkinson D	From Chain Drive to Turbo AFN Story	84	105		PSL		H	$100
Jenkinson D	Racing Driver Theory/Pract Fast....	58	203		Batsford/Bentley		X	$40
Jenkinson D	Porsche 356 Autohistory	81	136		Osprey	Autohistory	H	$40
Jenkinson D	Grand Prix Cars	59	297		Sports Car Press		H	$30
Jenkinson D	Story of Formula I 1954-1960	60	297		Tee & Whiten/Grenville		H	$50
Jenkinson D	Maserati 250 F Classic GP Car	75	172		Macmillan		H	$50
Jenkinson D	Profile No 08 Vanwall GP Car	66	298		Profile Publications		S	$20
Jenkinson D	Profile No 20 Frazer-Nash 1948-53	66	105		Profile Publications		S	$10
Jenkinson D	Porsche Past & Present	83	136		Gentry		H	$40
Jenkinson D	Profile No 54 300SLR Mercedes-Benz	67	130		Profile Publications		S	$30
Jenkinson D	Profile No 78 Maserati 250F GP Car	67	172		Profile Publications		S	$30
Jenkinson D	Racing Car Pocketbook	62	297		Batsford		H	$20
Jenkinson D	Racing Car Review 1950	50S	204		Grenville		H	$40
Jenkinson D	Racing Car Review 1951	50S	204		Grenville		H	$40
Jenkinson D	Profile No 89 BMW Type 328	67	106		Profile Publications		S	$30
Jenkinson D	Maserati 3011 Story of a Racing Car	87	172		Aries		H	$90
Jenkinson D	Jaguar E Type Autohistory	82	127		Osprey	Autohistory	H	$40
Jenkinson D	Racing Car Review 1947 (first)	47	204		Grenville		H	$50
Jenkinson D/Posthumus C	Vanwall Story of Tony Vandervell...	75	298		PSL		H	$60
Jenkinson D/Verstappen P	Schlumpf Obsession	77	401		Doubleday/Hamlyn		H	$125
Jenkinson K A	Preserving Commercial Vehicles	82	309		PSL		H	$30
Jenkinson K A	Preserved Lorries	77	306		Ian Allen		H	$30
Jennings G	Two-Stroke Tuners Handbook	73	609		HP		S	$50
Jensen P	Building Model Trucks	73	703		Auto-World/Haessner		H	$40
Jerome J	Truck On Rebldg P/U & Other Advntrs	77	306		Houghton/Bodley Head		H	$20
Jewell B	Allard to Zodiac Brit Prod Cars 60s	85	406		Alderman Press		H	$60
Jewell B	Motor Badges & Figureheads	78	507		Midas		X	$50
Jewell D	Man & Motor 20th Cent Love Affair	67	401		Walker		H	$30
Jewell F B	Model Car Collecting	63	704		Temple		H	$20
Jezierski C	Speed Indy Car Racing	85	299		Abrams		H	$50
Johnson A	Driving in Competition(Johnson)	71+	203		Bond-Parkhurst/Haessner		H	$30
Johnson B	Three-56 Porsche Rest Gd Authent...	87	136		356 Registry		S	$40
Johnson E	Dawn of Motoring How Car Came Brit	86	130	401	Mercedes U K		H	$40
Johnson J	Big Rigs Down Under	79	306		Golden/Taylor-Type		H	$30
Johnson M B	Interstaters (Australian Trucking)	83	306		Savvas/Truckin Life		H	$40
Johnson R	Corvette Restoration Srce Bk 53-67	78	114		Johnson		S	$60
Johnston R	Our First 50 Years 1905-55	55	105		Nuffield/BMC		H	$70
Jolly F	Delahaye Sport et Prestige	81	120		Editions Presse Audio.		H	$80
Jones A/Botsford K	Driving Ambition Alan Jones	81	205		Atheneum		H	$30
Jones B	Story of Panther Motor Cycles	83	606		PSL/Thorsons		H	$50
Jones C	Road Race	77	297		McKay		H	$40
Jones C R	Convert your Compact Car to Elec...	81	417		Domus		S	$20
Jones E	High Gear	55	416		Bantam		S	$20
Jones G/Allen J	Ford That Beat Ferrari History GT40	85	169		Kimberley's		H	$180
Jones T F	Enduro	70	602		Chilton		S	$10
Judge A W	Carburettors and Fuel Systems	25+	405		Chapman & Hall/Bentley	Motor Manuals	H	$20
Judge A W	Mechanism of Car	25+	405		Bentley	Motor Manuals	H	$20
Judge A W	Car Maintenence & Repair	28+	405		Chapman & Hall/Bentley	Motor Manual	H	$20
Judge A W	Modern Electrical Equip for Autos	62	405		Bentley	Motor Manuals	H	$10
Juratovic J	Automotive Fine Art (AFAS Catalog)	87	506		GP Publishing		S	$20
Jute A	Designing and Building Special Cars	85	405		David & Charles		H	$50
Kahn M	Mexico or Bust (World Cup Rally 70)	70	209		Harrap		H	$30
Kahn M	World Motor Racing/Rallying H/B 70	70	209		Mayflower		S	$20
Kahn M	Day I Died	74	205		Gentry/Wren		H	$40
Karolevitz R F	This Was Trucking A Pictorial Hist	66	306		Superior/Bonanza		H	$40
Karolevitz R F	This Was Pioneer Motoring	68	401		Superior		H	$40
Karslake K	Racing Voiturettes	50	298		MRP		H	$150
Karslake K	French Grand Prix 1906-1914(S/B #7)	49	206		MRP		S	$50
Karslake K/Pomeroy L	From Veteran to Vintage	56	401		Temple		H	$150
Kato S	My Years with Toyota	81	126		Toyota		H	$40
Katz F	Art Afons Fastest Man On Wheels	65	211	205	Rutledge		H	$40
Kaye D	Buses and Trolleybuses 1919 to 1945	70			Blandford		H	$20
Kaye D	Buses and Trolleybuses Before 1919	72			Blandford		H	$20
Keats J	Insolent Chariots	58+	419		Lippincott/Fawcett/Crest		X	$30
Keith K/Hooker S	Achievement of Excell...Rolls-Royce	77	139		Newcomen Society		S	$30
Kelley K	Pickup Parade Light Truck Handbook	67+	301		Auto Book Press/Sincere		X	$30
Kelley L	Hot Rod Corvette No 02	78	114		Petersen		S	$10
Kelly M A	Overtype Steam Road Waggon	71	303		Goose		H	$40
Kennett P	Dennis - World Trucks No 6	79	303		PSL	World Trucks	H	$30
Kennett P	DAF - World Trucks No 5	79	303		PSL	World Trucks	H	$30
Kennett P	Seddon Atkinson - World Trucks No 3	78	303		PSL/Aztex	World Trucks	H	$30

Author	Title	Pub date	Subjects		Publisher	Series	Bind	Price
Kennett P	ERF - World Trucks No 1	78	303		PSL/Aztex	World Trucks	H	$30
Kennett P	Scania World Trucks No 2	78	303		PSL/Aztex	World Trucks	H	$30
Kennett P	MAN World Trucks No 04	78	303		PSL/Aztex	World Trucks	H	$30
Kennett P	Volvo World Trucks No 7	79	303		PSL	World Trucks	H	$30
Kennett P	Fiat World Trucks No 9	80	303		PSL	World Trucks	H	$30
Kennett P	Berliet - World Trucks No 12	81	303		PSL	World Trucks	H	$30
Kennett P	Magirus World Trucks No 13	83	303		PSL	World Trucks	H	$30
Kennett P	Leyland World Trucks No 14	83	303		PSL	World Trucks	H	$30
Kennett P	AEC - World Trucks No 10	80	303		PSL	World Trucks	H	$30
Kennett P	International - World Trucks #11	81	301		PSL	World Trucks	H	$40
Kennett P	Scammell - World Trucks No 8	79	303		PSL	World Trucks	H	$30
Kenyon J W	Racing Wheels	41	603	416	Nelson		H	$40
Kenyon L	Handbook High Performance Driving	75	203		Dodd, Mead		H	$30
Kestler P	Bugatti Evolution of Style	77	107		Edita		H	$100
Kettlewell M	Autocourse 1978-79	78	204		Hazleton		H	$300
Kettlewell M	Autocourse 1975-76	75	204		Hazleton		H	$180
Kettlewell M	Autocourse 1976-77	76	204		Hazleton		H	$150
Kettlewell M	Autocourse 1977-78	78	204		Hazleton		H	$180
Kettlewell M	Autocourse 1972-73	73	204		Haymarket		H	$300
Kettlewell M	Autocourse 1973-74	74	204		Haymarket		H	$400
Kettlewell M	Autocourse 1974-75	75	204		Haymarket		H	$400
Key M	Lead Sleds Chopped & Low '35 - '54	84	422		Osprey		S	$40
Key M/Thacker T	Fins & Fifties Cars Chrome Culture	87	403		Osprey		H	$50
Keyser M	Speed Merchants	73	297		Rutledge/Prentice-Hall		H	$50
Kidner R W	Steam Lorry	48+	303		Oakwood	Locomotion Pprs	S	$10
Kidner R W	Military Traction Engines & Lorries	75	308		Oakwood	Locomotion Pprs	S	$10
Kidner R W	Hist of Motorized Vehcls 1769-1946	49	401		Clymer		S	$30
Kieselbach R J F	Streamlined Cars in Germany	82	408		W. Kohlhammer GmbH		H	$100
Kieselbach R J F	Stromlinienbusse in Deshld(English)	83			Kohlhammer edition		H	$100
Kimberley W	Comp Gd Triumph TR7 & TR8	81	146		Dalton Watson		H	$40
Kimes B R	American Car Since 1775	71	403		Automobile Quarterly		H	$50
Kimes B R	Golden Anniv Lincoln MC 1921-1971	70	161		AQ		X	$50
Kimes B R	Cars That Henry Ford Built	78	122		AQ		H	$40
Kimes B R	Classic Tradition of Lincoln MC	68	161		Automobile Quarterly		H	$50
Kimes B R	Automobile Quarterlys Gt Cars Gd Mq	76	401		Aq/Bonanza		H	$40
Kimes B R	Packard Hist of MC & Co (leather)	78	159		AQ		L	$125
Kimes B R/Langworth R M	Oldsmobile First Seventy-Five Years	72	162		AQ		X	$40
Kimes B R/Paddock L C	Legend of Lincoln	85	161		Automobile Quarterly		S	$20
Kimzey L	Earlyriders Motorcycling thru Years	78	601		Paisano		S	$20
Kincaid P	Rule of Road Intl Gd Hist/Practice	86	401		Greenwood		H	$20
King A C	Oliver Advertising History	81	901		King		S	$20
King B	All Color Book of Racing Cars	73	297		Octopus Books		H	$10
Kingdon J G	True's Automobile Yearbook #4 1955	55	410		Fawcett		S	$20
Kingman W	Profile No 35 Cord 810 & 812	66	116		Profile Publications		S	$30
Kingsford P W	F W Lanchester Life of Engineer	60	105		Arnold		H	$125
Kinsella D	Allard	77	105		Haynes		H	$40
Kirby G	PPG Indy Car World Series 1981('80)	81	204		Competition Images		S	$20
Kirchberg P	Grand Prix Rpt Auto Union(German)	84	124		transpress VEB Verlag		H	$40
Kirchberg P	Bildatlas Auto Union	87	124		Transpress		H	$70
Kitihara T	Cars Tin Toy Dreams	84	703		Chronicle		S	$30
Klapper C F	British Lorries 1900-1945	73	303		Ian Allen		H	$20
Klass G	Fire Apparatus Pict Hist LA Fire D	74	302		Ruccione		S	$50
Kleinfield S	Month at Brickyard	77	208		Holt		H	$40
Klemantaski L	Motor Racing Circuits of Europe	58	298		Batsford		H	$60
Klemantaski L	British Racing Green 1946-1956	57	298		Bodley		H	$60
Klemantaski L/Frostick M	Vanwall Story	58	298		H Hamilton		H	$70
Klemantaski L/Frostick M	Racing Sports Cars	56	298		Macmillan/Bodley		H	$60
Klemantaski L/Frostick M	Drivers in Action	55	298		Bodley		H	$70
Klemantaski L/Frostick M	For Practice Only	59	298		Bodley		H	$60
Klemantaski L/Frostick M	Le Mans (Klemantaski)	60	206		Macmillan		H	$180
Kling K/Molter G	Pursuit of Victory Story of Rac Dri	56	205		Bodley Head		H	$80
Knepper M	Corvair Affair	82	113		MBI		H	$40
Knight R	Racing & Tuning Production Mtcycles	70	604		Speed & Sports		S	$30
Knight R J/Randle J N	Discussion of Alt Spts Cr Concepts	77	405	127	SAE		S	$30
Knittel S	Mercedes 190SL Auto Classic #3	80S	130		Podzun-Pallas	Auto-Classic	S	$20
Knittel S	Mercedes 300SL Auto Classic #5	83	130		Podzun-Pallas	Auto Classic	S	$20
Knittel S	Opel GT Coupe Auto-Classic #4	80S	124		Albion Scott	Auto-Classic	S	$20
Knittel S	Borgward Isabella Auto-Classic #6	80S	124		Podzun-Pallas	Auto Classic	S	$20
Knittel V S	Deutsche Krader im Kriege		606		Podzun-Pallas-Verlag	Waffen-Arsenal	S	$20
Knowles A	Donald Campbell CBE	69	205	211	Allen & Unwin/Barnes		H	$30
Knowles A	Auto-Biography My 40 Yrs of Motrng	70	205		Allen & Unwin		H	$30
Knudson R L	MG International 1977	77	131		MRP		H	$30
Knudson R L	Land Speed Record Breakers	81	211		Lerner		H	$30
Knudson R L	Fabulous Cars of 1920s & 1930s(Juv)	81	401		Lerner		H	$20
Knudson R L	T Series MG	73	131		Motorcars Unlimited		X	$60
Knudson R L	Classic MG Yearbook 1973	74	131		Motorcars Unlimited		H	$40
Knudson R L	MG Sports Car America Loved First	75	131		Motorcars Unlimited		H	$50
Kobayashi S	America Classic Cars (Japanese)	61	403		Nigensha Co. Ltd.		H	$150

Author	Title	Pub date	Subjects		Publisher	Series	Bind	Price
Kobayashi S	Lincoln Car Graphic Lib (Japanese)	71	161		Car Graphic/Nigensha	Car Grap Lib 47	S	$40
Kobayashi S	Porsche (Kobayashi)	73	136		MBI		S	$40
Kobayashi S	Alfa Romeo Car Grap Lib(Japanese)	70S	101		Car Graphic/Nigensha	Car Grap Lib 26	S	$40
Koblenz J	Corvette Americas Sports Car (84)	84	114		Pub Intl/Cons Gd/Beekman	Consumer Gd	H	$30
Koch G M	Bestattungswagen (German) (Hearses)	87	304		Diesel Queen		H	$70
Konrad A	VW Beetle Handbook Tun Hand Maint	70	150		Foulis		H	$30
Kopec R J	Shelby Buyers Guide	78	109	122	SAAC		S	$30
Kopec R J	Shelby American Guide	78+	109	122	SAAC		S	$50
Korff W H	Designing Tomorrow's Cars	80	502		M-C Publ		H	$50
Kosbab W H	Motorcycle Dictionary/Terminology	84	601		Career		S	$20
Kovacik B	Sports Cars of World(Petersen 1971)	71	401		Petersen		S	$10
Kowal B	Jaguar (Exeter)	83+	127		Exeter/Bookthrift/S&S		H	$10
Kroon R	Hors Ligne Special Ferrari/1985	85	121		Hors Ligne		S	$40
Kroth K A	Das Werk Opel	30S	124		Max Schroder		H	$40
Krueger R	Gypsy on 18 Wheels Truckers Tale	75	301		Praeger		S	$20
Kubisch U	Motorroller Mobil (scooters etc)	85	401	606	Elefanten Press		S	$40
Kuipers J F J	Hist of Comm. Vehicles of World	72	306		Oakwood Press		H	$40
Kuipers J F J	Buses on Continent 1898-1976	77			Oakwood	Locomotion Pprs	S	$10
Kuipers J F J	Great Trucks (Consumer Gd)	83	306		Publications Intl	Consumer Gd	H	$20
Kumano M etc	Toyota Motor Sports (Japanese)	88	126				S	$50
Kuns R F	Comp Ray Kunz Auto Racing Book	?	299		Ray Kuns		S	$50
Kuns R F	Automobile Racing 6E (Kuns)	47	202		Kuns		S	$60
Kuns R F	Automotive Essentials	35+	405		Bruce		H	$30
Kuns R F	Automobile Racing 5E (Kuns)	39	202		Kuns		S	$60
Kupelian Y/J	Histoire del Automobile Belge (Fr)	70S	402		Paul Legrain		H	$80
Kutner R M	Comp Gd to Kit Cars	77+	423		Auto Logic		S	$10
Laas W	Ford Bk of Styling	63	122	502	Ford Motor Co		S	$40
Laban B	Chrome Glamour Cars of Fifties	82	401		Gallery/Orbis/Smith		H	$40
Laban B	Ferrari (Laban)	84	121		Multimedia/Smith/Gallery		H	$20
Labric R/Ham G	Les 24 Heures du Mans (Labric)	49	206	504			S	$1500
Labro P	Twenty-Four Heures Impress. (Otis)	82	206		Otis		H	$100
Lacombe C	Motorcycle (Lacombe)	74	601		Denoel/Guiness/Grosset		H	$30
Lamm J	De Lorean Stainless Steel Illusion	83	168		Newport Press		H	$100
Lamm M	Great Camero	78+	111		Lamm-Morada Publ. Inc.		H	$30
Lamm M	Camaro Book From A Through Z28	84	111		Lamm-Morada		H	$70
Lamm M	Fabulous Firebird	79	138		Lamm-Morada		H	$50
Lampe M	Ferrari 512 V-12 Competition Cars	82	121		Manfred Lampe		H	$300
Lancia	Sixty anni della Lancia	67	157		Lancia		S	$40
Landau R/Phillippi J	Airstream (trailers)	84	306		Gibbs M Smith		S	$30
Lane A	Austerity Motoring 39-50 Shire 183	87	406		Shire Pub	Shire Album	S	$10
Lane M R	Pride of Road Pict St Tract....	76	903		New English Library		H	$50
Lane R W/Boylston H D	Travels with Zenobia Paris to Alb..	83	122	212	University of Missouri		H	$20
Lang H	Grand Prix Driver (Lang)	53	205	130	Foulis		H	$70
Lang H P/Lang P G	Danhausens World Modelcar Book '85	84	702		Danhausen		S	$20
Lang H P/Lang P G	Danhausens World Modelcar Book '86	85	702		Danhausen		S	$20
Langworth R M	Hudson Postwar Years	77	163		MBI	Postwar Years	H	$60
Langworth R M	Studebaker Postwar Years	79	145		MBI		H	$60
Langworth R M	Thunderbird Story Personal Luxury	80	147		MBI		H	$80
Langworth R M	Automobile Quarterlys World of Cars	71	401		AQ		H	$20
Langworth R M	Chrysler & Imperial Postwar Years	76	112		MBI		H	$60
Langworth R M	Porsche Tradition of Greatness (H)	83	136		Publications Int	Consumer Guide	H	$40
Langworth R M	Comp Hist Ford Motor Company	87	122		Pub Int/Beekman/Crown	Consumer Guide	H	$40
Langworth R M	Tiger Alpine Rapier Sporting Cars..	82	105		Osprey		H	$50
Langworth R M	Cars That Never Were Prototypes	81	401		Pub Int/Beekman/Crown	Consumer Gd	H	$30
Langworth R M	Comp Bk Collectible Cars 40-80	85	401		Publications Intl		H	$30
Langworth R M	Mercedes-Benz First Hundred Years	84	130		Publications Int/Beekman	Consumer Gd	H	$40
Langworth R M	Ency of American Cars 1930-1980	84	403		Publications Intl		H	$50
Langworth R M	Great American Convertible (Lngwth)	88	403		Pub Intl/Beekman House	Consumer Gd	H	$40
Langworth R M	New Comp Bk Coll Cars see COMP BK..	87	401		Publications Intl		H	$0
Langworth R M	Porsche Tradition of Greatness (S)	84	136		Publications Intl	Consumer Gd	S	$10
Langworth R M	Cadillac Standard of Excellence	80	110		Publications Intl	Consumer Guide	H	$20
Langworth R M	Mustang Car That Started Ponycar...	79	122		Publications Intl	Consumer Guide	H	$20
Langworth R M/ Norbye J	Comp Hist Chrysler Corp 1924-1985	85	112		Pub Intl/Beekman/Crown	Consumer Guide	X	$40
Langworth R M/Consumer Gd	Ency of American Cars 1940-1970	80	403		Publications Intl		H	$40
Langworth R M/Consumer Gd	Great Cars From Ford	82	122		Publications Intl		S	$20
Langworth R M/Norbye J P	Chevrolet 1911-1985	84	111		Publications Intl	Consumer Guide	H	$40
Langworth R M/Norbye J P	Comp Hist General Motors	86	160		Publications Intl	Consumer Guide	H	$50
Langworth R M/Robson G	Comp Bk Collectible Cars 30-80	82+	401		Pub Intl/Beekman/Crown	Consumer Guide	H	$40
Larew W B	Carburetors & Carburetion	67	405		Chilton		H	$30
Lartigue J H	J H Lartigue Et Les Autos	74	510		Chene		H	$150
Lartigue J H	Boyhood Photos of J-H Lartigue	66	510		Ami Guichard		H	$500
Lartigue J-H	Jacques-Henri Lartigue(English)	86	510		Centre National/Pantheon		S	$20
Lastu J M/Lastu D	Ferrari Miniatures au 1/43 1962-83	80S	121	702	Editions Adepte		H	$70
Lauda N	My Years With Ferrari	78	205	121	MBI		H	$50
Lauda N	New Formula One Turbo Age	82	202		Verlag Orac/MBI/Kimber		H	$60
Lauda N	Art and Science of GP Driving	77	203		Verlag Orac/MBI		H	$50
Laux J M	In First Gear French Auto Ind to 14	76	407		Liverpool U		H	$40
Lawrence M	Directory of Classic Spts-Rac Cars	87	297		Aston		S	$40

Author	Title	Pub date	Subjects		Publisher	Series	Bind	Price
Lawrence M	Mille Miglia (Lawrence)	88	206		Miura/Batsford	Wld Grt Mtr Cmp	H	$80
Leake G	Concise Cat. 1-75 Series Matchbox	81	702		Leake		S	$20
Lee B	Tokheim Pump Co 1901-1980	80	507		Lee		S	$30
Lee R	Fit for Chase Cars & Movies	69	509		Barnes/Castle		H	$30
Leefe C	Rolls-Royce Alpine Compendium......	73	139		Transport Bookmen		H	$50
Legate T	Cobra (Legate)	84	109		Chambers Green/Haynes/MBI		H	$90
Lehwald E A	El Camino Source Book	83	111		Bookman	Source Book	S	$30
Lehwald E A	Cadillac 1940-1984 ID Guide	84	110		Bookman Dan	ID Guide	S	$30
Lehwald E A	Chevelle SS Vol II A Source Book	85	111		Bookman	Source Boo	S	$30
Lehwald E A	Monte Carlo Classic Source Book	85	111		Bookman	Source Book	S	$20
Lehwald E A	Big Chevys Source Book	83	111		Bookman	Source Book	S	$20
Leicester City Transport	Fifty Years of Motorbuses 1924-1974	74			Leicester City Transport			$20
Leland W/Millbrook	Master of Precision Henry Leyland	66	404		Wayne University Press		H	$80
Lent H B	X Cars Detroit's 1-of-a-kind Autos	71	403		Putnam		H	$40
Lesberg S/Goldberg N	Hammer Down Heavy Truckers Romance.	77	301		Peebles		X	$10
Leslie S W	Boss Kettering Wizard of GM	83	160	404	Columbia		X	$40
Lessner E	Famous Auto Races Rallies	56	297		Hanover House		H	$40
Levin H	Grand Delusions Cosmic...(DeLorean)	83	168		Viking Penguin		H	$40
Levine L	Ford Dust and Glory Racing History	68	169		Macmillan		H	$250
Lewandowski J	Porsche 959: Art & Car Edition	86	136		Sudwest	Art & Car	H	$800
Lewandowski J	Maserati Geschichte Technik........	82	172		Motorbuch Verlag		H	$70
Lewandowski J	Mercedes-Benz 300SL (Art & Car Ed)	88	130		Sudwest	Art & Car	H	$400
Lewandowski J	Mercedes-Benz 1886-1986 (2 volumes)	86	130		Edita		H	$350
Lewandowski J	Ferrari GTO (Art & Car)	87	121		Sudwest	Art & Car	H	$600
Lewis D L	Automobile & American Culture	81	419		U of Mich Press		S	$50
Lewis D L/McCarville.....	Ford 1903 to 1984 (Consumer Guide)	83	122		Pub Intl/Beekman/Crown		H	$30
Lewis E	Motor Memories Saga Whirling Gears	47	401		Alved/Clymer		H	$30
Lewis P	Alf Francis Racing Mechanic	57+	205		Foulis/Motoraces BC		H	$60
Lewis P	Dicing With Death	61	298		Daily Mirror		S	$40
Libby B	Champions of Indianapolis 500	76	208		Dodd Mead		H	$20
Libby B	Andretti	70	205		Grosset & Dunlap		X	$30
Libby B	Great American Race Drivers	70	205		Cowles Book		H	$30
Libby B	Parnelli Story of Auto Racing	69	205		E P Dutton		H	$40
Libby B	AJ Foyt Racing Champion	74	205		Hawthorn		H	$40
Libby B	Heroes of Stock Car Racing	75	205		Random	Sports Library	H	$20
Libby B	Foyt	74	205		Hawthorn		H	$40
Libby B/Petty R	King Richard Richard Petty Story	77	205		Doubleday		H	$30
Lichty R	Collecting & Rest Antique Fire Engs	81	302		Tab		S	$30
Lidz J	Rolling Homes	79	306		A&W Visual Library		S	$20
Lief A	Firestone Story	51	418		Whittlesey/McGraw		H	$30
Lienert R M	Automotive News GM 75th Anniv Issue	83	160		Crain		S	$40
Lienert R M	Automotive News Centennial of Car	85	401		Crain		S	$30
Lindh B	Volvo Car From 20's to 80's	84	165		Förlagshuset Norden		H	$125
Lingnau G	Freiheit auf zwei Radern BMW	82	606		ECON		H	$80
Lini F/Costantini L	Addio Bandini (Italian)	67	205		LEA		S	$40
Lintern M	Comp Gd to American Cars 66-76	77	403		AutoMedia		S	$30
Liska H	Liska Portfolio(1953 copyright)	53	130	504	Daimler-Benz AG		H	$0
Liska H	Liska Portfolio(1954 copyright)	54	130	504	Daimler-Benz AG		H	$0
Liska H	Liska Portfolio(1955 copyright)	55	130	504	Daimler-Benz AG		H	$250
Little K/Rosenhan K	Chicago Fire Department Engines	72	302		Little/Rosenhan		S	$50
Lloyd I	Rolls-Royce Years of Endeavour	78	139		Macmillan		H	$60
Lloyd I	Rolls-Royce Merlin at War	78	139		Macmillan		H	$60
Lloyd I	Rolls-Royce Growth of Firm	78	139		Macmillan		H	$60
Lloyd J	Worlds Veteran to Vintage Cars	60	401		Macdonald/Hanover		H	$20
Lloyd N	V-16 BRM Grand Prix Car(7" record)	50S	298		Schofield Productions	Sound Stories		$20
Lloyd N	Monaco Grand Prix 1959(12" record)	50S	206		Schofield Productions	Sound Stories		$40
Lloyd N	Vingt-Q'tre du Mans(7" record Eng)	50S	206		Schofield Productions	Sound Stories		$20
Lloyd N/Pomeroy L	Three Pointed Star (12" record)	50S	130		Schofield Productions	Sound Stories		$40
Locke B W	Sports Car Bodywork	54+	202		Bentley		H	$50
Lockwood N	Designing and Building Sports Car	60	405		Scientific/Foulis		H	$40
Loeper J J	Galloping Gertrude by Motorcar 1908	80	419		Atheneum		H	$20
Loewy R	Industrial Design(Spec sig ltd ed)	79	502	145	Overlook Press		H	$500
Loewy R	Industrial Design	79	502	145	Overlook		H	$125
Logas A	Auto-Universum 1970	69	410		Int Auto Parade			$50
Logoz A	Auto-Parade 1958 (Vol II)	58	410		Int Auto Parade		H	$70
Logoz A	Auto-Parade 1962 #5	61	410		Int Auto Parade/Chilton		H	$60
Logoz A	Auto-Parade 1963 #6	62	410		Int Auto Parade/Macmillan		H	$60
Logoz A	Auto-Parade 1960 #3	60	410		Int Auto Parade/Chilton		H	$60
Logoz A	Auto-Universum 1966	65	410		Int Auto Parade		H	$60
Logoz A	Auto-Parade 1961 #4	61	410		Int Auto Parade/Chilton		H	$60
Logoz A	Auto-Universum 1967	66	410		Int Auto Parade		H	$60
Logoz A	Auto-Universum 1965	65	410		Int Auto Parade/A Barker		H	$60
Logoz A	Auto-Universum 71	70	410		Int Auto Parade		H	$50
Logoz A	Auto-Universum 1969	68	410		Int Auto Parade		H	$60
Logoz A	Auto-Universum 1964	63	410		Int Auto Parade		H	$60
Logoz A	Auto-Parade 1957(1st)(Int Auto Cat)	57	410		Int Auto Parade		S	$100
Logoz A	Auto-Universum 1968	67	410		Int Auto Parade			$60
Longstreet S	Century on Wheels Story Studebaker	52	145		Holt/Greenwood		H	$40

Author	Title	Pub date	Subjects	Publisher	Series	Bind	Price
Longstreet S	Boy in the Model-T	56	122	Simon & Schuester/Paperb		S	$20
Losch A	World Cars '80	80	410	Auto Club Italy/Herald		H	$50
Losch A	World Cars '79	79	410	Auto Club Italy/Herald		H	$70
Losch A	World Cars '82	82	410	Auto Club Italy/Herald		H	$50
Losch A	World Cars '83	83	410	Auto Club Italy/Herald		H	$50
Losch A	World Cars '78	78	410	Auto Club Italy		H	$90
Losch A	World Cars '81	81	410	Auto Club Italy/Herald		H	$70
Losch A	World Cars '84	84	410	Auto Club Italy/Herald		H	$30
Losch A	World Cars '85 (last)	85	410	Auto Club Italy/Herald		H	$30
Louis H/Currie B	Story of Triumph Motorcycles	75+	606	PSL		H	$50
Loup S	Renault (Loup)	57	120	Dumont/Bodley Head		H	$40
Lowe	Kaingaroa Super Trucks	83	306	Lodestar Press		S	$20
Lowry R	Monte Carlo Rally	50S	209	Foulis		H	$30
Lozier H	Car of Kings	67	130	Chilton Book Co.		H	$350
Lozier H	Getting Started in Model-Building	71	704	Hawthorn		H	$30
Lozier H	Auto Racing Old and New(Fawcett 184	53	297	Fawcett		S	$10
Lucas T/Riess F	HT Convert to Electric Car	80	417	Michelman/Crown		H	$30
Lucero J R	Legion Ascot Speedway 1920s-1930s	82	206	Orecul Pub.		H	$90
Ludvigsen K E	Gurneys Eagles	76	299	MBI		H	$125
Ludvigsen K E	Group 7 Wld's Most Pwfl Rac Cars	71+	297	World/Arco		H	$90
Ludvigsen K E	Mercedes-Benz Racing Cars	71	130	Bond/Parkhurst		H	$150
Ludvigsen K E	Mercedes-Benz Guide	59	130	Sports Car Press		S	$40
Ludvigsen K E	Inside Story of Fastest Fords	69	122	Style Auto		H	$80
Ludvigsen K E	Guide to Corvette Speed	69	114	Sports Car Press	Mod Sports	S	$30
Ludvigsen K E	Tribute to Turbo (Carrera)	75	136	Porsche		H	$0
Ludvigsen K E/Wise D B	Comp Ency of American Automobile	77+	403	Orbis		H	$30
Ludvigsen K E/Wise D B	Ency of American Automobile(Ldvgsn)	74+	403	Orbis/Chartwell		H	$30
Lukins A H	Floyd Clymer Catalog Brit Cars 1951	51	406	George Ronald/Clymer		S	$20
Lurani G	Nuvolari (SCP)	63	205	Sports Car Press	Mod Sports Car	S	$20
Lurani G	Nuvolari	59	205	Morrow/Cassell		H	$125
Lurani G	Mille Miglia 1927-57 (English)	81	206	Edita		H	$125
Lurani G	Hist of Racing Car	72	297	Crowell		H	$50
Lurani G	La Storia Della Mille Miglia	79	206	Instituto Geografico.....		H	$80
Lush T	Allard Inside Story	77	105	MRP		H	$70
Lyndon B	Circuit Dust	34	298	John Miles		H	$125
Lyndon B	Grand Prix (Lyndon)	35	298	John Miles		H	$250
Lyndon B	Combat Motor Racing History	33	298	Heinemann		H	$150
Lyons P	Road Racing Annual 1977	77	204	Oxman		S	$40
Lyons P	Road Racing Annual 1978	78	204	Oxman		H	$50
Lyons P	Cars in Profile 04 Chaparral 2.....	72	299	Profile Publications		S	$20
Lyons P	Comp Bk Lamborghini	88	128	Pub Intl/Haynes/Guild	Consumer Guide	H	$40
Lyons P	James Hunt	75	205	Augustus Books		S	$10
Lyons P/Gilligan V	Formula One 74(only book in series)	74	204	Oxman		H	$40
Lyons P/Knepper/Gilligan	Road Racing Annual 1976('75 season)	75	204	Oxman		S	$80
MacDonald J	Under Green Comp Gd to Auto Racing	79	297	Peebles		H	$30
MacKellar C	Yamaha Two-Stroke Twins	85	606	Osprey	Osprey Coll Lib	H	$50
MacManus/Beasley	Men Money & Motors	29	401	Harper		H	$30
MacMinn S	Sports Cars of Future	59	401	Sports Car Press	Mod Sports Cars	S	$10
MacPherson T	Dragging and Driving (juv)	60	201	Putnam		H	$10
Macauley T	Yamaha Legend	79	606	St. Martins		H	$40
Macauley T	Mike the Bike Again	80	610	Cassell		H	$30
Macauley T	International Motor Cycle Rac Book	71	603	Souvenir		H	$30
Macbeth G	Observers Book of Motor Sport	75+	297	Warne		H	$10
Mack R F	Historic Commercial Vehicles	72	306	Turntable		S	$10
Mackerle J	Air-cooled Motor/Auto Engines	61+	405	Cleaver-Hume/Halsted		H	$50
Maclay J L S	Triumph TR Maintenance Mod & Tuning	67	146	Haynes		H	$30
Madaro G	Tutte Le Fiat	70	152	Editoriale Domus		H	$70
Madaro G	Ferrarissima #02 (Original Ed)	85	121	Automobilia		H	$125
Madaro G	Ferrarissima #04 (Original Ed)	86	121	Automobilia		H	$125
Madaro G	Ferrarissima #03 (Original Ed)	85	121	Automobilia		H	$125
Madaro G	Ferrarissima #01 (Original Ed)	84	121	Automobilia		H	$125
Madow M	Pikes Peak Race to Clouds	79	206	Marc Madow		S	$30
Magayne J H	Ford Retractable 1957-59 Photofacts	83	122	MBI	CMB Photofacts	S	$50
Mahla U	Six Hundred Thirty Days To Top	84	106	BMW AG		S	$40
Mahoney D	Trio at Top	70	205	Robert Hale		H	$30
Mahoney J	Indianapolis 1969-1972 Yearbook	80	208	Hungness		H	$200
Mahoney T	Story of George Romney	60	102	Harper		H	$30
Main-Smith B	First AMC(motorcycle) Racing Scene	80	603	BMS		S	$20
Main-Smith B	Second Post-Vintage Rac Scene 31-53	78	603	BMS		S	$20
Main-Smith B	Second Post-Vintage Scene 1931-1953	78	603	BMS		S	$20
Main-Smith B	First Knocker Norton Scene	79	606	BMS		S	$10
Main-Smith B	Book of Super Bike Road Tests	72	601	BMS		S	$20
Main-Smith B	Vincent-HRD Motorcycles 1947-1955	60+	606	Temple/BMS		S	$20
Main-Smith B	First Velocette Scene	77	606	BMS		S	$20
Mallet J	Fire Engines of World	81	302	Vilo		H	$50
Mallet J	Great American Fire Engines	84	302	EPA/Outlet/Crescent		H	$30
Mandel L	American Cars (From Harrah's Coll)	82	403	Stewart, Tabori		H	$60
Mandel L	William Fisk Harrah Life &.....	81	404	Doubleday		H	$30

Author	Title	Pub date	Subjects		Publisher	Series	Bind	Price
Mandel L	Driven American Four-Wheeled Love..	77	419		Stein and Day		H	$30
Mandell L	Fast Lane Summer N American Rd Rac	81	299		Squarebooks		H	$40
Mann D/Scalzo J	Motorcycle Ace Dick Mann Story	72	610		Regnery		H	$30
Manso P	Vrooom!! Conversations with...	69	205		Funk & Wagnalls		H	$40
Manwaring L A	Observers Book of Automobiles 1967	67	410		Warne		H	$20
Manwaring L A	Observers Book of Automobiles 1957	57	410		Warne		H	$40
Manwaring L A	Observers Book of Automobiles 1958	58	410		Warne		H	$40
Manwaring L A	Observers Book Commercial Veh(1966)	66	306		Warne		H	$20
Manwaring L A	Observers Book of Autos 11E 1965	65	410		Warne		H	$10
Manwaring L A	Observers Book of Autos 09E 1963	63	410		Warne		H	$10
Marchiano M	Zagato	84	501		Automobilia		H	$180
Marchiano M	Le Zagato Fulvia Sport Junior Z	86	157	101	Libreria dell Automobile		H	$70
Marchiano M/Bowler	Zagato Aston Martin Vantage Zagato	86	103	501	Aston Martin		S	$30
Margolies J	End of the Road Vanishing Architect	77	506		Penguin		S	$30
Markmann C	Book of Sports Cars	59	401		Putnam		H	$70
Marsh P/Collett P	Driving Passion Psychology of Car	86	419		Faber & Faber		H	$30
Marshall D/Fraser I	BMC 1100s Maint Tuning & Mod	67	131	105	Foulis		H	$20
Marshall G	Competition Driving	79	203		Foulsham		H	$20
Marshall P	Wheels of London(boxed with access)	72	306		Sunday Times Magazine		H	$200
Marston H I	Big Rigs (juvenile)	79	306		Dodd Mead		H	$20
Martells J	Antique Automotive Collectibles	80	507		Contemporary		H	$60
Martin W H/Hot Rod Eds	Volkswagen Handbook	63	150		Petersen	Hot Rod	S	$30
Martin W H/Hot Rod Eds	Chrysler Corp Cars Perf Handbook	62	112		Petersen	Hot Rod	S	$30
Martin W H/Hot Rod Eds	Pontiac Performance Handbook	63	138		Petersen	Hot Rod	S	$30
Martin W H/Hot Rod Eds	Selecting and Bldg Hot Rod Engines	64	202		Petersen	Hot Rod	S	$20
Martin W H/Hot Rod Eds	Speed Tuning & Trouble Shooting	63	202		Petersen	Hot Rod	S	$20
Martin W H/Hot Rod Eds	Hot Rod Magazine Yearbook #1 1961	61	201		Petersen	Hot Rod	S	$40
Martinez A/Nory J L	American Automobiles of 50s and 60s	86	403		EPA/Vilol/MBI		H	$40
Martinez A/Nory J L	European Automobiles of 50s and 60s	82	401		EPA/Vilo		H	$40
Martinez A/Poulain H	Setton Collection of Automobiles	88	298		EPA		H	$125
Marvin K/Arnheim A	What Was McFarlan?	67	158		Arnheim		S	$60
Marvin K/Homan A L	Cars of 1923	57	403		Automobilists of UHV		S	$30
Marvin R B	Ferrari Register V2	85	121		Ferrari Data Bank		H	$100
Marvin R B	Packard Guide	87	159		Packard Data Bank		S	$60
Marvin R B	Ferrari Register (V1)	83	121		Ferrari Data Bank		S	$100
Mase A	Great Drivers (Mase)	81	205	510	Libro Port		H	$125
Massini M/Box R de la	Ferrari 250LM	83	121		Osprey		H	$70
Massucci E	Cars For Kids (Bebe Auto)	82	703		Automobilia		H	$100
Massucci E	Color Treasury of Autos & Model Crs	72	702		Orbis/Crescent		H	$20
Massucci E	Bebe Auto (same as Cars for Kids)	82+	703		Automobilia		H	$70
Mathieson T A S O	Pictorial Survey Rac Cars 1919-39	63	298		MRP		H	$125
Mathieson T A S O	Grand Prix Racing 1906-1914	65	298		Connoisseur Automobile		H	$180
Matsuda Y	Racing Porsches Matsuda Collection	82	136		Matsuda		H	$125
Matteucci M	Hist of Motor Car	70	401		Crown		H	$20
Maxim H P	Horseless Carriage Days	36+	401		Harper & Bros/Dover		X	$40
May C A N	Formula 3 Record of 500cc Racing	51	298		Foulis		H	$50
May C A N	Shelsley Walsh	46	206		Foulis		H	$40
May C A N	More Wheelspin Post-war Comp Mtrng	48	298		Foulis		H	$40
May C A N	Wheelspin Abroad Continental.......	49	298		Foulis		H	$40
May C A N	Speed Hill-Climb	62	298		Foulis		H	$40
May D	Pastmasters Of Speed	58	610		Temple		H	$60
May G S	Most Unique Machine Michigan.......	75	401		Eerdmans		H	$30
May G S	R E Olds Auto Industry Pioneer	77	404		Eerdmans		H	$30
Mayborn M	Studebaker Second 50 Yrs 02-52 (Ads)	73	145		Highland Enterprises		S	$20
Mayborn M	Buick When Better Automobiles (Ads)	72+	108		Highland		S	$20
Mayborn M	Studebaker Last Years 1952-66 (Ads)	73	145		Highland		S	$20
Mays R	Split Seconds My Racing Years	51	205		Foulis		H	$60
Mays R/Roberts P	BRM S	64	298		Pan		S	$30
Mays R/Roberts P	BRM H	62+	298		Cassell		H	$60
McCahill T	Modern Sports Car	54	401		Prentice		H	$20
McCarthy M	Classic Porsche	83	136		Bison/Fell/Exeter		H	$20
McCollister J E	Roar In City (Long Beach GP)	75	206		Performance Marketing		H	$40
McComb F W	Aston Martin V8s Autohistory	81	103		Osprey	Autohistory	H	$50
McComb F W	MGB Autohistory	82	131		Osprey	Autohistory	H	$40
McComb F W	AC(Shelby) Cobra Autohistory	84	109		Osprey	Autohistory	H	$40
McComb F W	Veteran Cars	74	401		Hamlyn		H	$20
McComb F W	MGA Autohistory	83	131		Osprey	Autohistory	H	$40
McComb F W	Profile No 45 MG Midget M Type	66	131		Profile Publications		S	$10
McComb F W	Morgan (French)	85	164		EPA	Toute L'Hist...	S	$20
McComb F W	MG by McComb	78+	131		Osprey		H	$50
McComb F W	Mercedes-Benz V8s Autohistory	80	130		Osprey	Autohistory	H	$50
McComb F W	Profile No 86 18/80 MG	67	131		Profile Publications		S	$20
McComb F W	Profile No 15 MG Magnette K3	66	131		Profile Publications		S	$30
McComb F W	MG (Shire-McComb)	85	131		Shire	Shire Album 152	S	$10
McFarland J	Great Manifold Bolt-On Edelbrock	82	202		Edelbrock		S	$30
McFarland K/Sparks J C	Midget Motors and Karting	61	214		Dutton		H	$20
McGaughey W H	American Automobile Album	54	403		Dutton		H	$40
McGonegal R	Chevrolet Celebrating 75 Yrs Perf..	86	111		Petersen	Magazine Spec'l	S	$10

Author	Title	Pub date	Subjects		Publisher	Series	Bind	Price
McGovern C	Alpine Classic Sunbeam	80	105		Gentry/Haynes		H	$90
McGovren J	Muscle Cars	84	403		Quintet/Apple/Chartwell		H	$30
McGovren J	Worlds Fastest Cars Ill Gd to......	85	412		Quintet/Book Sls/Chtwell		H	$20
McKay P/Naismith B	Le Mans 24 Heures Du Mans 1(84 Eng)	84	206		Garry Sparke		H	$40
McLaren B	From Cockpit	63+	205		Muller/MBC		H	$60
McLellan J	MG Art of Abingdon	82	131		MRP		H	$70
McLintock J D	Renault Cars & Charisma	83	120		PSL		H	$50
McPherson T	American Funeral Cars & Ambulances	73	304		Crestline	Crestline	H	$50
McPherson T A	Dodge Story	75	115		Crestline	Crestline	H	$100
Mclellan J	AC and Cobra	82	105	109	Dalton Watson	Dalton Watson	H	$60
Mclellan J	Great Automobile Designs	74	502		Arco		H	$40
Mclellan J	Bodies Beautiful Hist of Car Styl..	75	502		David & Charles		H	$50
Meier A E/Hoschek	Over the Road History of Intercity	75			Motor Bus Society		H	$60
Mellors T/Davison G S	Continental Circus	49	603		T T Special		H	$60
Melton J/Purdy K	Bright Wheels Rolling	54	401		Macrae Smith		H	$30
Merlin D	Audi Une Tradition Sportive	81	124		Editia, S.A.		H	$30
Merlin D	Pininfarina Prestige & Trad.1930-80	80	501		Edita S.A.		H	$100
Merlin O	Fangio Racing Driver	59	205		Desclee Brouwer/Bat/Bent		H	$60
Merritt R	Ferrari Brochures & Sales Lit	77	121		Barnes		S	$150
Merritt R	Ferrari Oper Maint Serv HB 1948-63	75	121		Barnes		S	$150
Merz C	And Then Came Ford	29	415		Doubleday		H	$30
Metternich M G W	Maybach (German/English)	73+	124		Uhle & Kleimann		H	$125
Metternich M G W	Das Maybach-Register	81	124		Sieger Verlag		H	$70
Meyer J C	California Classics Vol I	77	401		Classic Car Club of SC		H	$30
Meyer J C	California Classics Vol III	80	401		Classic Car Club of SC		H	$30
Meyer J C	California Classics Vol II	78	401		Classic Car Club of SC		H	$30
Meyer J C	Forest Domain of Pierce-Arrow	84	170		South Cal Region PA Soc		H	$30
Meynell L	Rolls Man of Speed	53	139		Bodley Head		H	$50
Michels P	Vom Blitzkarren zum Groben Borgward	82	124		Barbel Michels		H	$150
Miklues R L	Bowser V1	78	507		Miklues		S	$40
Millanta C/Orsini/Zagari	Ferrari Automobili 1947-1953	85	121		Editoriale Olimpia		H	$150
Miller D	Source Book of Fire Engines	83	302		Ward Lock Ltd		S	$20
Miller D	Ill Ency of Trucks Buses	82+	306		Quarto/Hamlyn		H	$50
Miller D	Ill Hist of Trucks and Buses	82	306		Quarto/A&W/Galahad		H	$10
Miller E K	Century on Wheels Story of Am Auto	87	418		Pioneer		H	$40
Miller J	Fast Company Men Machines Am Racing	72	299		Follett		H	$30
Miller P	Fast Ones	64	297		Arco		H	$30
Miller R	Chevrolet Coming of Age 1911-42	76	111		Evergreen		H	$80
Miller R	Motorcyclists Encyclopedia	72	601		BMS		S	$20
Miller S	Porsche Year 1982	82	136		Carrera International		X	$60
Miller S	Sammy Miller on Trials	69+	601		Parkhurst		H	$30
Miller S	Porsche 911/912 Source Book	84	136		Bookman	Source Boo	S	$30
Mills B	Restoring Convertibles Rags to.....	77	405		MBI		S	$30
Mills B	Adventures In Rest Antique Cars	78	401		Dodd/Mead		H	$30
Mills J	Construction of Ford Specials	60	156		Batsford		H	$40
Mills W	Down the Grid	65	297		Ian Allen		H	$20
Millspaugh B	Z Car Enthusiasts Guide (Datsun)	86	126		Millspaugh		S	$60
Milton F	Automobilist Abroad (early travel)	07	401		Page		H	$125
Minchin G R N	Under My Bonnet	50	139		Foulis		H	$30
Minchin N	Silver Lady	61	139		Foulis		H	$30
Mineau W	Stirling Moss's Book of Motor Sport	55	297		Cassell		H	$40
Minerbi M	Alfa Romeo Zagato SZ TZ (Italian)	85	101		La Mille Miglia Editrice		H	$90
Minter D	Racing All My Life Derek Minter	65	610		Barker		H	$40
Minton D	BMW Story	79	606		Phoebus/BPC		S	$20
Miska K H	Berlinetta Lusso	78	121		Barnes		X	$80
Moe D	Ferrari Library	83	121		MMC		S	$30
Mohs B	Amazing Mr Mohs	84	158		Mohs		S	$20
Moity C	Le Mans 24-Hours Race 1978	79	206		Pub Intl/Edita		H	$80
Moity C	Les 24 Heures du Mans 1981	81	206		Publications Intl		H	$80
Moity C	Le Mans 24-Hour Race 1949-73	74	206		Edita		H	$150
Moity C	Les 24 Heures du Mans 1980	80	206		Publications Intl		H	$80
Moline M	Best of Ford	73	415		Rumbleseat		H	$20
Molloy E/Lanchester G H	Automobile Engineers Reference Bk		405		Newnes		L	$70
Moloney J H	Ency of American Cars 1930-1942	77	403		Crestline	Crestline	H	$60
Molter G	Automobile Year 1962-63 #10	63	204		Edita S.A.		H	$200
Molter G	Automobile Year 1963-64 #11	64	204		Edita S.A.		H	$125
Molter G	Automobile Year 1964-65 #12	65	204		Edita S.A.		H	$100
Molter G	Automobile Year 1965-66 #13	66	204		Edita S.A.		H	$150
Molter G	Juan Manuel Fangio	56	205		Foulis		H	$50
Molter G	German Racing Cars and Drivers	50	298		Clymer		S	$50
Monkhouse G L	Motor Racing with Mercedes-Benz	45	130		Foulis/Clymer		X	$60
Monkhouse G L	Motoraces of Grand Prix Racing	47	298		Clymer		X	$30
Monkhouse G L/King-Farlow	Grand Prix Racing Facts & Figures	50+	297		Foulis		H	$50
Monroe T	Clutch & Flywheel Handbook	77	202		H P Books		S	$30
Montagu	Lost Causes of Motrg Europe Vol 1	71	401		Cassell/Barnes		H	$50
Montagu	Lost Causes of Motrg Europe Vol 2	71	401		Cassell/Barnes		H	$40
Montagu	Lost Causes of Motoring	60+	401		Cassell		H	$70
Montagu	Jaguar (Ballantine)	71	127		Ballantine	Ballantine #10	S	$30

Author	Title	Pub date	Subjects		Publisher	Series	Bind	Price
Montagu	Gordon Bennett Races	53+	206		Cassell/MBC		H	$70
Montagu	Jaguar (Foulis)	75+	127		Foulis/Haynes	Minimarque	H	$30
Montagu	Antique Cars (Montagu)	80S	401		Camden House	Golden Hglts	H	$10
Montagu	Jaguar Biography	61	127		Cassell/Norton		H	$50
Montagu	Jaguar Lord Montagu of Beaulieu	67	127		Barnes		H	$40
Montagu	Rolls of Rolls-Royce	67	139		Cassell/MBC		H	$50
Montagu/Bird A	Steam Cars 1770-1970	71	414		Cassell/St Martins		H	$100
Montagu/Frostick	Royalty on Road	80	401		Collins		H	$50
Montagu/McComb F W	Behind Wheel Magic & Manners...	77	401		Paddington		H	$30
Montaut E	Ten Ans de Courses (Montaut)	08?	504	297	Montaut Mabileau Editeurs		S	$3000
Montville J	Mack Living Legend of Highway	79	301		Aztex		X	$60
Montville J	Mack	73	301		Haessner		H	$70
Moon H	Aurelia	71	157		American Lancia Club		S	$50
Moore S	Immortal 2.9 Alfa-Romeo 8C 2900 A/B	86	101		Parkside		H	$150
Moreland F W	Green Fields Fairer Lanes	69	415		Five Star		H	$50
Moretti V	La Scommessa di Gianni Lancia(Ital)	86	157		Edizioni di Autocritica		H	$70
Moretti V	Le Auto dei Papi/Pontiffs' Cars	81	401		Edizioni di Autocritica		H	$90
Moretti V	Gioachino Colombo Le Origini del...	85	121		Sansoni Autocritica		H	$80
Moretti V	Enzo Ferrari Pilota	87	121		Edizioni di Autocritica		H	$60
Morgan D	Souping Volkswagen	59	150		Clymer		S	$30
Moritz M/Seaman B	Going for Broke Chrysler Story	81	112		Doubleday		H	$40
Morland A	Street Rods Pre-48 American Rods	83	422		Osprey	Osprey Color	S	$30
Morland A	Custom Motorcycles St Bikes on Show	83	601		Osprey	Colour Lib	S	$30
Morland A	Street Machines 49 and on Custom...	84	201		Osprey		S	$30
Morley D	Classic British Scramblers	86	606		Osprey	Coll Lib	H	$50
Morris L	Antique Cars (Morris)	70	401		Casa Editore/Grosset		H	$10
Morrison I	Guiness Bk of Formula One	89	297		Guiness		H	$50
Morrissey C B	Modern Buses and Coaches (juv)	52			Temple		H	$20
Morrow H	Formula Junior Guide	61	297		Sports Car Press	Mod Sports Car	S	$90
Mortimer C	Brooklands and Beyond	74	206		Goose & Son		H	$30
Mortimer C	Racing a Sports Car	51	298		Foulis		H	$50
Mortimer C	Constant Search Coll Motoring Books	82	507		Haynes		H	$60
Morton C W	Hist of Rolls-Royce Motor Cars Vol1	64	139		Foulis		H	$150
Moses D	Buses of World	82			Ian Allan Ltd		H	$30
Moses S	Fast Guys Rich Guys and Idiots	86	297		September Press		H	$60
Mosquera C/Coma-Cros E	Ricart Pegaso La Pasion del Auto...	88	173		Arcris Ediciones		H	$200
Moss S	In Track of Speed	57+	205		Frederick Muller		H	$40
Moss S	Le Mans '59 (Moss)	59	206		Cassell/Hanover		H	$80
Moss S	HT Watch Motor Racing	75	297		Gentry		H	$30
Moss S	Turn at the Wheel	61	205		Kimber		H	$40
Moss S/Lloyd N	XVme Grand Prix Monaco 57 (7" rec)	50S	206		Schofield Productions	Sound Stories		$30
Moss S/Pomeroy L	Design and Behaviour of Racing Car	63	202		Kimber		H	$70
Motor	Motor Road Test Annual 1979	79	410		IPC		S	$20
Motor	Highlights of Hist 25 Yrs w/ Motor	29	401		Motor(US)		H	$80
Motor Cycle	British Motorcycle Engines	50S	609		Iliffe/Clymer		S	$30
Motor Cycle	Two-Stroke Motorcycles How Get Best	67	609		Iliffe/Clymer		S	$30
Motor Racing staff	Motor Racing Year 1966-7	66	204		Knightsbridge		H	$30
Motor Racing staff	Motor Racing Year 1967-8	67	204		Knightsbridge		H	$30
Motor Racing staff	Motor Racing Year 1968-9	68	204		Knightsbridge		H	$30
Muller B	Racedrivers	63	205	510	Motor-Presse-Verlag		H	$150
Munaron G	Ferrari Le 4 Cilindri Sport	87	121		La Mille Miglia Editrice		H	$400
Muncaster H	Model Stationary Engines Design....	12	704		Tee		S	$20
Murani P/Pasini S/Orsini	Ferrari Testarossa	85+	121		Automobilia		H	$90
Murray C	Petersens Basic HT Tune Your Car	79	405		Petersen		S	$10
Murray D	Ecurie Ecosse Scotlands Racing Team	62	127		S Paul/MBC		H	$80
Murray J	Handbook of Motocross (juv)	78	602		Putnam		H	$10
Murray S	Petersens Big Book of Auto Repair	76+	405		Petersen		H	$30
Murray S	HT Tune Your Car(Petersen's)	75+	405		Petersen		H	$20
Murray S	Petersens Compl Bk Eng Swapping 4E	75	405		Petersen/Hot Rod		S	$20
Murray S	Special Interest Am Cars(1930-1960)	76	403		Petersen	Petersen	S	$20
Murray S	Petersens Compl Ford Book 4E	76	122		Petersen		S	$20
Murray S	Petersens Compl Ford Book 1E	70	122		Petersen		S	$30
Murray S	Petersens Compl Ford Book 2E	72	122		Petersen		S	$20
Murray S	Petersens Compl Chevrolet Book 4E	75	111		Petersen		S	$30
Murray S	Petersens Compl Volkswagen Book 3E	73	150		Petersen		S	$20
Murray S	Petersens Compl Bk Plym Dodge Chrys	73	132		Petersen		S	$30
Murray S	Petersens Compl Bk Japanese Import	72	167	126	Petersen		S	$20
Murray S	Petersens Compl Ford Book 3E	73	122		Petersen		S	$20
Murray S	Petersens Compl Bk Engines 10E	74	202		Petersen		S	$20
Murray S	Petersens Basic Ignit/Elec Systems	77	405		Petersen		S	$10
Murray S	Petersens Comp Bk Pickups & Vans	72	306		Petersen		S	$20
Murray S	Petersens Compl Chevrolet Book 3E	73	111		Petersen		S	$20
Murray S/Hall A	Petersens Compl Bk Pinto	77	122		Petersen		S	$10
Murray T C	License Plate Book	78+	507		Murray		S	$30
Musciano W A	Building and Operating Model Cars	56	701		Funk & Wagnells		H	$30
Musgrove C	Moggie The Purch, Maint & Enjoy....	80	164		Quills		H	$80
Musselman M M	Get a Horse! Story of Auto America	50	401		Lippincott		H	$20
Mutch R	Last of Great Road Races	75	603		Transport Bookman		S	$30

Author	Title	Pub date	Subjects		Publisher	Series	Bind	Price
Myers C	Honda (Myers)	84	606		Arco		H	$20
Nader Group	Small on Safety....Volkswagen	72	150		Grossman		H	$30
Nader R	Unsafe At Any Speed	65	113		Grossman		X	$20
Nagle E	Old Cars World Over	58	401		Arco		H	$30
Nagle E	Veterans of Road Story of VCC..	55	401		Arco		H	$20
Nagle E	Other Bentley Boys	64	139		Harrap		H	$50
Naidu G M/Tesar G/Udell G	Electric Car Alternative to the...	74	417		Pub Sciences Group		S	$20
Nakajima N	Model Cars of World	77	702		Hoikusha	ColorBooks #34	S	$30
Nakajima N	Model Cars of Japan	77	702		Hoikusha	Color Books	S	$30
Nallinger F	Annals of Mercedes-Benz Motor Veh	61	130		Daimler-Benz		H	$50
Nallinger F	Gottlieb Daimler Karl Benz(leaflet)	?	130		Im Propylaen-Verlag		S	$40
Nankivell E	Jowett Jupiter Car that Leaped.....	81	105		Batsford		H	$50
Narus D J	Great American Woodies & Wagons	77	403		Crestline	Crestline	H	$100
Naul G M	Specification Book US Cars 20-29	78	403		MBI		S	$30
Naul G M	Specification Book US Cars 30-69	80	403		MBI		S	$30
Neeley W	Daytona U.S.A.	79	206		Aztex		H	$50
Neeley W	Playboy Gd Rally Rac Spts Cr Drivg	81	203		Playboy		H	$20
Neeley W/Lamm J	Cars to Remember 37 Great Autos....	75	401		Regnery		H	$40
Nelson R	Worlds Largest Mtrng Spectacle	72	401		Directional		S	$10
Nelson W H	Small Wonder Amazing Story of VW	65	150		Little Brown		X	$20
Nencini F	Effetto Alfa (includes record)(Eng)	80S	101		Alfa Romeo		S	$150
Nesbitt D	Fifty Year of Am Auto Design 30-80	85	502		Publications Intl		H	$10
Neubauer A	Speed Was My Life	58	205		Clarkson Potter/Barrie		H	$70
Neubauer A	Herr Uber 1000 PS	59	130	205	HDV		H	$40
Neubauer H O	Volkswagen Beetle & Derivatives	79	150		Dalton Watson/Beaulieu B		H	$40
Neubecker W	Antique Automobile Body Const/Rest	12+	405		Post		S	$30
Neumann B	Model Car Building	71	702		Putnam	Here is yr Hobb	H	$20
Neville B	Real Steel An Investor's and.......	75+	401		Running Press		S	$20
Nevins A/Hill F E	Ford Times Man Company	54	122		Scribners	Nevins Triology	H	$60
Nevins A/Hill F E	Ford Expansion & Challenge 1915-33	57	122		Scribners	Nevins Triology	H	$70
Nevins A/Hill F E	Ford Decline and Rebirth 1933-1962	62	122		Scribners	Nevins Triology	H	$40
Newall R	Morris Minor Ser MM Super Profile	84	105		Haynes		H	$20
Newcomb T P/Spurr R T	Automobile Brakes & Braking Systems	69	405		Robert Bentley Inc.	Motor Manuals	H	$20
Newell D	Incompleat Corvair Story	79	113		Bob Terkelson		S	$40
Neyhart L A	Henry Ford Engineer (juv)	50	415		Houghton Mifflin		H	$30
Nichols M	Ferrari Berlinetta Boxer Autohist.	79	121		Osprey	Autohistory	H	$60
Nichols R	Classic Corvette	83	114		Bookthrift/Exeter/Bison		H	$20
Nichols R	Ency of Sports Cars	86	401		Bookthrift			$0
Nichols R	Exotic Cars (Nichols)	85	401		Bison		H	$30
Nichols R	Classic American Cars	86	403		Bison/Bookthrift/Exeter		H	$20
Nichols R	Classic Cars (Nichols)	84	401		Bison/Bookthrift/Exeter		H	$20
Nichols R	Muscle Cars (Nichols)	85	403		Brompton		H	$20
Nicholson J B	Modern Motorcycle Mechanics	42+	609		Nicholson		H	$40
Nicholson T R	Isotta-Fraschini(Ballantine)	71	118		Ballantine	Ballantine #3	S	$20
Nicholson T R	Car Badges of World	70	507		American Heritage/Cassell		H	$60
Nicholson T R	Worlds Motor Museums	70	401		Lippincott		H	$60
Nicholson T R	Wild Roads Story Transcon. Motoring	69	212		Norton		H	$30
Nicholson T R	Adventurers Road	57	212		Rinehart		H	$30
Nicholson T R	Sports Cars 1928-1939	69	401		Blandford/Macmillan		H	$20
Nicholson T R	Sports Cars Book Two 1907-1927	70	401		Blandford/Macmillan		H	$20
Nicholson T R	Racing Cars & Rec Break 1898-1921	71	297		Blandford/Macmillan		H	$20
Nicholson T R	Passenger Cars 1913-23	72	401		Macmillian		H	$20
Nicholson T R	Passenger Cars 1863-1904	70	401		Macmillian		H	$20
Nicholson T R	Profile No 11 Alvis Speed 20,25,etc	66	105		Profile Publications		S	$20
Nicholson T R	Profile No 62 Amilcar 1920-1929	67	120		Profile Publications		S	$10
Nicholson T R	Profile No 06 Duesenberg J & SJ	66	116		Profile Publications		S	$30
Nicholson T R	Passenger Cars 1905-12	71	401		Macmillan		H	$20
Nicholson T R	Birth of British Mtr Cr 1 1769-1842	82	419		Macmillan		H	$50
Nicholson T R	Birth of British Mtr Cr 2 1842-1893	82	419		Macmillan		H	$50
Nicholson T R	Birth of British Mtr Cr 3 1894-1897	82	419		Macmillan		H	$50
Nicholson T R	Profile No 74 Isotta Fraschini T8	67	118		Profile Publications		S	$20
Nicks M	Golden Oldies Classic Bike Tests	81	601		PSL		H	$40
Nicol G	Volvo	75	165		St Martins	Great Cars	H	$30
Nitske R	Comp Mercedes Story	55	130		Macmillan		H	$30
Nitske R	Amazing Porsche and VW Story	58	150	136	Comet Press Books		H	$50
Nixon C	Racing with David Brown Aston Vol 2	80	103		Transport Bookman		H	$80
Nixon S J C	Invention of Automobile	36	130		Country Life		H	$30
Nixon S J C	Daimler 1896 to 1946 50 Years of...	46	105		Foulis		H	$70
Nixon S J C	Antique Automobile (Nixon)	56	401		Cassell		H	$50
Nockolds H	Lucas 1st 100 Years V2 Successors	78	418		David & Charles		H	$70
Nockolds R	Magic of a Name	45+	139		Foulis		H	$40
Nockolds R	Magic of a Name(Color ed)	49	139		Foulis		H	$100
Nolan W F	Phil Hill Yankee Champion	62	205		Putnam		H	$125
Nolan W F	Men of Thunder Fabled Daredevils...	64	205		Bantam		S	$20
Nolan W F	Barney Oldfield Life and Times of..	61	205		Putnam		H	$70
Nolan W F/Beaumont C	When Engines Roar	64	205		Bantam		S	$10
Norback C T	Chiltons Comp Bk of Auto Facts	81	412		Chilton		X	$30
Norbye J P	Oldsmobile Postwar Years	81	162		MBI	Marques America	H	$50

Author	Title	Pub date	Subjects		Publisher	Series	Bind	Price
Norbye J P	Wankel Engine Design...............	71	405		Chilton		H	$50
Norbye J P	Pontiac Postwar Years	79	138		MBI		H	$40
Norbye J P	De Tomaso Pantera Autohistory	80	118		Osprey	Autohistory	H	$50
Norbye J P	BMW Bavaria's Driving Machine	84	106		Publications Intl	Consumer Guide	H	$30
Norbye J P	Gas Turbine Engine Design..........	75	202		Chilton		H	$40
Norbye J P	New Fiat Guide	69	152		Sports Car Press/Crown	Mod Sports Car	S	$20
Norbye J P	Streamling & Car Aerodynamics	77	202		Tab	Mod Spts Car	S	$20
Norbye J P	Comp HB Front Wheel Drive Cars	79	405		Tab		S	$20
Norbye J P	Comp Hist German Car 1886..........	87	408		Ervin/Crown/Portland		H	$30
Norbye J P/Dunne J	Buick Postwar Years	78	108		MBI	Marques America	H	$50
Nordberg N	Resa Kungligt(Swedish)	76	173		Raben & Sjogren		H	$30
Norman E	Supercharge	69	202		Norman		S	$20
Norris I	Automobile Year 1981-82 #29	82	204		Edita S.A.		H	$80
Norris I	Automobile Year 1982-83 #30	83	204		Edita S.A.		H	$80
Norris I	Automobile Year 1983-84 #31	84	204		Edita S.A.		H	$60
Norris I	Automobile Year 1984-85 #32	85	204		Edita S.A.		H	$60
North P	Shelby Source Book V2	85	109	122	Bookman Dan	Source Book	S	$30
North P	Four-4-2 Vol II Source Book	85	162		Bookman Dan	Source Book	S	$30
North P	Barracuda Challenger V2 Source Bk	85	137		Bookman	Source Book	S	$30
North P	Road Runner V2 Source Book	85	137		Bookman Dan	Source Book	S	$30
North P	Hurst Source Book	85	162	201	Bookman	Source Book	S	$30
North P	Charger V2 Source Book	85	115		Bookman	Source Boo	S	$20
Nowak S	Automobile Restoration Guide	81+	405		Tab	Mod Auto	S	$20
Nye D	Story of Lotus 1961-1971	72	129		MRP/Bentley		H	$80
Nye D	Racers Inside Story of Williams	82	298		Barker		H	$50
Nye D	Cooper Cars	83+	298		Osprey		H	$100
Nye D	ELC2 The MG K3 Magnette	81	131		Horseless Carriages	Sports Car P...	S	$50
Nye D	Dino The Little Ferrari	79	121		Barnes/Osprey		H	$60
Nye D	Single Seat-Lotus F-1 & Indy Cars	78	129		Newport Press		H	$60
Nye D	Theme Lotus (prior to '86 editions)	78+	129		MRP		H	$100
Nye D	Autocourse Hist of the GP Car 66-85	86	297		Hazleton		H	$40
Nye D	Colonels Ferraris Maranello Con...	80	121		Ampersand/Maranello		H	$40
Nye D	Motor Racing Mavericks	74	297		Batsford		H	$40
Nye D	United States Grand Prix 1908-1977	78	206		Batsford		H	$50
Nye D	Classic Single-Seaters Donington	74	298		Macmillan		H	$40
Nye D	Grand Prix Tyrrells	75	298		Macmillan	Donington MM	H	$50
Nye D	Ferrari 365 GTB/4 Dayt World S/C#1	84	121		Albion Scott/Moto-Art		H	$10
Nye D	Cars in Profile 03 F1 Repco-Brabham	72	298		Profile Publications		S	$40
Nye D	Powered by Jaguar Cooper HWM.......	80	127	105	MRP		H	$40
Nye D	Carl Benz and Motor Car	73	130		Priory Press	Pioneers S & D	H	$10
Nye D	Racing Cars (Nye)	80	297		Grisewood/Booktft/Exeter		H	$40
Nye D	Racing Car Oddities	75	297		Arco		H	$60
Nye D	Famous Racing Cars Fifty of the....	89	297		Guild Pub		H	$40
Nye D	British Cars of Sixties	70	406		Nelson		S	$30
Nye D	Mighty Jaguar Sports Car	80S	127		Speed - Sporting Cars		H	$10
Nye D	Sports Cars (Nye)	80+	401		Grisewood/Bookthft/Exeter		H	$30
Nye D	Great Racing Drivers (Nye)	77	205		Hamlyn		H	$10
Nye D	International Motor Racing (Nye)	73	297		Macmillan/Crowell	Leisureguides	H	$60
Nye D/Goddard G	Great Racing Cars of Donington Coll	74	297		Macmillan		H	$30
O'Connell J/Myers A	Safety Last An Indictment Auto Ind.	66	419		Random		X	$20
O'Connor P	Black Tiger at Le Mans (Juv fict)	58	206	213	Washburn/Scholastic		H	$30
O'Kane D	HT Repair Your Foreign Car	68	405		Doubleday		H	$20
O'Leary M/Haslam J	Great Automobile Club (juvenile)	68	416		Constable/Longmans		S	$30
O'Shea P	Guide to Competition Driving	57	203		Sports Car Press		S	$20
OC Editors	Best of Old Cars V3	83	401		Krause		S	$20
OC Editors	Best of Old Cars V1	76	401		Krause		S	$30
OC Editors	Best of Old Cars V2	79	401		Krause		S	$30
OC Editors	Best of Old Cars V4	83	401		Krause		S	$30
OC Editors	Best of Old Cars V6	87	401		Krause		H	$60
Obert E F/Jennings B H	Internal Combustion Eng Analysis...	44+	405		International Textbook		H	$30
Octpobc.../H	Abtomo....(Russian)	68	401		in Moscow		X	$40
Oldham J	New Mercedes-Benz Guide	77	130		Tab	Mod Sports Car	H	$40
Oldham W J	Hyphen in Rolls-Royce	67	139		Foulis		H	$100
Oldham W J	Rolls-Royce 40/50hp Ghosts Phntms..	74	139		Haynes		H	$60
Oliver G A	Rover	71	105		Cassell		H	$70
Oliver G A	Cars and Coachbuilding 100 Years...	81	501		Sotheby		S	$30
Oliver G A	Profile No 02 Rolls Royce Phantom I	66	139		Profile Publications		S	$10
Oliver G A	Profile No 67 Argylls 1911-1928	67	158		Profile Publications		S	$20
Oliver G A	Profile No 49 1905 3-cy Rolls-Royce	67	139		Profile Publications		S	$30
Oliver G A	Profile No 07 Bentley 3 1/2 & 4 1/4	66	139		Profile Publications		S	$20
Oliver G A	Profile No 29 4 1/2-litre Lagonda	66	105		Profile Publications		S	$10
Oliver G A	Cars in Profile 12 Rolls-Royce P2	73	139		Profile Publications		S	$20
Oliver S H	Autos & Motorcyles in US Nat Museum	57	297		Smithsonian		S	$40
Oliver S H	Profile No 94 Packard 8/12 1923-42	67	159		Profile Publications		S	$20
Oliver S H/Berkebile D H	Smithsonian Autos & Motorcycles S	68	401		Smithsonian		S	$20
Oliver S H/Berkebile D H	Wheels and Wheeling Smithsonian....	74	601		Smithsonian		H	$30
Olney R R	Janet Guthrie First Woman at Indy	78	205		Harvey House		H	$30
Olney R R	Daredevils of Speedway	66	205		Grosset & Dunlap		H	$30

Author	Title	Pub date	Subjects		Publisher	Series	Bind	Price
Phipps D	Autocourse 1967-68	68	204		Haymarket		H	$200
Phipps D	Autocourse 1970-71	71	204		Haymarket		H	$200
Phipps D	Autocourse 1964-65 (1965)	65	204		Haymarket		H	$300
Phipps D	Autocourse 1965-66 (1966)	66	204		Haymarket		H	$250
Phipps D	Autocourse 1968-69	69	204		Haymarket		H	$250
Phipps D	Autocourse 1969-70	70	204		Haymarket		H	$250
Phipps D	Autocourse 1971-72	72	204		Haymarket		H	$250
Phipps D	Profile No 48 Lotus Elite	67	129		Profile Publications		S	$30
Piccard J R	Automobile Year 1985-86 #33	85	204		Edipresse		H	$80
Piccard J R	Automobile Year 1986-87 #34	86	204		Edipresse		H	$80
Piccard J R	Automobile Year Bk of Dream Cars	81	502		Edita/Crown/Crescent		H	$90
Pick C	Cars in Color	79	401		Octopus		H	$10
Pickard D	British 250 Racer	84	603		Pickard		S	$10
Pietruska R	Perpetuating Porsche Paranoia	81	136		R P Design		S	$20
Pihera L	Making of Winner Porsche 917	72	136		Lippincott		H	$50
Pininfarina	Pininfarina Cinquantanni(English)	80	501		Edizioni Pininfarina		H	$150
Pininfarina E	Cara Automobile	68	504				H	$250
Pirsig R M	Zen and Art of Motorcycle Maint....	74	601		Bantam		S	$10
Pitrone J M/Elwart J P	Dodges Auto Family Fortune & Misfor	81	115	404	Icarus Press		H	$50
Plummer J	Best Loved Cars of World	79	401		Sackett & Squire/Chartwl		H	$10
Poltronieri M	Storia della Formula 1(Italian)4Vol		297		Edzioni Equipe		H	$300
Pomeroy L	Grand Prix Car Vol II	54	297		MRP/Temple		H	$400
Pomeroy L	Grand Prix Car Vol I	54	297		MRP/Temple		H	$400
Pomeroy L	Motor Year Book 1955	55	410		Temple		H	$30
Pomeroy L	Motor Year Book 1951	51	410		Temple		H	$30
Pomeroy L	Motor Year Book 1952	52	410		Temple		H	$30
Pomeroy L	Motor Year Book 1953	53	410		Temple		H	$30
Pomeroy L	Motor Year Book 1954	54	410		Temple		H	$30
Pomeroy L	Evolution of Racing Car	66	298		Kimber		H	$80
Pomeroy L	Motor Year Book 1956	56	410		Temple		H	$50
Pomeroy L	Motor Year Book 1950	50	410		Temple		H	$40
Pomeroy L	Formula One G P Car (12" record)	50S	297		Schofield Productions	Sound Stories		$50
Pomeroy L	Profile No 21 Vauxhall 1914 GP	66	105		Profile Publications		S	$10
Pomeroy L	Grand Prix Car 1906-1939	49	297		MRP/Temple		H	$600
Pomeroy L	Motor Year Book 1957 (last)	57	410		Temple		H	$30
Pomeroy L	Motor Year Book 1949 (first)	49	410		Temple		H	$90
Pomeroy L	Racing Car Explained (juv)	63	202		Temple		H	$30
Pope N B	Full Chat	52	610		MRP		H	$100
Popular HR	Corvette Performance	77	114		Argus		H	$20
Porazik J	Motor Cars 1770-1940	81	401		Slovart/Smith/Galley	Handbook Guide	H	$10
Porter L	BMC and Leyland B-series Eng Data	85	131	406	Osprey		H	$60
Porter P	Jaguar Complete Ill History	84	127		Warne/Haynes		H	$50
Posey S	Mudge Pond Express	76	205		Putnam		H	$50
Post D R	Classic Cord	52	116		Post		X	$70
Post D R	Rolls-Royce Living Legend	58	139		Post		H	$70
Post D R	Rolls-Royce An Album....British R-R	53	139		Post		X	$90
Posthumus C	Classic Racing Cars	77	297		Rand McNally/Hamlyn		H	$40
Posthumus C	Mercedes & MB Racing Car Gd 1901-55	78	130		Transport Bookman		S	$20
Posthumus C	Bentley Toute L'Histoire	83	139		EPA	Auto Histoire	S	$20
Posthumus C	Profile No 59 Auto Union 1934-1937	67	124		Profile Publications		S	$20
Posthumus C	Profile No 79 1906-08 GP Renaults	67	120		Profile Publications		S	$10
Posthumus C	Cars in Profile 02 4.5 Lago-Talbot	72	120		Profile Publications		S	$20
Posthumus C	British Racing Cars	48	298		Vitesse/Floyd Clymer		S	$20
Posthumus C	Roaring Twenties Album of Early....	80	297		Blandford		H	$40
Posthumus C	German Grand Prix	66	206		Temple	Classic Mtr Rac	H	$50
Posthumus C	British Competition Car	59	406		Batsford		H	$40
Posthumus C	Profile No 18 1926-27 1 1/2 Delage	66	120		Profile Publications		S	$30
Posthumus C	World Sports Car Championship	61	297		MacGibbon		H	$40
Posthumus C/Tremayne D	Land Speed Record	71+	211		Osprey/Crown		H	$60
Potherat J	Le Mans 1923-39 (French)	72	206		Ed. del'automobiliste		H	$60
Potter J E	Motor Trend World Auto. Yr.Bk. 1967	67	410		Petersen		S	$20
Poulain H	L'Art et L'Automobile	73	504		Les Clefs du Temps		H	$300
Pound A	Turning Wheel Story of GM 1908-1933	34	160		Doubleday		H	$40
Pourret J G	Ferrari 275GTB 275GTS..... (French)	84	121		Publications Intl		H	$100
Pourret J G	Ferrari GTO Anniversary	87	121		ACLA		H	$60
Pratt P R	World Understanding On Two Wheels	80	601		Pratt		S	$20
Pressland D	Art of Tin Toy	76	703		New Cavendish/Crown		H	$150
Pressland D	Toy Autos 1890-1939 (Ottenheimer)	84	703		Ingram/Harper & Row		H	$80
Presto K/Bryce J	Power Basics of Auto Racing	86	203		Hope		S	$20
Preston C	Jokeswagen Book	66	150		Bernard Geis/Random		H	$20
Pritchard A	Competition Cars of Europe	70	298		Bobbs-Merrill		H	$30
Pritchard A	Grand Prix Championship(1950-1970)	71	297		Grosset & Dunlap		H	$30
Pritchard A	Porsche (Pritchard)	69	136		Pelham		H	$30
Pritchard A	Historic Motor Racing	69	297		Grosset & Dunlap		H	$20
Pritchard A	Maserati History	76	172		David & Charles		H	$30
Pritchard A	Motor Racing Year (1969-Pritchard)	70	204		MRP		H	$40
Pritchard A	Sports Car Championship	72	297		Hale		H	$50
Pritchard A	Ford vs Ferrari (Zuma/US edition)	84	122	121	Zuma		H	$70

Author	Title	Pub date	Subjects	Publisher	Series	Bind	Price
Rhodes A	Louis Renault	69	120	Cassell		H	$30
Ricardo H	High Speed Internal Combustion Eng	23+	405	Blackie/Interscience		H	$250
Rice G	Relics of the Road #3 International	75	301	Hastings	Relics of Road	H	$70
Rice G	Relics of the Road #2 Keen Kenworth	73	301	Hastings	Relics of Road	H	$70
Rice G	Relics of the Road #1 GMC Gems	71+	301	Hastings House	Relics of Road	H	$70
Richard Y	Renault 1898-1965	65	120	Pierre Tisne		H	$60
Richards N/Richards P	Trucks and Super-Trucks (juvenile)	80	301	Mus of Science/Doubleday		H	$10
Richards W C	Last Billionaire Henry Ford	48	415	Scribner		H	$30
Richardson L D	Triumph Mtrcycl Mechanics Handbook	75	609	Hi-Torque		S	$20
Richardson P	Vincent (Richardson)	55+	606	Pearson	Mtr Cycl Maint	S	$40
Richardson S	Minic Lines Bros Tinplate Vehicles	81	703	Mikansue		S	$30
Rickenbacker E V	Rickenbacker Autobiography	68	205	Prentice/Hutchinson		H	$40
Ridgley D W	Ferrari 410 Superamerica Series III	83	121	Ridgley		S	$50
Rieman K	Happy Wheels Appr. Metropolitan	80	158	Sterner Stuff		S	$40
Ritch O C	Lincoln Continental	63	161	Clymer/MBI		S	$40
Ritch O C	One Hundred of Worlds Finest Autos	60	401	Clymer		S	$30
Ritch O C	Indianapolis 1963 Yearbook	63	208	Clymer		X	$80
Ritch O C	Indianapolis 1962 Yearbooks	62	208	Clymer		S	$50
Ritch O C	Corvair Performance Handbook	63	113	Petersen		S	$20
Ritch O C/Hot Rod Editors	Chevrolet Performance Handbook	63	111	Petersen	Hot Rod	S	$30
Rivers Fletcher A F	V-16 Story of BRM Engine	54	298	MRP		H	$90
Robbin I	Great Cars of All Time	60	401	Grosset		H	$30
Robbins K	Trucks of Every Sort (juvenile)	81	301	Crown		H	$20
Roberts P	Competitive Driving	64	203	Stanley Paul		H	$30
Roberts P	Shell Book of Epic Motor Races	65	297	Arco		H	$30
Roberts P	Any Color so Long as it's Black	76	503	Morrow		H	$90
Roberts P	Racing Cars & Hist of Mtr Sport	73	297	Octopus		H	$20
Roberts P	Collector's History of Automobile	78	401	Ottenheimer/Crown/Bon		H	$20
Roberts P	Veteran and Vintage Cars	63	401	Hamlyn		H	$20
Roberts P	Pictorial Hist of Automobile (P.R.)	77	401	Ottenheimer/Grosset		H	$30
Roberts P	Everyones Color Bk of Classic Cars	80	401	Hamlyn		H	$10
Roberts P	What Car is That?	80	401	Mandarin/Octopus		H	$10
Roberts P	Automobiles of the World (Roberts)	64	401	Gautier-Languereau/Follet		H	$20
Roberts P	Crescent Color Gd to Classic Cars	80	401	Hamlyn/Crown/Crescent		H	$10
Roberts P	Great German Cars	85	408	Multimedia/Smith/Gallery		H	$20
Roberts P	Pictorial Hist of Car	78	401	Mandarin/Octopus		H	$30
Robinson D	Lucky Lott Hell Driver	85	205	Boston Mills		S	$20
Robinson W F	Cadillac Toute L'Histoire(French)	85	110	EPA	Auto Histoire	S	$20
Robotham W	Silver Ghosts & Silver Dawn	70	139	Constable		H	$150
Robson G	Story of Triumph Sports Cars	73	146	MRP		H	$60
Robson G	Talbot Sunbeam-Lotus MRP Rally Lib	85	120	MRP	Rally Library 3	S	$20
Robson G	Fiat Sports Cars From 1945 to X1/9	84	152	Osprey		H	$70
Robson G	Magnificent Mercedes	81	130	Bsghl/Haynes/Morrow/Otlet		H	$50
Robson G	Range Rover/Land-Rover	79	105	David & Charles		H	$40
Robson G	Rolls-Royce Silver Cld Autohistory	80	139	Osprey	Autohistory	H	$50
Robson G	Lancia Stratos Super Profile	83	157	Haynes	Super Profile	H	$30
Robson G	Ency of Worlds Classic Cars	77	401	Salamander/Chartwell		H	$30
Robson G	Jaguar D Type & XKSS Autohistory	83	127	Osprey	Autohistory	H	$40
Robson G	Mighty MGs Twin Cam MGC MGB GT V8..	82	131	David & Charles		H	$70
Robson G	Rover Story A Century of Success	77	105	PSL		H	$40
Robson G	Ill History of Rallying	81	209	Osprey		H	$40
Robson G	Ency of Eur Spts & GT Cars from 61	80	412	Haynes		H	$70
Robson G	Saab Turbo Autohistory	83	173	Osprey	Autohistory	H	$40
Robson G	Third Generation Lotuses Coll Guide	83	129	MRP	Coll Guide	H	$50
Robson G	Rolls-Royce Silver Spirit Autohist.	85	139	Osprey	Autohistory	H	$40
Robson G	Monte Carlo Rally (Robson)	89	209	Miura/Batsford	Wld Grt Mtr Cmp	H	$80
Roebuck N	Mario Andretti World Champion	79	205	Hamlyn		H	$40
Roebuck N/Townsend	Grand Prix World Formula One C/S 85	85	204	GS Publications		H	$70
Rogliatti G	Le Ferrari (large format)	66	121	L'Editrice del Auto......		H	$250
Rogliatti G	Le Piu Belle Vetture D'Epoca	70	401	LEA		H	$60
Rogliatti G	Great Collectors Cars	73	401	Mondadori/Grosset		H	$40
Rogliatti G	Ferrari Story #01	84	121	Stamperia Artistica		S	$30
Rogliatti G	Ferrari Story #03	85	121	Stamperia Artistica		S	$30
Rogliatti G	Ferrari Story #06	86	121	Stamperia Artistica		S	$30
Rogliatti G	Ferrari Story #08	86	121	Stamperia Artistica		S	$30
Rogliatti R	Ferrari (Rogliatti)	73	121	LEA/Crowell/Hamlyn		H	$100
Roll R M	American Trucking 75 Year Odyssey	79	301	MBI		H	$100
Rolls-Royce	Rolls-Royce Catalogue 1910/1911	73	139	EP/Crown/Bonanza		H	$30
Rolofson B	Sportscar Specials (Trend 178)	60	401	Trend	Trend Book	S	$20
Rolt L T C	Motoring History	64	401	Studio Vista/Dutton		S	$30
Rolt L T C	Horseless Carriage(Rolt)	50	297	Constable		H	$40
Rolt L T C	Landscape with Machines	71+	404	Sutton		X	$20
Rosberg K/Botsford K	Keke Autobiography	85	205	Hutchinson		H	$40
Rose A	Nineteen 84 Paper Corvette	84	114	Dolphin/Doubleday		S	$30
Rose A C/Rakeman C	Historic American Roads	76	401 419	Crown		H	$20
Rose G	Record of Motor Racing 1894-1908	49	297	MRP/Autobooks		H	$200
Rose J	Ginetta G15 Super Profile	86	105	Haynes	Super Profile	H	$20
Rosfeldt K	Die Geschichte der Marken R-R/Bentl	81	139	Verlag Karl Brinkman		H	$100

Author	Title	Pub date	Subjects		Publisher	Series	Bind	Price
Schneiders R	ISDT'73 Olympics of Motorcycling	73	602		Chilton		H	$20
Schofield M	Petersens Compl Bk Engines 08E	72	202		Petersen		S	$20
Schofield M/Hot Rod Eds	Petersens Basic Engine Hot Rodding	72	201		Petersen	Hot Rod	S	$30
Scholfield M/Hot Rod Eds	Off-Road Fun Cars	70	311		Petersen	Hot Rod	S	$20
Schorr M L	Mopar Performance Years V1 Dodge...	82	132		Quicksilver	Quicksilver	S	$20
Schorr M L	Mopar Performance Years V2	84	132		Quicksilver	Quicksilver	S	$20
Schorr M L	Mopar Street Performance Handbook	85	132		Quicksilver	Quicksilver	S	$20
Schorr M L	Buick V-8 & V-6 Performance Years	83	108		Quicksilver		S	$20
Schorr M L	Ford Street Performance Handbook	85	122		Quicksilver		S	$30
Schorr M L	Oldsmobile Performance Years	83	162		Quicksilver	Quicksilver	S	$20
Schorr M L	Ford Small-Block HT High Perf Eng..	76	122		Performance Pub		S	$20
Schorr M L	Camaro Three Gen Premier Perf Cars	82	111		Quicksilver	Quicksilver	S	$20
Schorr M L	Pontiac Performance Years	82	138		Quicksilver	Quicksilver	S	$20
Schorr M L	Ford Performance Years V1	83	122		Quicksilver	Quicksilver	S	$20
Schorr M L	Mustang Performance Years	82	122		Quicksilver	Quicksilver SC	S	$20
Schorr M L	Mopar Performance Years V3	84	132		Quicksilver	Quicksilver	S	$20
Schorr M L	Pontiac Trans-Am High Perf Handbook	81	138		Quicksilver	Supercar	S	$20
Schorr M L	Pontiac GTO Americas Premier S/C	78	138		Performance Publications		S	$20
Schorr M L	Z/28 Camaro No 1 Teams Cafe Racer	78	111		Performance		S	$20
Schorr M L	Mopar Big-Block HT High Perf Eng...	76	132		Performance Pub		S	$20
Schorr M L	Off-Road Book (technical)	79	311		Perf Pub		S	$10
Schrader H	BMW History	79	106		Bleicher Verlag/AQ		H	$90
Schrader H	Mercedes-Benz Vom 28/95PS zum SSKL	82	130		BLV	M-B Automobile	H	$90
Schrader H	Schlumpf Automobile Coll(3 lang)	79	401		Schrader/BLV		X	$150
Schrader H	BMW History L	79	106		Bleicher Verlag/AQ		L	$100
Schrader H	Porsche 356 Auto Classic #1	82	136		Podzun-Pallas/Albion	Auto Classic	S	$30
Schrader H	One Hundred Yrs Porsche Mirrored...	76	136		Porsche		H	$90
Schrader H	Datsun Automobiles from Japan	76	167		Schrader		H	$40
Schrader H	Jaguar Mk II Auto-Classic #2	80S	127		Albion Scott	Auto-Classic	S	$20
Schrader H/Demand C	Supercharged Mercedes	79	130		Edita		H	$100
Schrauzer G N	Rolls-Royce Humour	78	139		RROC		H	$40
Schreib L	Comp Gd Bolt-On Performance	78	202		SA		S	$30
Schroeder J J	Wonderful World of Automobiles	71	401		DBI Books		S	$20
Schroeder M/Schroeder S	Ferrari Own Club Monterey 1984	85	121		Ferrari Owners Club		H	$50
Schroeder M/Schroeder S	Ferrari Own Club 25 Yrs Honoring...	86	121		Ferrari Owners Club		H	$50
Schuster G/Mahoney T	Longest Auto Race	66	212		John Day Co. Inc.		H	$50
Scibor-Rylski A J	Road Vehicle Aerodynamics	75+	202		Pentech		H	$70
Scott M	Barry Sheene Will to Win	83	610		Allen & Unwin		S	$30
Scott M G H	Packard Complete Story	85	159		Tab		H	$60
Scott M/Cutts J	Worlds Fastest Motorcycles	86	601		Quintet/Chartwell		H	$20
Scott Moncrieff D	Veteran and Edwardian Motor Cars	55+	401		Batsford		S	$10
Scott-Moncrieff D	Classic Cars 1930-40	63	401		Batsford/Bentley		H	$30
Scott-Moncrieff D	Three-Pointed Star Story of MB	55+	130		Cassell/Norton/MBI/Haynes		H	$50
Scott-Moncrieff D	Veteran Motor Car	56	401		Scribners		H	$40
Seal R R	Maryland Automobile History 1900-42	85	403		Adams		H	$40
Sears	Nineteen 09-1912 Sears Mot Bug Cat	73	158		Digest		S	$10
Sears S W	Automobile in America	77	401		American Heritage/S & S		H	$70
Sedgwick M	Cars of 1930's	70	401		Robert Bentley, Inc.		H	$40
Sedgwick M	Cars of 30s and 40s	80	401		Nordbok/Crown/Hamlyn		H	$40
Sedgwick M	Cars of 50s and 60s	83	401		Nordbok/Beekman/Crown		H	$40
Sedgwick M	Early Cars (Sedgwick)	62	401		Weidenfeld		H	$20
Sedgwick M	Vauxhall Pictorial Tribute	81	105		Dalton Watson		S	$50
Sedgwick M	Antique Cars	81	401		Exeter		H	$20
Sedgwick M	Cars in Profile 07 Facel Vega	73	120		Profile Publications		S	$20
Sedgwick M	Profile No 23 Fiat Tipo 508S	66	121		Profile Publications		S	$10
Sedgwick M	Profile No 31 Delaunay-Bellevilles	66	105		Profile Publications		S	$10
Sedgwick M	Profile No 37 Sunbeam 1911-1913	66	105		Profile Publications		S	$10
Sedgwick M	Profile No 52 Morris 8 1935-1948	67	105		Profile Publications		S	$10
Sedgwick M	Profile No 82 Lea-Francis 1927-32	67	105		Profile Publications		S	$10
Sedgwick M	Fiat	74	152		Arco		H	$60
Sedgwick M	Profile No 95 Citroen 1934-1955	67	153		Profile Publications		S	$30
Sedgwick M	Motor Car 1946-56	79	401		Batsford		H	$70
Sedgwick M	Vintage Cars (Sedgwick)	80+	401		Grisewood/Bookthft/Exeter		H	$10
Sedgwick M	Profile No 47 6-cy Hotchkiss 29-54	67	120		Profile Publications		S	$30
Sedgwick M	Passenger Cars 1924-1942	75	401		Blandford		H	$20
Sedgwick S	How & Where of 8-litre Bentleys	72	139		BDC		S	$40
Sedgwick S	Motoring My Way	76	404		Batsford		H	$40
Seidel W E	Mercedes-Benz Klassische (juvenile)	85	130	424	Podszun		H	$20
Seidler E	Champion of World	70	205		Automobile Year		H	$80
Seidler E	Romance of Renault	73	120		Edita		H	$70
Seidler E	Renault Challenge	81	120		Edita		S	$30
Seidler E	Lets Call It Fiesta	76	169		Edita		S	$20
Seifert E	BMW (Pocket History)	80	106		Libreria dell'Automobile	Comp Hist	S	$20
Seiff I	Great Classics Auto Eng in Gold Age	82+	401		Hoffman/Orbis/Smith/Gall		H	$40
Seiffert U/Walzer P	Future for Automotive Technology	84	405	150	Pinter		H	$40
Sessions R	Turbo Hydra-Matic 350 Handbook	85	405		H P Books		S	$30
Sessions R	HT Hotrod Your Buick V6	86	108		HP		X	$30
Setright L J K	Bristol Cars and Engines	74	105		MRP		H	$180

Author	Title	Pub date	Subjects		Publisher	Series	Bind	Price
Smith P H	Tuning and Maintenance of MG Cars	52+	131		Foulis/Haynes		H	$40
Smith P H/Morrison J C	Scientific Design Exhaust Intake Sy	62+	202		Bentley		H	$30
Solinger	Porsche Guide	58	136		Sports Car Press		S	$30
Sommers D	Eddie Called Me Boss	79	205		Warren		H	$40
Sorensen C E	My Forty Years With Ford	56	415		Norton		H	$40
Sorensen L	American Ford	75	122		Silverado	Fordiana	H	$80
Sorensen L	Ford Road 75th Anniv Ford Motor Co	78	122		Silverado		H	$50
Sorensen L	Open Fords	77	122		Silverado	Fordiana	H	$125
Soutter A W	American Rolls-Royce	76	139		Mowbray		H	$125
Sox R/Martin B/Neeley B	Sox and Martin Bk of Drag Racing	74	201		Regnery		H	$80
Spafford R	My Mistress Death	56	207		Fawcett		S	$10
Spain R	GT40 Individual Hist & Race Record	86	156		Osprey		H	$180
Speed J F	British Motor Cars	52	406		Foulis		H	$30
Spence J/Brown G	Motorcycle Racing in America	74	602		O'Hara		S	$20
Spiegel M	NASCAR 25 Years of Racing Thrills	74	299		Scholastic		S	$10
Spiegel M	Cycle Jumpers	73	601		Scholastic/Berkley		S	$10
Sporting Motorist Staff	Autocourse 1961-62	62	204		Trafalgar Press		H	$200
Sporting Motorist Staff	Autocourse 1959	60	204		Trafalgar Press		S	$300
Sporting Motorist Staff	Autocourse 1960-61 Part Two	61	204		Trafalgar/Victoria House		S	$180
Spurring Q	Year of Silver Arrows Wld C/S 89-90	90	130		Q Editions		S	$20
Stambler I	Great Moments in Auto Racing	68	297		Four Winds		X	$30
Stambler I	Automobile Engines Today & Tomorrow	72	405		Grosset & Dunlap		H	$30
Stambler I	Top Fuelers Drag Racing Royalty	78	201	213	Putnam		H	$30
Stambler I	Dream Machines Vans & Pickups(juv)	80	301		Putnam		H	$20
Stambler I	Unusual Autos of Today/Tomorrow	72	424		Putnam		H	$30
Stambler I	New Automobiles of the Future	78	424		Putnam		H	$20
Stambler I	Racing Sprint Cars (juvenile)	79	299	213	Putnam		H	$30
Stambler I	Guide to Model Car Racing	67	701		Norton		H	$20
Stanford D	Red Car (MG, juvenile)	54	131	207	Scholastic		S	$40
Stanford J	Profile No 32 30-98 hp Vauxhall	66	105		Profile Publications		S	$10
Stanford J	Sports Car Development and Design	57	401		Batsford		H	$30
Staniforth A	High Speed Low Cost 140mph Mini	69	171		PSL		H	$40
Stanley L T	Grand Prix Wld Chmpshp 60(GP Year)	61	204		Barnes	GP Wld Chmpshp	H	$90
Stanley L T	Grand Prix Wld Chmpshp 64	65	204		Macdonald/Doubleday	GP Wld Chmpshp	H	$70
Stanley L T	Grand Prix Wld Chmpshp 65	66	204		Macdonald	GP Wld Chmpshp	H	$125
Stanley L T	Grand Prix Wld Chmpshp 59	60	204		Barnes	GP Wld Chmpshp	H	$90
Stanley L T	Grand Prix Wld Chmpshp 61	62	204		Barnes	GP Wld Chmpshp	H	$90
Stanley L T	Grand Prix Wld Chmpshp 62	63	204		Barnes	GP Wld Chmpshp	H	$90
Stanley L T	Grand Prix Wld Chmpshp 63	64	204		Barnes	GP Wld Chmpshp	H	$90
Stanley L T	Grand Prix Wld Chmpshp 66	67	204		Macdonald	GP Wld Chmpshp	H	$80
Stanley L T	Grand Prix Wld Chmpshp 68(GP #10)	69	204		Allen/McKay	GP Wld Chmpshp	H	$60
Stanley L T	Grand Prix Wld Chmpshp 69(GP #11)	70	204		McKay	GP Wld Chmpshp	H	$60
Stanley L T	Grand Prix Wld Chmpshp 67	68	204		Macdonald	GP Wld Chmpshp	H	$150
Stanley L T	Behind Scenes	85	297		Queen Anne		H	$30
Stanley L T	BRM Story	66	298		Parrish		H	$80
Stathatos J	Long Drive An Accont London-Sydney	78	209		Pelham/Atheneum		H	$40
Stefanini A	Raid Ferrari D'Epoca Modena 81(Eng)	81	121		Cons Centro Creativo		H	$90
Stefanini A	Ferrari Days (Modena 83)	83	121		Editore NiuItaly		H	$90
Stein R	Treasury of Automobile	61	401		Ridge/Crown		H	$20
Stein R	Sports Cars of World (Stein)	52+	401		Scribner		H	$50
Stein R	World of Automobile	73	401		Ridge Press		H	$40
Stein R	Great Cars	67	401		Grosset & Dunlap/Ridge		H	$30
Stein R	American Automobile (Stein)	75	403		Ridge/Random/Galahad		H	$40
Stein R	Greatest Cars	79	401		Ridge/Simon Schuster/WHS		H	$40
Stein R	Vintage and Classic Cars	77	401		Ridge/Bantam	All-Color Guide	S	$10
Stein R	Vintage and Classic Cars (Stein)	77	401		Ridge/Bantam		S	$10
Steinwedel L W	Mercedes-Benz Story	69	130		Chilton	Sebring	H	$50
Steinwedel L W	Beetle Book America's 30 Yr Love...	81	150		Prentice		H	$30
Steinwedel L W	Golden Age of Sports Cars	72	401		Chilton		H	$20
Steinwedel L W/Newport J	Duesenberg (Steinwedel/Newport)	70+	116		Chilton/Nelson/Norton		H	$40
Stephens P J	Ford Specials	60	156		Foulis/Scientific		H	$40
Stern J	Trucker A Portrait Am Cowboy	75	301		McGraw		S	$20
Stern J/Stern M	Auto Ads	78	503		David Obst/Random		H	$40
Stern P V	Pictorial Hist of Automobile(Motor)	53	401		Hearst/Viking		H	$50
Stern P V	Tin Lizzie Story of Fab Model T....	55	122		Simon & Schuster		H	$30
Stern P V/Brindle M	Famous GM Cars GM Family Album	62	160	504	GM		S	$20
Stevens E M G	Know Thy Beast Vincent	72+	606		Vincent Pub		H	$60
Stevens-Stratten S W	British Lorries 1945-1975	78	303		Ian Allen		H	$30
Stewart J	Jackie Stewarts Princ(autographed)	86	205	203	Hazleton/MBI		H	$100
Stewart J	Jackie Stewarts Owner Driver Book	73	405		Dodd Mead		H	$20
Stewart J/Dymock E	Jackie Stewart World Champion	70	205		Regnery		H	$20
Stewart J/Dymock E	Jackie Stewart World Champ(Signed)	70	205		Regnery/Pelham		H	$100
Stewart J/Manso	Faster Racers Diary	72	205		Farrar/Straus/Giroux		X	$30
Stobbs W	Motor Museums of Europe	83	401		Barker/Weidenfeld		H	$50
Stone H W/Knudson R	MG Mania Insomnia Crew	83	131		New England T Register		S	$50
Stone W S	Guide to American Sports Car Racing	60+	297		Hanover/Doubleday		H	$40
Stone W S	Profile No 90 Ford GT	67	122		Profile Publications		S	$30
Stone W S	So You're Going to Buy Used Spts Cr	67	401		Sports Car Press		S	$10

Author	Title	Pub date	Subjects		Publisher	Series	Bind	Price
Thompson J	Ferrari Cabriolets & Spyders AH	85	121		Osprey	Autohistory	H	$40
Thompson M/Borgeson G	Challenger Mickey Thompsons Story	64	205 211		Prentice Hall		X	$40
Thompson/Rabagliati/Sheld	Formula One Record Bk 1961 - 65	74	297		Leslie Frewin Publishers		H	$150
Thoms D/Donnelly T	Motor Car Industry in Coventry.....	85	419		St Martins		H	$30
Throm E L/Crenshaw J S	Popular Mechanics Auto Album	52	401		Popular Mechanics		X	$20
Tippette G	Brave Men	72	297		Macmillan		H	$30
Toboldt B	Fix Your Ford V-8's&6's 1932-1952	52	122		Goodheart-Willcox		H	$20
Toboldt B	Fix Your Chevrolet V8&6 1966-1975	75	111		Goodheart-Willcox		H	$20
Tommasi T	Chris Amon (Italian)	69	205		L'Editrice Dell'Automobil		H	$20
Tommasi T	Graham Hill (Italian)	69	205		L'Editrice dell'Automobil		H	$30
Tommasi T	Jackie Stewart (Italian)	71	205		Auto.Club d Italia		S	$40
Tommasi T	From Indianapolis/Brands to Le Mans	74	297		Derbi Books		H	$40
Tompkins E S	Speed Camera (How-to)	46	297 510		Foulis		H	$40
Torrens	Whos Who in Motor Cycling	35	610		Esso		S	$40
Torres E	Jeepney	79	306		GCF Books		H	$40
Tours H	Profile No 26 Leyland 8 1922-1926	66	105		Profile Publications		S	$10
Tours H	Parry Thomas Designer Driver	59	205		Batsford		H	$50
Townroe P M	Social and Political Conseq of M/C	74	419		David & Charles		H	$20
Tragatsch E	Ill Ency of Motorcycles	77+	601		Quarto/Chartwell/Hamlyn		H	$40
Tragatsch E	Comp Ill Ency of World Motorcycles	77	601		Holt Rinehart Winston		H	$60
Traisler R	All About Electric & Hybrid Cars	82	417		Tab		H	$30
Trickey C	Tuning Mini	69+	171		Speedsport		S	$30
Trickey C	More Mini Tuning	68+	171		Speed Sport	Speed Sport	S	$30
Trinkle F M	Coast to Coast in Brush Rnabout	52	158 212		Clymer		S	$30
Trow N	Lancia the Shield and Flag	80	157		David & Charles		H	$60
Troyer H	Four Wheel Drive Story	54	311		McGraw-Hill		H	$80
Truscott L K	Comp Van Book	76	307		Harmony/Crown		S	$20
Tubbs D	Rolls-Royce Phantoms	64	139		Hamish Hamilton		H	$50
Tubbs D	Art and Automobile	78	504		Quarto/Arlington/Grosset		H	$50
Tubbs D	Profile No 16 Jowett Javelin&Jupitr	66	105		Profile Publications		S	$10
Tubbs D	Profile No 27 Talbot 14/45,75,90etc	66	105		Profile Publications		S	$10
Tubbs D	Profile No 39 Austin 7	66	105		Profile Publications		S	$20
Tubbs D	Profile No 70 Wolseley Hornet	67	105		Profile Publications		S	$10
Tubbs D	Profile No 44 Lancia Lambda	67	157		Profile Publications		S	$20
Tuck B	Mountain Movers	84	306		PSL		H	$30
Tuck B	Mammoth Trucks Modern Day Heavy....	85	306		Osprey	Osprey Col Lib	S	$30
Tuck B	Hauling Heavyweights Moving Extra..	86	306		PSL		S	$30
Tuck B	Move It! Ill Hist Heavy Haulage Veh	87	306		PSL		S	$30
Tuckey B	Ultimate Excitement(Snowdon photos)	67	297 510		Murray Australia		H	$40
Tuckey W P	Book of Australian Motor Racing	65	298		Murray		H	$40
Turner	Ford Popular	84	156		Osprey		H	$50
Turner M/Roebuck N	Formula One Cars & Drivers (Turner)	83	297 504		Temple		H	$150
Turner S	Way to Win	74	209		MRP		H	$30
Turner S/Mason T	Drive It! Compl Bk of Rallying	78+	209		Haynes		H	$20
Turner S/Mason T	Getting Started in Motorsport	85	297		Haynes		H	$20
Turner S/Organ J	MGB Handbook/Comphnsv Owners Manual	68	131		Foulis/Bentley		H	$40
Turnquist R E	Packard Story Car & Company	65	159		Barnes		H	$50
Tuthill R N	American Auto Sales Lit 1928-1942	79	505		Bookman Dan		S	$40
Twite M L	Worlds Racing Cars 2E	64	297		Macdonald/Doubleday		H	$30
Twite M L	Worlds Racing Cars 3E	66	297		Macdonald/Doubleday		H	$30
Twite M/Taylor R/Windsor	Prototype 1968-70	69	298		Pelham		H	$60
Twork E O	Henry Ford and Benjamin B Lovett A	82	415		Harlo		H	$30
Ukon T	Clubman Racer P2 Daytona (Japanese)	86	602		Neko		S	$30
Ullyett K	Book of Silver Ghost	63	139		Max Parrish		X	$50
Ullyett K	Triumph Companion	62	146		Stanley Paul/Autobooks		H	$40
Ullyett K	Mercedes-Benz Companion	66	130		Stanley Paul		H	$40
Ullyett K	Book of Bentley	65	139		Max Parrish		H	$100
Ullyett K	Rolls-Royce Companion	69	139		Stanley Paul & Co.		H	$50
Ullyett K	Book of Phantoms	64	139		Max Parrish		H	$80
Ullyett K	Eleven Hundred Companion	67	131 105		S Paul		H	$30
Ullyett K	Porsche and Volkswagen Companion	62	136 150		S Paul/Autobooks		H	$30
Ullyett K	Jaguar Companion	59	127		Stanley Paul	Companion	H	$40
Ullyett K	Book of Mini	64	171		Parrish		H	$40
Ullyett K	Beauty of Cars	62	510		Parrish		H	$50
Ulmann A E	Sebring Story	69	206		Chilton	Sebring	H	$40
Ulmann A E	Mercedes Pioneer of an Industry	53	130		Carroll Press		S	$50
Underwood	Whatever Became of Baby Austin	65	158		Heritage		S	$125
Unser B/Scalzo J	Bobby Unser Story	79	205		Doubleday		H	$30
Urich M	Holly 5200 Carburetor Handbook	82	202		H P Books		S	$20
Uskali G/Johnson C	HT Restore Antique & Classic Cars	54	405		Popular Mechanics		H	$40
Valent H	Road Racing at Watkins Glen	58	206		Watkins Glen C of C		H	$200
Valentini F	Lessico Della Carrozzeria	79	501		Automobilia		H	$40
Van Damm S	No Excuses	57	209 205		Putnam		H	$30
Van Kempen R	Nelson Piquet Story of 83 Champshp.	80S	205		Kimberley's	Driver's Guides	S	$20
Van Loon A J	Australian Motoring Yearbook 73	73	204		Motoring News Intl		S	$80
Van Loon A J	Australian Competition Yearbook 74	74	204		Motoring News Intl		S	$70
Van Valkenburgh P	Chevrolet=Racing 14 Years of.......	72	111		Haessner		H	$180
Van den Abeele A	Automobile Year Bk Mdls #3 84(last)	83	704		Editions 24 Heures		H	$80

Author	Title	Pub date	Subjects	Publisher	Series	Bind	Price
Van den Abeele A	Automobile Year Bk Mdls #1 82	81	704	Edita		H	$80
Van den Abeele A	Automobile Year Bk Mdls #2 83	82	704	Edita		H	$80
Van der Feen D	IMSA '84 Yearbook	84	204	IMSA		S	$30
Van der Feen D	IMSA '86 Yearbook	86	204	Intl Mtr Spts Association		S	$30
Vanderveen B H	American Cars of 1930s	71	403	Warne	Olyslager	H	$30
Vanderveen B H	Half Tracks	70S	308	Warne	Olyslager	H	$40
Vanderveen B H	Jeep(Olyslager)	70	117	Warne	Olyslager	H	$30
Vanderveen B H	American Cars of 1960s	77	403	Haynes/Warne	Olyslager	H	$30
Vanderveen B H	American Trucks of Late Thirties	75	301	Warne	Olyslager	H	$30
Vanderveen B H	British Cars of Early Forties	74	406	Olyslager/Warne/Haynes	Auto Library	H	$30
Vanderveen B H	British Cars of Late Forties	74	406	Warne/Haynes/Foulis	Olyslager	H	$30
Vanderveen B H	Fire Crash Vehicles from 1950	76	302	Warne	Olyslager	H	$30
Vanderveen B H	American Cars of 1950s	73	403	Warne/Haynes	Olyslager	H	$30
Vanderveen B H	Wreckers & Recovery Vehicles	72+	306	Haynes/Warne	Olyslager	H	$30
Vanderveen B H	American Cars of 1940s	72	403	Warne	Olyslager	H	$30
Vanderveen B H	Observers Fighting Veh Dir WW II	69	308	Warne		H	$40
Vanderveen B H	Buses and Coaches from 1940	74		Warne	Olyslager	H	$30
Vanderveen B H	Fire-Fighting Vehicles 1840-1950	76	302	Warne	Olyslager	H	$30
Vanderveen B H	Scammell Vehicles	71	303	Warne	Olyslager	H	$30
Vanderveen B H	American Trucks of Early Thirties	74	301	Warne	Olyslager	H	$30
Vanderveen B H	Observer's Army Vehicles Directory	74	308	Warne		H	$30
Vanderveen B H	British Cars of Late Thirties	73	406	Warne	Olyslager	H	$30
Vanderveen B H	Motorcycles to 1945	75	601	Warne	Olyslager	H	$30
Vanderveen B H	Fairground and Circus Transport	73	306	Warne	Olyslager Lib	H	$20
Vandiest C L	Jaguar Cars Practical Guide........	61	127	Pearson		H	$40
Various	Profiles Complete 96 Copy Set		401	Profile Publications		S	$200
Various	Think Small VW	67	150	Volkswagen of America		H	$30
Varisco F	Nardi	87	118	Libreria dell'Auto		H	$50
Venables R	British Trials Motorcycles(Ven'bls)	85	606	BMS		S	$30
Venables R	British Scrambles Motorcycles	86	603	Bruce Main-Smith		S	$50
Vetten H	BMW (factory history)	73	106	BMW		S	$90
Vetten H	Das Buch Von Volkswagen 1938-1988	88	150	Volkswagen AG		H	$50
Viart B	Jaguar Tradition of Sports Cars	85	127	EPA/MBI/Haynes		H	$80
Vieyra D I	Fill'er Up Archit History Gas Stat	79	401	Macmillan/Collier		S	$50
Villa L	Life With Speed King (Campbell)	79	205 211	Marshall Harris	Kaleidoscope	H	$40
Villa L/Gray T	Record Breakers	69	211	Hamlyn/Transatlantic		H	$70
Villard H S	Great Road Races 1894-1914	72	212	Barker		H	$40
Villavecchia I M	Two Wheel Horse Enj Dynamic Balance	71	601	Editorial Fullgraf Spain		H	$20
Vincent P C	PCV Autobiography of Philip Vincent	76	610	Vincent		H	$40
Vizard D	HT Rebuild Yr 1.3,1.6, 2.0 OHC Ford	80	169	HP		S	$40
Vizard D	HT Hotrod Your 2.0-liter OHC Ford	84	169	Fountain/HP		S	$40
Vizard D	Tuning Ford Escorts & Capris	72	156	SpeedSport		S	$20
Vizard D	HT Modify Ford SOHC Engines	84	169	Fountain		S	$30
Vizard D	HT Modify Your Mini	87	171	Fountain Press		S	$40
Vizard D	Tuning Twin Cam Fords	69+	156	Speedsport Motobooks		S	$20
Voller D J	British Cars of Early Sixties	81	406	Warne/Haynes	Olyslager	H	$30
Voller D J	British Cars of Late Sixties	82	406	Warne	Olyslager	H	$30
Voller D J	British Cars of Early Fifties	75	406	Olyslager/Warne/Haynes	Auto Library	H	$30
Voller D/Alexander C	Observers Book of Autos 21E 1978	78	410	Warne		H	$10
Von Fersen H	Autos In Deutschland 1885-1920(Ger)	65	408	Motorbuch Verlag		H	$50
Von Fersen H	Klassische Wagen I	71	401	Hallwag		H	$40
Von Fersen H	Sportwagen in Deutschland	68	408	Motorbuch Verlag		H	$50
Von Fersen H	Autos in Deutschland 1920-1939(Ger)	63	408	Motorbuch Verlag		H	$100
Von Frankenberg R	Porsche Double World Champs.1900-77	78	136	Haynes		H	$40
Von Frankenberg R	Christophorus 1970 Yearbook	70	136	Porsche		S	$30
Von Frankenberg R	Porsche Man & His Cars	61+	136	Bentley		H	$50
Von Mende H	Styling Automobile Design	79	502	Motorbuch Verlag		H	$30
Vose K	Dream Cars Past & Present	89	401	Image Bank/Mallard		H	$50
Vyse H	Automobile Connoisseur 05	71	410	Speed & Sport Pub. Ltd		H	$30
Vyse H	Automobile Connoisseur 04	70	410	Speed & Sports		H	$30
Waar B	HT Hotrod & Race Your Datsun	84	167	Steve Smith		S	$40
Waar B	Off Road Handbook/Back Country Tips	75	311	HP		S	$20
Waar B	Baja-Prepping VW Sedans/Dune.......	70	150	HP		S	$20
Wade Wells A	Hail to Jeep (original)	46	117	Harper		H	$80
Wagner C L	Automobile Year 1966-67 #14	67	204	Edita S.A.		H	$150
Wagner F J	Saga of Roaring Road	49	205	Floyd Clymer		S	$40
Wagner R	Golden Wheels	86	401	Western Reserve/Zubal		H	$40
Wagstaff J S	London RT Bus (Wagstaff)	73		Oakwood	Locomotion Pprs	S	$10
Wakefield R	Road & T Guide Sports & GT 1982	81	410	CBS		S	$20
Wakefield R	Road & T Guide Sports & GT 1983	82	410	CBS		S	$20
Wakefield R	Road & T Guide Sports & GT 1984	83	410	CBS		S	$20
Wakefield R	New BMW Guide	79	106	Tab	Mod Sports Car	S	$20
Walker G	Senior Tourist Trophy 1958(10" rec)	50S	603	Schofield Productions	Sound Stories		$30
Walker G	Isle of Man TT 1959(12" record)	50S	603	Schofield Productions	Sound Stories		$40
Walker G	Isle of Man TT '60 Pt 1(12" record)	50	603	Schofield Productions	Sound Stories		$40
Walker G	Isle of Man TT '60 Pt 2(12" record)	50S	603	Schofield Productions	Sound Stories		$40
Walker M	Ducati Singles	85+	606	Osprey	Coll Lib	H	$50
Walker M	Moto Guzzi Twins	86	606	Osprey	Osprey Coll Lib	H	$50

Author	Title	Pub date	Subjects	Publisher	Series	Bind	Price
Walker T	Around Houses Hist MR West Aust	80	298	Racing Car News		S	$30
Walkerley R	Races That Shook World H		297	Sports Car Press/Temple	Mod Sports Car	H	$30
Walkerley R	Sports Cars Today	62	401	Arthur Barker Ltd		H	$10
Walkerley R	Moments That Made Racing History	59	297	Temple/Sports Car Press		H	$20
Walkerley R	Races That Shook World S	59	297	Arco/Mod Sports Car Press		S	$20
Walkerley R	Grands Prix 1934-1939	48+	297	MRP		H	$70
Walkerley R	Famous Motor Races	63	298	Barker		H	$30
Walkerley R	Motor Racing Facts & Figures	61+	297	Batsford/Bentley		H	$50
Walkerley R	Racing Cars Today	62	298	Barker		H	$30
Walkerley R	Automobile Racing (Walkerley)	62	298	Temple		H	$30
Wallace P J	Brooklands (Ballantine)	71	206	Ballantine Books	Ballantine	S	$20
Walton J	Escort Mk 1 2 & 3 Dev & Comp Hist	85	156	Haynes		H	$40
Walton J	Unbeatable BMW	79	106	Osprey		H	$60
Walton J	Doble Steam Cars Buses, Lorries...	65+	158	Light Steam Power		H	$100
Walton J	Great Marques BMW	83	106	Octopus		H	$30
Walton J	Racing Mechanic 7 Yrs Ferr (Cuoghi)	80+	297 121	Osprey		H	$50
Walton J	R S Fords	87	156	Menoshire			$0
Walton J	Lotus Esprit Autohistory	82+	129	Osprey	Autohistory	H	$40
Walton J	Fiat X1/9 Autohistory	82	152	Osprey		H	$40
Walton J	Audi Quattro Dev & Comp History	84	124	Haynes		H	$70
Walton J	BMW 6 Series	85	106	Cadogan/Prentice Hall	High Performnce	H	$40
Walton J/Caddell L	Supercars Worlds Finest (Walton)	88	401	Macdonald/Longmeadow		H	$30
Wankel F	Rotary Piston Machines	65	405	Deutsche Verlag/Iliffe		H	$60
Warburton L	Electroplating for the Amateur	50+	405	Argus		S	$30
Ward I	World of Motorcycles (Comp Set 22)	79	601	Orbis/CBS		H	$250
Ward I	World of Automobiles (Comp set 22)	74	401	Orbis/CBS/Quattroruote		H	$125
Ward I	Lotus Elan Autohistory	84	129	Osprey	Autohistory	H	$40
Ward I/Caddell L	Great British Bikes	76	606	Orbis			$40
Ward L	Concise Ill Bk Modern Sports Cars	89	401	Brian Trodd/W H Smith		H	$10
Warnock C G	Edsel Affair	80	158	Pro West		H	$60
Warren P/Linskey M	Taxicabs Photographic History	76	401	Almark		H	$50
Watkins M	British Sports Cars Since the War	73	406	Arco		H	$40
Watkins M	AC (Foulis Mini Marque)	76	105 109	Haynes	Mini-Marque	H	$30
Watkins M	Automobile Connoisseur 01	69	410	Speed & Sports		H	$40
Watkins M B	Suspension & Brakes Tuning Comp	70	202	Speed Sport	Tuning Comp #3	S	$20
Watkins M B	Tuning Stromberg Carburetters	73	202	Speed Sport		S	$10
Watson D	Glory Road	73	297	Stadia		S	$10
Watson/Janota	Turbocharging Internal Comb. Engine	83	202	Wiley/Macmillan		H	$250
Watts B	Three Wheeler	70	164	Morgan 3 Wheeler Club		S	$20
Webb C	Investors Ill Gd to Am Conv 1946-76	79	403	Barnes		H	$50
Webb I	Ferrari Dino 206GT etc Autohistory	80	121	Osprey	Autohistory	H	$50
Webb I	Ferrari 275GTB & GTS Autohistory	81	121	Osprey	Autohistory	H	$50
Webb N C	From Last to First Neil Bonnett....	79	205	Strode		H	$40
Weernink W	La Lancia 70 Years of Excellence	79	157	MRP		H	$80
Weernink W	Lancia Fulvia & Flavia Coll Guide	84	157	MRP	Coll Guide	H	$50
Weis B J	Arrow 100th Anniv Meet 1978 issue	78	170	Pierce-Arrow Society		S	$30
Weisberger B A	Dream Maker William C Durant GM	79	160	Little Brown		H	$30
Weitmann J	Porsche Story	68	136	Arco		H	$50
Wells G	Land Transport Tomorrow	70	419	Clifton Books		H	$20
Wells K	Cosworth	87	297	Kimberley		S	$30
Werking N P	Speedway Driver History	48	208	Clymer		S	$40
Werstein I ed	Roaring Road Best Auto Rac Stories	57	297	Automotive Periodicals		S	$10
Wheatley R	Restoration of Antique&Classic Cars	64+	405	Bentley		H	$30
Wheatley R/Morgan B	Restoration Vintage & Thorbrd Cars	57+	405	Batsford		H	$30
Wherry J H	MG Story	67	131	Chilton		H	$40
Wherry J H	Alfa Romeo Story	67	101	Chilton	Sebring	H	$50
Wherry J H	Jaguar Story	67	127	Chilton	Sebring	H	$30
Wherry J H	Antique and Classic Cars(Trend 193)	60	401	Trend	Trend Book	S	$10
Wherry J H	MG Sports Car Supreme	82	131	Barnes		H	$40
Wherry J H	Automobiles of the World (Wherry)	68	412	Chilton/Galahad		H	$60
Wherry J H	Concours d'Elegance	69	401	Howell North		H	$30
Wherry J H	Economy Car Blitz	56	412	Associated Booksellers		H	$30
White A J	Assassination of Corvair	69	113	Readers Press		H	$40
Whitehead R A	Kaleidoscope of Steam Wagons	79	306	Marshall Harris		H	$40
Whiteman J/Steinemann R	Project Porsche 928	78	136	Porsche/Motorbuch Verlag		H	$180
Whitener B	Electric Car Book	81	417	Love Street Books		S	$20
Whiteside T	Investigation of Ralph Nader	72	401	Arbor		H	$30
Whitt D	Petersens Basic Atmtv Tools........	74	405	Petersen		S	$10
Whyte A	Jaguar SS90 & SS100 Super Profile	84	127	Haynes	Super Profile	H	$20
Whyte A	Centenary of Car 1885-1985	84	401	Octopus/Longmeadow/Walden		H	$30
Whyte A	Volvo 1800 and Family Autohistory	84	165	Osprey		H	$40
Whyte A	Touch of Class 101 Great Marques...	85	401	Mandarin/Octopus/Lngmdw		H	$20
Whyte A	Cars Old Classics From Early Days..	83	401	Mandarin/Octopus		H	$20
Whyte A	Jaguar History Great British Car	80+	127	PSL/Sterling		H	$60
Whyte A	Jaguar XJ40 Evolution of Species	87	127	PSL		H	$50
Whyte R I	Daimler & Lanchester Owners' Comp	81	105	DLOC		S	$20
Wieder R/Hall G	Great American Convertible (Wieder)	77	403	Baron Wolman/Doublday		S	$30
Wiegersma F	La Belle Chauffeusse	81	506	VOC Angel Books		H	$50

Author	Title	Pub date	Subjects		Publisher	Series	Bind	Price
Wieland J/Force E	Corgi Toys Ones with Windows	81	702		MBI		S	$40
Wik R M	Henry Ford & Grass-roots America	72	415		Univ of Mich		X	$40
Wilk P	Collecting & Restoring Antique Cars	78	401		Book Creations/Cornerston		S	$20
Wilkie D J	Esquires American Autos and Makers	63	403		Esquire/Harper & Row		H	$20
Wilkins G	Automobile Year 1961-62 #9	62	204		Edita S.A.		H	$250
Wilkins M/Hill F E	American Business Abroad Ford......	64	169		Wayne		H	$40
Wilkinson S	Stainless Steel Carrot	73	299		Houghton		H	$20
Wilkinson S	World of Racing Endurance Racing	81	213		Childrens Press		H	$10
Willamson C N/A M	Lightning Conductor Discov America	00S	212		Country Life Press		H	$40
Williams G	World of Model Cars (Williams)	76	704		G P Putnam's Sons		H	$30
Williams G	Sands of Speed (Babs)	73	211		Davies		H	$40
Williams M	British Tractors for World Farming	80	904		Blandford Press		S	$20
Williams M	Road Movies Comp Gd Cinema on Whls	82	509		Proteus/Scribner		S	$30
Williams M	Ford & Fordson Tractors	85	904		Blandford		H	$50
Williams P J	Grand Prix Racing (Williams - juv)	67	213		Scholastic		S	$10
Williams W C	Motoring Mascots of World 1E	77	507		MBI		H	$60
Williamson C N/A M	Lightning Conductor Strange Adven..	02+	212		Methuen/Henry Holt		H	$40
Willinger K/Gurney G	American Jeep in War & Peace	83	117		Crown		S	$30
Willoughby G	Ferrari 308 & Mondial Autohistory	82	121		Osprey	Autohistory	X	$50
Willoughby V	Back to Basics	81	609		Haynes		S	$20
Willoughby V	Classic Motorcycles	75	601		Hamlyn/Dial		H	$50
Willoughby V	Racing Motor Cycle	80	603		Hamlyn		H	$40
Wilson E	Alfa Romeo Giulietta	82	101		Osprey		H	$125
Wilson P C	Chrome Dreams Auto Styling Since 93	76	502		Chilton		H	$30
Wilson S	British Motor Cycles Since 1950 V1	82	606		PSL		H	$50
Wilson S	British Motor Cycles Since 1950 V2	83	606		PSL		H	$50
Wilson S	British Motor Cycles Since 1950 V4	87	606		PSL		H	$70
Wilson T	HT Rebuild Your Honda Car Engine	85	126		HP		S	$20
Wimpff J	Compleat Hist Corvair for Nut V1	78+	113		Clark's Corvair Parts		S	$40
Wimpff J	Compleat Hist Corvair for Nut V2	80	113		Vair Press		S	$30
Wineland L/Hot Rod Eds	Motorcycle Sport Book	70S	602		Petersen	Hot Rod	S	$20
Wingrove G	Comp Car Modeller	78	702		Crown/New Cav/Eyre Meth..		H	$90
Wingrove G	Model Cars of Gerald Wingrove	79	702		New Cavendish/Methuen		H	$125
Wingrove G	Unimat Lathe Projects	79	704		New Cavendish		S	$30
Wise D B	Ill History of Automobiles	80	401		Quarto/A&W		H	$10
Wise D B	Steam on Road	73	414		Hamlyn		H	$20
Wise D B	Classics of the Road	78	401		Orbis		H	$20
Wise D B	Motor Car Illustrated Intl History	77+	401		Orbis		H	$30
Wise D B	Veteran and Vintage Cars (Wise)	70	401		Hamlyn/Grosset		H	$10
Witzenburg G	Camaro From Challenger to Champion	81	111		Automobile Quarterly		H	$60
Wolfe A S	Vans Vanners and Vanning	76	307		Greatlakes Living Press		H	$20
Wolfe C	Buick Riviera 1963-73 all series...	86	108		MBI		S	$40
Wolfe T	Kandy-Kolored Tangerine-Flake......	66	416		Cape/Pan		S	$30
Wolfson V	ARRC 1971 & SCAA Road Racing Annual	72	204		Haessner & Associates		S	$20
Wood D F	Chevy El Camino 1959-82 Photofacts	82	111		MBI	CMB Photofacts	S	$40
Wood E V	Story of Hudson Motor Car 1909-1957	73	163		Triangle Press		S	$20
Wood G/Renstrom R C	Great Motorcycles Hist 22 Famous...	72	606		Bond Parkhurst		S	$20
Wood J	Profile No 64 1 1/2-litre Squire	67	105		Profile Publications		S	$20
Wood J	Famous Marques of Britan	83+	406		Mandarin/Octopus/etc		H	$60
Wood J	Great Marques Rolls-Royce	82	139		Mandarin/Octopus		H	$30
Wood J	Great American Cars	85	401		Multimedia/Smith/Gallery		H	$20
Wood J	Ford Cortina Mk 1 62-66 Autohistory	84	156		Osprey	Autohistory	H	$40
Wood J	Great Marques of America	86	403		Mandarin/Octopus		H	$30
Wood J	Rolls-Royce (Shire-Wood)	87	139		Shire	Shire Album 198	S	$10
Wood T	Drive It! Compl Bk of Formula 2	84	297		Haynes		H	$20
Woodbury G	Story of Stanley Steamer S	67	158		Clymer		S	$60
Woodbury G	Story of Stanley Steamer H	50	158		Norton		H	$70
Woodhams J	Old Lorries Shire Album 138	85	303		Shire Pub	Shire Album	S	$10
Woollett M	Yamaha	84	606		Arco		S	$20
Woollett M	Honda (Woollett)	83	606		Temple/Newnes/Hamlyn		H	$40
Woollett M	Speedbikes	83	601		Arco		H	$20
Woollett M	World Championship Motor Cycl Rac	73	604		Hamlyn		H	$40
Woollett M	Lightweight Bikes	81	601		Batsford	Batsford PB	S	$10
Wortham J/Whitener B	Forget Gas Pumps Make Your Own Fuel	79	417		Love Street Books		S	$20
Worthington-Williams M	Automobilia Guided Tour for Coll...	79	507		Hastings/Batsford		H	$50
Worthington-Williams M	Vintage Car Annual #1	79	401		Marshall Harris		H	$40
Worthington-Williams M	From Cyclecar to Microcar	81	406		Dalton Watson		H	$50
Woudenberg P R	Ford in Thirties	76	122		Petersen		H	$20
Woundenberg P R	Lincoln & Continental Postwar Years	80	161		MBI	Marques Amer	H	$60
Wren J A/Wren G J	Motor Trucks of America	79	301		Univ of Michigan		S	$30
Wright N	Camaro (Gallery)	85	111		Gallery/Smith		H	$20
Wright N	Mustang (Wright)	85	122		Multimedia/Gallery/Smith		H	$20
Wright N	Ultimate Mustang Book	86	122		Gallery/Smith		H	$40
Wright O D/White E L D	London to Calcutta 1938	88	212		Little Hills		H	$40
Wyatt R J	Austin 1905-1952	81	105		David & Charles		H	$60
Wyatt R J	Austin Seven 1922-1939	68+	105		David & Charles		H	$50
Wyer J	Motor Racing Management	56	103	297	Bodley Head		H	$40
Wyer J	Certain Sound 30 Years of Motor Rac	81	298		Edita/Haynes		H	$125

Author	Title	Pub date	Subjects		Publisher	Series	Bind	Price
Wyer J/Nixon C	Racing with David Brown Aston Vol 1	80	103		Transport Bookman		H	$80
Wymer N	Harry Ferguson Life of (juv)	61	404	901	Phoenix	Liv Biog	H	$50
Wyss W A	Super Fords	79	122		Zuma Marketing		S	$30
Wyss W A	De Tomaso Automobiles	81	118		Osprey		H	$90
Wyss W A	Shelbys Wildlife (hardbound)	77+	109		MBI		H	$30
Yale S	Mopar 273 318 etc Perf Gd & Catalog	75	132		Phase III		S	$10
Yamaguchi J K	RX-7 New Mazda RX-7 and Mazda Rot..	85	126		Dai Nippon/St Martins		H	$60
Yamaguchi J K/Thompson J	Miata Mazda MX-5 (2 volume set)	89	126		Dai Nippon/St Martins		H	$60
Yamamoto K	Rotary Engine	81	405		Sankaido/Toyo Kogyo/Mazdq		H	$50
Yarborough C/Neeley W	Cale Hazardous Life and Times of...	86	205		Times		H	$30
Yarnell D	Auto Pioneering Story of R E Olds	49	404		R E Olds		H	$50
Yates B	Sunday Driver	72	205		Farrar,Straus/Doubleday		X	$40
Yates B	Indianapolis 500(Yates)	56+	213	208	Harper		H	$30
Yates B	Decline and Fall Am Auto Industry	83	419		Empire		H	$30
Yates B	Racers & Drivers Fastest Men/Cars..	68	205		Bobbs Merrill		H	$30
Yates B	Guide to Racing Cars	63	297		Sterling/Crown/Bonanza		H	$20
Yates R F/Yates B W	Sport and Racing Cars	54	297		Harper & Row		H	$30
Yost S K	Great Old Cars Where are they Now?	60	401		Wayside		S	$20
Young E S	McLaren Man Cars & Team	71	298		Bond/Parkhurst		H	$70
Young E S	Bruce McLaren Man & His Rac T'm	71	298		Eyre & Spottiswoode		H	$60
Young E S	James Hunt Against All Odds	77	205		Hamlyn		H	$30
Young R	Boss Ket Life of Charles Kettering	61	404		McKay		H	$40
Young R	Peak of Performance Pikes Peak.....	82	206		Ron Young		S	$40
Zavitz R P	Chevelle 64-73 Databook & Price Gd	86	111		Bookman Dan		S	$30
Zavitz R P	Canadian Cars 1946-1984	85	413		Bookman		S	$30
Zavitz R P	Buick Gran Sports Source Book	84	108		Bookman	Source Book	S	$30
Zavitz R P	Barracuda/Chall 64-74 Data Bk/P Gd	85	115	137	Bookman Dan		S	$30
Zavitz R P	Riviera Classic Source Book	84	108		Bookman Publishing	Source Boo	S	$30
Zavitz R P	Big Buick Source Book	84	108		Bookman	Source Book	S	$20
Zavitz R P	Four-4-2 64-86 Data Bk/Price Guide	85	162		Bookman		S	$30
Zavitz R P	Cadillac Data Bk & Price Gd 1960-69	85	110		Bookman		S	$30
Ziegler R	Messerschmitt Kabinenroller	80S	124		Freunde		S	$70
Zweigardt M	Auto im Zeitblick Mercedes 1949-53	80	130		Gourmandise Verlag		S	$20

AUTOMOBILIA, CREATIVE, COLLECTIBLES, COACHBUILDING (Continued)

DESIGN/STYLING

AUTOMOBILIA, CREATIVE, COLLECTING,COACHBUILDING (Continued)
PAINTING/DRAWING/SCULPTURE (Continued)

Title	Year	Author	Publisher	Bind	Price
Manifold Pressures Motoring........	58	Brockbank R	Temple	H	$30
More Sketches by Casque	30S	Davis S C H	Iliffe	H	$80
Motor Racing Drivers Past & Present	56	Sallon	Shell-Mex	S	$40
Motor Racing Sketchbook	50S	Demand C	Foulis	H	$125
Oldtimers (Art book - German text)	61	Buergle K/Simsa P	Motor-Presse-Verlag	H	$40
Racing Cars (Nelson)	50S	Groves R	Nelson	H	$30
Sixty Vetture ai Raggi X	67	Cavara G	Auto Club d'Italia	S	$150
Spirit Celebrating 75 Yrs of R-R...	79	Dallison K	Spirit Group	H	$300
Ten Ans de Courses (Montaut)	08?	Montaut E	Montaut Mabileau Editeurs	S	$3000
Walter Gotschke and M-B Racing Car*	80	Gotschke W	Barnes/Rights Marketing	H	$400
Yumping Yarns (F1 cartoons)	88	Bamber J	Tudor Journals	S	$20

PERIODICALS (CAR STYLING, STYLE AUTO)

Title	Year	Author	Publisher	Bind	Price
Car Styling No 01	73	Fujimoto A	San'ei Shobo	H	$100
Car Styling No 02	73	Fujimoto A	San'ei Shobo	H	$100
Car Styling No 03	73	Fujimoto A	San'ei Shobo	H	$90
Car Styling No 04	73	Fujimoto A	San'ei Shobo	H	$90
Car Styling No 05	73	Fujimoto A	San'ei Shobo	H	$90
Car Styling No 06	73	Fujimoto A	San'ei Shobo	H	$80
Car Styling No 07	74	Fujimoto A	San'ei Shobo	H	$80
Car Styling No 08	74	Fujimoto A	San'ei Shobo	H	$80
Car Styling No 09	75	Fujimoto A	San'ei Shobo	H	$80
Car Styling No 10	75	Fujimoto A	San'ei Shobo	H	$80
Car Styling No 11	75	Fujimoto A	San'ei Shobo	H	$70
Car Styling No 12	75	Fujimoto A	San'ei Shobo	H	$70
Car Styling No 13	76	Fujimoto A	San'ei Shobo	H	$70
Car Styling No 14	76	Fujimoto A	San'ei Shobo	H	$70
Car Styling No 15	76	Fujimoto A	San'ei Shobo	H	$70
Car Styling No 16	76	Fujimoto A	San'ei Shobo	H	$60
Car Styling No 17	77	Fujimoto A	San'ei Shobo	H	$60
Car Styling No 18	77	Fujimoto A	San'ei Shobo	H	$60
Car Styling No 19	77	Fujimoto A	San'ei Shobo	H	$50
Car Styling No 19 - Bertone	77	Fujimoto A	San'ei Shobo	H	$60
Car Styling No 20	77	Fujimoto A	San'ei Shobo	H	$60
Car Styling No 21	78	Fujimoto A	San'ei Shobo	H	$60
Car Styling No 22	78	Fujimoto A	San'ei Shobo	H	$60
Car Styling No 23	78	Fujimoto A	San'ei Shobo	X	$60
Car Styling No 24	78	Fujimoto A	San'ei Shobo	H	$60
Car Styling No 25	79	Fujimoto A	San'ei Shobo	H	$60
Car Styling No 26	79	Fujimoto A	San'ei Shobo	X	$60
Car Styling No 27	79	Fujimoto A	San'ei Shobo	X	$60
Car Styling No 28	79	Fujimoto A	San'ei Shobo	X	$60
Car Styling No 29	80	Fujimoto A	San'ei Shobo	H	$60
Car Styling No 30	80	Fujimoto A	San'ei Shobo	H	$60
Car Styling No 31	80	Fujimoto A	San'ei Shobo	H	$60
Car Styling No 31 1/2 Porsche/Desg	80	Fujimoto A	San'ei Shobo	S	$70
Car Styling No 32	80	Fujimoto A	San'ei Shobo	H	$60
Car Styling No 33	81	Fujimoto A	San'ei Shobo	H	$60
Car Styling No 34	81	Fujimoto A	San'ei Shobo	H	$50
Car Styling No 35	81	Fujimoto A	San'ei Shobo	H	$50
Car Styling No 35 1/2 - Giugiaro	81	Fujimoto A	San'ei Shobo	S	$70
Car Styling No 36	81	Fujimoto A	San'ei Shobo	H	$50
Car Styling No 37	82	Fujimoto A	San'ei Shobo	H	$50
Car Styling No 38	82	Fujimoto A	San'ei Shobo	H	$50
Car Styling No 39	82	Fujimoto A	San'ei Shobo	H	$50
Car Styling No 40	82	Fujimoto A	San'ei Shobo	H	$50
Car Styling No 41	83	Fujimoto A	San'ei Shobo	H	$50
Car Styling No 42	83	Fujimoto A	San'ei Shobo	H	$50
Car Styling No 43	83	Fujimoto A	San'ei Shobo	X	$50
Car Styling No 44	83	Fujimoto A	San'ei Shobo	H	$50
Car Styling No 45	84	Fujimoto A	San'ei Shobo	X	$50
Car Styling No 46	84	Fujimoto A	San'ei Shobo	S	$50
Car Styling No 47	84	Fujimoto A	San'ei Shobo	S	$50
Car Styling No 48	84	Fujimoto A	San'ei Shobo	S	$50
Car Styling No 49	85	Fujimoto A	San'ei Shobo	S	$50
Car Styling No 50	85	Fujimoto A	San'ei Shobo	S	$50
Car Styling No 51	85	Fujimoto A	San'ei Shobo	S	$50
Car Styling No 52	85	Fujimoto A	San'ei Shobo	S	$50
Car Styling No 53	86	Fujimoto A	San'ei Shobo	S	$50
Car Styling No 54	86	Fujimoto A	San'ei Shobo	S	$50
Car Styling No 55	86	Fujimoto A	San'ei Shobo	S	$50
Car Styling No 56	86	Fujimoto A	San'ei Shobo	S	$50
Car Styling No 57	87	Fujimoto A	San'ei Shobo	S	$50
Car Styling No 58	87	Fujimoto A	San'ei Shobo	S	$50
Car Styling No 59	87	Fujimoto A	San'ei Shobo	S	$50
Car Styling No 60	87	Fujimoto A	San'ei Shobo	S	$50
Car Styling No 61	87	Fujimoto A	San'ei Shobo	S	$50
Car Styling No 62	88	Fujimoto A	San'ei Shobo	S	$50

AUTOMOBILIA, CREATIVE, COLLECTING,COACHBUILDING (Continued)
PERIODICALS (CAR STYLING, STYLE AUTO) (Continued)

Car Styling No 63	88	Fujimoto A	San'ei Shobo	S	$50
Car Styling No 64	88	Fujimoto A	San'ei Shobo	S	$50
Car Styling No 65	88	Fujimoto A	San'ei Shobo	S	$50
Car Styling No 66	88	Fujimoto A	San'ei Shobo	S	$50
Car Styling No 67	88	Fujimoto A	San'ei Shobo	S	$50
Car Styling No 68	89	Fujimoto A	San'ei Shobo	S	$50
Style Auto - 01 (Italian)	63	Cinti F	Edistyle	H	$70
Style Auto - 02 (Italian)	63	Cinti F	Style Auto	H	$50
Style Auto - 03 (Italian)	64	Cinti F	Style Auto	H	$50
Style Auto - 04 (English)	64	Bellia G	Style Auto	X	$50
Style Auto - 05 (English)	64		Style Auto	X	$30
Style Auto - 06 (English)	65	Bellia G	Style Auto	H	$50
Style Auto - 07 (English)	65	Bellia G	Style Auto	X	$50
Style Auto - 08 (English)	65	Bellia G	Style Auto	S	$50
Style Auto - 09 (English)	65	Dinarich M	Style Auto	S	$50
Style Auto - 10 (English)		Bellia G	Style Auto	S	$50
Style Auto - 11 (English)		Bellia G	Style Auto	S	$50
Style Auto - 12 (English)		Bellia G	Style Auto	X	$50
Style Auto - 13 (English)	67	Dinarich M	Style Auto	H	$50
Style Auto - 14 (English)			Style Auto	X	$30
Style Auto - 15 (English)			Style Auto	X	$50
Style Auto - 16 (English)	68	Dinarich M	Style Auto	S	$50
Style Auto - 17 (English)	68	Dinarich M	Style Auto	H	$50
Style Auto - 18 (English)			Style Auto	X	$50
Style Auto - 19 (English)			Style Auto	X	$50
Style Auto - 20 (English)	69	Dinarich M	Style Auto	H	$60
Style Auto - 21 (English)	69	Dinarich M	Style Auto	H	$40
Style Auto - 22 (English)	69		Style Auto	S	$30
Style Auto - 23 (English)			Style Auto	X	$30
Style Auto - 24 (English)			Style Auto	X	$30
Style Auto - 25 (English)			Style Auto	X	$30
Style Auto - 26 (English)			Style Auto	X	$30
Style Auto - 27 (English)			Style Auto	X	$30
Style Auto - 28 (English)	70		Style Auto		30
Style Auto - 29 (English)	71	Dinarich M	Style Auto	H	$30
Style Auto - 30 (English)			Style Auto	X	$30
Style Auto - 31 (English)			Style Auto	X	$30
Style Auto - 32 (English)			Style Auto	X	$30
Style Auto - 33 (English)			Style Auto	X	$30
Style Auto - 34/35 (English)			Style Auto	X	$30
Style Auto - 36 (English)			Style Auto	X	$30
Style Auto - 37 (English) (last)	78	Dinarich M	Style Auto	H	$30

PHOTOGRAPHY

Automotive Photog. of Peter Coltrin	78	Coltrin P	Barnes	S	$40
Beauty of Cars	62	Ullyett K	Parrish	H	$50
Boyhood Photos of J-H Lartigue	66	Lartigue J H	Ami Guichard	H	$500
Comp Pirelli Cal-see HEAVENLY B					
Eighty Jahre Camera und Automobil	63	Beer H	Terhag-Verlag	H	$125
Gas Food and Lodging	82	Baeder J	Cross River/Abbeville	H	$50
Great Drivers (Mase)	81	Mase A	Libro Port	H	$125
Heavenly Bodies Pirelli Calendar	75		Harmony Books/Pan	S	$100
J H Lartigue Et Les Autos	74	Lartigue J H	Chene	H	$150
Jacques-Henri Lartigue(English)	86	Lartigue J-H	Centre National/Pantheon	S	$20
Looking Back	82	Alexander J	At Speed Press	H	$80
New Matadors	65	Baumann H H	Bond	H	$70
Photo Formula-I Best Auto Yr 53-78	79		Edita	H	$150
Racedrivers	63	Muller B	Motor-Presse-Verlag	H	$150
Speed Camera (How-to)	46	Tompkins E S	Foulis	H	$40
Ultimate Excitement(Snowdon photos)	67	Tuckey B	Murray Australia	H	$40
Victorian and Edwdn Cyclng/Motoring	77	Demaus A B	Batsford	H	$30

SALES LITERATURE (ABOUT)

American Auto Sales Lit 1928-1942	79	Tuthill R N	Bookman Dan	S	$40

CLASSIC MOTORBOOKS CATALOGS

Classic Motorbooks 1970 Catalog	69		S	$50
Classic Motorbooks 1971 Catalog	70		S	$40
Classic Motorbooks 1972 Catalog	71		S	$40
Classic Motorbooks 1973 Catalog	72		S	$40
Classic Motorbooks 1974 Catalog	73		S	$40
Classic Motorbooks 1975 Catalog	74		S	$30
Classic Motorbooks 1976 Catalog	75		S	$30
Classic Motorbooks 1977 Catalog	76		S	$30
Classic Motorbooks 1978 Catalog	77		S	$30
Classic Motorbooks 1978 Mtcycl Cat	77		S	$20
Classic Motorbooks 1979 Catalog	78		S	$20
Classic Motorbooks 1980 Catalog	79		S	$20
Classic Motorbooks 1981 Catalog	80		S	$20

CLASSIC MOTORBOOKS CATALOGS (Continued)

Classic Motorbooks 1982 Catalog	81			S	$20
Classic Motorbooks 1983 Catalog	82			S	$20
Classic Motorbooks 1984 Catalog	83			S	$10
Classic Motorbooks 1985 Catalog	84			S	$10
Classic Motorbooks 1986 Catalog	85			S	$10

GENERAL
ALTERNATE PROPULSION - ELECTRIC, ALCHOHOL. ETC.

All About Electric & Hybrid Cars	82	Traisler R	Tab	H	$30
Brown's Alchohol Motor Fuel Cookb'k	79+	Brown M H	Desert Publ	S	$30
Comp Bk Electric Vehicles	81+	Shacket S R	Domus/Quality	X	$30
Convert your Compact Car to Elec...	81	Jones C R	Domus	S	$20
Electric Car Alternative to the...	74	Naidu G M/Tesar G/Udell G	Pub Sciences Group	S	$20
Electric Car Book	81	Whitener B	Love Street Books	S	$20
Electric Vehicles Des/Build Yr Own	77+	Hackleman M	Earthmind/Peace Press	S	$30
Forget Gas Pumps Make Your Own Fuel	79	Wortham J/Whitener B	Love Street Books	S	$20
HT Convert to Electric Car	80	Lucas T/Riess F	Michelman/Crown	H	$30
Solargas HT Easily Make Your Own...	79	Hoye D	Intl Publishing	S	$20

ANNUALS, PERIODICALS, CAR CATALOGS, ETC (EXCEPT AQ)

Auto 1953	52	Di Ruffia C B	Alfieri Editore	H	$80
Auto 1954	53	Di Ruffia C B	Alfieri Editore/Tudor	H	$80
Auto 1955	54	Di Ruffia C B	Alfieri Editore/Tudor	H	$80
Auto 1956	56	Di Ruffia C B	Alfieri Editore/Tudor	H	$80
Auto-Parade 1957(1st)(Int Auto Cat)	57	Logoz A	Int Auto Parade	S	$100
Auto-Parade 1958 (Vol II)	58	Logoz A	Int Auto Parade	H	$70
Auto-Parade 1960 #3	60	Logoz A	Int Auto Parade/Chilton	H	$60
Auto-Parade 1961 #4	61	Logoz A	Int Auto Parade/Chilton	H	$60
Auto-Parade 1962 #5	61	Logoz A	Int Auto Parade/Chilton	H	$60
Auto-Parade 1963 #6	62	Logoz A	Int Auto Parade/Macmillan	H	$60
Auto-Universum 1964	63	Logoz A	Int Auto Parade	H	$60
Auto-Universum 1965	65	Logoz A	Int Auto Parade/A Barker	H	$60
Auto-Universum 1966	65	Logoz A	Int Auto Parade	H	$60
Auto-Universum 1967	66	Logoz A	Int Auto Parade	H	$60
Auto-Universum 1968	67	Logoz A	Int Auto Parade		60
Auto-Universum 1969	68	Logoz A	Int Auto Parade	H	$60
Auto-Universum 1970	69	Logas A	Int Auto Parade		50
Auto-Universum 71	70	Logoz A	Int Auto Parade	H	$50
Automobil Revue '51	51		Hallwag	S	$80
Automobil Revue '56	56		Hallwag	S	$70
Automobil Revue '59	59		Hallwag	S	$70
Automobil Revue '61	61		Hallwag	S	$60
Automobil Revue '62	62		Hallwag	S	$60
Automobil Revue '63	63		Hallwag	S	$60
Automobil Revue '64	64		Hallwag	S	$60
Automobil Revue '65	65		Hallwag	S	$60
Automobil Revue '66	66		Hallwag	S	$60
Automobil Revue '67	67		Hallwag	S	$60
Automobil Revue '68	68		Hallwag	S	$60
Automobil Revue '69	69		Hallwag	S	$60
Automobil Revue '70	70		Hallwag	S	$50
Automobil Revue '71	'71		Hallwag	S	$50
Automobil Revue '72	72		Hallwag	S	$50
Automobil Revue '73	73		Hallwag	S	$50
Automobil Revue '74	74		Hallwag	S	$50
Automobil Revue '75	75		Hallwag	S	$50
Automobil Revue '76	76		Hallwag	S	$50
Automobil Revue '78	78		Hallwag	S	$50
Automobil Revue '79	79		Hallwag	S	$50
Automobil Revue '80	80		Hallwag	S	$40
Automobil Revue '81	81		Hallwag	S	$40
Automobil Revue '82	82		Hallwag	S	$40
Automobil Revue '84	84		Hallwag	S	$40
Automobil Revue '85	85		Hallwag	S	$60
Automobil Revue '86	86		Hallwag	S	$60
Automobil Revue '87	87		Hallwag	S	$60
Automobil Revue '88	88		Hallwag	S	$60
Automobil Revue '89	89		Hallwag	S	$60
Automobil Revue '90	90		Hallwag	S	$60
Automobile Almanac 1967	67	Ash D	Essandess/Simon Schuster	S	$30
Automobile Almanac 1971	70	Ash D	Morrow	H	$20
Automobile Almanac 1972	71	Ash D	Automobile Almanac	S	$20
Automobile Almanac 1973	73	Ash D	Automobile Almanac/Crowel	H	$20
Automobile Almanac 1975	75	Ash D	Automobile Almanac	H	$20
Automobile Almanac 1977	77	Ash D	Automobile Almanac	S	$10
Automobile Connoisseur 01	69	Watkins M	Speed & Sports	H	$40
Automobile Connoisseur 03	70		Speed & Sports	H	$30
Automobile Connoisseur 04	70	Vyse H	Speed & Sports	H	$30

GENERAL (Continued)
ANNUALS, PERIODICALS, CAR CATALOGS, ETC (EXCEPT AQ) (Continued)

Automobile Connoisseur 05	71	Vyse H	Speed & Sport Pub. Ltd		H	$30
Automobile World 1969 see AUTO-UNIV						60
Automobiles 1951 (Japanese MV Ind)	51		Soc Auto Engineers Japan		H	$50
High Performance Cars 1958-1959	57	Grant G/Bolster J	Autosport		S	$20
High Performance Cars 1961-1962	61	Grant G/Bolster J	Autosport		S	$20
High Performance Cars 1965-1966	65	Grant G/Bolster J	Autosport		S	$20
Le Grandi Automobili 01	82		Automobilia		S	$30
Le Grandi Automobili 02	82		Automobilia		S	$30
Le Grandi Automobili 03	83		Automobilia		S	$30
Le Grandi Automobili 04	83		Automobilia		S	$30
Le Grandi Automobili 05	83		Automobilia		S	$30
Le Grandi Automobili 06	83		Automobilia		S	$30
Le Grandi Automobili 07	84		Automobilia		S	$30
Le Grandi Automobili 08	84		Automobilia		S	$30
Le Grandi Automobili 09	84		Automobilia			30
Le Grandi Automobili 10	84		Automobilia		S	$30
Le Grandi Automobili 11	85		Automobilia		S	$30
Le Grandi Automobili 12	85		Automobilia		S	$30
Le Grandi Automobili 13	85		Automobilia		S	$30
Le Grandi Automobili 14	85		Automobilia		S	$30
Le Grandi Automobili 15	86		Automobilia		S	$30
Le Grandi Automobili 16	86	Alfieri B	Automobilia		S	$40
Le Grandi Automobili 17	86	Alfieri B	Automobilia		S	$30
Le Grandi Automobili 18	87	Alfieri B	Automobilia		S	$50
Motor Road Test Annual 1969	69		Hamlyn		S	$30
Motor Road Test Annual 1970	70		Hamlyn		S	$30
Motor Road Test Annual 1971	71		IPC		S	$30
Motor Road Test Annual 1972	72		IPC		S	$30
Motor Road Test Annual 1973	73		IPC		S	$30
Motor Road Test Annual 1974	74		IPC		S	$30
Motor Road Test Annual 1975	75		IPC		S	$30
Motor Road Test Annual 1979	79	Motor	IPC		S	$20
Motor Road Test Annual 1985	85		Specialist & Professional		S	$40
Motor Road Test Annual 1986	86		Prospect		S	$50
Motor Road Test Annual 1987	87		Prospect		S	$50
Motor Trend World Auto. Yr.Bk. 1966	66		Motor Trend		H	$20
Motor Trend World Auto. Yr.Bk. 1967	67	Potter J E	Petersen		S	$20
Motor Year Book 1949 (first)	49	Pomeroy L	Temple		H	$90
Motor Year Book 1950	50	Pomeroy L	Temple		H	$40
Motor Year Book 1951	51	Pomeroy L	Temple		H	$30
Motor Year Book 1952	52	Pomeroy L	Temple		H	$30
Motor Year Book 1953	53	Pomeroy L	Temple		H	$30
Motor Year Book 1954	54	Pomeroy L	Temple		H	$30
Motor Year Book 1955	55	Pomeroy L	Temple		H	$30
Motor Year Book 1956	56	Pomeroy L	Temple		H	$50
Motor Year Book 1957 (last)	57	Pomeroy L	Temple		H	$30
Motoring Annual (1957)	57	Douglas A	Ian Allen		H	$30
Observers Book of Automobiles 1955	55	Parsons R T	Warne		H	$70
Observers Book of Automobiles 1956	56	Parsons R T	Warne		H	$60
Observers Book of Automobiles 1957	57	Manwaring L A	Warne		H	$40
Observers Book of Automobiles 1958	58	Manwaring L A	Warne		H	$40
Observers Book of Automobiles 1967	67	Manwaring L A	Warne		H	$20
Observers Book of Autos 09E 1963	63	Manwaring L A	Warne		H	$10
Observers Book of Autos 11E 1965	65	Manwaring L A	Warne		H	$10
Observers Book of Autos 21E 1978	78	Voller D/Alexander C	Warne		H	$10
Road & T Guide Sports & GT 1982	81	Wakefield R	CBS		S	$20
Road & T Guide Sports & GT 1983	82	Wakefield R	CBS		S	$20
Road & T Guide Sports & GT 1984	83	Wakefield R	CBS		S	$20
Road & T Road Test/BG Ann 1982	82	Simanatis D	CBS		S	$20
Road & T Road Test/BG Ann 1983	83	Bryant T L	CBS		S	$20
Road & T Road Test/BG Ann 1984	84	Simanatis D	CBS		S	$20
Road & T Road Test/BG Ann 1985	85	Clendenin D	CBS		S	$20
Trend Book 1955 Mtr Trnd Auto Yr Bk	55	Carroll W	Trend	Trend Bk #118	S	$10
Trend Book 1957 Comp Gd Cars World	57	Bayless K M	Trend	Trend Book #142	S	$10
Trend Book 1958 Auto Gd Cars World	58	Bayless K M	Trend	Trend Book #167	S	$10
Trend Book 1959 Gd to Cars of World	59	Bayless K M	Trend	Trend Book #182	S	$10
True's Automobile Yearbook #1 1952	52	Barnard C N	Fawcett		S	$20
True's Automobile Yearbook #2 1953	53	Barnard C N	Fawcett		S	$20
True's Automobile Yearbook #3 1954	54	Barnard C N	Fawcett		S	$20
True's Automobile Yearbook #4 1955	55	Kingdon J G	Fawcett		S	$20
True's Automobile Yearbook #5 1956	56	Barnard C N	Fawcett		S	$20
True's Automobile Yearbook #6 1957	57	Barnard C N	Fawcett		S	$20
True's Automobile Yearbook #7 1958	58	Eisinger L	Fawcett		S	$20
True's Automobile Yearbook #8 1959	59	Eisinger L	Fawcett		S	$20
True's Automobile Yearbook #9 1960	60	Eisinger L	Fawcett		S	$20
World Cars '62(World Car Catalogue)	62	D'Angelo S	LEA		H	$180
World Cars '63(World Car Catalogue)	63	D'Angelo S	LEA		H	$180

GENERAL (Continued)
ANNUALS, PERIODICALS, CAR CATALOGS, ETC (EXCEPT AQ) (Continued)

GENERAL (Continued)
AUTOMOBILE QUARTERLY (Continued)

Automobile Quarterly Vol 08-3	69	AQ		AQ	H	$80
Automobile Quarterly Vol 08-4	70	AQ		AQ	H	$90
Automobile Quarterly Vol 09-1	70	AQ		AQ	H	$90
Automobile Quarterly Vol 09-2	70	AQ		AQ	H	$20
Automobile Quarterly Vol 09-3	70	AQ		AQ	H	$70
Automobile Quarterly Vol 09-4	71	AQ		AQ	H	$70
Automobile Quarterly Vol 10-1	72	AQ		AQ	H	$50
Automobile Quarterly Vol 10-2	72	AQ		AQ	H	$20
Automobile Quarterly Vol 10-3	72	AQ		AQ	H	$20
Automobile Quarterly Vol 10-4	72	AQ		AQ	H	$30
Automobile Quarterly Vol 11-1	73	AQ		AQ	H	$20
Automobile Quarterly Vol 11-2	73	AQ		AQ	H	$20
Automobile Quarterly Vol 11-3	73	AQ		AQ	H	$30
Automobile Quarterly Vol 11-4	73	AQ		AQ	H	$20
Automobile Quarterly Vol 12-1	74	AQ		AQ	H	$20
Automobile Quarterly Vol 12-2	74	AQ		AQ	H	$20
Automobile Quarterly Vol 12-3	74	AQ		AQ	H	$30
Automobile Quarterly Vol 12-4	74	AQ		AQ	H	$20
Automobile Quarterly Vol 13-1	75	AQ		AQ	H	$30
Automobile Quarterly Vol 13-2	75	AQ		AQ	H	$40
Automobile Quarterly Vol 13-3	75	AQ		AQ	H	$30
Automobile Quarterly Vol 13-4	75	AQ		AQ	H	$20
Automobile Quarterly Vol 14-1	76	AQ		AQ	H	$20
Automobile Quarterly Vol 14-2	76	AQ		AQ	H	$20
Automobile Quarterly Vol 14-3	76	AQ		AQ	H	$30
Automobile Quarterly Vol 14-4	76	AQ		AQ	H	$20
Automobile Quarterly Vol 15-1	77	AQ		AQ	H	$20
Automobile Quarterly Vol 15-2	77	AQ		AQ	H	$30
Automobile Quarterly Vol 15-3	77	AQ		AQ	H	$20
Automobile Quarterly Vol 15-4	77	AQ		AQ	H	$20
Automobile Quarterly Vol 16-1	78	AQ		AQ	H	$40
Automobile Quarterly Vol 16-2	78	AQ		AQ	H	$30
Automobile Quarterly Vol 16-3	78	AQ		AQ	H	$40
Automobile Quarterly Vol 16-4	78	AQ		AQ	H	$30
Automobile Quarterly Vol 17-1	79	AQ		AQ	H	$20
Automobile Quarterly Vol 17-2	79	AQ		AQ	H	$20
Automobile Quarterly Vol 17-3	79	AQ		AQ	H	$20
Automobile Quarterly Vol 17-4	79	AQ		AQ	H	$20
Automobile Quarterly Vol 18-1	80	AQ		AQ	H	$30
Automobile Quarterly Vol 18-2	80	AQ		AQ	H	$20
Automobile Quarterly Vol 18-3	80	AQ		AQ	H	$20
Automobile Quarterly Vol 18-4	80	AQ		AQ	H	$20
Automobile Quarterly Vol 19-1	81	AQ		AQ	H	$30
Automobile Quarterly Vol 19-2	81	AQ		AQ	H	$30
Automobile Quarterly Vol 19-3	81	AQ		AQ	H	$20
Automobile Quarterly Vol 19-4	81	AQ		AQ	H	$20
Automobile Quarterly Vol 20-1	82	AQ		AQ	H	$30
Automobile Quarterly Vol 20-2	82	AQ		AQ	H	$30
Automobile Quarterly Vol 20-3	82	AQ		AQ	H	$30
Automobile Quarterly Vol 20-4	82	AQ		AQ	H	$60
Automobile Quarterly Vol 21-1	83	AQ		AQ	H	$30
Automobile Quarterly Vol 21-2	83	AQ		AQ	H	$30
Automobile Quarterly Vol 21-3	83	AQ		AQ	H	$50
Automobile Quarterly Vol 21-4	83	AQ		AQ	H	$50
Automobile Quarterly Vol 22-1	84	AQ		AQ	H	$30
Automobile Quarterly Vol 22-2	84	AQ		AQ	H	$30
Automobile Quarterly Vol 22-3	84	AQ		AQ	H	$30
Automobile Quarterly Vol 22-4	84	AQ		AQ	H	$30
Automobile Quarterly Vol 23-1	85	AQ		AQ	H	$100
Automobile Quarterly Vol 23-2	85	AQ		AQ	H	$80
Automobile Quarterly Vol 23-3	85	AQ		AQ	H	$60
Automobile Quarterly Vol 23-4	85	AQ		AQ	H	$30
Automobile Quarterly Vol 24-1	86	AQ		AQ	H	$30
Automobile Quarterly Vol 24-2	86	AQ		AQ	H	$50
Automobile Quarterly Vol 24-3	86	AQ		AQ	H	$30
Automobile Quarterly Vol 24-4	86	AQ		AQ	H	$30
Automobile Quarterly Vol 25-1	87	AQ		AQ	H	$30
Automobile Quarterly Vol 25-2	87	AQ		AQ	H	$30
Automobile Quarterly Vol 25-3	87	AQ		AQ	H	$30
Automobile Quarterly Vol 25-4	87	AQ		AQ	H	$30
Automobile Quarterly Vol 26-1	87	AQ		AQ	H	$30
Automobile Quarterly Vol 26-2	88	AQ		AQ	H	$30
Automobile Quarterly Vol 26-3	88	AQ		AQ	H	$30
Automobile Quarterly Vol 26-4	88	AQ		AQ	H	$30
Automobile Quarterly Vol 27-1	89	AQ		AQ	H	$20
Automobile Quarterly Vol 27-2	89	AQ		AQ	H	$20
Automobile Quarterly Vol 27-3	89	AQ		AQ	H	$20

GENERAL (Continued)
AUTOMOBILE QUARTERLY (Continued)

GENERAL (Continued)
GENERAL (Continued)

Early Cars (Sedgwick)	62	Sedgwick M	Weidenfeld		H	$20
Eighty-five Jahre Berliner Auto....	82	Stuhlemmer R	Dalton Watson	Dalton Watson	H	$40
El Automovil en el Uruguay 1900-30	81	Tatlock A C	Ediciones Banda Oriental		S	$30
Elite Cars Exciting Look Exp.......	80	Consumer Gd	Publications Intl	Consumer Gd	S	$10
Elite Cars Fastest and Finest	87	Consumer Gd	Publications Intl	Consumer Gd	H	$20
Ency of Motorcar	79+	Drackett P	Mandarin/Octopus/Crown		H	$40
Ency of Sports Cars	86	Nichols R	Bookthrift			20
Ency of Worlds Classic Cars	77	Robson G	Salamander/Chartwell		H	$30
European Automobiles of 50s and 60s	82	Martinez A/Nory J L	EPA/Vilo		H	$40
European Classic Cars Survivors	75	Rasmussen H	Picturama	Survivors	H	$60
European Sports Cars of 50's	78	Rasmussen H	Picturama	Survivors	H	$60
Everyones Color Bk of Classic Cars	80	Roberts P	Hamlyn		H	$10
Exotic Cars (Brown)	85	Brown S	Gallery/Smith/Multimedia		H	$20
Exotic Cars (Nichols)	85	Nichols R	Bison		H	$30
Fabulous Cars of 1920s & 1930s(Juv)	81	Knudson R L	Lerner		H	$20
Famous Auto Museums 2 Museo...Turin	79	Fujimoto A	San'ei Shobo Pub		H	$40
Famous Old Cars	57+	Bowman H W	Fawcett/Arco	Arco Auto Lib	X	$30
Fill'er Up Archit History Gas Stat	79	Vieyra D I	Macmillan/Collier		S	$50
Fill'er Up! Story 50 Years Motoring	52	Partridge B	McGraw		H	$20
Floyd Clymer Hist Motor Scrap Bk#1H	44	Clymer F	Clymer		H	$30
Floyd Clymer Hist Motor Scrap Bk#1S	44	Clymer F	Clymer		S	$30
Floyd Clymer Hist Motor Scrap Bk#2	44	Clymer F	Clymer		X	$30
Floyd Clymer Hist Motor Scrap Bk#3	46	Clymer F	Clymer		X	$30
Floyd Clymer Hist Motor Scrap Bk#4	47	Clymer F	Clymer		H	$30
Floyd Clymer Hist Motor Scrap Bk#5	48	Clymer F	Clymer		H	$30
Floyd Clymer Hist Motor Scrap Bk#6	50	Clymer F	Clymer		H	$30
Floyd Clymer Hist Motor Scrap Bk#7	54	Clymer F	Clymer		H	$30
Floyd Clymer Hist Motor Scrap Bk#8	50S	Clymer F	Clymer		S	$30
Floyd Clymer Hist S/B 1899	55	Clymer F	Clymer		S	$30
From Veteran to Vintage	56	Karslake K/Pomeroy L	Temple		H	$150
Fun of Old Cars Coll & Rest Ant....	67	Stubenrauch B	Dodd Mead		H	$40
Gas Food and Lodging	82	Baeder J	Cross River/Abbeville		H	$50
Get a Horse! Story of Auto America	50	Musselman M M	Lippincott		H	$20
Golden Age of Luxury Car	80	Hildebrand G	Dover		S	$20
Golden Age of Motoring	82	Fondin J	Edita		H	$50
Golden Age of Sports Cars	72	Steinwedel L W	Chilton		H	$20
Golden Wheels	86	Wagner R	Western Reserve/Zubal		H	$40
Grand Tour 1982-83 (Harrahs Coll)	82		Graphics Etc		S	$20
Great American Automotive Story	76	Automotive Industries	Chilton		H	$20
Great American Autos from 1890-1930	72	Brooks L	Scholastic		S	$20
Great American Cars	85	Wood J	Multimedia/Smith/Gallery		H	$20
Great American Race 1984	84		Greatrace Ltd		S	$30
Great Auto Trivia Book	85	Frumkin	Crown/Outlet		S	$20
Great Car Collections of the World	86	Eves E/Burger D	Multimedia/Smith/Gallery		H	$30
Great Cars	67	Stein R	Grosset & Dunlap/Ridge		H	$30
Great Cars (New English Library)	71	Howell M	New English Library		H	$10
Great Cars in Profile (V4 Misc Pfs)	71	Harding A	Profile Publications		S	$30
Great Cars of All Time	60	Robbin I	Grosset		H	$30
Great Cars of Golden Age	79	Brazendale K	Geografico/Orbis/Crescent		H	$30
Great Classics Auto Eng in Gold Age	82+	Seiff I	Hoffman/Orbis/Smith/Gall		H	$40
Great Collectors Cars	73	Rogliatti G	Mondadori/Grosset		H	$40
Great Old Cars Where are they Now?	60	Yost S K	Wayside		S	$20
Greatest Cars	79	Stein R	Ridge/Simon Schuster/WHS		H	$40
Guide to Used Sports Cars	57	Christy J	Sports Car Press	Mod Sports Car	S	$20
Guiness Bk of Car	87	Harding A/Allport W/etc	Guiness		H	$40
Harrahs Auto Coll (cat)	74		Harrah's		S	$10
Harrahs Auto Coll Annotation (cat)	65		Harrah's		S	$10
Harrahs Auto Coll Roster (cat)	60S		Harrah's		S	$10
Harrahs Auto Coll Special Edition	75		Harrah's		S	$20
Harrahs Auto Coll(Batchelor)	84	Batchelor D/Lamm M	GP Publishing		H	$80
Hershey P.A.	71		Directional Advertising		S	$20
Highlights of Hist 25 Yrs w/ Motor	29	Motor	Motor(US)		H	$80
Hist of Motor Car	70	Matteucci M	Crown		H	$20
Hist of Motorized Vehcls 1769-1946	49	Kidner R W	Clymer		S	$30
Hist of Sports Cars	70	Georgano G N	Rainbird/Dutton		H	$50
Hist of Worlds Classic Cars	63	Hough R/Frostick M	Allen & Unwin		H	$60
Hist of Worlds Sports Cars	61	Hough R	Harper		H	$40
Hist on Road Vintage Car Miscellany	58	Anderson J R L	Hamish Hamilton		H	$40
Historic American Roads	76	Rose A C/Rakeman C	Crown		H	$20
Horseless Carriage Days	36+	Maxim H P	Harper & Bros/Dover		X	$40
HT Import European Car	85	Duguay J	Williamson		S	$30
Il Museo dell'Automobile Torino	66	Biscaretti di Ruffia R	Auto Club d'Italia		H	$60
Ill History of Automobiles	80	Wise D B	Quarto/A&W		H	$10
Ill History of Road Transport	86	Burgess-Wise D/Miller D	Quarto/New Burlington		H	$30
Ill Motor Cars of World	71	Olyslager P	Grosset & Dunlap		H	$20
Imported Car Spotter's Guide	79	Burness T	MBI		S	$40
Inside 100 Great Cars	88	Hodges D	M Cavendish/Orbis/Foulis		H	$40

GENERAL (Continued)
GENERAL (Continued)

Title	Year	Author	Publisher		Type	Price
Investigation of Ralph Nader	72	Whiteside T	Arbor		H	$30
Ken Purdys Book of Automobiles	72	Purdy K W	Playboy		X	$20
Kings of Road (S)	61	Purdy K W	Bantam		S	$20
Kings of Road (H)	49+	Purdy K W	Little/Hutchinson/Bnza		H	$40
Klassische Wagen I	71	Von Fersen H	Hallwag		H	$40
Klassische Wagen II	74	Hediger F	Hallwag		H	$40
L A Freeway Appreciative Essay	81	Brodsly D	Univ of California		S	$20
Last American Convertibles	79	Hirsch J/Weith W	Collier		S	$20
Le Auto dei Papi/Pontiffs' Cars	81	Moretti V	Edizioni di Autocritica		H	$90
Le Piu Belle Vetture D'Epoca	70	Rogliatti G	LEA		H	$60
Les Voitures de Police/Gangsters	78	Borge J/Viasnoff N	Balland		S	$30
Light Car Technical History	70	Caunter C F	Her Majestys Stat Office		S	$30
London Motor Show 1930	70	Dalton L	Dalton Watson	Dalton Watson	H	$40
Lost Causes of Motoring	60+	Montagu	Cassell		H	$70
Lost Causes of Motrg Europe Vol 1	71	Montagu	Cassell/Barnes		H	$50
Lost Causes of Motrg Europe Vol 2	71	Montagu	Cassell/Barnes		H	$40
Make Money Owning Your Car	76	Olson J R	MBI		X	$30
Man & Motor 20th Cent Love Affair	67	Jewell D	Walker		H	$30
Man and Motor Cars(auto safety etc)	66	Black S	Norton		H	$20
Manual for Old Car Rest. & Colls.	60S	Pulfer H	Harry Pulfer		S	$20
Men Money & Motors	29	MacManus/Beasley	Harper		H	$30
Merry Old Mobiles on Parade	51	Sibley H	Goodheart-Willcox		S	$10
Modern Classics Grt Crs Pstwr Era	78+	Taylor R	Scribners/Beekman		H	$40
Modern Sports Car	54	McCahill T	Prentice		H	$20
Monarch Illus Gd to Basic Car Care	77	Pettis A	Simon & Schuster		S	$10
Money-Wise Guide to Sports Cars	82	Bohr P	Harcourt,Brace,Jnovch		S	$20
Montagu Motor Museum	59		Cassell		S	$20
Most Unique Machine Michigan.......	75	May G S	Eerdmans		H	$30
Motor Car 1765-1914	60	Bird A	Batsford		H	$30
Motor Car 1946-56	79	Sedgwick M	Batsford		H	$70
Motor Car Illustrated Intl History	77+	Wise D B	Orbis		H	$30
Motor Car Lovers Companion	65	Hough R	Harper & Row		H	$20
Motor Cars 1770-1940	81	Porazik J	Slovart/Smith/Galley	Handbook Guide	H	$10
Motor Memories Saga Whirling Gears	47	Lewis E	Alved/Clymer		H	$30
Motor Museums of Europe	83	Stobbs W	Barker/Weidenfeld		H	$50
Motor Sports Car Road Tests 1E	61		Temple		S	$10
Motor Sports Car Road Tests 2E	65		Temple		S	$10
Motor Trend Presents 100 Yrs of Auto	86		Motor Trend		S	$30
Motorcars of Golden Past	65	Purdy K W	Little Brown		H	$90
Motoring & Mighty	71	Garrett R	Stanley		H	$30
Motoring History	64	Rolt L T C	Studio Vista/Dutton		S	$30
Motorists Weekend Book	60	Frostick M/Harding A	Batsford/Bentley		H	$30
Motorroller Mobil (scooters etc)	85	Kubisch U	Elefanten Press		S	$40
Museo Dell'Automobile CatalogoGen'l	62	Biscaretti diRuffia,C	Museo Dell'Auto.		S	$20
New Comp Bk Coll Cars see COMP BK..	87	Langworth R M	Publications Intl		H	$
New Encyclopaedia Motorcars 1885 on	68+	Georgano G N	Dutton/Crescent		H	$70
Old Car Book (Fawcett 207)	53	Bentley J	Fawcett	Fawcett	S	$10
Old Car Value Guide	68	Craft Q	Quentin Craft	SemiAnnual	S	$30
Old Car Value Guide Vol 3-1	71	Craft Q	Quentin Craft	Semi Annual	S	$20
Old Car Value Guide Vol. 2-4	70	Craft Q	Quentin Craft	SemiAnnual	S	$20
Old Car Value Guide Vol. 3-2	72	Craft Q	Quentin Craft	SemiAnnual	S	$20
Old Car Value Guide Vol. 4-1	73	Craft Q	Quentin Craft	SemiAnnual	S	$20
Old Cars World Over	58	Nagle E	Arco		H	$30
Oldtime Automobile(Fawcett 134)	51	Bentley J	Fawcett	Fawcett	S	$10
Olympian Cars	76	Carson R B	Knopf		H	$125
One Hundred of Worlds Finest Autos	60	Ritch O C	Clymer		S	$30
One Hundred Yrs of Auto 1886-1986	84	Ruiz M	Gallery/Smith/Mondadori		H	$40
Passenger Cars 1863-1904	70	Nicholson T R	Macmillian		H	$20
Passenger Cars 1905-12	71	Nicholson T R	Macmillan		H	$20
Passenger Cars 1913-23	72	Nicholson T R	Macmillian		H	$20
Passenger Cars 1924-1942	75	Sedgwick M	Blandford		H	$20
Passion for Cars	74	Gibbs A	David & Charles/Scribners		H	$20
Petersens World of Wheels	71	Tanner H	Petersen		S	$20
Pictorial Hist of Automobile (P.R.)	77	Roberts P	Ottenheimer/Grosset		H	$30
Pictorial Hist of Automobile(Motor)	53	Stern P V	Hearst/Viking		H	$50
Pictorial Hist of Car	78	Roberts P	Mandarin/Octopus		H	$30
Popular Mechanics Auto Album	52	Throm E L/Crenshaw J S	Popular Mechanics		X	$20
Presidents on Wheels	71	Collins H R	Acropolis/Bonanza		H	$40
Private Motor Car Collections of GB	73	Hugo P	Dalton Watson	Dalton Watson	H	$50
Profiles Complete 96 Copy Set		Various	Profile Publications		S	$200
Prototype Cars Cars That Never Were	81	Consumer Guide	Consumer Gd		S	$20
Real Steel An Investor's and.......	75+	Neville B	Running Press		S	$20
Review/Preview 85/86	85	Bonsall T E	Bookman Dan		S	$20
Road & T Exotic Cars:5	87	Bryant T L	CBS		S	$10
Road is Yours Story of Auto & Men	51	Cleveland R M	Greystone		H	$20
Royalty on Road	80	Montagu/Frostick	Collins		H	$50
Rule of Road Intl Gd Hist/Practice	86	Kincaid P	Greenwood		H	$20

GENERAL (Continued)
GENERAL (Continued)

GENERAL (Continued)
GENERAL (Continued)

GENERAL (Continued)
MIXED MAKES OF AUTOS - AMERICAN (Continued)

MIXED MAKES OF AUTOS - BRITISH

GENERAL (Continued)
MIXED MAKES OF AUTOS - BRITISH (Continued)

Year	Author	Publisher		Type	Price
74	Vanderveen B H	Olyslager/Warne/Haynes	Auto Library	H	$30
81	Voller D J	Warne/Haynes	Olyslager	H	$30
74	Vanderveen B H	Warne/Haynes/Foulis	Olyslager	H	$30
82	Voller D J	Warne	Olyslager	H	$30
73	Vanderveen B H	Warne	Olyslager	H	$40
70	Nye D	Nelson		H	$40
82		Neko	Neko	S	$40
59	Posthumus C	Batsford		H	$40
52	Speed J F	Foulis		H	$30
73	Watkins M	Arco		H	$40
47+	Grant G	Foulis/Clymer		X	$30
49	Chambers P	Clymer		S	$20
74	Culshaw D/Hoffobin P	Walter Parrish/Morrow		H	$150
83+	Wood J	Mandarin/Octopus/etc		H	$60
51	Lukins A H	George Ronald/Clymer		S	$20
81	Worthington-Williams M	Dalton Watson		H	$50
72	Hudson B	Foulis		H	$30
81	Hudson B	Haynes		H	$40
48	Greenwood G	Clymer		H	$30
86	Pritchard A	Osprey		H	$60
74	Filby P	David & Charles		H	$40

MIXED MAKES OF AUTOS - CANADIAN

Year	Author	Publisher		Type	Price
70	Bondt J D	Oberon		H	$40
85	Zavitz R P	Bookman		S	$30
73	Durnford H/Baechler G	McClelland & Stewart		H	$150
69	Collins R	Collins/Ryerson		H	$50

MIXED MAKES OF AUTOS - FRENCH

Year	Author	Publisher		Type	Price
78	Dumont P	Warne		H	$50
64	Bolster J	Autosport/Batsford		H	$60
82	Saka P/Menu J/Dauliac J-P	Fernand Nathan		H	$50
76	Laux J M	Liverpool U		H	$40
71	Bishop C W	Editions Genin		S	$30
87	Sabates F	Editions CH Massin		H	$30
83	Bellu R	Delville		H	$125
77	Dumont P	EPA		H	$40

MIXED MAKES OF AUTOS - GERMAN

Year	Author	Publisher		Type	Price
75	Granz P/Kirchberg P	Transpress VEB		H	$40
65	Von Fersen H	Motorbuch Verlag		H	$50
63	Von Fersen H	Motorbuch Verlag		H	$100
66	Oswald W	Motorbuch Verlag		H	$50
87	Norbye J P	Ervin/Crown/Portland		H	$30
82	Oswald W	Motorbuch		H	$80
83	Oswald W	Motorbuch		H	$80
65	Sloniger J/von Fersen H	Batsford/Bentley		H	$50
85	Roberts P	Multimedia/Smith/Gallery		H	$20
68	Von Fersen H	Motorbuch Verlag		H	$50
82	Kieselbach R J F	W. Kohlhammer GmbH		H	$100

MIXED MAKES OF AUTOS - ITALIAN

Year	Author	Publisher		Type	Price
62	ANFIA	ANFIA(Italian Auto Ind)		H	$200
83		Neko	Neko	S	$30
67	Pritchard A/Davey K	Allen & Unwin/Bentley		H	$60
67	Cavara G	Auto Club d'Italia		S	$150

MIXED MAKES OF AUTOS - JAPANESE

Year	Author	Publisher		Type	Price
61	Clymer F	Clymer		S	$50

MIXED MAKES OF AUTOS - OTHER COUNTRIES

Year	Author	Publisher		Type	Price
72	Goode J	Lansdowne		H	$20
58				H	$40
67	Schmid E	Edition du Chateau de....		H	$90
70S	Kupelian Y/J	Paul Legrain		H	$80
70	Ciuro J	CEAC		H	$40
85	Harding M	View Productions		H	$50
68	Paynting H H	James Flood		H	$150
78	Schmid E	Edita		H	$60
76	Paynting H H	James Flood Charity Trust	Early Motoring	H	$150

REFERENCE

Year	Author	Publisher		Type	Price
68	Wherry J H	Chilton/Galahad		H	$60
54	Shwetzer E L	Heinrich Klammes Press		S	$30
71+	Harding A	Sterling/Guinness		H	$20
81	Norback C T	Chilton		X	$30
78	Casucci P	Mondadori/Rand McNally	R-M Col Ill Gds	S	$20
56	Wherry J H	Associated Booksellers		H	$30
67	Angelucci E	Odhams		H	$40
80	Robson G	Haynes		H	$70
85	Georgano G N	Bison		H	$30
82	Garvey J	Pelham		S	$30
81		Automotive Info Clearing		S	$30

GENERAL (Continued)
REFERENCE (Continued)

GENERAL (Continued)
TECHNICAL (Continued)

MARQUES (ONE MAKE BOOKS)
ABARTH

ALFA ROMEO

MARQUES (ONE MAKE BOOKS) (Continued)
ALFA ROMEO (Continued)

AMERICAN - MISC.

AMERICAN MOTORS

ASTON MARTIN

MARQUES (ONE MAKE BOOKS) (Continued)
ASTON MARTIN (Continued)

Aston Martin 1914-1940 Pict. Review	76	Hunter I	Transport Bookman		H	$40
Aston Martin 1963-1972	75	Gershon D	Oxford Illustrated		H	$40
Aston Martin and Lagonda	77	Frostick M	Dalton Watson	Dalton Watson	H	$60
Aston Martin Britain's Mst Colorful	76	Garnier P Editor	IPC Transport Press	Autocar	S	$40
Aston Martin Coll Rd Tests 1921-42	74	Feather A M	Feather		H	$30
Aston Martin Coll Rd Tests 1948-59	79	Feather A M	Feather		S	$30
Aston Martin Guide from 1948	79	Stowers R	Transport Bookman		S	$20
Aston Martin Postwar Road Cars	88	Rasmussen H	MBI/Haynes		H	$90
Aston Martin Register 1963	63	AMOC	AMOC		S	$70
Aston Martin Story of a Sports Car	57	Coram D	MRP		H	$300
Aston Martin V-8	85	Bowler M	Gentry/Arco		H	$40
Aston Martin V8s Autohistory	81	McComb F W	Osprey	Autohistory	H	$50
David Brown's	60	Donnelly	Collins		H	$125
Lionel Martin Biography	80	Demaus A B	Transport Bookman		H	$40
Motor Racing Management	56	Wyer J	Bodley Head		H	$40
Power Behind Aston Martin	78	Courtney G	Oxford Ill		H	$40
Profile No 33 AstonMartin 1 1/2 Int	67	Coram D	Profile Publications		S	$20
Racing with David Brown Aston Vol 1	80	Wyer J/Nixon C	Transport Bookman		H	$80
Racing with David Brown Aston Vol 2	80	Nixon C	Transport Bookman		H	$80
Zagato Aston Martin Vantage Zagato	86	Marchiano M/Bowler	Aston Martin		S	$30

AUBURN, CORD & DUESENBERG

Classic Cord	52	Post D R	Post		X	$70
Cord Front Drive - O/M Mod.810-812	51		Floyd Clymer		S	$10
Cord Front-Drive	57+	Huntington R	Clymer/MBI		X	$40
Cord Sales Catalog			Floyd Clymer		S	$10
Duesenberg (Steinwedel/Newport)	70+	Steinwedel L W/Newport J	Chilton/Nelson/Norton		H	$40
Duesenberg J Owners Manual(reprint)	51		Clymer		S	$20
Duesenberg Worlds Finest Motorcar	79		Royco Enterprises		S	$20
Jimmy Murphy and White Dusbg (juv)	68	Briggs R/Carter B	Hamilton		H	$50
Profile No 06 Duesenberg J & SJ	66	Nicholson T R	Profile Publications		S	$30
Profile No 09 Auburn Straight-eight	66	Betts Jr C	Profile Publications		S	$30
Profile No 35 Cord 810 & 812	66	Kingman W	Profile Publications		S	$30
Profile No 57 Duesenberg 1920-1927	67	Betts Jr C	Profile Publications		S	$10
Rolling Sculpture Designer & Work	75	Buehrig G M	Haessner		H	$125
Worlds Finest Motor Car(SC reprint)	70S		Duesenberg		S	$20

AUSTIN HEALEY

Austin Healey (Healey/Wisdom)	59	Healey D/Wisdom T/Boyd M	Cassell		H	$100
Austin Healey 100 1952-1959	80	Clarke R M	Brooklands	Brooklands	S	$30
Austin Healey Guide	59	Healey D/Wisdom T	Sports Car Press	Mod Sports Car	S	$30
Austin Healey Story Big Healeys	77	Healey G	Gentry/Haynes		H	$60
Austin Healey Year Book 1979-80	80	Skilleter P	Magpie		H	$30
Healey (Autocar)	83	Garnier P	Temple/Hamlyn		H	$50
Healey Handsome Brute	78	Harvey C	Oxford Ill/St Martins		H	$80
Healey Specials	80	Healey G	Gentry/Haynes		H	$50
Healeys and Austin-Healeys	70	Browning P/Needham L	Foulis/MBI		H	$80
Hillman Minx Guide	63	Page S F	Sports Car Press		H	$20
More Healeys Frog-eyes Sprites.....	78	Healey G	Gentry Books		H	$60
Tuning BMC Sports Cars	69	Garton M	Speed Sport		S	$30

BMW

BMW (Bladon)	85	Bladon S	Multimedia/Smith/Gallery		H	$10
BMW (factory history)	73	Vetten H	BMW		S	$90
BMW (Pocket History)	80	Seifert E	Libreria dell'Automobile	Comp Hist	S	$20
BMW 1979(Japanese)	79	Inouye K	Neko	Neko	S	$30
BMW 6 Series	85	Walton J	Cadogan/Prentice Hall	High Performnce	H	$40
BMW Bavaria's Driving Machine	84	Norbye J P	Publications Intl	Consumer Guide	H	$30
BMW Book of Car	83	Slater D	Winchmore/Smith/Gallery		H	$20
BMW Complete Story from 1928	82	Oswald W/Walton J	Motorbuch Verlag/Haynes		H	$60
BMW History	79	Schrader H	Bleicher Verlag/AQ		H	$90
BMW History L	79	Schrader H	Bleicher Verlag/AQ		L	100
Freude am Fahren BMW Charakter.....	83	Simsa P	ECON		H	$60
Great Marques BMW	83	Walton J	Octopus		H	$30
New BMW Guide	79	Wakefield R	Tab	Mod Sports Car	S	$20
Profile No 89 BMW Type 328	67	Jenkinson D	Profile Publications		S	$30
Six Hundred Thirty Days To Top	84	Mahla U	BMW AG		S	$40
Unbeatable BMW	79	Walton J	Osprey		H	$60
Une Saison avec Luigi Racing(Eng)	76	Strebelle H	Strebelle		S	$30

BRITISH - MISC.

AC (Foulis Mini Marque)	76	Watkins M	Haynes	Mini-Marque	H	$30
AC and Cobra	82	Mclellan J	Dalton Watson	Dalton Watson	H	$60
Allard	77	Kinsella D	Haynes		H	$40
Allard Inside Story	77	Lush T	MRP		H	$70
Alpine Classic Sunbeam	80	McGovern C	Gentry/Haynes		H	$90
Alvis in Thirties	61	Clarke R M	Brooklands	Brooklands	S	$30
Armstrong Siddeley Cars 1945-1960	72	Clarke R M	Brooklands	Brooklands	S	$30
Aston Martin and Lagonda	77	Frostick M	Dalton Watson	Dalton Watson	H	$60
Austin 1905-1952	81	Wyatt R J	David & Charles		H	$60
Austin A30 & A35 1951-1962	83	Clarke R M	Brooklands	Brooklands	S	$30

MARQUES (ONE MAKE BOOKS) (Continued)
BRITISH - MISC. (Conitinued)

MARQUES (ONE MAKE BOOKS) (Continued)
CHEVROLET (INCLUDING CAMARO) (Continued)

Title	Year	Author	Publisher	Series	Fmt	Price
Chevrolet Power	78		Chevrolet Motors		S	$10
Chevrolet Racing Engine	76	Jenkins B	SA		S	$30
Chevrolet Small/Big Block Parts Gd	76		Phase III		S	$20
Chevrolet Speed Manual	54	Fisher B	Clymer		S	$30
Chevrolet=Racing 14 Years of.......	72	Van Valkenburgh P	Haessner		H	$180
Chevy El Camino 1959-82 Photofacts	82	Wood D F	MBI	CMB Photofacts	S	$40
Chevy Spotter's Guide 1920-1980	81	Burness T	MBI		S	$20
El Camino Source Book	83	Lehwald E A	Bookman	Source Book	S	$30
Fix Your Chevrolet V8&6 1966-1975	75	Toboldt B	Goodheart-Willcox		H	$20
Great Camero	78+	Lamm M	Lamm-Morada Publ. Inc.		H	$30
HT Hop Up Chevrolet & GMC 6 cy Eng	51	Huntington R	Clymer		S	$20
Louis Chevrolet Memorial	75		Indianapolis Speedway		S	$10
Monte Carlo Classic Source Book	85	Lehwald E A	Bookman	Source Book	S	$20
Muscle Chevys!	85	Bonsall T E	Bookman Publishing		S	$20
Petersens Compl Bk Vega			Petersen		S	$10
Petersens Compl Chevrolet Book 3E	73	Murray S	Petersen		S	$20
Petersens Compl Chevrolet Book 4E	75	Murray S	Petersen		S	$30
Sixty Years of Chevrolet	72	Dammann G H	Crestline	Crestline	H	$40
Z/28 Camaro No 1 Teams Cafe Racer	78	Schorr M L	Performance		S	$20

CHRYSLER

Title	Year	Author	Publisher	Series	Fmt	Price
Bailout (Chrysler)	80	Stuart R	and Books		S	$20
Chrysler & Imperial Postwar Years	76	Langworth R M	MBI		H	$60
Chrysler 300 1955-1961 Photofacts	82	Gunnell J	MBI	CMB Photofacts	S	$40
Chrysler 300 Source Book	81	Bonsall T E/Shields S A	Bookman	Source Book	S	$30
Chrysler Cars 1930-1939	80	Clarke R M	Brooklands	Brooklands	S	$30
Chrysler Corp Cars Perf Handbook	62	Martin W H/Hot Rod Eds	Petersen	Hot Rod	S	$30
Chrysler Corp Story of American Co	55	Chrysler	Chrysler		S	$30
Comp Hist Chrysler Corp 1924-1985	85	Langworth R M/ Norbye J	Pub Intl/Beekman/Crown	Consumer Guide	X	$40
Going for Broke Chrysler Story	81	Moritz M/Seaman B	Doubleday		H	$40
Life of American Workman Chrysler	37+	Chrysler W P/Sparkes B	Curtis/Dodd Mead		H	$40
New Deals Chrysler Revival.........	85	Reich R B/Donahue J D	Times		H	$30
Pictorial Hist Chrysler Corp. Cars	66+		Chrysler Corp.		S	$30
Seventy Years of Chrysler	74	Dammann G H	Crestline	Crestline	H	$80

CITROEN

Title	Year	Author	Publisher	Series	Fmt	Price
Andre Citroen Les Chevrons de la G	80	Sabates F/Schweitzer	EPA		H	$70
Black Journey - Africa with Citroen	27+	Haardt G/Audouin-Dubreuil	Cosmopolitan/Bles		H	$180
Citroen (Great Cars Series)	75	Broad R	Luscombe	Great Cars	H	$40
Citroen 2CV Collectors Guide	83	Taylor J	MRP	Coll Gd	H	$50
Citroen Great Marque of France	76	Dumont P	Interauto/MBI/EPA		H	$100
Citroen SM 1970-1975	85		EPA	Les Archives...	S	$40
Citroen SM Autohistory	81	Daniels J	Osprey	Autohistory	H	$50
Citroen Traction Avant 1934-1957	83	Sabates F	Vu Par La Presse	Coll Auto Achvs	S	$20
Citroen Traction Avant 34-39 (#3)	83	Sabates F/Didier L	Vu Par La Presse		S	$40
Fifty Years Traction Avant Citroen	85	Sabates F	Edition N7		S	$50
L'Album de la DS	83	Borge J/Viasnoff N	EPA		H	$70
La 2CV	77	Borge J/Viasnoff N	Veyrier/Balland		H	$40
La DS Citroen	86	Puiboube D	Editions Atlas	Les Voitures...	H	$30
Les Prestigieuses Citroen	86	Sabates F	Editions CH Massin		H	$50
Profile No 95 Citroen 1934-1955	67	Sedgwick M	Profile Publications		S	$30
Toutes les Citroen	79	Bellu R	Jean-Pierre Delville		H	$125
Traction Avant 7-11-15-22	84	De Serres O	EPA		H	$80
Travels with 2CV Epic Journey......	88	Earwaker N	Javelin		S	$30
Why Citroen	77+	Chassin J P	Northfield Industries		S	$40

COBRA/SHELBY

Title	Year	Author	Publisher	Series	Fmt	Price
AC (Foulis Mini Marque)	76	Watkins M	Haynes	Mini-Marque	H	$30
AC and Cobra	82	Mclellan J	Dalton Watson	Dalton Watson	H	$60
AC Cobra 1962-1969	80	Clarke R M	Brooklands	Brooklands	S	$30
AC Cobra 260-289-427(French)	84	Hazan P	EPA	Grand Tourisme	H	$50
AC(Shelby) Cobra Autohistory	84	McComb F W	Osprey	Autohistory	H	$40
Carroll Shelby Story	67	Shelby C/Bentley J	Pocket Books		S	$30
Carroll Shelbys Racing Cobra S	86	Friedman D/Christy J	Newport/Petersen		S	$20
Cobra (Legate)	84	Legate T	Chambers Green/Haynes/MBI		H	$90
Cobra Story	65+	Shelby C/Bentley J	Trident/MBI		H	$50
Ford Cobra Guide	64	Carroll W	Sports Car Press	Mod SportsCar	S	$40
Profile No 60 A.C. Cobra	67	Pritchard A/Davey K	Profile Publications		S	$20
Shelby American Guide	78+	Kopec R J	SAAC		S	$50
Shelby Buyers Guide	78	Kopec R J	SAAC		S	$30
Shelby Source Bk Cobras & Mustangs	84	Ackerson R C	Bookman	Source Book	S	$30
Shelby Source Book V2	85	North P	Bookman Dan	Source Book	S	$30
Shelbys Wildlife (hardbound)	77+	Wyss W A	MBI		H	$30

CORVAIR

Title	Year	Author	Publisher	Series	Fmt	Price
Assassination of Corvair	69	White A J	Readers Press		H	$40
Compleat Hist Corvair for Nut V1	78+	Wimpff J	Clark's Corvair Parts		S	$40
Compleat Hist Corvair for Nut V2	80	Wimpff J	Vair Press		S	$30
Corvair 1959-1968	84	Clarke R M	Brooklands	Brooklands	S	$30
Corvair Affair	82	Knepper M	MBI		H	$40
Corvair Decade	80	Fiore T	Corvair Society		H	$50

MARQUES (ONE MAKE BOOKS) (Continued)

CORVAIR (Continued)

Title	Year	Author	Publisher		Bind	Price
Corvair Hist & Restoration Guide	84	Artzberger B	Aztex		S	$50
Corvair Performance Handbook	63	Ritch O C	Petersen		S	$20
Corvair SAE Papers	79		SAE		S	$20
Incompleat Corvair Story	79	Newell D	Bob Terkelson		S	$40
Unsafe At Any Speed	65	Nader R	Grossman		X	$20

CORVETTE

Title	Year	Author	Publisher		Bind	Price
Best of Corvette Restorer 1953-1967	80	Bruce M	M Bruce Assoc		S	$50
Chevrolet Corvette 68-82 Autohist..	83	Falconer T	Osprey		H	$40
Classic Corvette	83	Nichols R	Bookthrift/Exeter/Bison		H	$20
Competition Corvette	80	Consumer Gd	Publications Intl		S	$10
Corvette (Coleman)	83+	Coleman B	Wncmr/Smith/Gallery/CP		H	$20
Corvette Americas Only	78	Antonick M	Michael Bruce Associates		H	$50
Corvette Americas Only True Spts Cr	78	Consumer Gd	Publications Intl/Mayflwr	Consumer Gd	H	$10
Corvette Americas Only(leather)	78	Antonick M	Michael Bruce Associates		L	150
Corvette Americas Sports Car (84)	84	Koblenz J	Pub Intl/Cons Gd/Beekman	Consumer Gd	H	$30
Corvette Body Repair Guide V2 68-82	81	Schiro R J	Glas-Ra		S	$70
Corvette Cars 1955-1964	79	Clarke R M	Brooklands	Brooklands	S	$30
Corvette Guide	58	Thompson D	Sports Car Press/Arco		H	$30
Corvette Past Present Future	84	Consumer Gd	Publications Intl	Consumer Guide	H	$10
Corvette Performance	77	Popular HR	Argus		H	$20
Corvette Restoration Srce Bk 53-67	78	Johnson R	Johnson		S	$60
Corvette Sensuous Am 1-1 thru 3-3	78	Antonick M	Michael Bruce Associates		H	$500
Corvette Sensuous Am 83-1 thru 85-3	83+	Antonick M	Michael Bruce Associates		H	$500
Corvette Sports Car of America	80	Antonick M	Michael Bruce Associates		H	$60
Corvettes for Road	84	Rasmussen H	MBI	Survivors	H	$40
Corvettes Technically Speaking	77	Harrison M C	M & H Engineering		S	$125
Guide to Corvette Speed	69	Ludvigsen K E	Sports Car Press	Mod Sports	S	$30
Hot Rod Corvette No 02	78	Kelley L	Petersen		S	$10
New 1984 Corvette(Consumer Guide)	83	Consumer Gd	Pub Intl		S	$10
Nineteen 84 Paper Corvette	84	Rose A	Dolphin/Doubleday		S	$30

DATSUN/NISSAN

Title	Year	Author	Publisher		Bind	Price
Datsun 240Z & 260Z 1970-1977	80	Clarke R M	Brooklands	Brooklands	S	$30
Datsun Automobiles from Japan	76	Schrader H	Schrader		H	$40
Datsun Z-Cars (Consumer Guide)	81	Consumer Gd	Pub Intl/Castle	Consumer Guide	H	$30
HT Hotrod & Race Your Datsun	84	Waar B	Steve Smith		S	$40
HT Modify Datsun 510/610/240Z......	73	Fisher B/WaarB	HP		S	$30
HT Modify Your Nissan/Datsun OHC En	86	Honsowetz F	HP		S	$30
Nissan/Datsun History Nissan in US	82	Rae J B	McGraw		H	$40
Petersens Compl Bk Datsun	75	Hall A	Petersen		S	$20
Petersens Compl Bk Japanese Import	72	Murray S	Petersen		S	$20
Road & T Gd to Nissan 300ZX	89	Paddock L C	Diamandis		S	$20
Skyline GT-R - Datsun(Japanese)	82		Neko	Neko	H	$50
Skyline Symbol 25 Yrs Quality (Jap)	83		Kodansha		S	$50
Tuning Datsuns	78	Davies P	Speedsport		S	$20

DE LOREAN

Title	Year	Author	Publisher		Bind	Price
De Lorean Stainless Steel Illusion	83	Lamm J	Newport Press		H	$100
DeLorean	85	DeLorean J Z	Zondervan		H	$40
DeLorean Tapes	84	Eddy P	Collins		S	$30
Dream Maker Rise & Fall of DeLorean	83	Fallon I/Srodes J	Putnam		H	$40
Grand Delusions Cosmic...(DeLorean)	83	Levin H	Viking Penguin		H	$40
Hard Driving My Yrs with DeLorean	85	Haddad W	Random		H	$40

DODGE

Title	Year	Author	Publisher		Bind	Price
Barracuda/Chall 64-74 Data Bk/P Gd	85	Zavitz R P	Bookman Dan		S	$30
Charger V2 Source Book	85	North P	Bookman	Source Boo	S	$20
Dodge Cars 1924-38	78	Clarke R M	Brooklands	Brooklands	S	$20
Dodge Military Vehicles Coll. 1	84	Clarke R M	Brooklands	Brooklands	S	$30
Dodge Story	75	McPherson T A	Crestline	Crestline	H	$100
Dodges Auto Family Fortune & Misfor	81	Pitrone J M/Elwart J P	Icarus Press		H	$50
Muscle Dodges!	85	Bonsall T E	Bookman Pub		S	$20

FERRARI

Title	Year	Author	Publisher		Bind	Price
Auto Test Ferrari 1 1962-71(French)	83		EPA	Auto Test	S	$30
Berlinetta Lusso	78	Miska K H	Barnes		X	$80
Boxer Ferrari Flat-12 Rac & GT Cars	81	Thompson J	Newport Press/Osprey		H	$60
Cars in Profile 01 246 P4 Ferraris	72	Frere P	Profile Publications		S	$10
Cavallino No. 01 (Vol 01-1)	78		John W. Barnes		S	$500
Cavallino No. 01 (Vol 01-1) reprint	87		Barnes		S	$20
Cavallino No. 02 (Vol 01-2)	78		Barnes		S	$300
Cavallino No. 03 (Vol 01-3)	79		Barnes		S	$80
Cavallino No. 04 (Vol 01-4)	79		Barnes		S	$80
Cavallino No. 05 (Vol 01-5)	79		Barnes		S	$80
Cavallino No. 06 (Vol 01-6)	79		Barnes		S	$80
Cavallino No. 07 (Vol 02-1)	79		Barnes		S	$100
Cavallino No. 08 (Vol 02-8)	79		Barnes		S	$80
Cavallino No. 09	79		Barnes		S	$100
Cavallino No. 10	80		Barnes		S	$80
Cavallino No. 11	80		Barnes		S	$70
Cavallino No. 12	81		Barnes		S	$80

MARQUES (ONE MAKE BOOKS) (Continued)
FERRARI (Continued)

Cavallino No. 13	81		Barnes	S	$50
Cavallino No. 14	82		Barnes	S	$80
Cavallino No. 15	82		Barnes	S	$80
Cavallino No. 16	83		Cavallino	S	$80
Cavallino No. 17	83		Cavallino	S	$80
Cavallino No. 18	83		Cavallino	S	$80
Cavallino No. 19	83		Cavallino	S	$30
Cavallino No. 20	84		Cavallino	S	$30
Cavallino No. 21	84		Cavallino	S	$80
Cavallino No. 22	84		Cavallino	S	$80
Cavallino No. 23	84		Cavallino	S	$20
Cavallino No. 24	85		Cavallino	S	$20
Cavallino No. 25	85		Cavallino	S	$20
Cavallino No. 26	85		Cavallino	S	$80
Cavallino No. 27	85		Cavallino	S	$20
Cavallino No. 28	85		Cavallino	S	$20
Cavallino No. 29	86		Cavallino	S	$20
Cavallino No. 30	86		Cavallino	S	$20
Cavallino No. 31	86		Cavallino	S	$20
Cavallino No. 32	86		Cavallino	S	$60
Cavallino No. 33	86		Cavallino	S	$80
Cavallino No. 34	86		Cavallino	S	$80
Cavallino No. 35	86		Cavallino	S	$80
Cavallino No. 36	86		Cavallino	S	$30
Cavallino No. 37	87		Cavallino	S	$20
Cavallino No. 38	87		Cavallino	S	$80
Cavallino No. 39	87		Cavallino	S	$80
Cavallino No. 40	87		Cavallino	S	$30
Cavallino No. 41	87		Cavallino	S	$60
Cavallino No. 42	87		Cavallino	S	$60
Cavallino No. 43	88		Cavallino	S	$60
Cavallino No. 44	88		Cavallino	S	$30
Cavallino No. 45	88		Cavallino	S	$30
Cavallino No. 46	88		Cavallino	S	$30
Cavallino No. 47	88		Cavallino	S	$30
Cavallino No. 48	88		Cavallino	S	$30
Cavallino No. 49	89		Cavallino	S	$60
Cavallino No. 50	89		Cavallino	S	$20
Cavallino No. 51	89		Cavallino	S	$30
Cavallino No. 52	89		Cavallino	S	$20
Cavallino No. 53	89		Cavallino	S	$60
Classic Ferrari (Eaton)	83	Eaton G	Exeter/Bison/Bookthrift	H	$20
Colonels Ferraris Maranello Con...	80	Nye D	Ampersand/Maranello	H	$40
Dino The Little Ferrari	79	Nye D	Barnes/Osprey	H	$60
Dossier Auto GTO Ferrari	84	Pascal D	EPA	S	$20
Enciclopedia Ferrari (Italian)	85	D'Argenzio R	Casa Editrice	S	$30
Enzo Ferrari 50 Years of Motoring	80	Casucci P	Mondadori/Crown/Greenwich	H	$60
Enzo Ferrari 50 Years of Motoring	80	Casucci P	Mondadori/Crown/Greenwich	H	$60
Enzo Ferrari Le Mythe	80S	Pascal D	Ch Massin	H	$40
Enzo Ferrari Memoirs (Hamilton)	63+	Ferrari E	Hamilton	H	$125
Enzo Ferrari Memoirs (MBC)	63	Ferrari E	Motoraces Book Club	H	$50
Enzo Ferrari Pilota	87	Moretti V	Edizioni di Autocritica	H	$60
Enzo Ferrari Story Autobiography	63	Ferrari E	Macmillan/Hamish Hamilton	H	$180
Ferrari (Ballantine/Foulis Mini)	71+	Setright L J K	Ballantine/Foulis	X	$30
Ferrari (Exeter)	83		Col Lib/Exeter/S&S	H	$10
Ferrari (Foreword by Niki Lauda)	82	Eaton G	Col Lib/Crescent	Colour Library	H	$20
Ferrari (Laban)	84	Laban B	Multimedia/Smith/Gallery	H	$20
Ferrari (Rogliatti)	73	Rogliatti R	LEA/Crowell/Hamlyn	H	$100
Ferrari (Tanner) 1E	59	Tanner H	Foulis/Bentley	H	$125
Ferrari (Tanner) 2E	64	Tanner H	Foulis/Bentley	H	$90
Ferrari (Tanner) 3E	68	Tanner H	Bentley	H	$80
Ferrari (Tanner) 4E	74	Tanner H	Foulis	H	$70
Ferrari (Tanner) 5E	79	Tanner H/Nye D	Haynes	H	$70
Ferrari 126 C3 (Italian)	83	Chiavegato C	Forte Editore	H	$70
Ferrari 126 C4	84	Chiavegato C	Forte Editore	H	$70
Ferrari 25 Years of Formula One	74	Barnes J W	John W. Barnes Jr.	H	$40
Ferrari 250 GTO Autohistory	83	Clarke D	Osprey	Autohistory	H	$40
Ferrari 250 GTO Super Profile	82	Harvey C	Haynes	Super Profile	H	$30
Ferrari 250LM	83	Massini M/Box R de la	Osprey	H	$70
Ferrari 275 330GT 330GTC Parts Book	70S		Carbooks	S	$40
Ferrari 275GTB & GTS Autohistory	81	Webb I	Osprey	Autohistory	H	$50
Ferrari 275GTB 275GTS..... (French)	84	Pourret J G	Publications Intl	H	$100
Ferrari 308 & Mondial Autohistory	82	Willoughby G	Osprey	Autohistory	X	$50
Ferrari 365 GTB/4 Dayt World S/C#1	84	Nye D	Albion Scott/Moto-Art	H	$50
Ferrari 365 GTB/4 Daytona	82	Braden P/Roush G	Newport/Osprey	H	$80
Ferrari 410 Superamerica Series III	83	Ridgley D W	Ridgley	S	$50
Ferrari 512 V-12 Competition Cars	82	Lampe M	Manfred Lampe	H	$300

MARQUES (ONE MAKE BOOKS) (Continued)
FERRARI (Continued)

MARQUES (ONE MAKE BOOKS) (Continued)
FERRARI (Continued)

Ferrari Yearbook 1963 (Italian)	64		Ferrari		S $1000
Ferrari Yearbook 1963 (reprint)	78		C Dedolph		S $90
Ferrari Yearbook 1964 (Italian)	64		Ferrari		S $800
Ferrari Yearbook 1965 (Italian)	65		Ferrari		S $600
Ferrari Yearbook 1966(Italian)46-66	66		Ferrari		S $800
Ferrari Yearbook 1966(reprint)46-66	77				S $90
Ferrari Yearbook 1967 (Italian)	67		Ferrari		S $600
Ferrari Yearbook 1968-69-70(Italian	70		Ferrari		S $400
Ferrari's Drivers	80	Fenu M	Kimber		H $30
Ferraris for Road	80	Rasmussen H	MBI	Survivors	H $40
Ferrarissima #01 (Original Ed)	84	Madaro G	Automobilia		H $125
Ferrarissima #02 (Original Ed)	85	Madaro G	Automobilia		H $125
Ferrarissima #03 (Original Ed)	85	Madaro G	Automobilia		H $125
Ferrarissima #04 (Original Ed)	86	Madaro G	Automobilia		H $125
Ford vs Ferrari (Zuma/US edition)	84	Pritchard A	Zuma		H $70
Ford vs Ferrari 1E	68	Pritchard A	Pelham Books		H $100
Formula Ferrari(Italian)	84	Chiavegato C	Forte Editore		S $50
Gioachino Colombo Le Origini del...	85	Moretti V	Sansoni Autocritica		H $80
Grand Prix Ferrari	74	Pritchard A	Hale		H $50
Grand Prix Intl Spec Iss Ferrari 86	86	Renvoize P P	GPI/GELT		S $30
GT Granturismo Story 1 Ferr Testa..	87		GT Granturismo e Comp....		S $20
Guide to Ferrari Cars Since 1959	74+		Maranello Concessionaires		S $20
Hors Ligne Special Ferrari/1985	85	Kroon R	Hors Ligne		S $40
Kimberley GP Team Gd 03 Ferrari	83	Constanduros B	Kimberley's		S $30
Kimberley GP Team Gd 13 Ferrari	84	Henry A	Kimberley's		S $30
L'Indimenticabile 82 della Ferrari	82	Rossi A	FOR-VEM		S $30
La Ferrari in tuta	80	Borsari G	Auto Sprint		S $50
Le Ferrari (large format)	66	Rogliatti G	L'Editrice del Auto......		H $250
Le Origini del Mito	85	Colombo G	Sansoni/Autocritica		H $80
Les Fabuleuses Ferrari(French)	83	Bellu S	EPA	Les Fabuleux	H $30
My Years With Ferrari	78	Lauda N	MBI		H $50
Piloti che gente 1E	83	Ferrari E	Enzo Ferrari		H $250
Piloti che gente 1E(English)	83	Ferrari E	Enzo Ferrari		H $200
Piloti che gente 4E	87	Ferrari E	Enzo Ferrari		H $700
Profile No 12 Ferrari Tipo 625&555	66	Davey K/Pritchard A	Profile Publications		S $30
Profile No 23 Fiat Tipo 508S	66	Sedgwick M	Profile Publications		S $10
Profile No 84 Ferrari Tipo 340/375	67	Davey K/Pritchard A	Profile Publications		S $30
Racing Mechanic 7 Yrs Ferr (Cuoghi)	80+	Walton J	Osprey		H $50
Raid Ferrari D'Epoca Modena 81(Eng)	81	Stefanini A	Cons Centro Creativo		H $90
Road & T Ferrari	87	Bryant T L	CBS		S $20
Scuderia Ferrari: Racing 1929-1939	81	Orsini L/Zagari/Nye	Osprey		H $300
Spyder California Ferrari of.....	76	Carrick G M	John W.Barnes		S $40
Superfast Type 410 Superamerica	78	Dethlefsen D	Dethlefsen		S $30

FIAT

Abarth Fiat/Simca/Porsche..........	83	Braden P/Schmidt G	Newport/Osprey		H $70
Alle Fiat Automobile 1899-1986	86	Schmarbeck W	Motorbuch Verlag		H $60
Fiat	74	Sedgwick M	Arco		H $60
Fiat (Pocket History)	81	Bernabo F	Automobilia	Comp History	S $20
Fiat (Shimwell)	77	Shimwell R	Luscombe	Great Cars	H $40
Fiat A Fifty Years Record	51		Arnoldo Mondadori		H $70
Fiat Sports Cars From 1945 to X1/9	84	Robson G	Osprey		H $70
Fiat X1/9 1972-1980	81	Clarke R M	Brooklands	Brooklands	S $30
Fiat X1/9 Autohistory	82	Walton J	Osprey		H $40
Forty Years of Design with Fiat	79	Giacosa D	Automobilia		H $100
Le Grandi Fiat	67	Anselmi A T	Auto Club d'Italia		H $100
New Fiat Guide	69	Norbye J P	Sports Car Press/Crown	Mod Sports Car	S $20
Project X1/9 Cmpl Gd to Rac Prep...	79	Fiat	Fiat Motors of NA		S $30
Tutte Le Fiat	70	Madaro G	Editoriale Domus		H $70

FORD-ALL

American Business Abroad Ford......	64	Wilkins M/Hill F E	Wayne		H $40
Automotive News Ford 75th Ann Issue	78	Ford Motor Company	Crain		S $50
Fiesta Concept of Economical Veh	78	Aigner J/Franz F	SAE		S $20
Ford Book of Competition Motoring	65	Clark J/Brinton A	S Paul		H $30
Ford Competition Cars	76+	Frostick M/Gill B	Haynes		H $40
Ford Dust and Glory Racing History	68	Levine L	Macmillan		H $250
Ford That Beat Ferrari History GT40	85	Jones G/Allen J	Kimberley's		H $180
Ford vs Ferrari 1E	68	Pritchard A	Pelham Books		H $100
Formula Ford Book	77	Brittan N	PSL		H $40
Ghia Ford's Carrozzeria	85	Burgess-Wise D	Osprey		H $60
HT Hotrod Your 2.0-liter OHC Ford	84	Vizard D	Fountain/HP		S $40
HT Modify Ford SOHC Engines	84	Vizard D	Fountain		S $30
HT Rebuild Yr 1.3,1.6, 2.0 OHC Ford	80	Vizard D	HP		S $40
Lets Call It Fiesta	76	Seidler E	Edita		S $20
Racing Fords	68	Tanner H	Meredith		H $150

FORD-AMERICAN

American Ford	75	Sorensen L	Silverado	Fordiana	H $80
Best of Times (Ford Times)	77		Ford		H $10

MARQUES (ONE MAKE BOOKS) (Continued)
FORD-AMERICAN (Continued)

	Year	Author	Publisher	Series	Type	Price
Book of Ford-Powered Perf Cars	67	Engel G S	Pocket Books		S	$20
Boss 302 Registry	84	Ream R/Eby T	Ream/Eby		S	$30
Boy in the Model-T	56	Longstreet S	Simon & Schuester/Paperb		S	$20
Cars That Henry Ford Built	78	Kimes B R	AQ		H	$40
Comp Hist Ford Motor Company	87	Langworth R M	Pub Int/Beekman/Crown	Consumer Guide	H	$40
Drive It! Compl Bk of Formula Ford	84	Bingham P	Haynes		H	$30
Fix Your Ford V-8's&6's 1932-1952	52	Toboldt B	Goodheart-Willcox		H	$20
Floyd Clymer Hist S/B Ford Mod T		Clymer F	Clymer		S	$30
Ford 1903 to 1984 (Consumer Guide)	83	Lewis D L/McCarville.....	Pub Intl/Beekman/Crown		H	$30
Ford Agency Pictorial History	81	Dominguez H	MBI		S	$30
Ford at Fifty 1903-1953	53		Simon & Schuster		H	$30
Ford Bk of Styling		Laas W	Ford Motor Co		S	$40
Ford Decline and Rebirth 1933-1962	63	Nevins A/Hill F E	Scribners	Nevins Triology	H	$40
Ford Expansion & Challenge 1915-33	62	Nevins A/Hill F E	Scribners	Nevins Triology	H	$70
Ford GT 40 SAE Papers	57		SAE		S	$60
Ford GT 40 Sports Cars Profile #1	79		Sapphire		S	$20
Ford GT40 Anglo-Am Comp Classic	84	Archibald S	MRP		H	$80
Ford GT40 Prototypes and Sports Crs	84	Hodges D	Leventhal/Arco		H	$50
Ford in Thirties	70	Hodges D	Petersen		S	$20
Ford Methods and Ford Shops	76	Woudenberg P R	Engineering Magazine		H	$150
Ford Models V-8 B & A Cars	15	Arnold H L/Faurote F L	Norman W Henley		H	$30
Ford Motor Cars - 1912 Catalog	33	Page V W	Floyd Clymer		S	$10
Ford Mustang 1967-1973			Brooklands	Brooklands	S	$30
Ford Performance Cars 1963-1973	82	Clarke R M	Special Interest Cars		S	$20
Ford Performance Handbook (Hot Rod)	62	Brock R/Hot Rod Editors	Petersen	Hot Rod	S	$30
Ford Performance Years V1	83	Schorr M L	Quicksilver	Quicksilver	S	$20
Ford Ranchero 1957-1979 Photofacts	84	Siuru B/Holder B	MBI	CMB Photofacts	S	$40
Ford Retractable 1957-59 Photofacts	83	Magayne J H	MBI	CMB Photofacts	S	$50
Ford Road 75th Anniv Ford Motor Co	78	Sorensen L	Silverado		H	$50
Ford Small-Block HT High Perf Eng..	76	Schorr M L	Performance Pub		S	$20
Ford Spotters Guide 1920-1980	81	Burness T	MBI		S	$30
Ford Street Performance Handbook	85	Schorr M L	Quicksilver	Quicksilver	S	$30
Ford Times Man Company	54	Nevins A/Hill F E	Scribners	Nevins Triology	H	$60
Ford Treasury of Station Wag Living	57	Reck F M/Moss W	Simon & Schuster		H	$20
Ford vs Ferrari (Zuma/US edition)	84	Pritchard A	Zuma		H	$70
Great Cars From Ford	82	Langworth R M/Consumer Gd	Publications Intl		S	$20
Henrys Wonderful Model T 1908-1927	55	Clymer F	Clymer/McGraw/Bonanza		H	$40
Inside Story of Fastest Fords	69	Ludvigsen K E	Style Auto		H	$80
Model T Ford in Speed Sport	56	Pulfer H	Dan R Post		S	$50
Mustang (Carlyon)	84	Carlyon R	Winchmore/Haynes		H	$30
Mustang (Wright)	85	Wright N	Multimedia/Gallery/Smith		H	$20
Mustang Car That Started Ponycar...	79	Langworth R M	Publications Intl	Consumer Guide	H	$20
Mustang Complete Guide (Car Life)	65	Shattuck D	Bond Publishing		S	$20
Mustang Performance Years	82	Schorr M L	Quicksilver	Quicksilver SC	S	$20
New Ford Mustang(Press info reprint	64		Ford Motor Co		S	$20
Open Fords	77	Sorensen L	Silverado	Fordiana	H	$125
Petersens Compl Bk Pinto	77	Murray S/Hall A	Petersen		S	$10
Petersens Compl Ford Book 1E	70	Murray S	Petersen		S	$30
Petersens Compl Ford Book 2E	72	Murray S	Petersen		S	$20
Petersens Compl Ford Book 3E	73	Murray S	Petersen		S	$20
Petersens Compl Ford Book 4E	76	Murray S	Petersen		S	$20
Profile No 13 Ford Model T 1908-27	66	Bird A	Profile Publications		S	$10
Profile No 24 Ford Mustang	66	Stone W S	Profile Publications		S	$20
Profile No 90 Ford GT	67	Stone W S	Profile Publications		S	$30
Ranchero Source Book	83	Ackerson R C	Bookman	Source Book	S	$30
Shelby American Guide	78+	Kopec R J	SAAC		S	$50
Shelby Buyers Guide	78	Kopec R J	SAAC		S	$30
Shelby Source Bk Cobras & Mustangs	84	Ackerson R C	Bookman	Source Book	S	$30
Shelby Source Book V2	85	North P	Bookman Dan	Source Book	S	$30
Story of Ford in Canada			Ford of Canada		H	$30
Super Fords	79	Wyss W A	Zuma Marketing		S	$30
Thirty-two Ford Deuce	84	Thacker T	Osprey		H	$60
Tin Lizzie Story of Fab Model T....	55	Stern P V	Simon & Schuster		H	$30
Travels with Zenobia Paris to Alb..	83	Lane R W/Boylston H D	University of Missouri		H	$20
Ultimate Mustang Book	86	Wright N	Gallery/Smith		H	$40
V-8 Album	85	Early Ford V-8 Club	Early Ford V-8 Club		H	$80

FORD-FOREIGN

	Year	Author	Publisher	Series	Type	Price
Capri Muscle Cars 1969-1983	84	Clarke R M	Brooklands	Brooklands	S	$30
Construction of Ford Specials	60	Mills J	Batsford		H	$40
Escort Mk 1 2 & 3 Dev & Comp Hist	85	Walton J	Haynes		H	$40
Ford Cortina Mk 1 62-66 Autohistory	84	Wood J	Osprey	Autohistory	H	$40
Ford Escort Drawing Bd to Race Trk	68		Speed & Sports		S	$20
Ford Formula One Racing Cars	82	Geary L	Ian Henry	Transport	H	$20
Ford Panel Vans	80	Cole L	Ian Henry	Transport Ser	H	$20
Ford Popular	84	Turner	Osprey		H	$50
Ford RS Escorts 1968-80	82	Clarke R M	Brooklands	Brooklands	S	$30
Ford Specials	60	Stephens P J	Foulis/Scientific		H	$40

MARQUES (ONE MAKE BOOKS) (Continued)
GERMAN - MISC. (Continued)

Das Maybach-Register
Das Werk Opel
DKW Auto Union Guide
Grand Prix Rpt Auto Union(German)
Kimberley Rally Team Gd 01 Audi
Maybach (German/English)
Messerschmitt Kabinenroller
Opel GT Coupe Auto-Classic #4
Opel Wheels to the World
Profile No 59 Auto Union 1934-1937
Twenty Thou Miles Afri Jungle (DKW)
Vom Blitzkarren zum Groben Borgward

81	Metternich M G W	Sieger Verlag		H	$70
30S	Kroth K A	Max Schroder		H	$40
61	Ayling K	Sports Car Press/Crown	Mod Sports Car	S	$30
84	Kirchberg P	transpress VEB Verlag		H	$40
84	Buhlmann K	Kimberley's		S	$10
73+	Metternich M G W	Uhle & Kleimann		H	$125
80S	Ziegler R	Freunde		S	$70
80S	Knittel S	Albion Scott	Auto-Classic	S	$20
75		AQ		H	$40
67	Posthumus C	Profile Publications		S	$20
57+	Brom J L	Gollancz/Pop Bk Club		H	$30
82	Michels P	Barbel Michels		H	$150

HUDSON

Cars That Hudson Built
Hist of Hudson
Hudson & Railton Cars 1936-1940
Hudson Postwar Years
Story of Hudson Motor Car 1909-1957

80	Conde J	Arnold-Porter		H	$60
82	Butler D	Crestline	Crestline	H	$60
76	Clarke R M	Brooklands	Brooklands	S	$30
77	Langworth R M	MBI	Postwar Years	H	$60
73	Wood E V	Triangle Press		S	$20

ITALIAN - MISC.

Cisitalia
De Tomaso Automobiles
De Tomaso Pantera Autohistory
Isotta Fraschini (Anselmi)
Isotta Fraschini 8C Monterosa Cat
Isotta-Fraschini(Ballantine)
Maserati etc Car Grap Lib(Japanese)
Moretti (Italian)
Nardi
Pantera & Mangusta 1969-1974
Pantera 1970-1973
Panteras for Road
Profile No 38 O.M. 1920-31 6-cylndr
Profile No 61 Italias/Racing1907-08
Profile No 74 Isotta Fraschini T8
Quel Mondo Dipinto (Italian)

80	Balestra N/De Agostini C	Automobilia		H	$150
81	Wyss W A	Osprey		H	$90
80	Norbye J P	Osprey	Autohistory	H	$50
77	Anselmi A T	G. Milani/MBI/Albion		H	$180
50S		Clymer		S	$30
71	Nicholson T R	Ballantine	Ballantine #3	S	$20
70S	Takashima S	Car Graphic/Nigensha	Car Grap Lib 30	S	$40
89	Ruberi M	Ruberi		S	$50
87	Varisco F	Libreria dell'Auto		H	$50
80	Clarke R M	Brooklands	Brooklands	S	$40
80	Clarke R M	Brooklands	Brooklands	S	$40
82	Rasmussen H	MBI	Survivors	H	$60
66	Armstrong D	Profile Publications		S	$10
67	Clutton C	Profile Publications		S	$20
67	Nicholson T R	Profile Publications		S	$20
78	Franzini P/Delllanzo L	Editrice Lombarda		H	$70

JAGUAR

Cars in Profile 11 Jaguar D-Type
Case History Story of Jaguar.......
Discussion of Alt Spts Cr Concepts
Ecurie Ecosse Scotlands Racing Team
Great Marques Jaguar
Great Marques Poster Book Jaguar
Jaguar (Ballantine)
Jaguar (Exeter)
Jaguar (Foulis)
Jaguar (Pocket History)
Jaguar 1979 (Japanese)
Jaguar Biography
Jaguar Cars 1948-1951
Jaguar Cars 1951-1953
Jaguar Cars 1954-1955
Jaguar Cars 1955-1957
Jaguar Cars 1957-1961
Jaguar Cars Practical Guide........
Jaguar Companion
Jaguar Complete Ill History
Jaguar D Type & XKSS Autohistory
Jaguar Defin Hist SEE Jaguar Hist
Jaguar Drivers Yearbook 1977(first)
Jaguar Drivers Yearbook 1978
Jaguar Drivers Yearbook 1979-80
Jaguar Drivers Yearbook 1980-81
Jaguar E Type 1961-66
Jaguar E Type Autohistory
Jaguar Guide
Jaguar History Great British Car
Jaguar Il Fascino di......(Italian)
Jaguar Lord Montagu of Beaulieu
Jaguar Mk II Auto-Classic #2
Jaguar Motor Racing & Manufacturer
Jaguar Since 1945
Jaguar Sports (Autocar)
Jaguar Sports Cars 1957-1960
Jaguar SS Cars 1931-1937
Jaguar SS Cars 1937-1947
Jaguar SS90 & SS100 Super Profile
Jaguar Story

73	Appleton J	Profile Publications		S	$10
64		Jaguar Cars		S	$40
77	Knight R J/Randle J N	SAE		S	$30
62	Murray D	S Paul/MBC		H	$80
82	Harvey C	Mandarin/Octopus		H	$30
85	Harvey C	Octopus/Woodbury/Dalton		S	$20
71	Montagu	Ballantine	Ballantine #10	S	$30
83+	Kowal B	Exeter/Bookthrift/S&S		H	$10
75+	Montagu	Foulis/Haynes	Minimarque	H	$30
80	Frostick M	Automobilia	Complete Book	S	$20
		Neko		S	$30
61	Montagu	Cassell/Norton		H	$50
71	Clarke R M	Brooklands	Brooklands	S	$30
71	Clarke R M	Brooklands	Brooklands	S	$30
71	Clarke R M	Brooklands	Brooklands	S	$30
72	Clarke R M	Brooklands	Brooklands	S	$30
72	Clarke R M	Brooklands	Brooklands	H	$40
61	Vandiest C L	Pearson		H	$40
59	Ullyett K	Stanley Paul	Companion	H	$50
84	Porter P	Warne/Haynes		H	$40
83	Robson G	Osprey	Autohistory	H	$40
78	Skilleter P	Magpie		H	$50
79	Skilleter P	Magpie		H	$50
80	Skilleter P	Magpie		H	$50
81	Skilleter P	Magpie		H	$40
75	Clarke R M	Brooklands	Brooklands	S	$30
82	Jenkinson D	Osprey	Autohistory	H	$40
57	Bentley J	Sports Car Press	Mod Sports Car	S	$30
80+	Whyte A	PSL/Sterling		H	$60
79	Casucci P			S	$100
67	Montagu	Barnes		H	$40
80S	Schrader H	Albion Scott	Auto-Classic	S	$20
78	Berry R	Aztex		S	$20
82	Busenkell	Norton		H	$40
75	Garnier P	Hamlyn		H	$40
72	Clarke R M	Brooklands	Brooklands	S	$30
70	Clarke R M	Brooklands	Brooklands	S	$40
70	Clarke R M	Brooklands	Brooklands	S	$40
84	Whyte A	Haynes	Super Profile	H	$20
67	Wherry J H	Chilton	Sebring	H	$30

MARQUES (ONE MAKE BOOKS) (Continued)
JAGUAR (Continued)

MARQUES (ONE MAKE BOOKS) (Continued)
LINCOLN (Continued)

MARQUES (ONE MAKE BOOKS) (Continued)
MERCEDES (Continued)

MERCURY

MG

MARQUES (ONE MAKE BOOKS) (Continued)
MG (Continued)

Title	Year	Author	Publisher		Bind	Price
MG Mania Insomnia Crew	83	Stone H W/Knudson R	New England T Register		S	$50
MG MGB GT 1965-1980	80	Clarke R M	Brooklands	Brooklands	S	$30
MG Sports 4 cyl TB from Abingdon	80S	Autocar	Autocar		S	$20
MG Sports Car America Loved First	75	Knudson R L	Motorcars Unlimited		H	$50
MG Sports Car Supreme	82	Wherry J H	Barnes		H	$40
MG Sports Cars (Autocar)	74+	Garnier P	Hamlyn/St Martins		H	$40
MG Story	67	Wherry J H	Chilton		H	$40
MG TC 1945-1949	84	Clarke R M	Brooklands	Brooklands	S	$30
MG TD 1949-1953	84	Clarke R M	Brooklands	Brooklands	S	$30
MG TF 1953-1955	84	Clarke R M	Brooklands	Brooklands	S	$30
MG Workshop Manual	52	Blower W E	MRP/Bentley		H	$40
MGA Autohistory	83	McComb F W	Osprey	Autohistory	H	$40
MGA Collection #1 1955-1982	84	Clarke R M	Brooklands	Brooklands	S	$20
MGB Autohistory	82	McComb F W	Osprey	Autohistory	H	$40
MGB GT 1965-1980	85	Clarke R M	Brooklands	Brooklands	S	$30
MGB Handbook/Comphnsv Owners Manual	68	Turner S/Organ J	Foulis/Bentley		H	$40
Mighty MGs Twin Cam MGC MGB GT V8..	82	Robson G	David & Charles		H	$70
Motor Tramp	35	Heygate J	Cape		H	$70
Postwar MG & Morgan	79	Blakemore/Rasmussen	Picturama	Survivor S	H	$50
Profile No 15 MG Magnette K3	66	McComb F W	Profile Publications		S	$30
Profile No 45 MG Midget M Type	66	McComb F W	Profile Publications		S	$10
Profile No 86 18/80 MG	67	McComb F W	Profile Publications		S	$20
Red Car (MG, juvenile)	54	Stanford D	Scholastic		S	$40
T Series MG	73	Knudson R L	Motorcars Unlimited		X	$60
Tuning and Maintenance of MG Cars	52+	Smith P H	Foulis/Haynes		H	$40
Tuning BMC Sports Cars	69	Garton M	Speed Sport		S	$30

MINI

Title	Year	Author	Publisher		Bind	Price
Book of Mini	64	Ullyett K	Parrish		H	$40
High Speed Low Cost 140mph Mini	69	Staniforth A	PSL		H	$40
HT Modify Your Mini	87	Vizard D	Fountain Press		S	$40
Introduction to Mini	84		Mini City		S	$30
Mini-Cooper 1961-1971	81	Clarke R M	Brooklands	Brooklands	S	$30
More Mini Tuning	68+	Trickey C	Speed Sport	Speed Sport	S	$30
Tuning Mini	69+	Trickey C	Speedsport		S	$30
Works Minis	71+	Browning P	Haynes		S	$30

MOPAR

Title	Year	Author	Publisher		Bind	Price
Mopar 273 318 etc Perf Gd & Catalog	75	Yale S	Phase III		S	$10
Mopar Big-Block HT High Perf Eng...	76	Schorr M L	Performance Pub		S	$20
Mopar Oval Track Modifications	83	Shepard L S	Mopar		S	$40
Mopar Oval Track Performance Book	83	Chrysler Corporation	Chrysler Corporation		S	$40
Mopar Performance Years V1 Dodge...	82	Schorr M L	Quicksilver	Quicksilver	S	$20
Mopar Performance Years V2	84	Schorr M L	Quicksilver	Quicksilver	S	$20
Mopar Performance Years V3	84	Schorr M L	Quicksilver	Quicksilver	S	$20
Mopar Street Performance Handbook	85	Schorr M L	Quicksilver	Quicksilver	S	$20
Muscle Mopars	85	Bonsall T E	Bookman Dan		S	$20
Petersens Compl Bk Plym Dodge Chrys	73	Murray S	Petersen		S	$30

MORGAN

Title	Year	Author	Publisher		Bind	Price
Book of Morgan Three-Wheeler	50S	Clarke R M	Brooklands	Brooklands	S	$40
Four Wheeled-Morgan Vol 1 Flat Rad	77	Hill K	MRP		H	$100
Moggie The Purch, Maint & Enjoy....	80	Musgrove C	Quills		H	$80
More Morgan Pictorial History of...	76	Bowden G H	Gentry		H	$40
Morgan (French)	85	McComb F W	EPA	Toute L'Hist...	S	$20
Morgan 3 Whlr H/B Ford Engine Mdls	81	Birks T	Morgan 3 Wheeler Club		S	$20
Morgan 3-Wheeler 1930-52	80	Clarke R M	Brooklands	Brooklands	S	$40
Morgan Cars 1936-1960	79	Clarke R M	Brooklands	Brooklands	S	$30
Morgan Cars 1960-1970	79	Clarke R M	Brooklands	Brooklands	S	$30
Morgan Cars 1969-1979	80	Clarke R M	Brooklands	Brooklands	S	$30
Morgan First and Last of Real......	72+	Bowden G H	Gentry/Haynes		H	$70
Morgan Four Wheeler Workshop Manual		Dowdeswell J	Dowdeswell		S	$40
Morgan History of Famous Car			Morgan		S	$20
Morgan Sweeps Board 3-Wheeler..	78+	Alderson J D	Gentry/Haynes		H	$50
Morgans in Colonies	78	Sheally J H	Jordan & Co/MBI		H	$70
Morgans Pride of British	82	Sheally J H	Tab		H	$60
Postwar MG & Morgan	79	Blakemore/Rasmussen	Picturama	Survivor S	H	$50
Profile No 65 Plus Four Morgan	67	Dymock E	Profile Publications		S	$30
Seventy Years of Morgan Motoring	80	Chapman C	Morgan Clubs		S	$20
Three Wheeler	70	Watts B	Morgan 3 Wheeler Club		S	$20
Vintage Years of Morgan 3 Wheeler		Boddy W	Grenville		S	$30

OLDSMOBILE

Title	Year	Author	Publisher		Bind	Price
Four-4-2 64-86 Data Bk/Price Guide	85	Zavitz R P	Bookman		S	$30
Four-4-2 Vol II Source Book	85	North P	Bookman Dan	Source Book	S	$30
Hurst Source Book	85	North P	Bookman	Source Book	S	$30
Oldsmobile (French)	87	Baillon A	EPA	Toute L'Hist.	S	$20
Oldsmobile 1904 SalesBrochure			Floyd Clymer		S	$10
Oldsmobile First Seventy-Five Years	72	Kimes B R/Langworth R M	AQ		X	$40
Oldsmobile Performance Years	83	Schorr M L	Quicksilver	Quicksilver	S	$20
Oldsmobile Postwar Years	81	Norbye J P	MBI	Marques America	H	$50

MARQUES (ONE MAKE BOOKS) (Continued)
OTHER - MISC.

Title	Year	Author	Publisher	Series	Bind	Price
Bricklin	77	Fredricks H A/Chambers A	Brunswick Press		H	$30
Holden First 25 Years	73		Holden		S	$20
Monteverdi (German)	80	Gloor G/Wagner C L	Automobile Monteverdi		H	$300
Resa Kungligt(Swedish)	76	Nordberg N	Raben & Sjogren		H	$30
Ricart Pegaso La Pasion del Auto...	88	Mosquera C/Coma-Cros E	Arcris Ediciones		H	$200
Saab Guide	61	Ayling K	Sports Car Press/Crown	Mod Sports Car	S	$30
Saab Innovator	80	Chatterton M	David & Charles		H	$50
Saab Turbo Autohistory	83	Robson G	Osprey	Autohistory	H	$40
Saab Way	84	Sjögren G	Saab		S	$60
So Great a Change Story of Holden	79	Buttfield N	Ure Smith		S	$20
Sonett & All other SAAB Sports Cars	83	Svallner B	Allt om Hobby AB		H	$40

PACKARD

Title	Year	Author	Publisher	Series	Bind	Price
Coachbuilt Packard	73	Pfau H	Dalton Watson	Dalton Watson	H	$150
Packard 1942-1962	75	Dawes N T	Barnes		H	$70
Packard Cars 1920-1942	77	Clarke R M	Brooklands	Brooklands	S	$40
Packard Complete Story	85	Scott M G H	Tab		H	$60
Packard Eight Owners H/B 1929			Floyd Clymer		S	$10
Packard Guide	87	Marvin R B	Packard Data Bank		S	$60
Packard Hist of MC & Co (leather)	78	Kimes B R	AQ		L	125
Packard Service Letters		Abbott R	Abbott		S	$40
Packard Story Car & Company	65	Turnquist R E	Barnes		H	$50
Profile No 94 Packard 8/12 1923-42	67	Oliver S H	Profile Publications		S	$40

PIERCE-ARROW

Title	Year	Author	Publisher	Series	Bind	Price
Arrow 100th Anniv Meet 1978 issue	78	Weis B J	Pierce-Arrow Society		S	$30
Forest Domain of Pierce-Arrow	84	Meyer J C	South Cal Region PA Soc		H	$30
Pierce-Arrow 1919 Sales Catalog			Floyd Clymer		S	$10
Pierce-Arrow (Ballantine)	71	Hendry M D	Ballantine Books	Ballantine #4	S	$30
Pierce-Arrow (Ralston)	80	Ralston M	Barnes		H	$50
Pierce-Arrow Golden Age	84	Ralston M	Ralston		H	$60

PLYMOUTH

Title	Year	Author	Publisher	Series	Bind	Price
Barracuda Challenger V2 Source Bk	85	North P	Bookman	Source Book	S	$30
Barracuda/Chall 64-74 Data Bk/P Gd	85	Zavitz R P	Bookman Dan		S	$30
Plymouth and DeSoto Story	78	Butler D	Crestline	Crestline	H	$100
Plymouth Barracuda 1964-1974	85	Clarke R M	Brooklands	Brooklands	S	$30
Road Runner V2 Source Book	85	North P	Bookman Dan	Source Book	S	$30

PONTIAC

Title	Year	Author	Publisher	Series	Bind	Price
Fabulous Firebird	79	Lamm M	Lamm-Morada		H	$50
Fiero Facts Book	83		Fiero Owners Club of Amer		S	$30
Firebird (Carlyon)	84	Carlyon R	Gallery/Smith		H	$20
Grand Prix Classic Src Bk (Pontiac)	85	Sass D	Bookman Dan	Source Book	S	$20
GTO A Source Book	83	Bonsall T E	Bookman	Source Book	S	$30
Pontiac 1926-1966 ID Guide	82	Bonsall T E	Bookman	ID Guide	S	$20
Pontiac Complete History 1926-1986	85	Bonsall T E	Bookman Publishing		H	$60
Pontiac Firebird 1967-73	82	Clarke R M	Brooklands	Brooklands	S	$30
Pontiac GTO Americas Premier S/C	78	Schorr M L	Performance Publications		S	$20
Pontiac Performance Handbook	63	Martin W H/Hot Rod Eds	Petersen	Hot Rod	S	$30
Pontiac Performance Years	82	Schorr M L	Quicksilver	Quicksilver	S	$20
Pontiac Postwar Years	79	Norbye J P	MBI		H	$40
Pontiac Show Cars Experimentals....	86	Sass D	Bookman		S	$20
Pontiac Trans-Am High Perf Handbook	81	Schorr M L	Quicksilver	Supercar	S	$20
Seventy-5 Years of Pontiac-Oakland	82	Gunnell J	Crestline	Crestline	H	$100

PORSCHE

Title	Year	Author	Publisher	Series	Bind	Price
Abarth Fiat/Simca/Porsche..........	83	Braden P/Schimidt G	Newport/Osprey		H	$70
Amazing Porsche and VW Story	58	Nitske R	Comet Press Books		H	$50
Auto Test Porsche 911 #1 (French)	83		EPA	Auto Test	S	$30
Car Styling No 31 1/2 Porsche/Desg	80	Fujimoto A	San'ei Shobo		S	$70
Cars in Profile 05 Porsche 917	73	Frere P	Profile Publications		S	$20
Christophorus 1970 Yearbook	70	Von Frankenberg R	Porsche		S	$30
Classic Porsche	83	McCarthy M	Bison/Fell/Exeter		H	$20
Derek Bell My Racing Life (Spcl ed)	88	Bell D/Henry A	PSL		L	150
Fabulous Porsche 917	76	Hinsdale P	Haessner		S	$100
First Porsche Parade in Japan	80S		Neko		H	$40
Liebe Zu Ihm (5 lang)	60		Porsche		H	$500
Making of Winner Porsche 917	72	Pihera L	Lippincott		H	$50
New Porsche Guide	68	Sloniger J	Sports Car Press	Mod Sports Car	S	$20
One Hundred Yrs Porsche Mirrored...	76	Schrader H	Porsche		H	$90
Perpetuating Porsche Paranoia	81	Pietruska R	R P Design		S	$20
Porsche (Cotton)	82	Cotton M	Col Lib/Crown/Crescent		H	$20
Porsche (in Japanese) V5	71		Car Graphic Library	Car Grap L	S	$30
Porsche (Kobayashi)	73	Kobayashi S	MBI		S	$40
Porsche (Pritchard)	69	Pritchard A	Pelham		H	$30
Porsche 1978(Japanese)	78	Inouye T	Neko		S	$30
Porsche 1979 (Japanese)	79	Inouye T	Neko	Neko	S	$30
Porsche 1980 (Japanese)	80	Inouye T	Neko	Neko	S	$30
Porsche 356 Auto Classic #1	82	Schrader H	Podzun-Pallas/Albion	Auto Classic	S	$30
Porsche 356 Autohistory	81	Jenkinson D	Osprey	Autohistory	H	$40
Porsche 4 Cyl 4 Cam Spts & Rac Cars	77	Sloniger J	Batchelor/MBI		S	$60

MARQUES (ONE MAKE BOOKS) (Continued)
PORSCHE (Continued)

ROLLS-ROYCE & BENTLEY

MARQUES (ONE MAKE BOOKS) (Continued)
ROLLS-ROYCE & BENTLEY (Continued)

MARQUES (ONE MAKE BOOKS) (Continued)
STUDEBAKER (Continued)

MODELS/TOYS
GENERAL

MOTORCYCLE (Continued)
ANNUALS/PERIODICALS (Continued)

MOTORCYCLE (Continued)
MAKES - FOREIGN (Continued)

Ariel Postwar Models	83+	Bacon R	Osprey	Osprey Coll Lib	H	$50
Ariel Story	80	Hartley P	Argus Books Ltd		S	$30
Best Twin Story of Douglas Mtcycl	74	Clew J	Goose		H	$50
BMW Story	79	Minton D	Phoebus/BPC		S	$20
Book of AJS	41+	Haycraft W C	Pitman	Mtr Cycl Lib	S	$40
Book of P & M (motorcycles)	31+	Haycraft W C	Pitman	Mtr Cycl Lib	H	$40
Book of Royal Enfield	35+	Haycraft W C	Pitman	Mtr Cycl Lib	X	$40
Book of the Triumph (motorcycles)	39+	Brown E T/Davies A C	Pitman	Mtr Cycl Lib	S	$40
British Motor Cycles Since 1950 V1	82	Wilson S	PSL		H	$50
British Motor Cycles Since 1950 V2	83	Wilson S	PSL		H	$50
British Motor Cycles Since 1950 V4	87	Wilson S	PSL		H	$70
British Trials Motorcycles(Ven'bls)	85	Venables R	BMS		S	$30
Brough Superior Rolls-Royce of MCs	64+	Clark R H	Goose/Haynes		H	$50
BSA Motorcycles 1935 to 1940	59		Temple/Hamlyn/BMS		S	$20
Classic British Scramblers	86	Morley D	Osprey	Coll Lib	H	$50
Deutsche Krader im Kriege		Knittel V S	Podzun-Pallas-Verlag	Waffen-Arsenal	S	$20
Douglas (Carrick)	82	Carrick P	PSL	World Motor Cy	H	$30
Ducati Singles	85+	Walker M	Osprey	Coll Lib	H	$50
First Knocker Norton Scene	79	Main-Smith B	BMS		S	$10
First Velocette Scene	77	Main-Smith B	BMS		S	$20
Floyd Clymer Catalog Brit Mtrcycles	51	Ashby J B/Angier D J	Clymer		S	$30
Floyd Clymer Hist S/B For Mtcyl V1	55	Clymer F	Clymer		S	$40
Freiheit auf zwei Radern BMW	82	Lingnau G	ECON		H	$80
Giants of Small Heath(BSA)	80	Ryerson B	Haynes		H	$40
Great British Bikes	76	Ward I/Caddell L	Orbis			40
Great British Motorcycles of 50s	80	Currie B	Hamlyn		H	$30
Great Motorcycles Hist 22 Famous...	72	Wood G/Renstrom R C	Bond Parkhurst		S	$20
Honda (Myers)	84	Myers C	Arco		H	$20
Honda (Woollett)	83	Woollett M	Temple/Newnes/Hamlyn		H	$40
Honda Early Classic Motorcycles	85	Bacon R	Osprey	Osprey Coll Lib	H	$50
Italian Motorcycles	84	Parker T	Osprey	Osprey Col Lib	S	$30
Italian Motorcycles Guide	85	Ayton C J	Temple/Newnes/Hamlyn		H	$20
Japanese Motor Cycles(Hamlyn Guide)	82	Ayton C J	Hamlyn		H	$20
Know Thy Beast Vincent	72+	Stevens E M G	Vincent Pub		H	$60
KSS Velocette Super Profile	84	Clew J	Haynes	Super Profile	H	$20
Moto Guzzi Genius & Sport	83	Colombo M	Automobilia		H	$40
Moto Guzzi Twins	86	Walker M	Osprey	Osprey Coll Lib	H	$50
Moto MM Alla ricerca della.........	88	Ruffini E/Tozzi G	Nada		H	$125
Motorroller Mobil (scooters etc)	85	Kubisch U	Elefanten Press		S	$40
Norton Story	72	Holliday B	PSL		X	$40
Norton(Ballantine)	72	Howard D	Ballantine	Ballantine	S	$30
Postwar British Motorcycles	82	Ayton C J	Hamlyn		H	$30
Royal Enfield Motor Cycles	48+	Booker C A E	Pearson		H	$40
Royal Enfield Postwar Models	82	Bacon R	Osprey	Osprey Coll Lib	H	$50
Story of BMW Motorcycles	82	Croucher R	PSL		H	$40
Story of BSA Motor Cycles	78	Holliday B	PSL		H	$40
Story of Honda Motor Cycles	76	Carrick P	PSL		H	$50
Story of Kawasaki Motor Cycles	78	Carrick P	PSL		H	$40
Story of Manx	48	Davison G S	TT Special		H	$60
Story of Panther Motor Cycles	83	Jones B	PSL/Thorsons		H	$50
Story of Royal Enfield Motor Cycles	81	Hartley P	PSL		H	$40
Story of Rudge Motorcycles	85	Hartley P	PSL		H	$40
Story of Triumph Motorcycles	75+	Louis H/Currie B	PSL		H	$50
Story of Velocette	50S	Beresford G	T T Special		H	$40
Suzuki	80	Clew J	Haynes		H	$30
Suzuki Two-Strokes	84	Bacon R	Osprey	Osprey Coll Lib	H	$50
Team Suzuki	82	Battersby R	Osprey		H	$60
Triumph Singles	84	Bacon R	Osprey	Osprey Coll Lib	H	$40
Velocette Development History	82+	Burris R	Haynes		S	$40
Velocette Flat Twins	85	Bacon R	Osprey	Osprey Coll Lib	H	$50
Villiers Singles & Twins	83	Bacon R	Osprey	Osprey Coll Lib	H	$40
Vincent (Richardson)	55+	Richardson P	Pearson	Mtr Cycl Maint	S	$40
Vincent HRD Story	75+	Harper R	Vincent Publishing		H	$60
Vincent Vee Twins	82	Harper R	Osprey	Osprey Coll Lib	H	$50
Vincent-HRD Motorcycles 1947-1955	60+	Main-Smith B	Temple/BMS		S	$20
Whatever Happ Brit M/Cycle Industry	81	Hopwood B	Haynes		S	$20
Yamaha	84	Woollett M	Arco		S	$20
Yamaha Legend	79	Macauley T	St. Martins		H	$40
Yamaha Two-Stroke Twins	85	MacKellar C	Osprey	Osprey Coll Lib	H	$50

PERSONALITIES/BIOGRAPHIES

Barry Sheene Will to Win	83	Scott M	Allen & Unwin		S	$30
Evel Knievel on Tour	77	Saltman S/Green M	Dell		S	$20
Francis Beart Single Purpose	78	Clew J	Haynes		H	$40
Full Chat	52	Pope N B	MRP		H	$100
Kenny Roberts	82	Coleman B	Weidenfeld		H	$60
Leader of the Pack Barry Sheene	83+	Beacham I	Macdonald/Q Anne/Futura		S	$20
Lifes Bits & Pieces	73	Hoel J C (Pappy)	J C Hoel		S	$30

MOTORCYCLE (Continued)
PERSONALITIES/BIOGRAPHIES (Continued)

MOTORCYCLE (Continued)
TECHNICAL (Continued)

RACING, RALLY, DRIVING
ANNUALS (PERIODICALS)

RACING, RALLY, DRIVING (Continued)
ANNUALS (PERIODICALS) (Continued)

Title	Year	Author	Publisher	Series	Bind	Price
Automobile Year 1980-81 #28	81	Armstrong D	Edita S.A.		H	$80
Automobile Year 1981-82 #29	82	Norris I	Edita S.A.		H	$80
Automobile Year 1982-83 #30	83	Norris I	Edita S.A.		H	$80
Automobile Year 1983-84 #31	84	Norris I	Edita S.A.		H	$60
Automobile Year 1984-85 #32	85	Norris I	Edita S.A.		H	$60
Automobile Year 1985-86 #33	85	Piccard J R	Edipresse		H	$80
Automobile Year 1986-87 #34	86	Piccard J R	Edipresse		H	$80
Automobile Year 1987-88 #35	87	Hodges D	Editions Lamuniere		H	$100
Automobile Year 1988-89 #36	88	Hodges D	Editions JR		H	$80
Autosport Yearbook 1976	76	Phillips I	Haymarket		S	$20
CART 1988-89 Men and Machines......	88	Hughes J	Autosport Intl		H	$70
CART 1989 Media Guide	89	CART	CART Pub Relations		S	$20
CART 1989-90 Men and Machines......	89	Hughes J	Autosport Intl		H	$60
Canadian Motorsport Annual 1981-82	82	Chapman P	Wheelspin News		S	$30
Canadian Motorsport Annual 1983-84	84	Chapman P	Wheelspin News		S	$30
Car and Driver Racing Annual 66-67	67	Davis D E	Ziff-Davis		S	$30
Car Racing 1953 (52 season)	53	Gardner A T G	Country & Sporting		S	$50
Daytona 500 1985 Yearbook	85	Breslauer K C	Auto Racing Memories		S	$30
FIA Yr Bk of Automobile 1969	69		PSL		S	$30
FIA Yr Bk of Automobile Sport 1971	71		PSL		S	$20
FIA Yr Bk of Automobile Sport 1972	72		PSL		S	$20
FIA Yr Bk of Automobile Sport 1973	73		PSL		S	$20
FIA Yr Bk of Automobile Sport 1974	74		PSL		S	$20
FIA Yr Bk of Automobile Sport 1975	75		PSL		S	$20
FIA Yr Bk of Automobile Sport 1976	76		PSL		S	$20
FIA Yr Bk of Automobile Sport 1977	77		PSL		S	$20
Formula 1 86/87 World C/S Y/B 01	86	Braillon D	ACLA		H	$100
Formula 1 87-88 World C/S Y/B 02	87	Braillon D	ACLA		H	$80
Formula One 74(only book in series)	74	Lyons P/Gilligan V	Oxman		H	$40
Formula One YB 1987 (FOCA)	87		Grid		H	$90
Formula One YB 1988 (FIA) #2	87	Constanduros B	Grid		H	$90
Grand Prix Guide 71 Marlboro	72	Reust F	Kreuzer		S	$30
Grand Prix Guide 73 Marlboro	73	Reust F	SIL		S	$30
Grand Prix Guide 74	73	Reust F	SIL		H	$30
Grand Prix Wld Chmpshp 59	60	Stanley L T	Barnes	GP Wld Chmpshp	H	$90
Grand Prix Wld Chmpshp 60(GP Year)	61	Stanley L T	Barnes	GP Wld Chmpshp	H	$90
Grand Prix Wld Chmpshp 61	62	Stanley L T	Barnes	GP Wld Chmpshp	H	$90
Grand Prix Wld Chmpshp 62	63	Stanley L T	Barnes	GP Wld Chmpshp	H	$90
Grand Prix Wld Chmpshp 63	64	Stanley L T	Barnes	GP Wld Chmpshp	H	$90
Grand Prix Wld Chmpshp 64	65	Stanley L T	Macdonald/Doubleday	GP Wld Chmpshp	H	$70
Grand Prix Wld Chmpshp 65	66	Stanley L T	Macdonald	GP Wld Chmpshp	H	$125
Grand Prix Wld Chmpshp 66	67	Stanley L T	Macdonald	GP Wld Chmpshp	H	$80
Grand Prix Wld Chmpshp 67	68	Stanley L T	Macdonald	GP Wld Chmpshp	H	$150
Grand Prix Wld Chmpshp 68(GP #10)	69	Stanley L T	Allen/McKay	GP Wld Chmpshp	H	$60
Grand Prix Wld Chmpshp 69(GP #11)	70	Stanley L T	McKay	GP Wld Chmpshp	H	$60
Grand Prix World Formula One C/S 85	85	Roebuck N/Townsend	GS Publications		H	$70
IMSA '84 Yearbook	84	Van der Feen D	IMSA		S	$30
IMSA '86 Yearbook	86	Van der Feen D	Intl Mtr Spts Association		S	$30
IMSA '87 Yearbook	88		Paul Oxman Publishing		S	$30
IMSA '88 Yearbook	89	Burns G	IMSA		S	$30
International Motor Racing Bk #2	68	Drackett P	Souvenir		H	$20
International Motor Racing Bk #3	69	Drackett P	Souvenir		H	$20
International Motor Racing Bk #4	70	Drackett P	Souvenir Press		H	$20
International Motor Racing Bk(#1)	67	Drackett P	Souvenir Press		H	$30
Motor Racing 1946	48	Gibson J E	MRP		S	$70
Motor Racing 1947	49	Gibson J E	MRP		S	$80
Motor Racing International Way No 1	70	Brittan N	Kaye & Ward		H	$20
Motor Racing International Way No 2	71	Brittan N	Kaye & Ward		H	$20
Motor Racing Year (1969-Pritchard)	70	Pritchard A	MRP		H	$40
Motor Racing Year 1963-4	63	Blunsden J/Brinton A	Knightsbridge		H	$30
Motor Racing Year 1964-5	64	Blunsden J/Brinton A	Knightsbridge		H	$30
Motor Racing Year 1965-6	65	Blunsden J/Brinton A	Knightsbridge		H	$30
Motor Racing Year 1966-7	66	Motor Racing staff	Knightsbridge		H	$30
Motor Racing Year 1967-8	67	Motor Racing staff	Knightsbridge		H	$30
Motor Racing Year 1968-9	68	Motor Racing staff	Knightsbridge		H	$30
Motor Racing Year 1970	70	Blunsden J	MRP		H	$30
Motor Racing Year 1971	70	Blunsden J	MRP		H	$30
Motor Racing Year 1972	71	Blunsden J	MRP		H	$40
Motor Racing Year 1973	72	Blunsden J	MRP		H	$30
Motor Racing Year 1975	76	Blunsden J	MRP		S	$30
Motor Racing Year No 2 (1970)	71	Pritchard A	Pelham		H	$30
Motor Sport Yearbook 1972 J Player	72	Gill B	Q Anne		S	$20
Motor Sport Yearbook 1973 J Player	73	Gill B	Q Anne/Collier Books		S	$20
Motor Sport Yearbook 1974	73	Gill B	Brickfield/Collier		S	$20
Motor Sport Yearbook 1975 J Player	75	Gill B	Brickfield/Queen Anne		S	$20
Motor Sport Yearbook 1976	76	Gill B	Queen Anne Press		S	$20
PPG Indy Car World Series 1981('80)	81	Kirby G	Competition Images		S	$20

RACING, RALLY, DRIVING (Continued)
ANNUALS (PERIODICALS) (Continued)

RACING, RALLY, DRIVING (Continued)
BIOGRAPHIES (PERSONALITIES)(Continued)

RACING, RALLY, DRIVING (Continued)
BIOGRAPHIES (PERSONALITIES) (Continued)

RACING, RALLY, DRIVING (Continued)
EARLY TRANSCONTINENTAL RACES, RUNS & EXPEDITIONS (Continued)

Title	Year	Author	Publisher		Cond	Price
Lightning Conductor Strange Adven..	02+	Williamson C N/A M	Methuen/Henry Holt		H	$40
London to Calcutta 1938	88	Wright O D/White E L D	Little Hills		H	$40
Longest Auto Race	66	Schuster G/Mahoney T	John Day Co. Inc.		H	$50
Mad Motorists Great Peking-Paris...	65	Andrews A	Lippincott		H	$30
New York to Paris 1908 (Thomas)	51	Thomas Motor Co	Clymer		S	$20
Overland by Auto in 1913	81	Copeland E M	Indiana Historical Soc		S	$30
Peking to Paris	72	Barzini L	Library Press		H	$50
Road Race Round World NY to Paris	65	Jackson R B	Walck		S	$20
Round World in a Motorcar	09	Scarfoglio A	Mitchell Kennerley		H	$250
Travels with Zenobia Paris to Alb..	83	Lane R W/Boylston H D	University of Missouri		H	$20
Twenty Thou Miles Afri Jungle (DKW)	57+	Brom J L	Gollancz/Pop Bk Club		H	$30
Two Roads to Africa	39	Symons H E	Travel Book Club		H	$100
Wheels Round World	51	Hess A	Newman Neame		H	$20
Wild Roads Story Transcon. Motoring	69	Nicholson T R	Norton		H	$30

FICTION

Title	Year	Author	Publisher		Cond	Price
Carlotti Takes the Wheel (juv fict)	59	Hawthorn M	Childrens Book Club		H	$50
Fast Green Car	65+	Butterworth W E	Norton/Grosset/Tempo		X	$20
Fast One (novel)	78	Daley R	Crown		H	$20
Follow Circus	69	Hoy R	Pacific		H	$20
Grand Prix Driver (juvenile)	69	Butterworth W E	Norton		H	$20
Green Helmet	57	Cleary J	Fontana		X	$30
Le Mans 24 (Fiction)	71	Petitclerc D B	Harcourt Brace/Playboy		X	$30
My Mistress Death	56	Spafford R	Fawcett		S	$10
Out of Control (novel)	74	Gerber D	Prentice		H	$20
Racer	53	Ruesch H	Ballantine		S	$10
Red Car (MG, juvenile)	54	Stanford D	Scholastic		S	$40
Road Racer	67+	Butterworth W E	Norton/Grosset/Tempo		X	$20
Twenty-four Hours at Le Mans(fict)	57	Gregoire J A	John Day		H	$40

FOREIGN - GENERAL

Title	Year	Author	Publisher		Cond	Price
Around Houses Hist MR West Aust	80	Walker T	Racing Car News		S	$30
Auto Da Corsa I Documentari	68	Bernabo F	Instituto Geografico.....		H	$90
Automobile Racing (Walkerley)	62	Walkerley R	Temple		H	$30
Blue Blood Hist GP Cars in France	79	Bellu S	Warne/EPA		H	$50
Book of Australian Motor Racing	65	Tuckey W P	Murray		H	$40
Boys Book of Racing Cars	48		MRP		H	$30
BRM H	62+	Mays R/Roberts P	Cassell		H	$60
BRM S	64	Mays R/Roberts P	Pan		S	$30
BRM Collection Christie Catalog	81		Christies		S	$50
BRM Story	66	Stanley L T	Parrish		H	$80
Brabham Grand Prix Cars	85	Henry A	Hazleton		H	$50
Brabham Story of Racing Team	85	Drackett P	Weidenfeld/Barker		H	$50
British Racing Cars	48	Posthumus C	Vitesse/Floyd Clymer		S	$20
British Racing Green 1946-1956	57	Klemantaski L	Bodley		H	$60
British RDC Silver Jubilee Book	52		BRDC		H	$100
British Road Racing (Dudley)	50	Dudley J	Ian Allen/Clymer		S	$30
Bruce McLaren Man & His Rac T'm	71	Young E S	Eyre & Spottiswoode		H	$60
Cars in Profile 03 F1 Repco-Brabham	72	Nye D	Profile Publications		S	$10
Cars in Profile 08 McLaren M8	73	Hodges D	Profile Publications		S	$20
Cars in Profile 10 Matra MS80	73	Crombac G	Profile Publications		S	$10
Case History	58	Smith N	Autosport		H	$40
Certain Sound 30 Years of Motor Rac	81	Wyer J	Edita/Haynes		H	$125
Chequered Flag (Rutherford)	56	Rutherford D	Collins		H	$30
Circuit Dust	34	Lyndon B	John Miles		H	$125
Classic Single-Seaters Donington	74	Nye D	Macmillan		H	$50
Combat Motor Racing History	33	Lyndon B	Heinemann		H	$150
Comp Hist Grand Prix Motor Racing	86+	Cimarosti A	Hallwag/Bateman/Crescent		H	$50
Competition Cars of Europe	70	Pritchard A	Bobbs-Merrill		H	$30
Controlling Racing Car Team	51	Davis S C H	Foulis		H	$30
Cooper Cars	83+	Nye D	Osprey		H	$100
Dicing With Death	61	Lewis P	Daily Mirror		S	$40
Drivers in Action	55	Klemantaski L/Frostick M	Bodley		H	$70
Evolution of Racing Car	66	Pomeroy L	Kimber		H	$80
F 3000	88	Barbe S	L'Equipe		H	$60
Facts About Grand Prix Team Tyrrell	77	Gill B	Whizzard G		H	$40
Famous Motor Races	63	Walkerley R	Barker		H	$30
For Practice Only	59	Klemantaski L/Frostick M	Bodley		H	$60
Formula 2	53	Grant G	Foulis		H	$40
Formula 3 Record of 500cc Racing	51	May C A N	Foulis		H	$50
Formula Junior	61	Blunsden J	MRP		H	$70
Formula One Grand Prix Rac Since 46	66	Pritchard A	Allen & Unwin		H	$50
German Racing Cars and Drivers	50	Molter G	Clymer		S	$50
Grand Prix (Lyndon)	35	Lyndon B	John Miles		H	$250
Grand Prix Gift Book (juvenile)	67		Young World Prod (UK)		H	$30
Grand Prix Racing 1906-1914	65	Mathieson T A S O	Connoisseur Automobile		H	$180
Grand Prix Tyrrells	75	Nye D	Macmillan	Donington MM	H	$40
Great Motor Sport of Thirties	77	Dugdale J	Gentry/Two Continents		H	$60
Honda F1 1964-1968 (Japanese)	84	Car Graphic	Nigensha Publishing		H	$200

RACING, RALLY, DRIVING (Continued)
GENERAL (Continued)

RACING, RALLY, DRIVING (Continued)
GENERAL (Continued)

HOT ROD, DRAG

INDIANAPOLIS

RACING, RALLY, DRIVING (Continued)
INDIANAPOLIS (Continued)

Five Hundred Souvenir Book	80	Hungness C/Fox J	Hungness	S	$10
Ill History of Indianapolis 500	67+	Fox J C	World/Hungness	H	$150
Indianapolis 1946 Yearbook supp'm't	46	Clymer F	Clymer	S	$30
Indianapolis 1947 Yearbook	47	Clymer F	Clymer	S	$40
Indianapolis 1948 Yearbook supp'm't	48	Clymer F	Clymer	S	$50
Indianapolis 1949 Yearbook	49	Clymer F	Clymer	X	$30
Indianapolis 1950 Yearbook	50	Clymer F	Clymer	S	$90
Indianapolis 1951 Yearbook	51	Clymer F	Clymer	S	$90
Indianapolis 1952 Yearbook	52	Clymer F	Clymer	S	$125
Indianapolis 1953 Yearbook	53	Clymer F	Clymer	S	$90
Indianapolis 1954 Yearbook	54	Clymer F	Clymer	S	$90
Indianapolis 1955 Yearbook	55	Clymer F	Clymer	S	$90
Indianapolis 1956 Yearbook	57	Clymer F	Clymer	S	$100
Indianapolis 1957 Yearbook	58	Clymer F	Clymer	X	$90
Indianapolis 1958 Yearbook	59	Clymer F	Clymer	S	$150
Indianapolis 1959 Yearbook	59	Clymer F	Clymer	X	$100
Indianapolis 1960 Yearbook		Clymer F	Clymer		180
Indianapolis 1961 Yearbook	62	Clymer F	Clymer	S	$100
Indianapolis 1962 Yearbooks	62	Ritch O C	Clymer	S	$50
Indianapolis 1963 Yearbook	63	Ritch O C	Clymer	X	$80
Indianapolis 1964 Yearbook	64	Clymer F	Clymer	S	$50
Indianapolis 1965 Yearbook	65	Clymer F	Clymer	X	$50
Indianapolis 1966 Yearbook	66	Clymer F	Clymer	X	$50
Indianapolis 1967 Yearbook	67	Clymer F	Clymer	X	$50
Indianapolis 1968 Yearbook	68	Davidson D	Clymer	S	$50
Indianapolis 1969-1972 Yearbook	80	Mahoney J	Hungness	H	$200
Indianapolis 1973 Yearbook	73	Hungness C	Hungness	X	$100
Indianapolis 1974 Yearbook	74	Hungness C	Hungness	X	$30
Indianapolis 1975 Yearbook	75	Hungness C	Hungness	X	$30
Indianapolis 1976 Yearbook	76	Hungness C	Hungness	X	$30
Indianapolis 1977 Yearbook	77	Hungness C	Hungness	X	$30
Indianapolis 1978 Yearbook	78	Hungness C	Hungness	S	$30
Indianapolis 1979 Yearbook	79	Hungness C	Hungness	X	$30
Indianapolis 1983 Yearbook	83	Hungness C	Hungness	X	$40
Indianapolis 1984 Yearbook	84	Hungness C	Hungness	X	$30
Indianapolis 1985 Yearbook	85	Hungness C	Hungness	X	$30
Indianapolis 500 (Fox)	67	Fox J C	World	H	$125
Indianapolis 500(Devaney)	76	Devaney J & B	Rand McNally	H	$60
Indianapolis 500(Engel)	70	Engel L K	Four Winds	H	$30
Indianapolis 500(Yates)	56+	Yates B	Harper	H	$30
Indianapolis Race History	46		Floyd Clymer	X	$60
Indy 500 American Inst Under Fire	74	Dorson R	Bond/Parkhurst	H	$40
Indy 500 Mechanic	75	Brawner C/Scalzo J	Chilton	H	$40
Indy Race and Ritual	80	Reed T	Presidio	S	$20
Marlboro Salute 75th Anniv Indy 500	86	Davidson D	Marlboro	H	$30
Month at Brickyard	77	Kleinfield S	Holt	H	$40
One Hundred 32 Unusual Cars Indy	70	Engel L K	Arco	H	$60
Race	58	Angelopolous A/Verlin B	Bobbs-Merrill	H	$300
Speedway Driver History	48	Werking N P	Clymer	S	$40
Thirty Days in May Indy 500	71	Higdon H	Putnam	H	$30
Those Incredible Indy Cars	73	Calvin J	Sports Car Press	Mod Sports Car	S	$30

JUVENILE

Behind the Wheel Stories of..(juv)	64	Fenner P R	Morrow	H	$20
Black Tiger at Le Mans (Juv fict)	58	O'Connor P	Washburn/Scholastic	X	$20
Bonneville Cars (juvenile)	73	Radlauer E & R S	Watts	H	$20
Boys Book of Motor Sport	50S	Grant G	Foulis	H	$50
Buggy-Go-Round (dune buggy racing)	71	Radlauer E/Radlauer R S	Collins	H	$20
Carlotti Takes the Wheel (juv fict)	59	Hawthorn M	Childrens Book Club	H	$50
Champions at Speed	79	Corson R	Dodd Mead	H	$20
Checkered Flag (Gault - juvenile)	64	Gault W C	Dutton	H	$20
Formula One Ultimate in Rac Cars	74	Taylor R	Western	Golden Wheels	H	$10
Grand Prix Driver (juvenile)	69	Butterworth W E	Norton	H	$20
Grand Prix Gift Book (juvenile)	67		Young World Prod (UK)	H	$30
Grand Prix Racing (Williams - juv)	67	Williams P J	Scholastic	S	$10
Great Racing Cars (Sullivan)	87	Sullivan G	Dodd Mead	H	$20
Indianapolis 500(Yates)	56+	Yates B	Harper	H	$30
Quarter-Mile Combat (juvenile)	75	Jackson R B	Walck	H	$20
Racing Cars (Nelson)	50S	Groves R	Nelson	H	$30
Racing Sprint Cars (juvenile)	79	Stambler I	Putnam	H	$30
Road Race Round World NY to Paris	65	Jackson R B	Walck	S	$20
Showdown at Daytona	76	Higdon H	Putnam	H	$20
Six Seconds To Glory Don Prudhomme	75	Higdon H	Putnam	H	$30
Stock Car Racer (juv fict)	57	Jackson C	Follett	H	$30
Those Daring Young Men in their J..	69	Davies J/Annakin K/Searle	Putnam	H	$20
Top Fuelers Drag Racing Royalty	78	Stambler I	Putnam	H	$30
World of Racing Endurance Racing	81	Wilkinson S	Childrens Press	H	$10
Worlds Great Race Drivers (Juv)	72	Orr F	Random House	H	$20

RACING, RALLY, DRIVING (Continued)

JUVENILE (Continued)

RACING, RALLY, DRIVING (Continued)
RALLIES (INCLUDING RALLY ANNUALS) (Continued)

TECHNICAL (PERFORMANCE EMPHASIS)

TRACKS/RACES (EXCEPT INDY)

RACING, RALLY, DRIVING (Continued)
TRACKS/RACES (EXCEPT INDY) (Continued)

RACING, RALLY, DRIVING (Continued)
U.S. - GENERAL (Continued)

TRUCKS, COMMERCIAL, MILITARY
4-WHEEL DRIVE (OFF ROAD VEHICLES)

FIRE

FUNERAL CARS

GENERAL

TRUCKS, COMMERCIAL, MILITARY (Continued)
GENERAL (Continued)

TRUCKS, COMMERCIAL, MILITARY (Continued)
TRUCKS - AMERICAN (Continued)

Wild Mook 18 Big Rig (Japanese)	70S	Imai K	World Photo Press		S	$40
Wild Mook 23 (US Trucking-Japanese)	78	Imai K	World Photo Press		S	$40

TRUCKS - FOREIGN

AEC - World Trucks No 10	80	Kennett P	PSL	World Trucks	H	$30
Berliet - World Trucks No 12	81	Kennett P	PSL	World Trucks	H	$30
Berliet de Lyon	81	Borge J/Viasnoff N	EPA		H	$80
British Lorries 1900-1945	73	Klapper C F	Ian Allen		H	$20
British Lorries 1945-1975	78	Stevens-Stratten S W	Ian Allen		H	$30
DAF - World Trucks No 5	79	Kennett P	PSL	World Trucks	H	$30
Dennis - World Trucks No 6	79	Kennett P	PSL	World Trucks	H	$30
Emergency Service Vehicles of UK	80	Sturman C	Ian Allan		H	$20
ERF - World Trucks No 1	78	Kennett P	PSL/Aztex	World Trucks	H	$30
European Trucks On the Road in.....	83	Jacobs D	Osprey	Osprey Col Ser	S	$30
Fiat World Trucks No 9	80	Kennett P	PSL	World Trucks	H	$30
Ford Military Vehicles	83	Geary L	Ian Henry Pub	Transport Ser	H	$30
Ford Trucks Transport Since 45	78	Ingram A	MRP		H	$40
Heavy Haulage	70S	Hawthorne R	Steaming		S	$10
Kaleidoscope of Lorries & Vans	79	Baldwin N	Marshall Harris		H	$40
Les Poids Lourds (French)	75	Borge J/Viasnoff N	Balland		H	$50
Leyland Bus	84	Jack	Transport Publishing Co.		H	$70
Leyland World Trucks No 14	83	Kennett P	PSL	World Trucks	H	$30
MAN World Trucks No 04	78	Kennett P	PSL/Aztex	World Trucks	H	$30
Magirus World Trucks No 13	83	Kennett P	PSL	World Trucks	H	$30
Old Lorries Shire Album 138	85	Woodhams J	Shire Pub	Shire Album	S	$10
Overtype Steam Road Waggon	71	Kelly M A	Goose		H	$40
Scammell - World Trucks No 8	79	Kennett P	PSL	World Trucks	H	$30
Scammell Vehicles	71	Vanderveen B H	Warne	Olyslager	H	$30
Scania World Trucks No 2	78	Kennett P	PSL/Aztex	World Trucks	H	$30
Seddon Atkinson - World Trucks No 3	78	Kennett P	PSL/Aztex	World Trucks	H	$30
Sentinel V1 1875-1930	73	Hughes W J/Thomas J L	David & Charles		H	$40
Steam Lorry	48+	Kidner R W	Oakwood	Locomotion Pprs	S	$10
Vintage Lorry Annual # 1	79	Baldwin N	Marshall Harris		H	$40
Volvo World Trucks No 7	79	Kennett P	PSL	World Trucks	H	$30
Wreck and Recovery	87	Thomas A	PSL		S	$30

VANS

Comp Van Book	76	Truscott L K	Harmony/Crown	S	$20
Customizing Vans	78	Beedie M	Blaketon Hall/Arco	H	$20
Light Vans & Trucks 1919-39	77	Ingram A/Baldwin N	Almark	H	$20
Van People Great American..........	77	Hall D K	Crowell	S	$20
Vans and the Truckin' Life	77	Cook T	Abrams	S	$20
Vans Vanners and Vanning	76	Wolfe A S	Greatlakes Living Press	H	$20

STYLE AUTO

All issues of this Italian magazine on coachbuilding are indexed by subject.

Style Auto, continued

AUTOMOBILE
Quarterly Magazine

VOL 1 THRU 26 AUTOMOBILE QUARTERLY INDEXED BY SUBJECT

FOR A MORE DETAILED INDEX OF THE FIRST 20 VOLUMES WE SUGGEST THE PURCHASE OF "AUTOMOBILE QUARTERLY INDEX 01-20"